# THE SOCIAL PSYCHOLOGY OF MORALITY

Ever since Plato's *Republic* was written over 2,000 years ago, one of the main concerns of social philosophy and later empirical social science was to understand the moral nature of human beings. The faculty to think and act in terms of overarching moral values is as much a defining hallmark of our species as is our intelligence, so *Homo moralis* is no less an appropriate term to describe humans as *Homo sapiens*.

This book makes a strong case for the pivotal role of social psychology as the core discipline for understanding morality. The book is divided into four parts. First, the role of social psychological processes in moral values and judgments is discussed, followed by an analysis of the role of morality in interpersonal processes. The sometimes paradoxical, ironic effects of moral beliefs are described next, and in the final section the role of morality in collective and group behavior is considered.

This volume will be of interest to students and researchers in the social and behavioral sciences concerned with moral behavior, as well as professionals and practitioners in clinical, counseling, educational and organizational psychology where understanding morality is of importance.

**Joseph P. Forgas** is Scientia Professor of Psychology at the University of New South Wales, Sydney. He received his D.Phil. degree from the University of Oxford and a D.Sc degree, also from Oxford. His research investigates affective influences on social cognition, motivation, and behavior. He has published 26 books and over 200 journal articles and book chapters. In recognition of his scientific contribution, he received the Order of Australia in 2012, as well as the APS's Distinguished Scientific Contribution Award, the Humboldt Research Prize, and a Rockefeller Fellowship. Forgas is a Fellow of the Academy of Social Sciences in Australia, the Association for Psychological Science, the Society of Personality and Social Psychology, and the Hungarian Academy of Sciences.

**Lee Jussim** is Professor of Psychology at Rutgers University, where he was chair from 2010–2013. He is the author of over 100 articles and chapters, and several books, including *Social Perception and Social Reality: Why Accuracy Dominates Bias and Self-Fulfilling Prophecy*, which received the 2013 AAP Prose Award for best book in psychology. His contribution to *The Social Psychology of Morality* was completed while he was a Fellow and Consulting Scholar at Stanford's Center for Advanced Study in the Behavioral Sciences. His current work focuses primarily on scientific integrity and best practices in science.

**Paul A.M. Van Lange** is Professor of Social Psychology and chair of the Section of Social and Organizational Psychology at the Vrije Universiteit Amsterdam, and Distinguished Research Fellow at the University of Oxford. His research focuses on human cooperation and trust grounded in evolutionary theorizing, particularly the functions of forgiveness, generosity, empathy, fairness, morality, retaliation, and competition. He is a recipient of the Kurt Lewin Medal and has published around 150 articles and several books, including the *Atlas of Interpersonal Situations*, the *Handbook of Theories of Social Psychology*, *Power, Politics, and Paranoia,* and *Social Dilemmas*. Van Lange was associate editor of the *Journal of Personality and Social Psychology* and *Psychological Science*, is founding editor of a series on human cooperation (published by Oxford University Press), editor-in-chief of *Current Opinion in Psychology*, and has served as director of the Kurt Lewin Institute (KLI) and as president of the Society of Experimental Social Psychology (SESP).

# The Sydney Symposium of Social Psychology series

This book is Volume 18 in the *Sydney Symposium of Social Psychology* series. The aim of the Sydney Symposia of Social Psychology is to provide new, integrative insights into key areas of contemporary research. Held every year at the University of New South Wales, Sydney, each symposium deals with an important integrative theme in social psychology, and the invited participants are leading researchers in the field from around the world. Each contribution is extensively discussed during the symposium and is subsequently thoroughly revised into book chapters that are published in the volumes in this series. For further details see the website at www.sydneysymposium.unsw.edu.au

## Previous Sydney Symposium of Social Psychology volumes:

SSSP 1. FEELING AND THINKING: THE ROLE OF AFFECT IN SOCIAL COGNITION** ISBN 0–521–64223–X (Edited by J.P. Forgas). *Contributors*: Mahzarin Banaji, Len Berkowitz, Jim Blascovich, Herbert Bless, Eric Eich, Shelly Farnham, Klaus Fiedler, Joseph Forgas, Daniel Gilbert, Anthony Greenwald, Jamin Halberstadt, Sara Jaffee, EunKyung Jo, Leslie Kirby, Mark Leary, Dawn Macauley, Leonard Martin, Wendy Berry Mendes, Paula Niedenthal, Brian Nosek, Marshall Rosier, Laurie Rudman, Carolin Showers, Craig Smith, Bartholomeu Troccoli, Timothy Wilson, and Robert Zajonc.

SSSP 2. THE SOCIAL MIND: COGNITIVE AND MOTIVATIONAL ASPECTS OF INTERPERSONAL BEHAVIOR** ISBN 0–521–77092–0 (Edited by J.P. Forgas, K.D. Williams, and L. Wheeler). *Contributors*: Susan Andersen, Roy Baumeister, Joel Cooper, Bill Crano, Garth Fletcher, Joseph Forgas, Mike Hogg, Pascal Huguet, Martin Kaplan, Norb Kerr, William and Claire McGuire, John Nezlek, Fred Rhodewalt, Astrid Schuetz, Constantine Sedikides, Jeffry Simpson, Richard Sorrentino, Dianne Tice, Kip Williams, and Ladd Wheeler.

SSSP 3. SOCIAL INFLUENCE: DIRECT AND INDIRECT PROCESSES* ISBN 1–84169–038–4 (Edited by J.P. Forgas and K.D. Williams). *Contributors*: Herbert Bless, Martin Bourgeois, Shannon Butler, Robert Cialdini, Barbara David, Ap Dijksterhuis, Lara Dolnik, Joseph Forgas, Stephen Harkins, Miles Hewstone, Michael Hogg, John Jost, Eric Knowles, Bibb Latané, Martin Lea, Jay Linn, Robin Martin, Thomas Mussweiler, Sik Hung Ng, Richard

Petty, Tom Postmes, Mark Schaller, Gretchen Sechrist, Russell Spears, Charles Stangor, Fritz Strack, James Tedeschi, Deborah Terry, John Turner, Eva Walther, Susan Watt, and Kipling Williams.

**SSSP 4. THE SOCIAL SELF: COGNITIVE, INTERPERSONAL, AND INTERGROUP PERSPECTIVES**★★ ISBN 1–84169–062–7 (Edited by J.P. Forgas and K.D. Williams). *Contributors:* Art Aron, Roy F. Baumeister, Monica Biernat, Marilynn B. Brewer, Natalie Ciarocco, Anna Clark, Joel Cooper, Christian S. Crandall, Joseph P. Forgas, Thomas Gilovich, Edward R. Hirt, Michael Hogg, William Ickes, Emiko Kashima, Yoshihisa Kashima, Marianne LaFrance, Mark Leary, Diane M. Mackie, Bertram F. Malle, Sean M. McCrea, Stephanie J. Moylan, Sabine Otten, Cynthia L. Pickett, Frederick Rhodewalt, Brandon J. Schmeichel, Constantine Sedikides, Eliot R. Smith, Dianne M. Tice, Michael Tragakis, Linda R. Tropp, Jean M. Twenge, and Stephen C. Wright.

**SSSP 5. SOCIAL JUDGMENTS: IMPLICIT AND EXPLICIT PROCESSES**★★ ISBN 0–521–82248–3 (Edited by J.P. Forgas, K.D. Williams, and W. Von Hippel). *Contributors:* Herbert Bless, Marilynn Brewer, David Buss, Tanya Chartrand, Klaus Fiedler, Joseph Forgas, David Funder, Adam Galinsky, Martie Haselton, Denis Hilton, Lucy Johnston, Arie Kruglanski, Matthew Lieberman, John McClure, Mario Mikulincer, Norbert Schwarz, Philip Shaver, Diederik Stapel, Jerry Suls, William von Hippel, Michaela Waenke, Ladd Wheeler, Kipling Williams, and Michael Zarate.

**SSSP 6. SOCIAL MOTIVATION: CONSCIOUS AND UNCONSCIOUS PROCESSES**★★ ISBN 0–521–83254–3 (Edited by J.P. Forgas, K.D. Williams, and S.M. Laham). *Contributors:* Henk Aarts, Neal Ashkanasy, Trevor Case, Roland Deutsch, Trish Devine, Joseph Forgas, Jens Forster, Guido Gendolla, Judy Harackiewicz, Ran Hassin, Leanne Hing, Doug Kenrick, Michael Kernis, Paul Lewicki, Nira Liberman, Steve Neuberg, Tom Pyszczynski, Jeffrey Quinn, Fred Rhodewalt, Mark Schaller, Jonathan Schooler, Steve Spencer, Fritz Strack, Wayne Warburton, Howard Weiss, Kip Williams, Wendy Wood, Rex Wright, and Mark Zanna.

**SSSP 7. THE SOCIAL OUTCAST: OSTRACISM, SOCIAL EXCLUSION, REJECTION, AND BULLYING**★ ISBN 1–84169–424–X (Edited by K.D. Williams, J.P. Forgas, and W. Von Hippel). *Contributors:* Roy F. Baumeister, Marilynn B. Brewer, John T. Cacioppo, Kathleen R. Catanese, Tanya L. Chartrand, C. Nathan DeWall, Geraldine Downey, Naomi I. Eisenberger, Susan T. Fiske, Julie Fitness, Joseph P. Forgas, Lowell Gaertner, Marcello Gallucci, Wendi L. Gardner, Elisheva F. Gross, Louise C. Hawkley, Michael A. Hogg, Jonathan Iuzzini, Jaana Juvonen, Norbert L. Kerr, Rachell Kingsbury, Megan Knowles, Jessica L. Lakin, Mark R. Leary, Matthew D. Lieberman, Geoff MacDonald, Jaap W. Ouwerkerk, Cynthia L. Pickett, Rainer Romero-Canyas,

Yonata Rubin, Stephanie Shaw, Kristin L. Sommer, Dianne M. Tice, Jean M. Twenge, Paul A.M. Van Lange, William von Hippel, Kipling D. Williams, Mariko Yamamoto, and Lisa Zadro.

**SSSP 8. AFFECT IN SOCIAL THINKING AND BEHAVIOR**★ ISBN 1–84169–454–2 (Edited by J.P. Forgas). *Contributors*: Danu B. Anthony, Jamie Arndt, Roy F. Baumeister, John T. Blackledge, Herbert Bless, Chris Burke, John T. Cacioppo, Joseph Ciarrochi, Gerald L. Clore, Bieke David, Elizabeth W. Dunn, Eric Eich, Ralph Erber, Klaus Fiedler, Joseph P. Forgas, Martie G. Haselton, John G. Holmes, E.J. Horberg, Felicia A. Huppert, Eric R. Igou, Janice R. Kelly, Dacher Keltner, Timothy Ketelaar, Leslie D. Kirby, Simon M. Laham, Dawn Macaulay, Susan Markunas, Christopher Oveis, Clay Routledge, Constantine Sedikides, Craig A. Smith, Jennifer R. Spoor, Justin Storbeck, Dianne M. Tice, Yaacov Trope, Kathleen D. Vohs, Tim Wildschut, and Piotr Winkielman, and Carrie Wyland.

**SSSP 9. EVOLUTION AND THE SOCIAL MIND**★ ISBN 1–84169–458–0 (Edited by J.P. Forgas, M.G. Haselton, and W. Von Hippel). *Contributors*: Nicholas B. Allen, Paul B.T. Badcock, Andrew S. Baron, D. Vaughn Becker, Ross Buck, Abraham P. Buunk, Emily Chan, Andrew W. Delton, Pieternel Dijkstra, R.I.M. Dunbar, Lesley A. Duncan, Phoebe C. Ellsworth, Garth J.O. Fletcher, Joseph P. Forgas, Steven W. Gangestad, Stephen Garcia, Jamin Halberstadt, Martie Haselton, Jeffrey Hutsler, Matthew C. Keller, Douglas T. Kenrick, Rob Kurzban, Jonathon LaPaglia, Debra Lieberman, Karlijn Massar, Kimberly Rios Morrison, Steven L. Neuberg, Nickola C. Overall, Theresa E. Robertson, Jeffrey Sanchez-Burks, Mark Schaller, Jeffry A. Simpson, Jennifer R. Spoor, Randy Thornhill, Peter M. Todd, Mark Van Vugt, William von Hippel, Kipling D. Williams, and Oscar Ybarra.

**SSSP 10. SOCIAL RELATIONSHIPS: COGNITIVE, AFFECTIVE, AND MOTIVATIONAL PROCESSES**★ ISBN 978–1–84169–715–4 (Edited by J.P. Forgas and J. Fitness). *Contributors*: Linda K. Acitelli, Christopher R. Agnew, Ximena B. Arriaga, Anita Blakeley-Smith, Alice D. Boyes, Marilynn B. Brewer, Margaret S. Clark, W. Andrew Collins, Susan Conway, Eli J. Finkel, Julie Fitness, Garth J.O. Fletcher, Joseph P. Forgas, Shelly L. Gable, Gian C. Gonzaga, Steven M. Graham, Martie G. Haselton, Elaine Hatfield, Katherine C. Haydon, Edward P. Lemay, Mario Mikulincer, Rowland S. Miller, Sandra L. Murray, Patricia Noller, Julie Peterson, Richard L. Rapson, David P. Schmitt, Phillip R. Shaver, Jeffry A. Simpson, SiSi Tran, Erin Williams, Kipling D. Williams, Juan E. Wilson, and Lisa Zadro.

**SSSP 11. PSYCHOLOGY OF SELF-REGULATION: COGNITIVE, AFFECTIVE, AND MOTIVATIONAL PROCESSES**★ ISBN 978–1–84872–842–4 (Edited by J.P. Forgas, R. Baumeister, and D.M. Tice). *Contributors*:

Jessica L. Alquist, Roy F. Baumeister, Hart Blanton, Matthias Bluemke, Charles S. Carver, Thomas F. Denson, Paul W. Eastwick, Bob Fennis, Klaus Fiedler, Eli J. Finkel, Ayelet Fishbach, Gráinne M. Fitzsimons, Joseph P. Forgas, Jens Förster, Malte Friese, Justin Friesen, Peter M. Gollwitzer, Deborah L. Hall, Wilhelm Hofmann, Sarah E. Johnson, Sander L. Koole, Arie W. Kruglanski, Jannine D. Lasaleta, Nira Liberman, Daniel Memmert, Daniel C. Molden, Gabriele Oettingen, Edward Orehek, Henning Plessner, Richard Ronay, Carol Sansone, Michael F. Scheier, Constantine Sedikides, Dianne M. Tice, Christian Unkelbach, Kathleen D. Vohs, William von Hippel, and Michaela Wänke.

**SSSP 12. PSYCHOLOGY OF ATTITUDES AND ATTITUDE CHANGE★** ISBN 978–1–84872–908–7 (Edited by J.P. Forgas, J. Cooper, and W.D. Crano). *Contributors:* David M. Amodio, Jim Blascovich, Marcella H. Boynton, Zhansheng Chen, Joel Cooper, William D. Crano, Klaus Fiedler, Joseph P. Forgas, Cindy Harmon-Jones, Eddie Harmon-Jones, Allyson L. Holbrook, Blair T. Johnson, Jon A. Krosnick, Tina Langer, Alison Ledgerwood, Brenda Major, Cade McCall, Jennifer Peach, Benjamin Peterson, Radmila Prislin, Leonie Reutner, Frederick Rhodewalt, Steven J. Spencer, Sarah S.M. Townsend, Yaacov Trope, Eva Walther, Michaela Wänke, Duane Wegener, Kipling D. Williams, Emiko Yoshida, and Mark P. Zanna.

**SSSP 13. PSYCHOLOGY OF SOCIAL CONFLICT AND AGGRESSION★** ISBN 978–1–84872–932–2 (Edited by J.P. Forgas, A.W. Kruglanski, and K.D. Williams). *Contributors:* Daniel Ames, Craig A. Anderson, Joanna E. Anderson, Paul Boxer, Tanya L. Chartrand, John Christner, Matt DeLisi, Thomas F. Denson, Ed Donnerstein, Eric F. Dubow, Chris Eckhardt, Emma C. Fabiansson, Eli J. Finkel, Gráinne M. Fitzsimons, Joseph P. Forgas, Adam D. Galinsky, Debra Gilin, Georgina S. Hammock, L. Rowell Huesmann, Arie W. Kruglanski, Robert Kurzban, N. Pontus Leander, Laura B. Luchies, William W. Maddux, Mario Mikulincer, Edward Orehek, Deborah South Richardson, Phillip R. Shaver, Hui Bing Tan, Mark Van Vugt, Eric D. Wesselmann, Kipling D. Williams, and Lisa Zadro.

**SSSP 14. SOCIAL THINKING AND INTERPERSONAL BEHAVIOR★** ISBN 978–1–84872–990–2 (Edited by J.P. Forgas, K. Fiedler, and C. Sekidikes). *Contributors:* Andrea E. Abele, Eusebio M. Alvaro, Mauro Bertolotti, Camiel J. Beukeboom, Susanne Bruckmüller, Patrizia Catellani, Cindy K. Chung, Joel Cooper, William D. Crano, István Csertő, John F. Dovidio, Bea Ehmann, Klaus Fiedler, Joseph P. Forgas, Éva Fülöp, Jessica Gasiorek, Howard Giles, Liz Goldenberg, Barbara Ilg, Yoshihisa Kashima, Mikhail Kissine, Olivier Klein, Alex Koch, János László, Anne Maass, Andre Mata, Elisa M. Merkel, Alessio Nencini, Andrew A. Pearson, James W. Pennebaker, Kim Peters, Tibor Pólya, Ben Slugoski, Caterina Suitner, Zsolt Szabó, Matthew D. Trujillo, and Orsolya Vincze.

**SSSP 15. SOCIAL COGNITION AND COMMUNICATION\*** ISBN 978–1–84872–663–5 (Edited by J.P. Forgas, O. Vincze, and J. László). *Contributors*: Andrea E. Abele, Eusebio M. Alvaro, Maro Bertolotti, Camiel J. Beukeboom, Susanne Bruckmüller, Patrizia Catellani, István Cserto, Cindy K. Chung, Joel Cooper, William D. Crano, John F. Dovidio, Bea Ehmann, Klaus Fiedler, J.P. Forgas, Éva Fülöp, Jessica Gasiorek, Howard Giles, Liz Goldenberg, Barbara Ilg, Yoshihisa Kahima, Mikhail Kissine, Alex S. Koch, János László, Olivier Klein, Anne Maass, André Mata, Elisa M. Merkel, Alessio Nencini, Adam R. Pearson, James W. Pennebaker, Kim Peters, Tibor Pólya, Ben Slugoski, Caterina Suitner, Zsolt Szabó, Matthew D. Trujillo, and Orsolya Vincze.

**SSSP 16. MOTIVATION AND ITS REGULATION: THE CONTROL WITHIN\*** ISBN 978–1–84872–562–1 (Edited by J.P. Forgas and E. Harmon-Jones). *Contributors*: Emily Balcetis, John A. Bargh, Jarik Bouw, Charles S. Carver, Brittany M. Christian, Hannah Faye Chua, Shana Cole, Carsten K.W. De Dreu, Thomas F. Denson, Andrew J. Elliot, Joseph P. Forgas, Alexandra Godwin, Karen Gonsalkorale, Jamin Halberstadt, Cindy Harmon-Jones, Eddie Harmon-Jones, E. Tory Higgins, Julie Y. Huang, Michael Inzlicht, Sheri L. Johnson, Jonathan Jong, Jutta Joormann, Nils B. Jostmann, Shinobu Kitayama, Sander L. Koole, Lisa Legault, Jennifer Leo, C. Neil Macrae, Jon K. Maner, Lynden K. Mile, Steven B. Most, Jaime L. Napier, Tom F. Price, Marieke Roskes, Brandon J. Schmeichel, Iris K. Schneider, Abigail A. Scholer, Julia Schüler, Sarah Strübin, David Tang, Steve Tompson, Mattie Tops, and Lisa Zadro.

**SSSP 17. SOCIAL PSYCHOLOGY AND POLITICS\*** ISBN 978–1–13882–968–8 (Edited by Joseph P. Forgas, Klaus Fiedler, and William D. Crano). *Contributors*: Stephanie M. Anglin, Luisa Batalha, Mauro Bertolotti, Patrizia Catellani, William D. Crano, Jarret T. Crawford, John F. Dovidio, Klaus Fiedler, Joseph P. Forgas, Mark G. Frank, Samuel L. Gaertner, Jeremy Ginges, Joscha Hofferbert, Michael A. Hogg, Hyisung C. Hwang, Yoel Inbar, Lee Jussim, Lucas A. Keefer, Laszlo Kelemen, Alex Koch, Tobias Krüger, Mark J. Landau, Janos Laszlo, Elena Lyrintzis, David Matsumoto, G. Scott Morgan, David A. Pizarro, Felicia Pratto, Katherine J. Reynolds, Tamar Saguy, Daan Scheepers, David O. Sears, Linda J. Skitka, Sean T. Stevens, Emina Subasic, Elze G. Ufkes, Robin R. Vallacher, Paul A.M. Van Lange, Daniel C. Wisneski, Michaela Wänke, Franz Woellert, and Fouad Bou Zeineddine.

**SSSP 18. THE SOCIAL PSYCHOLOGY OF MORALITY\*** ISBN 978–1–138–92907–4 (Edited by Joseph P. Forgas, Lee Jussim, and Paul A.M. Van Lange). *Contributors*: Stephanie M. Anglin, Joel B. Armstrong, Mark J. Brandt, Brock Bastian, Paul Conway, Joel Cooper, Chelsea Corless, Jarret T. Crawford, Daniel Crimston, Molly J. Crockett, Jose L. Duarte, Allison K. Farrell, Klaus Fiedler, Rebecca Friesdorf, Jeremy A. Frimer, Adam D. Galinsky, Bertram Gawronski, William G. Graziano, Nick Haslam, Mandy Hütter, Lee Jussim,

Alice Lee, William W. Maddux, Emma Marshall, Dale T. Miller, Benoît Monin, Tom Pyszczynski, Richard Ronay, David A. Schroeder, Simon M. Laham, Jeffry A. Simpson, Sean T. Stevens, William von Hippel, and Geoffrey Wetherell.

* Published by Routledge
** Published by Cambridge University Press

# THE SOCIAL PSYCHOLOGY OF MORALITY

*Edited by Joseph P. Forgas, Lee Jussim, and Paul A.M. Van Lange*

Routledge
Taylor & Francis Group

NEW YORK AND LONDON

First published 2016
by Routledge
711 Third Avenue, New York, NY 10017

and by Routledge
2 Park Square, Milton Park, Abingdon, Oxon, OX14 4RN

*Routledge is an imprint of the Taylor & Francis Group, an informa business*

*Library of Congress Cataloging-in-Publication Data*
Social psychology of morality (Forgas, Jussim, and Lange)
   The social psychology of morality / edited by Joseph P. Forgas, Lee Jussim, and Paul A.M. Van Lange.
      pages cm
   Includes bibliographical references and index.
   1. Ethics.   2. Social ethics.   3. Values.   4. Social psychology.   I. Forgas, Joseph P., editor.   II. Jussim, Lee J., editor.   III. Lange, Paul A. M. Van, editor.   IV. Title.
   BJ45.S6353 2016
   171—dc23
   2015030614

ISBN: 978-1-138-92906-7 (hbk)
ISBN: 978-1-138-92907-4 (pbk)
ISBN: 978-1-315-64418-9 (ebk)

Typeset in Bembo
by Apex CoVantage

Printed and bound in the United States of America by
Edwards Brothers Malloy on sustainably sourced paper

# CONTENTS

# CONTRIBUTORS

Anglin, Stephanie M., Rutgers University, USA

Armstrong, Joel B., University of Western Ontario, Canada

Bastian, Brock, University of New South Wales, Australia

Brandt, Mark J., Tilburg University, The Netherlands

Conway, Paul, Florida State University, USA

Cooper, Joel, Princeton University, USA

Corless, Chelsea, Melbourne School of Psychological Sciences, University of Melbourne, Australia

Crawford, Jarret T., The College of New Jersey, USA

Crimston, Daniel, University of Queensland, Australia

Crockett, Molly J., Department of Experimental Psychology, University of Oxford, UK

Duarte, Jose L., Arizona State University, USA

Farrell, Allison K., University of Minnesota, USA

Fiedler, Klaus, University of Heidelberg, Germany

Forgas, Joseph P., University of New South Wales, Australia

Friesdorf, Rebecca, Wilfrid Laurier University, Canada

Frimer, Jeremy A., University of Winnipeg, Canada

Galinsky, Adam D., Columbia University, USA

Gawronski, Bertram, University of Texas at Austin, USA

Graziano, William G., Purdue University, USA

Haslam, Nick, University of Melbourne, Australia

Hütter, Mandy, University of Tübingen, Germany

Jussim, Lee, Rutgers University, and The Center for Advanced Study in the Behavioral Sciences, Stanford, USA

Laham, Simon M., Melbourne School of Psychological Sciences, University of Melbourne, Australia

Lee, Alice, Columbia University, USA

Maddux, William W., INSEAD, France

Marshall, Emma, University of Canterbury, New Zealand

Miller, Dale T., Stanford University, USA

Monin, Benoît, Stanford University, USA

Pyszczynski, Tom, University of Colorado, Colorado Springs, USA

Ronay, Richard, Vrije Universiteit Amsterdam, The Netherlands

Schroeder, David A., University of Arkansas, USA

Simpson, Jeffry A., University of Minnesota, USA

Stevens, Sean T., Rutgers University, USA

Van Lange, Paul A.M., Vrije Universiteit Amsterdam, The Netherlands

von Hippel, William, University of Queensland, Australia

Wetherell, Geoffrey, Valparaiso University, USA

# 1

# IN SEARCH OF *HOMO MORALIS*

## The Social Psychology of Morality

*Joseph P. Forgas, Lee Jussim, and Paul A.M. Van Lange*

Ever since Plato's *Republic* was written over 2,000 years ago, one of the main concerns of social philosophy and later empirical social science has been to understand the moral nature of human beings. The faculty to think and act in terms of overarching moral values is as much a defining hallmark of our species as is our intelligence, so *Homo moralis* is no less an appropriate term to describe humans as is *Homo sapiens*. If morality has a flavor of the goodness or badness of humankind, and the ways in which individuals, groups, and societies regulate, or should regulate, individual action and behavior, then there is little doubt that we are talking about one of the broadest topics possible.

Many basic questions about human nature have at least some moral flavor. One of the most enduring philosophical debates has centered on the question of whether people are naturally bad or good. Alas, there could hardly be more disagreement among philosophers than on this issue. For example, from Plato onwards, many thinkers believed in the fundamentally flawed, emotional, and selfish nature of humankind. Most Christian religious philosophers also assumed that humans are inherently sinful, although capable of redemption and moral behavior. Nietzsche was among those most strongly convinced that people are bad by nature, and Adam Smith formulated an entire—and hugely successful—theory of economic behavior based on the assumption that individual selfishness can in fact be harnessed in service of the common good. At the other extreme, Rousseau was among those who believed in the inherent moral goodness of humankind. Paradoxically, hugely influential communalistic theories such as Marxism based on an assumption of the fundamentally good nature of humans, such as our presumed communality, empathy, and selflessness, turned out in practice to produce some of the most horrific societies in human history.

Morality is also strongly involved in views of how a society should go about controlling or regulating individuals' selfish impulses, and aggressive or violent tendencies. Some philosophers thought that a government should strongly control individuals' behavior by administering punishment and designing strict laws to regulate norm violations. Others were more "lenient" in their political philosophy. For the purposes of this chapter, taking an avowedly social psychological orientation, we may functionally define morality in terms of social norms—and the related sanctions that accompany norm violations. Morality tends to be less manifest in actions that conform to norms and are perceived as morally acceptable than in actions that involve norm violations. In the second half of this chapter, we will discuss the nature, functions, and consequences of social norms as embodiments of moral principles.

Topics to do with morality were traditionally addressed by scientists working in a number of disciplines, including anthropology, biology, economics, mathematics, neuroscience, psychology, and political science. In the present book, we would like to argue that social psychology occupies a privileged position when it comes to understanding the nature of human morality. In this introductory essay in particular, we will start by making a case for the pivotal role of social psychology as the core discipline for studying morality. Next, we will discuss the two fundamental alternative theoretical positions for studying morality: morality as the outcome of a rational, analytic, and deliberative process; and morality as in intrinsic, universal, intuitive, and evolutionarily determined human faculty. We will then consider the often paradoxical social effects of morality, when higher moral principles lead to often immoral and sometimes evil actions.

Next, the tangible conceptualization of moral principles in terms of social norms will be discussed, and the functions of social norms in facilitating the social life of dyads, groups, or larger collectives will be considered. And finally, the essential role of morality in defining and maintaining a stable and positive self-concept, and in informing and justifying our evaluations of others, will be discussed.

## Social Psychology and Morality

Moral concerns do not occur in some abstract world characterized by ivory tower speculation—they are inherently and deeply social. Nearly all manifestations of morality involve, are based on, influence, and sometimes govern our relations with other people (see also Frimer; Haslam; Miller & Monin; and Simpson, Farrell, & Marshall, this volume). Indeed, the social bases of morality can be readily extended to other living and even nonliving things (see also Bastian & Crimston, this volume). The basic intuitive foundations of morality identified in the recent literature (e.g., Graham et al., 2013) include predominantly social concerns, such as care/harm, fairness/cheating, loyalty/betrayal, authority/subversion, and sanctity/degradation.

The first four of these moral concerns refer exclusively to our relationships with other people, and the last one, sanctity/degradation, usually does so as well. The famous "trolley problem," deciding whether to allow one person to die in order to save several others, also involves a fundamentally social decision: What value should we place on human life? Are all lives of equal value? Should such decisions be even accepted and made? At the risk of being self- or (at least) group-serving, it appears then that social psychologists are uniquely well suited among all the sciences and humanities to seek to understand the causes, consequences, and nature of morality. This book seeks to make a contribution to this quest, by surveying some of the most recent cutting-edge research by leading social psychologists on the issue of morality.

Indeed, many of the most cherished topics in social psychology—stereotyping, prejudice, discrimination, altruism, justice, inequality, obedience, conformity, group differences, intelligence, terror management theory, the fundamental attribution error, and even concern with the power of the situation—can be viewed as deeply infused with moral undertones and implications. Many forms of discrimination are clearly immoral (and, sometimes, illegal), and the moral outrage by many social psychologists at such injustices has likely fueled a century of scientific interest in these topics. Milgram's (1974) obedience studies as well as Henri Tajfel's social identity theory (Tajfel & Forgas, 1982) were inspired by revulsion at the horrors of the Nazi Holocaust, and a need to understand how such immoral mass behavior could be explained by social psychologists. Latané and Darley's (1970) studies were inspired by being morally appalled at reports of the failure of an entire apartment building of residents to prevent the brutal murder of Kitty Genovese (although, there are now some questions about this story; see Manning, Levine, & Collins, 2007). And of course, most research on prejudice and stereotyping, especially in the US, has long been motivated by a moral concern about overcoming the morally repugnant historical consequences of slavery and decades of entrenched racism (see also Jussim, Crawford, Stevens, Anglin, & Duarte, this volume).

## Morality: Rational or Intuitive?

### Historical Perspectives on Morality

The social and behavioral sciences have danced with and around issues of morality from the very beginning. One of the most basic approaches to morality is deontology, espousing the principle that the rightness or wrongness of actions is inherent in themselves, as opposed to alternative views that emphasize the rightness or wrongness of the consequences of those actions (consequentialism), or focus instead on the character and habits of social actors (virtue) (see also Gawronski, Conway, Armstrong, Friesdorf, & Hütter, this volume).

Often, however, what early scholars addressed only partially overlapped with what we currently think of as morality. Moral philosophy was actually a vibrant topic in the late 19th and early 20th centuries, with many articles and texts on moral instincts and moral education (e.g., Bryant, 1912; Lull, 1911; Royce, 1893), topics that have largely evaporated from current social science discourse. Indeed, the very term "moral instincts" has a somewhat archaic sound to it. And the idea of "moral education" is not a particularly vibrant topic in modern social psychology today.

Surprisingly, the contrast between these older approaches and more modern perspectives is not as striking as it may at first appear. Although psychologists discarded most of the "instinct" theories decades ago when describing human behavior, similar ideas have resurfaced in recent evolutionary and other approaches to psychology that have become increasingly influential (e.g., Buss, 1995; see also Laham & Corless; Pyszczynski; and von Hippel, Ronay, & Maddux, this volume). According to such views, certain moral values appear universal and have an evolutionary basis (Graham et al., 2013). In this light, approaches referring to "moral instincts" received new currency in recent years. Furthermore, Royce's (1893) early paper highlights two particular forms of morality, care (he uses terms like "love" and "charity") and justice, which again figure prominently in one of the most influential of modern psychological theories of morality, Moral Foundations Theory (Graham et al., 2013). It seems then that there are at least two fundamental psychological approaches to understanding morality: as the outcome of a rational, analytic process; and as a fundamental, universal, and intuitive human faculty. We shall turn to considering this dichotomy next.

## Morality as Rational

The modern scientific, empirical study of the psychology of morality can primarily be traced to the influential work of Kohlberg (e.g., Kohlberg & Hersh, 1977) some decades ago, who was clearly inspired by Piaget's stage theory of cognitive development. This line of thinking, linking morality to rationality, has its philosophical and intellectual roots in the ideology of the Enlightenment, and especially, in the work of Jeremy Bentham, John Stuart Mill, and David Hume. Utilitarian philosophy attempted to explain the complexity of moral concerns in terms of a simple rational principle, asserting that what is good and desirable is not inherent in the action itself (deontology), but can be determined by analyzing the hedonistic consequences of alternative courses of action (consequentialism; see also Gawronski et al., this volume). Such "utilitarian calculus" assumes a cool, rational, deliberative approach to questions of morality, and it is this principle that was embodied in Piaget's developmental theory, and Kohlberg's subsequent work on morality as well.

Kohlberg argued for a basically cognitive, maturation-based development of morality through essentially rational reasoning processes. The person starts, as a young child, with a simple view of morality as a function of rewards and punishments, and proceeds through a series of developmental stages until, as the capacity for more abstract reasoning increases, the person adopts a set of universal and abstract moral principles. Furthermore, Kohlberg's work (e.g., Boyd & Kohlberg, 1973; Kohlberg & Hersh, 1977) shows a close affinity with earlier movements advocating "moral education," also a derivative of earlier utilitarian philosophies, whose aim became, for Kohlberg, to increase the child's ability to think and reason abstractly about moral principles.

## Morality as Intuitive

Kohlberg's view predominated for the past several decades. However, Haidt (2001) disagreed with a fundamental assumption underlying much of Kohlberg's work—that morality generally resulted from rational *reasoning* of any type. Instead, Haidt demonstrated in a variety of contexts (see reviews in Haidt, 2001, 2012) that people frequently claimed that behaviors were immoral (e.g., having sex with a sibling) even when they *failed* to violate any rational moral principle for such prohibitions (e.g., one argument against sibling sex was the risk of deformed or deficient offspring—an argument readily neutralized if the siblings used contraception). When confronted with this inconsistency, people became "dumb-founded"—insisting that the action was immoral even when compelled to agree that there were no good, rational reasons or moral principles that were violated. They were often unable to articulate a reason justifying why they considered the action to be immoral, while still insisting on its immorality.

On the basis of such findings, Haidt (2001, 2012) concluded that: (1) moral beliefs were often not based on the conscious, controlled reasoning processes as presumed by Kohlberg, and indeed, by many philosophers since the Enlightenment; (2) they were, instead, based on largely nonconscious and largely nonrational intuitions; however, (3) people were very good at enlisting their cognitive and abstract analytic abilities post hoc in order to *justify* their moral intuitions in order to make it *appear* as if their moral judgments were rational and the result of deep abstract considerations. Evolutionary approaches yield somewhat similar predictions, assuming that morality can best be understood in terms of universal, evolved tendencies that have some adaptive value (see also Laham & Corless; Pyszczynski; and von Hippel et al., this volume). Indeed, Haidt's 2001 article was titled "The Emotional Dog and Its Rational Tail" to capture the idea that these gut-level moral intuitions generally drive the seemingly rational justifications for moral beliefs and values. These ideas have evolved over the last 15 years into a new, general theoretical approach to morality, Moral Foundations Theory (e.g., Graham, Haidt, & Nosek, 2009) which posits that five (or possibly six; Haidt, 2012) fundamental moral intuitions serve as the basis for most moral beliefs and values.

There have been many other recent productive avenues in the study of morality unrelated to Haidt's intuitionist Moral Foundations Theory. For example, a quick Google Scholar search for "trolley problem" and "moral" yielded almost 2,000 hits; and there is an entire journal devoted to social justice (*Social Justice Research*). Nonetheless, Haidt's 2001 paper was hugely influential in that it reinvigorated the social psychological interest in issues of morality. According to Google Scholar, the paper has now been cited over 4,000 times. Haidt's insight that morality is mostly based on nonrational intuitions, whether one agrees with it or not, has sparked an explosion of research based on this approach.

The recent growth of interest in intuitive morality can also be demonstrated through a simple citation count study. Using Google Scholar, one of us (Jussim) performed a search for the terms "social psychology" and "prejudice" or "social psychology" and "moral" for either 1950–2001 or 2002–2015. The field has been expanding for a long time, and there were almost 50% more hits for "prejudice" in the 2002–2015 period. However, there were over *three times as many* hits post-2001 for "social psychology" and "moral" than in the 1950–2001 period. This volume, summarizing and integrating some of the most recent social psychological approaches, thus arrives at an opportune time when interest in this field is growing by leaps and bounds.

## Paradoxical Effects of Morality

So far, we implied that moral evaluations in the social domain can be easily classified into good, desirable, and bad, undesirable categories. It turns out that this is a huge oversimplification: sometimes highly moral intentions can produce deeply immoral outcomes, a pattern we may call the *paradoxical or ironic effects of morality*. In Kohlberg's rational system, morality was clearly good, something to be strived for; abstract moral reasoning was a higher and preferable stage of development worth striving for. Morals, however, can be a double-edged sword. Is inequality immoral? An implicit assumption in many major social psychological perspectives (e.g., Social Dominance Orientation, System Justification Theory, and much of the prejudice literature) seems to assume that it is. How can we explain, then, that Mao and Stalin eventually murdered tens of millions of their own citizens in the name of ideological systems supposedly intended to advance equality?

It seems that morals sometimes have paradoxical effects, and inspire and justify immoral behavior. All sorts of heinous acts, up to and including mass murder and genocide, have been committed in the name of what the perpetrators claimed were high moral purposes. Political values are rooted in moral values (Forgas, Fiedler, & Crano, 2015; Graham et al., 2013), and yet people often so despise their political enemies that they readily express willingness to perpetrate all sorts of injustices on them (see Brandt, Wetherell, & Crawford, this volume). The stronger and more absolute and unquestionable a strongly held moral belief appears to be, the more likely that its adherents will be prepared to act immorally to advance their ostensibly moral objectives.

This kind of paradoxical, "the ends justify the means" morality permeates all human history. As Koestler (1967) argued, human beings are unique among species in their capacity to commit horrific, systematic, and premeditated violence against members of their own species. These acts of unspeakable violence are almost always committed not out of explicit evil intent, but in the name of higher moral principles. Human history is full of such examples. The Mayans cut out the living hearts of tens of thousands of captives a day in the name of their religion; Christians sent children to fight for the liberation of the Holy Land in the Crusades, and burnt thousands of people on the stake in order to save their "eternal souls"; Hitler believed that the Holocaust was necessary to defend European culture and the Aryan race; and of course, modern-day Islamic radicals kill innocents in the name of their God.

Paradoxical effects of moral beliefs can also be observed closer to home, in social psychology (see also Fiedler; and Haslam, this volume). It is even possible that high moral purposes can sometime undermine scientific ethics. When researchers believe they are working to advance some higher good (combating oppression, adopting policies to limit climate change, etc.), they may inadvertently, or sometimes intentionally, reach false and misleading conclusions to serve their objectives (see Jussim et al., this volume). In this context, it is interesting to note that even though Kohlberg and Hersh (1977) claimed not to be advocating any particular moral worldview, they nevertheless repeatedly elevated a very specific set of moral values as the ones reflecting the "highest" levels of moral reasoning (justice, equality, respect for individual rights). Thus, Kohlberg's repeated claims stressing the importance of form and process over content, focusing on the sophistication of the person's moral reasoning, actually disguised an underlying substantive moral bias. As far as we can tell, there is nothing "objectively" superior about holding values such as justice, equality, liberty, and so forth over many alternatives, yet this represents exactly the type of value embedding in psychological theory that can undermine scientific validity and credibility (see also Duarte et al., 2015).

Indeed, the paradoxical aspects of morality seem even more universal. Many moral values are intrinsically in conflict with each other. The French Revolution, the harbinger of the modern age, had three moral values at its core: liberty, equality, and brotherhood. These values have guided political philosophy and democratic practice for the last three hundred years in Western civilizations. Yet it turns out that their simultaneous realization is impossible. As Dahrendorf (1968) showed, any political attempt to increase liberty will necessarily limit equality, and any increase in equality is only achievable at the expense of some liberty. And of course, brotherhood, the "poor cousin" of these three core moral values, can be, and has been, compromised by the historical pursuit of both liberty and equality.

Thus, despite the universal popular assumption that we can readily distinguish what is good and what is bad, and what are moral and immoral *behaviors*, reality is far more complex. Morality often has paradoxical effects, and strongly held moral beliefs and values can sometimes lead to manifestly evil behaviors. We may even venture a guess that the stronger and more absolute a moral belief is, the more likely that it will result in paradoxical, immoral consequences (Koestler, 1967). One of the objectives of this book is to focus on the ironic, paradoxical nature of morality as it applies to many aspects of social life. In particular we will include some challenging examples that document the paradoxical behavior of scientists themselves (see Fiedler; Haslam; and Jussim et al., this volume).

## Social Norms and Morality

One of the few common themes in definitions of morality is the shared emphasis on a "code of conduct," or explicit social norms to be used by a group or a society, prescribing appropriate courses of action and related sanctions. Morality is mostly about regulating social behavior (see also Galinsky & Lee; Graziano & Schroeder; and Simpson et al., this volume). We will now turn to discussing the moral aspects of some basic social norms, as well as the primary functions of such norms in enhancing the functioning of dyads, groups, or larger collectives. And finally, we will consider the role of moral norms in defining and maintaining the self, and in evaluating others.

Of course, different norms might prescribe sometimes opposing courses of action. While the Ten Commandments, a deontological system of norms par excellence, clearly prohibit murder, popes, bishops, and priests throughout history exhorted their armies to kill their enemies in the name of God, king, and country. Such norm conflict is inevitable in moral decisions. Norms may operate at the level of the individual, the group, the entire collective, or society at large. For a clearer understanding of the psychology of morality, we need to consider the moral content of representative social norms.

One of the most important norms guiding our behavior is rooted in the "no harm principle." Harming others is often seen as a norm violation, whereas withholding help can sometimes be justifiable (e.g., when the cost of helping is too high). To take a concrete example, Crockett (this volume) describes a series of studies where the no-harm principle is strongly involved in the process whereby people may prefer to receive some shocks themselves rather than to make the decision (and be accountable) for another suffering harm.

Another pervasive norm is the norm of *social responsibility* for others who are strongly dependent on one's help, especially when external, uncontrollable factors are the primary cause for their need. Social responsibility can also be activated when the self is in a position of power, or is in a unique position to help. Conceptually, the norm of responsibility should be distinguished from empathy, which is more emotional and automatic (Batson, 2011; see also Graziano & Schroeder, this volume). The norm of social responsibility is often preceded by some (implicit or explicit) evaluation of the other in need, the ability to help, and the availability of alternative sources of help (Latané & Darley, 1968).

A norm that is especially important to social interaction is the norm of *reciprocity* (Gouldner, 1960), captured in words of wisdom and sayings such as "do onto others as you would have them do unto you" (e.g., Batson, 2011), "quid pro quo" (e.g., Van Lange, Ouwerkerk, & Tazelaar, 2002), or "tit for tat" (e.g., Axelrod, 1984; see also Galinsky & Lee; and Simpson et al., this volume). The reciprocity norm can be positive (reciprocating cooperative behavior) or negative (reciprocating noncooperative behavior; e.g., Perugini, Gallucci, Presaghi, & Ercolani, 2003). This norm also often serves as a simplifying heuristic, guiding quick reactions to others. It is also interesting to note that as an interaction style, reciprocity is often perceived as both fair, moral, and intelligent (McClintock & Liebrand, 1988).

*Fairness* is a broader norm that is also linked to the reciprocity norm. There are several norms of fairness (e.g., Deutsch, 1975), sometimes based on the principle of equality. This norm is often important in regulating informal relations, for example, among friends. This norm also often functions as a heuristic when it comes to distributing resources (see also Forgas, this volume). Violations of equality, such as one taking a bigger slice of the pizza, will be readily noticed. Another fairness norm is equity (Adams, 1965), when differences in "input" are considered when distributing "output." This norm is stronger in formal relations, where people who have invested more (in terms of skill, effort, or other resources) should receive a greater reward than those who invested less.

Another norm, the *compliance* norm, is focused on complying with social pressure or normative cues, especially in face-to-face interactions, as deviance is counter-normative in many situations. The compliance norm is different from the earlier ones, in that the protection of others is not the primary concern. Classic research by Milgram (1974) and others established that people have a strong tendency to comply with norms, especially in face-to-face situations, even when such compliance results in very poor outcomes for others. People can be easily induced to comply, even to the extent of admitting to nonexistent transgressions (see Cooper, this volume) or lying about an unethical or even dangerous experiment to others (see Bocchiaro, Zimbardo, & Van Lange, 2012). Numerous techniques have been developed based on the compliance norm to get people to "go along." Indeed, advertising and the psychological manipulation of people to consume is one of the engines of modern capitalism. The well-known foot-in-the-door technique is just one of many such compliance strategies.

## The Adaptive Functions of Norms

As we have seen, morality, as translated into social norms of conduct, is mostly about regulating social behavior. We have looked at five relatively distinct social norms as an example, and this list is far from exhaustive. Many other norms could be discussed, such as the honesty norm, the commitment norm (e.g., to do what one promises), and conventional norms with some moral flavor (e.g., to be polite). But what are the broader functions of norms? Norms exist to regulate behavior in a way that is ultimately functional for the self, the dyad, the group, or the larger collective. Most norms exist to protect oneself from exploitation, to obtain collectively good outcomes (reciprocity), to protect the weak (social responsibility), to minimize harm (the no-harm principle) and the protection of collective interest (fairness norms). If most people act in such "moral," other-regarding ways, individuals and collectives are more likely to flourish.

Norms typically provide relatively concrete codes for conduct and thus serve as a moral compass, even though they may at times be in strong competition with our basic impulses or needs. For example, the impulse to be selfish may be countered by the social norm of fairness (see Forgas, this volume). Social norms also provide us with guidelines for evaluating others' actions and behaviors, especially in situations where the pursuit of self-interest poses a threat to others' welfare or collective welfare (Van Lange & Balliet, 2014).

These so-called mixed-motive situations call for resisting temptations to act selfishly. Most of the norms described earlier may be activated in these "dilemmas." The reciprocity norms may be most relevant in dyadic interactions (see Galinsky & Lee; and Simpson et al., this volume), and the compliance norms are often more relevant in situations in which people cannot act anonymously (see also Cooper; and Crockett, this volume). By and large, social norms prevent people from blindly pursuing self-interest at a cost to others or the collective. Norms with a strong moral flavor function to protect collective outcomes, help others in need, and promote some degree of equality, equity, and fairness in outcomes among people.

### When Norms Are Not Clear

So far, we have painted a picture of norms in terms of concrete and clear codes of conduct. However, moral norms can often be conflicting. In many situations, different norms prescribe different behaviors. In experiments on obedience the compliance norm dictates obedience, but the no-harm principle mandates resistance. Scientists may sometimes face similar dilemmas, for example, whether to encourage or discourage a weak Ph.D. student (no-harm principle vs. social responsibility to the discipline; see Fiedler, this volume). The norms of equality and equity often also produce conflicting expectations. Should all members of a music band get an equal share of the profit (equality), or should the lead singer, who contributed most to composing the songs, get a greater share (equity)? Fundamental political ideologies ever since the French Revolution involve a similar moral conflict (Dahrendorf, 1968): should equality be the primary moral and social objective (left-wing, collectivist, social democratic ideology), or should it be individual liberty, equity, and reward (right-wing, conservative, individualist ideology)?

Norms are often also ambiguous in some so-called layered social dilemmas, where the interests of the individual, the ingroup (and outgroup), and the entire collective may differ (e.g., Bornstein, 1992; Wit & Kerr, 2002; see also Gawronski et al., this volume). Employees often must decide among pursuing their own self-interest, the interests of the unit or team, or the interests of the entire organization. Some have argued that there is an individual and a group-based form of moral-ity (Wildschut & Insko, 2006). But at the very least, what is clear is that various norms of morality are conflicting, especially when various levels of social links are involved.

## Moral Evaluations of Self and Others

Moral norms serve not only as guides for behavior, but also as the basis for evalu-ating our own and others' actions (see also Miller & Monin, this volume). By and large, people's moral evaluations are positive for norm-following behavior and negative for norm-violating behavior. Such evaluations are magnified with the activation of emotions, especially social emotions. For example, social emotions such as shame and guilt are strongly linked to maintaining normative standards, and often strengthen norm-congruent behavior. Thus, social emotions are inti-mately linked to norms and moral evaluations.

Do moral evaluations differ for the self and others? There is every reason to believe that they do. People have a strong desire to see themselves, and to be seen by others, as moral. A moral reputation is important for one's status in a group, while moral self-evaluation is important for one's self-esteem. Some beliefs we hold about others may be rooted in the conviction that other people are primarily or only motivated by self-interest (Miller, 1999; Miller & Ratner, 1998; see also Kruger & Gilovich, 1999; Van Lange, 2015; see also Brandt et al., this volume). Indeed, there is evidence showing that people see themselves as better than aver-age, and that this tendency to aspire to moral superiority is especially pronounced for moral traits, such as justice and honesty, and less so for other traits (Allison, Messick, & Goethals, 1989; Van Lange & Sedikides, 1998).

Thus, people have a strong tendency to view the self as moral. People seem quite skillful at rationalizing their immoral actions (Gino, in press), using justifi-cations that allow them to construe rule-violating behaviors as legitimate (e.g., Shalvi, Gino, Barkan, & Ayal, 2015). Yet is unlikely that people try to justify others' behavior with an equally strong motivation. The logic may be that people benefit from having a moral reputation and a moral self-concept, but they benefit most when they have a fairly accurate and even pessimistic moral evaluation of others. In fact, beyond accuracy, sometimes it may serve us to underestimate the morality of others, so that we can act in preemptive, self-protective ways (better safe than sorry) to avoid becoming the victim of others' immoral behavior (see Galinsky & Lee, this volume). There seems to be a self-interest when constructing beliefs about others, especially about others who have the power to harm us, such as leaders, managers, and politicians (Van Prooijen & Van Lange, 2014).

## Overview of the Volume

### Part I. The Nature of Moral Values and Decisions

The book is organized into four parts. The first part, after this introductory chapter, is devoted to discussing basic issues concerning the social psychology of *moral values and moral decisions*, perhaps the most central topic in the social psychology of morality.

Chapter 2 by **Tom Pyszczynski** offers a terror management theoretical perspective on morality, suggesting that the emergence of death awareness in humans is a critical turning point in both the moral evolution of our species and the moral development of children. Research shows that thoughts of death affect moral judgments and behavior related to each of the moral intuitions specified by Moral Foundations Theory (Graham et al., 2013), demonstrating the important role that death anxiety plays in moral judgments and behavior.

In Chapter 3, **Miller and Monin** develop a conceptual distinction between moral opportunities versus moral tests, suggesting that people regulate their moral identity in two distinct classes of situations: those providing *moral opportunities* and those providing *moral tests*. The chapter defines and illustrates these two classes of moral challenges and demonstrates the relevance of this distinction to understanding the nature of moral self-regulation. The practical relevance of the distinction to understanding the consequences of economic incentives will also be discussed.

**Laham and Corless** in Chapter 4 discuss the role of different kinds of threats in the development of moral values. They argue that we need to distinguish between various threat-related constructs and between types of threats. For example, sensitivities to different kinds of threats (e.g., social vs. pathogen) differently predict moral and political values. Their work demonstrates the utility of this approach in understanding moral and political values.

In Chapter 5, **Molly Crockett** develops a computational neuroscience approach to analyze how people make moral decisions about harming others for personal gain. She illustrates how computational models traditionally used to investigate perceptual and reward-based learning and decision-making can shed light on moral cognition, providing examples from recent studies and outlining novel research avenues that arise from these insights, such as how uncertainty in choice shapes morality.

Chapter 6 by **Gawronski, Conway, Armstrong, Friesdorf, and Hütter** looks at the mechanisms underlying deontological (rule-based) versus utilitarian (consequence-based) responses to moral dilemmas. The chapter suggests that deontological and utilitarian judgments are not opposites on a bipolar continuum, but are rooted in functionally independent processes. They present a formalized model that provides quantitative estimates of (1) deontological tendencies, (2) utilitarian tendencies, and (3) general action tendencies. Several studies show that both utilitarian and deontological tendencies are the product of resource-independent processes, supporting a model that integrates both proscriptive and prescriptive moral norms.

## Part II. Moral Aspects of Interpersonal Behavior

In Chapter 7, **Simpson, Farrell, and Marshall** develop a relational approach to understanding morality in close relationships, suggesting that it is essential to consider dyadic processes to understand when, how, and why partners in close relationships do or do not act in line with their moral convictions. The chapter discusses what happens when romantic partners (1) share the same moral convictions, and (2) have discrepant convictions, focusing on "partner effects," when moral behavior is influenced by a partner's moral convictions.

In Chapter 8, **Galinsky and Lee** analyze the role of perspective-taking in moral judgments and behavior. They demonstrate a general process of vicarious morality, showing that perspective-taking can produce both vicarious generosity and selfishness. In competitive contexts, perspective-taking can inflame already aroused competitive impulses, functioning as a relational amplifier. In cooperative contexts, it creates the foundation for prosocial impulses. In the context of competition, perspective-taking can pervert the age-old axiom "do unto others as you would have them do unto you" into "do unto others as you think they will try to do unto you."

**Joel Cooper** in Chapter 9 describes an extreme phenomenon when social pressures can produce a false confession to an immoral act. The paper shows that in law enforcement, police can often convince suspects to confess to a crime that they did not commit. In a similar way, in social life people may be accused of moral transgressions, and situational pressures can lead innocent people to make false confessions and accept moral blame. A model of the psychological and moral consequences of false confessions is presented, showing that people often believe that they actually committed the moral transgression. Implications for self-attributions of dispositional morality are also considered.

Chapter 10 by **Joseph Forgas** argues that everyday mood states can also have a significant influence on moral decisions involving a conflict between selfishness and fairness. Whereas positive mood promotes more internally oriented thinking, promoting selfishness, negative mood directs greater attention to external requirements, such as fairness norms. In a series of experiments using the dictator game and the ultimatum game, happy participants were consistently more selfish and negative mood participants were more fair when allocating resources. Thus negative mood consistently increased, and positive mood reduced concern with external moral norms. The implications of the findings for our understanding of moral decisions involving selfishness versus fairness are considered.

## Part III. Ironic and Paradoxical Effects of Morality

Chapter 11 by **Jussim, Crawford, Stevens, Anglin, and Duarte** discusses the paradoxical effects of strong moral and ideological commitment in psychological research. Even methodologically sound research can lead to false conclusions if interpreted inappropriately. Picking only supportive results, overemphasizing minor findings, and using double standards can all lead to misinterpretation in service of a preconceived moral or political agenda. Several areas are reviewed (self-fulfilling prophecy, stereotype accuracy, stereotype threat, climate attitudes) where high moral/ political purpose can lead to pervasively misleading conclusions. The role of strong moral and ideological commitment as a threat to scientific integrity is considered.

**Nick Haslam** in Chapter 12 discusses a related issue: conceptual creep in the moral dimension of psychology's expanding notions of harm. He argues that moral concern about "harm" has undergone a significant expansion in psychology. Concepts of harm broaden to capture qualitatively new phenomena and deepen to capture quantitatively less extreme phenomena. Moral concerns such as abuse, addiction, bullying, mental disorder, prejudice, and trauma have all expanded in recent decades, and their meaning has been diluted. This pattern of conceptual creep reflects a dominant moral agenda, increasing moral concern, but also producing an ever-expanding circle of potential moral victims and perpetrators.

Chapter 13 by **Klaus Fiedler** discusses morality in scientists' own behavior. He argues that current discussions about questionable research practices are often fueled by whistle-blowers who themselves do not live up to higher levels of morality. Rather, current debates illustrate the zeitgeist of compliance with unreflected norms, conformity, and obedience. Transgressions of arbitrary norms are given more weight than violations of fundamental norms (e.g., quality of reasoning, cost-benefit assessments). The norm of reciprocity is violated when powerful players (editors, reviewers, whistle-blowers) are treated differently than weaker players (authors, students, applicants). The practical and theoretical implications of biased moral values among scientists are discussed.

## Part IV. Morality and Collective Behavior

Chapter 14 by **Brandt, Wetherell, and Crawford** discusses the relationship between moralization and intolerance of ideological outgroups. The chapter shows that important attitudes tend to be moralized and over time become central to the self, explaining their potency in predicting political behaviors and perceptions.

Their work suggests that both political liberals and conservatives are intolerant toward ideological outgroups and that this intolerance is based on perceived moral and value differences. Neither liberals nor conservatives are uniquely (im)moral, but rather both seek to defend different but equally tenable fundamental moral beliefs.

Chapter 15 by **Graziano and Schroeder** explores the links between morality and prosocial behavior, developing a multilevel approach. They argue that the causal variables linking morality and prosocial behavior operate at multiple distinct levels, and their multilevel approach is illustrated in two novel topic areas, one from behavioral epidemiology and the other from linguistic analysis of moral language. Specifically, the authors apply the multilevel approach to understanding the impact of pathogen prevalence on the evolution of social structures relevant to helping, and the changes in the relations among concepts of sin, debt, reparations, and prosocial acts.

Chapter 16 by **Bastian and Crimston** applies moral psychology to understanding conflicts involving resource use. Resource decision making often involves moral conflicts between human needs and the protection of animal rights, rare species, and entire ecosystems that are increasingly accorded moral rights. The chapter reviews how moral arguments influence resource decisions, demonstrating that moral sensitivity to the needs and rights of nonhumans has clear costs for humans. By linking human needs to moral reasoning about nonhuman entities, the authors provide new insights into how research, policy, and practice may best be positioned to address the inevitable rise of resource conflicts.

In Chapter 17, **von Hippel, Ronay, and Maddux** take an evolutionary perspective, looking at the development of cooperation and competition in groups to analyze what makes group leaders behave in a moral (fair) or an immoral (selfish) fashion. They suggest that the presence of inequality of opportunity in a group is a predisposing factor, as increasing inequality makes immoral individuals more attracted to leadership, and also increases their tendency to behave immorally. The chapter reviews a fascinating range of evidence from anthropology supporting this view, and the implications of the theory for understanding the causes of moral and immoral leadership in modern societies are discussed.

In Chapter 18, **Jeremy Frimer** considers the ways that groups of people with a common moral cause often *create* moral superheroes to represent core values, promote cohesion, and attract new adherents. Frimer's research shows that moral heroes are more ordinary than one might expect. When heroes tell stories about helping, giving, kindness, and social justice, this "hero talk" is not an indicator of the speaker's inner features but a residue of the social processes that creates heroes. When ordinary individuals engage in hero talk, audiences *falsely* expect that the speaker will behave heroically, producing a self-fulfilling prophecy. Hero creation may be an evolved moral "technology" to promote cohesion among humans in large cooperative groups.

## Conclusions

Understanding the nature and characteristics of morality is one of the core questions for psychology. As this introductory review shows, despite literally hundreds of years of philosophical and empirical interest in this topic, a complete understanding of the nature, functions, and consequences of how human beings think about and use moral concepts remains as elusive as ever. Theories range from pessimistic predictions that see *Homo sapiens* as a fundamentally immoral and selfish creature to idealistic notions that emphasize goodness, altruism, and communality (Koestler, 1967). Moral rules or norms can be based either on deontological, a priori notions of the intrinsic moral character of an action, or alternatively, emphasize the calculable consequences of behavioral options.

The chapters included here represent some of the best contemporary work on the social psychology of morality, exploring how moral judgments and behavior are shaped by social psychological processes, and in turn, how morality is a key determinant of social behavior. We have learned a great deal about the cognitive, affective, and motivational mechanisms that influence moral behavior. The chapters included here, in their various ways, all confirm the proposition that the social psychological study of morality is a thriving and productive field today. We hope that readers will find this book an informative and interesting overview of the current status of this fascinating area of inquiry.

## References

Adams, J.S. (1965). Inequity in social exchange. *Advances in Experimental Social Psychology*, *62*, 335–343.

Allison, S.T., Messick, D.M., & Goethals, G.R. (1989). On being better but not smarter than others: The Muhammad Ali effect. *Social Cognition*, 7, 275–296.

Axelrod, R. (1984). *The evolution of cooperation*. New York: Basic Books.

Batson, C.D. (2011). *Altruism in humans*. New York: Oxford University Press.

Bocchiaro, P., Zimbardo, P.G., & Van Lange, P.A.M. (2012). To defy or not to defy: An experimental study of the dynamics of disobedience and whistle-blowing. *Social Influence*, 7, 35–50.

Bornstein, G. (1992). The free-rider problem in intergroup conflicts over step-level and continuous public goods. *Journal of Personality and Social Psychology*, *62*, 597–606.

Boyd, D., & Kohlberg, L. (1973). The is-ought problem: A developmental perspective. *Zygon*, 8, 358–372.

Bryant, S. (1912). The many-sideness of moral education. *International Journal of Ethics*, 22, 383–399.

Buss, D. (1995). Evolutionary psychology: A new paradigm for psychological science. *Psychological Inquiry*, 6, 1–30.

Dahrendorf, R. (1968). *Essays in the theory of society*. Stanford, CA: Stanford University Press.

Deutsch, M. (1975). Equity, equality, and need: What determines which value will be used as the basis of distributive justice? *Journal of Social Issues*, *31*, 137–149.

Duarte, J.L., Crawford, J.T., Stern, C., Haidt, J., Jussim, L., & Tetlock, P. (2015). Political diversity will improve social psychological science. *Behavioral and Brain Sciences, 38*, 1–13.

Forgas, J.P., Fiedler, K., & Crano, W.D. (2015). *Social psychology and politics.* New York: Psychology Press.

Gino, F. (in press). How moral flexibility constrains our moral compass. In J.W. Van Prooijen & P.A.M. Van Lange (Eds.), *Corruption, cheating, and concealment: The roots of dishonest behavior.* Cambridge: Cambridge University Press.

Gouldner, A.W. (1960). The norm of reciprocity: A preliminary statement. *American Sociological Review, 25*, 161–178.

Graham, J., Haidt, J., Koleva, S., Motyl, M., Iyer, R., Wojcik, S.P., & Ditto, P.H. (2013). Moral foundations theory: The pragmatic validity of moral pluralism. *Advances in Experimental Social Psychology, 47*, 55–130.

Graham, J., Haidt, J., & Nosek, B.A. (2009). Liberals and conservatives rely on different sets of moral foundations. *Journal of Personality and Social Psychology, 96*, 1029–1046.

Haidt, J. (2001). The emotional dog and its rational tail: A social intuitionist approach to moral judgment. *Psychological Review, 108*, 814–834.

Haidt, J. (2012). *The righteous mind: Why good people are divided by religion and politics.* New York: Pantheon Books.

Koestler, A. (1967). *The ghost in the machine.* New York: Macmillan.

Kohlberg, L., & Hersh, R.H. (1977). Moral development: A review of the theory. *Theory Into Practice, 16*, 53–59.

Kruger, J., & Gilovich, T. (1999). "Naive cynicism" in everyday theories of responsibility assessment: On biased assumptions of bias. *Journal of Personality and Social Psychology, 76*, 743–753.

Latané, B., & Darley, J.M. (1968). Group inhibition of bystander intervention in emergencies. *Journal of Personality and Social Psychology, 10*, 215–221.

Latané, B., & Darley, J.M. (1970). *The unresponsive bystander: Why doesn't he help?* New York: Appleton-Century-Crofts.

Lull, H.G. (1911). Moral instruction through social intelligence. *American Journal of Sociology, 17*, 47–60.

Manning, R., Levine, M., & Collins, A. (2007). The Kitty Genovese Murder and the social psychology of helping: The parable of the 38 witnesses. *American Psychologist, 62*, 555–562.

McClintock, C.G., & Liebrand, W.B.G. (1988). The role of interdependence structure, individual value orientation and other's strategy in social decision making: A transformational analysis. *Journal of Personality and Social Psychology, 55*, 396–409.

Milgram, S. (1974). *Obedience to authority: An experimental view.* New York: Harper & Row.

Miller, D.T. (1999). The norm of self-interest. *American Psychologist, 54*, 1053–1060.

Miller, D.T., & Ratner, R.K. (1998). The disparity between the actual and assumed power of self-interest. *Journal of Personality and Social Psychology, 74*, 53–62.

Perugini, M., Gallucci, M., Presaghi, F., & Ercolani, A.P. (2003). The personal norm of reciprocity. *European Journal of Personality, 17*, 251–283.

Royce, J. (1893). On certain aspects of moral training. *International Journal of Ethics, 3*, 413–436.

Shalvi, S., Gino, F., Barkan, R., & Ayal, S. (2015). Self-serving justifications: Doing wrong and feeling moral. *Current Directions in Psychological Science, 24*, 125–130.

Tajfel, S., & Forgas, J.P. (1982). Social categorisation: Cognitions, values and groups. In J.P. Forgas (Ed.), *Social cognition* (pp. 113–140). London: Academic Press.

Van Lange, P.A.M. (2015). Generalized trust: Lessons from genetics and culture. *Current Directions in Psychological Science, 24,* 71–76.

Van Lange, P.A.M., & Balliet, D. (2014). Interdependence theory. In J. Dovidio & J. Simpson (Eds.), *Handbook of personality and social psychology: Interpersonal relations and group processes* (Vol. 3, pp. 65–92). New York: American Psychological Association.

Van Lange, P.A.M., Ouwerkerk, J., & Tazelaar, M. (2002). How to overcome the detrimental effects of noise in social interaction: The benefits of generosity. *Journal of Personality and Social Psychology, 82,* 768–780.

Van Lange, P.A.M., & Sedikides, C. (1998). Being more honest but not necessarily more intelligent than others: Generality and explanations for the Muhammad Ali effect. *European Journal of Social Psychology, 28,* 675–680.

Van Prooijen, J.W., & Van Lange, P.A.M. (Eds.). (2014). *Power, politics, and paranoia: Why people are suspicious of their leaders.* Cambridge: Cambridge University Press.

Wildschut, T., & Insko, C.A. (2006). A paradox of individual and group morality: Social psychology as empirical philosophy. In P.A.M. Van Lange (Ed.), *Bridging social psychology* (pp. 377–384). Mahwah, NJ: Erlbaum.

Wit, A.P., & Kerr, N.L. (2002). "Me versus just us versus us all" categorization and cooperation in nested social dilemmas. *Journal of Personality and Social Psychology, 83,* 616–637.

**PART I**

# The Nature of Moral Values and Decisions

# 2

# GOD SAVE US

## A Terror Management Perspective on Morality

*Tom Pyszczynski*

*Awareness of death and the emergence of conceptions of noncorporeal souls, deities, and afterlives transform moral behavior from a means of staying in the good graces of others to a strategy for transcending death. Thus the emergence of death awareness is a critical turning point in the moral evolution of our species. Research has shown that thoughts of death affect judgments and behavior related to each of the moral intuitions specified by Moral Foundations Theory (Haidt & Joseph, 2004), that threats to many of them increase death thought accessibility (Hirschberger, 2006), and that terror management processes play an important role in both prosocial and antisocial behavior. From the perspective of terror management theory (TMT), awareness of the inevitability of death transforms the primitive moral intuitions that initially evolved to facilitate group living into a central means of managing anxiety regarding human vulnerability and mortality.*

Concerns about morality go back to the very beginnings of human history, and probably much further. Recent theoretical developments in social and cultural psychology (e.g., Haidt & Joseph, 2004; Shweder, Much, Mahapatra, & Park, 1997) build on evolutionary thinking to suggest that moral intuitions evolved long before the emergence of our species because they serve the adaptive function of facilitating cooperation within groups and against competitors. Moral Foundations Theory (MFT; Haidt, 2010; Haidt & Joseph, 2004) posits that, over the course of human history, these moral intuitions were edited and refined by cultures, leading to the moral values used by today's humans to regulate their own and other people's behavior. Terror management theory (TMT; Solomon, Greenberg, & Pyszczynski, 1991, 2015) posits that moral values are part of the cultural worldviews that people use to shield themselves from anxiety that results from awareness of the inevitability of death. Bringing these theories together yields unique insights into the processes emphasized by each and sheds light on some important questions about human morality. In particular, this chapter focuses on the role that religion and belief in God plays in morality, how concepts of souls and spirits counter bodily related anxiety and disgust, and how religious motivation centered on sanctity and holiness relates to other moral concerns.

## The Roots of Human Morality

### Moral Foundations Theory

Although it is often assumed that morality is a unique feature of the human species, behavior that appears to reflect caring, sharing, deference to leaders, ingroup favoritism, disgust, and rebelling against constraints has been observed in other species, including primates such as chimpanzees, gorillas, bonobos, and other mammals such as wolves, deer, elephants, and even vampire bats (Bekoff & Pierce, 2009). This led de Waal (2008) and others to suggest that the rudiments of moral motivation are relatively common evolutionary adaptations that function to regulate the behavior of animals that live in groups. Morality of some form or other appears to be a universal feature of human beings. Building on observations of the universal presence of certain moral tendencies across diverse cultures, Shweder and colleagues (1997) posited three core ethics that underlie human moral behavior: autonomy, community, and divinity. Haidt and colleagues' MFT (Graham et al., 2013; Haidt & Joseph, 2004) expanded on this conceptualization and integrated it with evolutionary thinking about morality. From this perspective, human morality is rooted in gut-level moral intuitions that evolved in social animals to facilitate group living by encouraging behavior that reduces costly conflicts, promotes the welfare of individuals, and binds them together.

MFT further posits that these evolved moral intuitions are the building blocks upon which cultures create more complex and differentiated moral values. Haidt (2010) likens them to the first draft of people's moral values, which are then edited by the diverse social and cultural influences that are experienced over the course of life. MFT initially posited five moral foundations, currently stated as opposing poles of each moral dimension (Graham et al., 2013): (1) care/harm, which reflects concerns about the welfare of others; (2) fairness/cheating, which reflects concerns about equity and justice; (3) loyalty/betrayal, which reflects concerns about promoting the welfare of one's group; (4) authority/subversion, which reflects deference to authority; and (5) sanctity/degradation, which reflects concerns about disgust, purity, and sacredness. MFT theorists recently tentatively added a sixth foundation, liberty/oppression, which reflects reactance and resentment toward those who limit one's freedom (Graham et al., 2013). Because the majority of the research conducted to date has focused on the original five foundations, our discussion will focus on those five.

Research on MFT has supported the contention that the five foundations are independent dimensions (for a review, see Graham et al., 2013) that differ across individuals, cultures, and subcultures. Much of this research has focused on differences in the moral foundations of political liberals and conservatives, showing that whereas liberals place greater emphasis on the individualizing foundations of care/harm and fairness/cheating over the binding foundations of loyalty/betrayal, authority/subversion, and sanctity/degradation, conservatives place roughly equal value on all five of these foundations. There is also evidence that liberals place greater value than conservatives on harm/care and fairness/cheating (e.g., Graham, Haidt, & Nosek 2009). It appears that liberals and conservatives both value the recently added liberty/oppression foundation, but interpret it in different ways, with liberals viewing government as the defender of liberty and conservatives viewing government as an oppressor (Koleva, Graham, Ditto, Iyer, & Haidt, 2012).

Although MFT acknowledges that evolved moral foundations are customized by cultures, it emphasizes the intuitive aspects of morality. This is, in part, a counterpoint to the cognitive theories of morality (e.g., Kohlberg, 1969) that dominated psychology for most of the past 50 years, which focused almost exclusively on people's reasoning about abstract moral principles, viewing some types of moral reasoning as primitive and childlike but others as advanced and sophisticated. MFT's moral intuitionist perspective views moral judgments as originating in gut-level emotional reactions that are sometimes later rationalized with more abstract thinking, and in even fewer cases, revised on the basis of cognitive appraisals and abstract principles. Consistent with the intuitionist view, Haidt, Koller, and Dias (1993) found that people have strong opinions about the morality of things that do no apparent harm (such as eating one's dog after it dies) but are usually unable to provide rational explanations for these reactions.

## Terror Management Theory

From the perspective of TMT (Solomon et al., 1991, 2015), moral behavior reflects attempts to maintain a protective shield against existential anxiety by living up to the values of one's cultural worldview. TMT posits that human beings are unique among living creatures in that they have cognitive capacities that make them aware of the inevitability of death. This awareness in an animal with diverse motive systems oriented toward staying alive creates the potential for overwhelming terror, which is both highly aversive and capable of disrupting goal-directed behavior. In short, awareness of death would make life unlivable unless effectively managed. TMT posits that our ancestors solved this problem by using the same sophisticated intellectual abilities that gave rise to this problem.

Toward this end, our ancestors created *cultural worldviews* that provide: (1) an explanation for existence that imbues human life with meaning, significance, structure, and permanence; (2) standards that specify what a good person should and should not do; and (3) various means of literally or symbolically transcending death. The hope of *literal immortality* is provided by cultural beliefs that life continues in some form after physical death; for example, in heaven, through reincarnation, or by merging with the spirits of one's ancestors. Although the specifics of these afterlife beliefs vary dramatically across cultures (see Solomon et al., 2015, for a discussion of the diversity of afterlife beliefs), virtually all cultures, past and present, include them in some form. The hope of *symbolic immortality* provided by cultures affords individuals the opportunity to be a valuable part of something greater than themselves that they believe will last forever. Group memberships, such as being part of a family, ethnic group, nation, or political party provide symbolic immortality, which is enhanced by leaving valued contributions to those groups, such as children, books, works of art, monuments, or deeds and stories that will continue after one is gone.

Because many of the most important aspects of cultural worldviews are abstract ideas and values with no directly visible referent, many of which run counter to observable reality, people rely on other people to consensually validate them. Those who share one's beliefs and values increase one's faith or certainty; those with different beliefs and values undermine this faith and certainty. Because of the protection from death-related anxiety that our worldviews provide, people react positively to others who share and thus validate their worldviews and negatively to dissenting or critical others that threaten them. TMT posits that the way others impinge on faith in our worldview and personal value, and thus our ability to manage anxiety, is a major determinant of how we think, feel, and act toward them.

Managing existential terror by qualifying for either literal or symbolic immortality requires that one both believe in the absolute validity of one's worldview and believe that one is living up to the standards of value that are part of it. Religious teachings about literal immortality usually posit that both faith and good behavior are required to gain admission to a desirable afterlife. Similarly, common experience and cultural teachings make it clear that not all who pass on are remembered, and that being a good group member who believes in and values the group while exemplifying its values is the best route to living on in the minds of one's fellows. Thus TMT posits that emotional security in the face of knowledge of the inevitability of death requires both faith in one's cultural worldview and living up to the standards of value that it proscribes. This sense of meaning and personal value is the essence of self-esteem, which provides the protection against anxiety that people need to live happy and effective lives.

A large literature, consisting of hundreds of studies conducted in diverse cultures the world over, provides support for hypotheses derived from TMT (for recent reviews, see Greenberg, Vail, & Pyszczynski, 2014; Kesebir & Pyszczynski, 2012). Research has shown that:

1. Boosting self-esteem reduces both self-report and physiological indicators of anxiety, along with death-denying cognitive distortions.
2. Reminders of death (referred to as mortality salience; MS) increase defensive reactions to people and ideas that impinge on one's worldview and self-esteem, striving to enhance one's self-esteem, discomfort when violating cultural norms, estimates of the extent to which one's attitudes are shared by fellow group members, and preference for well-structured information.
3. Threats to one's worldview or self-esteem increase the accessibility of death-related thoughts (death thought accessibility, or DTA).
4. Boosting self-esteem or affirming one's worldview decreases DTA and reduces or eliminates defensive responses to MS.
5. Apparent evidence for the existence of an afterlife reduces the increased worldview defense and self-esteem striving that MS would otherwise produce.

These five logically distinct lines of research provide converging evidence for TMT by documenting these effects across diverse aspects of worldviews and self-esteem, including political attitudes, legal decisions, belief in God, support for war and terrorism, physical aggression, charitable donations, romantic love, attitudes toward sex, desire for children, and many others. Although alternative explanations have been proposed for some aspects of some studies, we know of no viable alternative to TMT as a comprehensive explanation for this literature (for discussions of critiques and alternative explanations for TMT research, see Pyszczynski, Greenberg, Solomon, & Maxfield, 2006; Pyszczynski, Solomon, & Greenberg, 2015).

## The Invention of Spirits, Gods, and Religion

Although most cultures teach that morality is rooted in the preferences of deities or other, less personal spiritual forces that lie outside of the realm of human nature, contemporary theories of morality pay surprisingly little attention to the role of gods and spirits in morality. This is odd because both morality and religion are widely viewed as reflecting evolved propensities that facilitate group living. Indeed, for many and perhaps most people, staying in the good graces of God is viewed as the primary reason to behave morally, and declining religious faith is viewed as a portent of moral chaos. In this section we integrate TMT with other theories of the origins of morality and religion (e.g., Bloom, 2004; Boyer, 2004; Haidt & Joseph, 2004; Kirkpatrick, 2005; Norenzayan et al., 2014) to speculate about the relationship between gods, religion, morality, and death.

Cultural worldviews probably began as attempts to answer practical questions about how the world works, addressing things that helped early humans meet their needs and navigate their way through life, such as explaining how to find food, keep warm, and stay in the good graces of others. Meaning systems are, by definition, social in that they are ways of sharing information among people. Because of the important role that relationships with others play in most aspects of life, such relationships were probably an important topic of even the earliest meaning systems. MFT suggests that moral intuitions evolved in our prehuman ancestors long before the emergence of language and meaning systems because they were useful for maintaining cohesion within groups and minimizing conflict. With the emergence of more sophisticated intellectual capacities and language, these moral intuitions were verbalized and codified into cultural norms and values, and then integrated into the more comprehensive cosmologies. Thus moral values were tied to the emerging cultural worldviews that give meaning and purpose to life and explain why moral behavior is important. This created an important link between moral intuition and moral reasoning.

From the perspective of TMT, the dawning awareness of the inevitability of death was a seismic event that dramatically changed the nature of our species in general, and morality in particular. To manage the disruptive potential for terror that resulted from realizing that all living things, oneself included, eventually die, meanings and values took on a new function. In addition to providing pragmatic guides for effectively navigating the physical and social environments, meanings and values became part of the emerging terror management system. Ideas and values that helped minimize this new source of anxiety by transforming the problem of death into a journey to a better mode of being were thus especially appealing. Comforting death-transcending ideas such as these were especially likely to be invented, shared with others, and eventually institutionalized as cultural knowledge. Death-denying memes were powerful because of the protection from anxiety they provided and the widespread desire for such protection, thus leading them to spread and proliferate.

As others have suggested, the earliest precursors to deities and religion may have initially emerged as by-products of psychological tendencies that were selected for other purposes, such as inferring the content of other minds and therefore attributing agency to ambiguous stimuli (e.g., Atran & Norenzayan, 2004; Bloom, 2004). Based on observations of contemporary hunter-gatherer societies, anthropologists and religious historians speculate that the earliest spirits were conceived of as capricious beings that often cared little about the welfare of humans; but as our species progressed, these spirits became increasingly powerful and focused on human welfare and morality (e.g., Boehm, 2008; Wright, 2009). TMT suggests that emerging awareness of the inevitability of death led our ancestors to impute this and other new functions to the spirits they had invented. Gods, spirits, and other supernatural entities became increasingly powerful beings that could control nature and reverse the troubling reality of death by granting immortality to otherwise mortal humans. Thus the emerging awareness of death had a profound impact on the function and nature of the gods and religions that humankind was creating, which ultimately changed the dynamics of the moral intuitions and social norms that controlled behavior.

Probably because of the human tendency to anthropomorphize and imagine that the gods thought much like they did, people imputed their own preferences and moral intuitions to the gods they were creating. Thus they invented deities that granted immortality only to those who pleased them by believing in them, following their commands, and offering gifts and sacrifices to stay in their good graces. Because of the high value that people and groups place on moral behavior, they assumed that the gods were similarly focused on morality when judging who was worthy of immortality. Similarly, because defeating death seemed like something that only extremely powerful beings could accomplish, people used their own experiences with powerful others as inspiration for the wishes they attributed to their deities. Thus experiences with parents, group leaders, and other authority figures were likely to have been especially influential sources of inspiration for the gods that were created. This might explain the obedience, devotion, fealty, and sacrifice that people assumed the gods demanded in return for both improving the nature of earthly existence and granting admission to the afterlife. Worship may have emerged as a projection of the deference and submission that human leaders demanded onto the will of the gods.

This may help explain the rather egotistic, insecure, and cruel nature of many human conceptions of God, which comedians such as George Carlin and Louis C.K. have pondered as a source of humor. Ironically, the reason many people find such musings offensive is because of their fear that the gods might unleash their wrath and smite anyone who finds humor in such challenges to their desire for fealty. For example, a few days after the 9/11 terrorist attacks, American evangelist Jerry Falwell famously proclaimed that these attacks were God's punishment for the existence of feminists, homosexuals, and promiscuity.

Importantly, the regulation of moral behavior was transferred, at least in part, from the group and its leaders to these all-powerful deities who were created in the image of powerful human beings. Just as other humans granted favor to and withheld punishment from those who behaved in a moral manner, so too did the gods. Thus caring for others and not harming them, treating them fairly and not cheating them, being loyal to one's group and not betraying it, showing deference to the deity's ultimate authority, and staying pure by pursuing spiritual pursuits over carnal pleasures became ways of pleasing the gods and assuring one's transcendence of death. The fear of negative social consequences our prehuman ancestors experienced when they violated their moral intuitions was greatly intensified by the newfound fear of losing the immortality that could be granted only by beings far more powerful than even the greatest human leaders. Once one's fate after death became contingent on the judgment of one's deity, the consequences of moral and immoral behavior became far greater.

The relationship between the pursuit of earthly and heavenly goals is a reciprocal one. As moral behavior became the major criterion for admission to the afterlife by the deities, this further increased the importance that mortal humans put on it for their relationships with other humans. TMT suggests that part of the reason parents and other socializing agents place such great value on the moral behavior of children is their commitment to the death transcendence of their offspring—which, in turn, increases their own prospects for both literal and symbolic immortality. Parents' literal immortality is on the line because many cultures teach that their gods will reward or punish them for their children's devotion or lack thereof. And parents' symbolic immortality is on the line because their names and genes are passed on to their children, and thus their children's standing in the memory of the eternal culture is a major way they themselves will be remembered. This may help explain why moral values are generally the most highly valued bases of both self-esteem and social judgment (e.g., Skitka, Bauman, & Sargis, 2005).

Moral heroes, such as Mahatma Gandhi, Martin Luther King Jr., and Nelson Mandela (discussed by Frimer, this volume) may serve a related function. Elevation of particularly virtuous human beings to moral hero status may be a way of exemplifying morally exemplary behavior and providing people with guidance and inspiration as to how to behave morally. Whereas deities and saints serve this purpose for the religious faithful, those who eschew religious beliefs can find similar inspiration in secular upholders of righteousness. If moral heroes are an additional way of dealing with the problem of death, reminders of morality should increase their appeal. Though no research has assessed this specific possibility, research has shown that MS leads people to assign larger rewards to those who endure risks to their own well-being in order to do the right thing (Rosenblatt, Greenberg, Solomon, Pyszczynski, & Lyon, 1989). Other research has shown that MS led to increased admiration for former US president George W. Bush shortly after the 9/11 terrorist attacks, at a time when his rhetoric emphasized restoring justice by punishing "evil doers."

## Cleanliness and Godliness

Following Shweder et al. (1997) and Rozin, Haidt, and McCauley (1999), MFT posits a close link between disgust and the sanctity/degradation foundation. Disgust is generally thought to have evolved because it facilitates the avoidance of pathogens; the sanctity/degradation moral foundation favors the mind and spirit over the body and the rest of the natural world and vilifies sex and other pleasures of the body (Haidt & Joseph, 2004; Rozin et al., 1999). Research has supported the connection between disgust and moral judgments, showing that people report feelings of disgust in response to immoral acts (e.g., Rozin et al., 1999), are more likely to view certain acts as immoral if they are high in disgust sensitivity (Horberg, Oveis, Keltner, & Cohen, 2009), and judge moral transgressions more severely when induced to feel disgusted (e.g., Wheatley & Haidt, 2005). Presumably cleanliness and purity are ways of avoiding disgust that would be elicited by stimuli associated with contamination. But why are mind, spirit, and godliness associated with purity as antidotes to disgust? And why are bodily processes and activities construed as less noble than mental and spiritual ones? An integration of TMT and MFT provides a unique perspective on these questions.

From the perspective of TMT, the human motivation to distance from the body is rooted in the problem of death. The concepts of spirit and soul are common cultural devices to deny death by distancing people from their mortal bodies. Because human bodies quite clearly die and decay, belief that our lives continue after death requires a nonmaterial aspect of self that continues to exist after the body has died. The concept of an eternal noncorporeal soul was invented by our ancestors as a solution to this problem. If, as Rozin et al. (1999) and many others have suggested, disgust is an innate response to decaying flesh, realizing that such decay is our own inevitable fate upon death may be another factor that leads people to view their essence as something not tied to their bodies. Because the body is the repository of death and decay, and the spirit our best hope of transcending death, we desperately strive to be more than our bodies, and construe ourselves as minds and spirits.

## Empirical Evidence for the Relationship Between Death, Morality, God, and Religion

Consistent with the death-denying function of morality posited by TMT, research has shown that terror management processes affect reactions to violations of all five of the moral foundations initially posited by MFT (for a review, see Kesebir & Pyszczynski, 2011). Many studies have shown that MS leads people to rate moral transgressions based on the care/harm foundation (e.g., stealing from a fund designated for the education of young people) as more severe and to recommend harsher punishment for the transgressors (Florian & Mikulincer, 1997). Other research shows that MS increases charitable giving, especially to ingroup charities (e.g., Jonas, Schimel, Greenberg, & Pyszczynski, 2002; for an interesting discussion of the role of morality in prosocial behavior, see Graziano & Schroeder, this volume). Studies have shown that MS intensifies reactions to violations of the fairness dimension, for example, by increasing derogation of the victim of a random tragedy (Landau, Greenberg, & Solomon, 2004); conversely, learning about severely injured innocent victims elicits more death-related cognitions than learning about victims responsible for their condition (Hirschberger, 2006). In addition, MS increases the desire for justice, which mediates the link between death thoughts and increased support for military action (Hirschberger et al., 2015). A multitude of TMT studies has shown that MS increases ingroup loyalty in the form of ingroup favoritism, outgroup hostility, stereotyping, and perceptions of group entitativity (for a review, see Castano & Dechesne, 2005; see Brandt, Wetherell, & Crawford, this volume, for a discussion of the role of moralization in responses to outgroups). MS also increases deference to authority, in the form of support for leaders, especially those who proclaim the unique value of the ingroup (Cohen, Solomon, Maxfield, Pyszczynski, & Greenberg, 2004). And MS increases oft-found differences between liberals and conservatives in commitment to individuating and binding moral foundations (Bassett, Van Tongeren, Green, Sonntag, & Kilpatrick, 2015).

If awareness of death changes moral concerns by bringing gods and religion into the picture, one might expect the sanctity/degradation foundation to be especially likely to spill over into other moral domains, as when people talk about the "sanctity of life," "God's justice," "sacred duties to one's country," and the "divine right of kings." Thus one might expect the sanctity/degradation dimension to increase in relative importance when death concerns are salient, especially (or perhaps only—see later discussion) for people of religious faith. To date we know of no research that has directly tested this hypothesis regarding the weighting of sanctity/degradation relative to other moral foundations. However, research has shown that MS affects sanctity/degradation-related attitudes in many ways. MS increases the intensity of emotional reactions to disgust-eliciting stimuli, and viewing disgusting pictures increases DTA (e.g., Cox, Goldenberg, Pyszczynski, & Weise, 2007; Goldenberg et al., 2001). MS decreases the appeal of the physical aspects of sex, and thoughts of the physical aspects of sex increase DTA; these effects emerge most clearly when thoughts of similarities between humans and other animals have been primed and among persons high in neuroticism (Goldenberg et al., 2001). Other research has shown that MS leads to more negative evaluations of sexually provocative (Landau et al., 2006), pregnant (Goldenberg, Cox, Arndt, & Goplen, 2007), or breast-feeding women (Cox, Goldenberg, Arndt, & Pyszczynski, 2007), all of whom are construed as impure by many religious and cultural traditions. Indeed, the very first demonstration of the MS effect, showing that reminders of death lead to higher bond recommendations for a woman arrested for prostitution (Rosenblatt et al., 1989), can be viewed as an instance of increased punitiveness toward a violator of the purity/sanctity dimension.

Research has also shown that MS increases belief in an afterlife and the existence of supernatural beings, even those not associated with one's own faith (e.g., Batson & Stocks, 2004; Norenzayan, Dar-Nimrod, Hanson, & Proulx, 2009; Osarchuk & Tatz, 1973) and increased distress when handling a religious object in a disrespectful way (Greenberg, Simon, Porteus, Pyszczynski, & Solomon, 1995). Other research shows that challenges to one's religious beliefs increase DTA (Schimel, Hayes, Williams, & Jahrig, 2007). A growing literature documents increases in morally appropriate behavior among people primed with thoughts of God or religion. Studies have shown that inducing religious thoughts reduces cheating, curbs selfish behavior, increases fairness toward strangers, and promotes cooperation in anonymous settings (for a review, see Norenzayan, Henrich, & Slingerland, 2013). Interestingly, whereas greater belief in a punishing God is associated with reductions in moral transgressions, greater belief in a kind God is associated with increased transgressions (Shariff & Norenzayan, 2011). This suggests the potential for punishment, presumably by withholding a favorable afterlife, is driving the effects of religious priming, which are reversed when primed with thoughts of a benevolent God whose mercy would save one from eternal punishment.

The TMT analysis presented here suggests that death reminders should also increase the role that religious themes play in promoting particular types of moral behavior. If a person's moral behavior is aimed at pleasing God in order to transcend death, then the link between the behavior and his or her religious beliefs would be an important moderator of responses to MS. Consistent with this reasoning, Rothschild, Abdollahi, and Pyszczynski (2009) found that although MS increased support for military action against Iran among American religious fundamentalists, this effect was reversed when they were previously primed with New Testament verses promoting compassion, with MS leading to less support for war among fundamentalists. Importantly, this MS-induced increase in support for peace emerged only among fundamentalists and only when the compassionate values were clearly linked to Christian teachings. A follow-up study found parallel effects among Iranians when the primed compassionate values were linked to the Koran but not when they were linked to common wisdom; this effect was not moderated by religious fundamentalism, perhaps because religion plays a more central role in Iranian than American life.

Although the findings regarding the effects of MS and religious priming discussed in this section have been generally consistent among people of religious faith, there are conflicting findings regarding such effects among atheists. For example, Norenzayan et al. (2009) and Jong, Halberstadt, and Bluemke (2012) found that MS increased self-reports of belief in supernatural beings only among people of faith. However, Jong et al. (2012) found MS to produce increases in implicit measures of religious belief among nonreligious persons as well, and Willer (2009) found MS to produce significant increases in belief among nonreligious participants but only marginal increases among religious ones. Ochsmann (1984) failed to find an effect of MS on belief in an afterlife but did find it to increase materialism in his sample of mostly secular German college students; he interpreted these findings as suggesting material values may substitute for religious beliefs in atheists. These inconsistent findings suggest that additional research on the role that religious concepts play in coping with death anxiety among atheists is needed. Perhaps whether religious teachings and beliefs were an important part of atheists' socialization and childhood experience may affect these processes.

## What Is Gained From an Integration of Terror Management and Moral Foundations Theories?

As should be clear from the foregoing discussion, MFT and TMT are highly compatible conceptualizations that, when brought together, shed new light on the issues emphasized by each one. The MFT analysis of how cultures build moral values and virtues out of preverbal evolved moral intuitions helps explain why morality is such an important and deeply rooted component of the world-views that TMT views as functioning to protect people from existential anxiety. Although TMT claims that people acquire self-esteem and existential security by living up to their culture's standards of value, in and of itself it has little to say about which values are more or less important for these purposes. Although we hadn't devoted much attention to this issue in previous statements of TMT, we never assumed that death-denying cultural beliefs and values emerged fully formed out of nowhere as soon as our ancestors realized that death was inevitable.

Research in moral psychology has shown that moral values are especially important determinants of how people evaluate themselves and others (e.g., Skitka et al., 2005). The MFT analysis of the interplay between natural selection and cultural adaptation in the evolution of morality provides a good starting point for expanding the TMT analysis of what determines the content of death-denying cultural worldviews. Cultures seized on moral intuitions, which initially emerged in our prehuman ancestors to maintain social order, as the benchmarks used by their deities to judge worthiness for continued existence after physical death. Tying moral values to concepts of immortality, which we view as a human innovation that emerged to help manage the terror of death, further increased the impact of these values on individual behavior and social order, thus further minimizing within group conflict and maximizing success over other groups.

Like biological evolution, cultural evolution builds on already existing elements that often emerged to serve other functions. Although it is faster than biological natural selection, cultural evolution takes time for people to generate ideas, to communicate them with others, and for the adaptive utility of these ideas to lead them to be adopted as cultural wisdom. Thus it is not surprising that beliefs about the specific nature of deities and spirits changed over the course of cultural history and vary considerably across time and place.

TMT provides an important bridge between the initial emergence of spirit concepts, which others have suggested initially resulted from anthropomorphic-ally applying theory of mind to natural phenomena, and the elaborate death-transcending concepts of the religions that have played such a powerful role in human morality (and immorality) over the course of human history. Clearly the contents of human conceptions of deities and spirits could not be due to some random variations in neural pathways being more effective than others in promoting survival and reproduction. The elaborate nature of religious beliefs and the relatively short time span in which they emerged suggests they were likely the product of some form of "intelligent design." But rather than an all-powerful god creating human beings and the ideas and values by which they lived, *human beings were the designers who created gods* by using their intelligence to creatively solve the problem of death. As Feuerbach (1841/1989) famously put it many years ago, "man created god in his own image."

Bringing TMT into discussions of the psychology of morality and religion also sheds light on why most cultures elevate the mind and spirit above the body. Bodies die and decay. The most common cultural solution to this problem is to separate the mind and spirit from the body and elevate oneself—via one's mind and spirit—above one's body. This also helps explain why godliness and spirituality are typically viewed as contrary to our bodily nature, as exemplified by MFT conceptualizing the sanctity/degradation foundation as rooted in disgust. Only non-corporeal entities can plausibly escape death and the disgust that is inherent in it.

Most contemporary theories of morality and religion are primarily social in nature (e.g., Bloom, 2005; Norenzayan et al., 2014); indeed, Graham and Haidt (2010, p. 140) recently described the MFT conception of morality and God as "relentlessly social." They emphasize the role that morality and religion play in promoting the smooth functioning of groups and success in competition with other groups. From these perspectives, groups with morality-promoting gods persist because social cohesion facilitates group survival, which facilitates individual survival and reproduction, and ultimately, the transmission of genes.

Although the content of such death-transcending religious beliefs were (and are) no doubt effective in promoting social integration and group living, it is highly unlikely that they were initially invented to fulfill this function. This would imply that the early humans who imagined gods and created religion had the foresight to speculate about what beliefs would be effective for keeping people in line and the intent to use such beliefs to promote social control. Although there probably were cases of leaders who cynically used religion to promote their own power and influence without themselves believing what was taught to the masses, this seems likely to be more the exception than the rule. Perhaps one might argue that some random variations in the nature of the deities that our ancestors imputed to natural phenomena were more effective in promoting social control than others, and that religions evolved in the direction of "Big Gods" (Norenzayan et al., 2014) who intervened in human affairs, because of such differential effectiveness. But this would not explain why some such conceptions were more likely to be invented, accepted, and spread in the first place. Clearly there must have been something that made increasingly powerful gods that demanded morality appealing enough for them to be invented, accepted, and spread enough so that they have the effect of increasing social order.

TMT provides an explanation for this necessary step in the evolution of religion that is consistent with the finding of signs of ritual burial of the dead coinciding with the some of the earliest remnants of modern humans. Although we acknowledge the role of ideology, morality, and religion in promoting social cohesion, TMT emphasizes the death-denying function of these cultural innovations that dramatically changes the way people relate to them. From the perspective of TMT, the ability of gods and religions to provide the protection from death that people crave is a major reason they are so effective in bringing people together and committing them to values that promote the welfare of their groups. Explaining the forces that led to the invention of the most prominent features of the deities found across diverse cultures, along with the determinants of the appeal of particular religious beliefs to the individuals who make up societies, should be an important part of any comprehensive theory of religion. Answers to these questions help explain what creates the devotion to beliefs and adherence to values through which religions facilitate social cohesion and group living.

TMT also provides a somewhat different but complementary perspective on the social nature of religion and morality. Belief in unobservable entities, such as deities, spirits, souls, and the like, requires other people who share these beliefs to make them plausible—if everyone else believes in an unseen world, it must really exist. Without such social consensus, maintaining religious faith would be impossible and those who believed in such things would be viewed as delusional. From the perspective of TMT, this need for validation of death-denying beliefs played an important role in bringing people together and may have even been partly responsible for the shift toward larger settlements and cities. Recent analyses of large monuments at Göbekli Tepe in Turkey, thought to be of religious significance but with no signs of agriculture or animal husbandry and dating to at least 11,000 years ago, has led some to speculate that agriculture may have emerged as a consequence of large-scale religion rather than, as more widely assumed, religion emerging to help control the larger settlements that resulted from agriculture (Schmidt, 2009).

## Summary and Conclusions

The goal of this chapter was to consider the role that concepts of gods, afterlives, and religion play in morality. From the perspective of TMT, awareness of death led to the emergence of gods and spirits capable of reversing death and granting immortality to otherwise mortal human beings. Across diverse cultures, moral behavior is viewed as the primary determinant of one's fate after death. Thus we argue that awareness of death changed the goals that underlie moral behavior. Whereas MFT views morality as a way of staying in the good graces of others, TMT adds that with the dawning awareness of death that resulted from the evolution of increasingly sophisticated human cognitive abilities, morality took on the very important additional function of providing a means of transcending death. Thus the intended audience for one's moral behavior expanded from the real people in one's group who might observe one's actions to an all-knowing deity who could *always* observe one's actions.

This is not to say that the judgments of other people became irrelevant to moral control. Judgments of one's moral adequacy depend on consensual validation from others. Awareness of death also led to a desire for symbolic immortality, that is, continued existence in the minds of others after one's death. This requires maintaining a reputation for one's virtue and other characteristics valued by one's society. And of course, social groups continue to mete out tangible and social rewards and punishments for morally acceptable and unacceptable behavior. Awareness of death led to the invention of gods that added to, rather than replaced, the power of the community in enforcing moral mandates.

With relatively few exceptions, evolutionary psychologists pay little attention to the adaptive pressure of internal experience and focus their explanations on the external physical and social environment. We have argued that the internal environment of mind, ideas, and private experience also plays an important role in shaping human nature (Greenberg et al., 2014). TMT posits that internal thoughts about the inevitable end of life, along with the powerful emotional distress that such thoughts produce, were a major impetus for human innovations in how reality is construed. This led to the invention and proliferation of death-transcending spirits and deities and the important role that moral behavior plays in acquiring continued existence after physical death. Because of the death-denying value of these creative fruits of the human imagination, these ideas were, and continue to be, socially transmitted and institutionalized as cultural knowledge. This may have created new selective pressure for brains and neural structures that were suited to believing in such entities and capable of being comforted by such ideas. Modern versions of morality, gods, and religion are thus a product of this complex interplay between biological natural selection, internal experience, human innovation, and cultural progress, all of which are major influences on the nature of our species.

# References

Atran, S., & Norenzayan, A. (2004). Religion's evolutionary landscape: Counterintuition, commitment, compassion, communion. *Behavioral and Brain Sciences, 27*, 713–730.

Bassett, J.F., Van Tongeren, D.R., Green, J.D., Sonntag, M.E., & Kilpatrick, H. (2014). The interactive effects of mortality salience and political orientation on moral judgments. *British Journal of Social Psychology, 54*, 236–254.

Batson, C.D., & Stocks, E.L. (2004). Religion: Its core psychological function. In J. Greenberg, S.L. Koole, & T. Pyszczynski (Eds.), *Handbook of experimental existential psychology* (pp. 141–155). New York: Guilford.

Bekoff, M., & Pierce, J. (2009). *Wild justice: The moral lives of animals*. Chicago: University of Chicago Press.

Bloom, P. (2004). *Descartes' baby: How the science of child development explains what makes us human*. New York: Basic Books.

Bloom, P. (2005). Is God an accident? *Atlantic Monthly, 296,* 105. Retrieved from http://www.theatlantic.com/magazine/archive/2005/12/is-god-anaccident/304425/

Boehm, C. (2008). A biocultural evolutionary exploration of supernatural sanctioning. In J. Bulbulia, R. Sosis, C. Genet, R. Genet, E. Harris, & K. Wyman (Eds.), *The evolution of religion: Studies, theories, and critiques* (pp. 143–150). Santa Margarita, CA: Collins Foundation Press.

Boyer, P. (2004). Religion, evolution, and cognition. *Current Anthropology, 45,* 430–433.

Castano, E., & Dechesne, M. (2005). On defeating death: Group reification and social identification as immortality strategies. *European Review of Social Psychology, 16,* 221–255.

Cohen, F., Solomon, S., Maxfield, M., Pyszczynski, T., & Greenberg, J. (2004). Fatal attraction: The effects of mortality salience on evaluations of charismatic, task-oriented, and relationship-oriented leaders. *Psychological Science, 15,* 846–851.

Cox, C.R., Goldenberg, J.L., Arndt, J., & Pyszczynski, T. (2007). Mother's milk: An existential perspective on negative reactions to breast-feeding. *Personality and Social Psychology Bulletin, 33,* 110–122.

Cox, C.R., Goldenberg, J.L., Pyszczynski, T., & Weise, D. (2007). Disgust, creatureliness and the accessibility of death-related thoughts. *European Journal of Social Psychology, 37,* 494–507.

De Waal, F.B. (2008). Putting the altruism back into altruism: The evolution of empathy. *Annual Review of Psychology, 59,* 279–300.

Feuerbach, L. (1989). *The essence of Christianity*. Amherst, NY: Prometheus. (Original work published 1841)

Florian, V., & Mikulincer, M. (1997). Fear of death and the judgment of social transgressions: A multidimensional test of terror management theory. *Journal of Personality and Social Psychology, 73,* 369–380.

Goldenberg, J.L., Cox, C.R., Arndt, J., & Goplen, J. (2007). "Viewing" pregnancy as existential threat: The effects of creatureliness on reactions to media depictions of the pregnant body. *Media Psychology, 10,* 211–230.

Goldenberg, J.L., Pyszczynski, T., Greenberg, J., Solomon, S., Kluck, B., & Cornwell, R. (2001). I am not an animal: Mortality salience, disgust, and the denial of human creatureliness. *Journal of Experimental Psychology: General, 130,* 427–435.

Graham, J., & Haidt, J. (2010). Beyond beliefs: Religion binds individuals into moral communities. *Personality and Social Psychology Review, 14,* 140–150.

Graham, J., Haidt, J., Koleva, S., Motyl, M., Iyer, R., Wojcik, S., & Ditto, P.H. (2013). Moral foundations theory: The pragmatic validity of moral pluralism. *Advances in Experimental Social Psychology, 47,* 55–130.

Graham, J., Haidt, J., & Nosek, B.A. (2009). Liberals and conservatives rely on different sets of moral foundations. *Journal of Personality and Social Psychology, 96,* 1029–1046.

Greenberg, J., Simon, L., Porteus, J., Pyszczynski, T., & Solomon, S. (1995). Evidence of a terror management function of cultural icons: The effects of mortality salience on the inappropriate use of cherished cultural symbols. *Personality and Social Psychology Bulletin, 21,* 1221–1228.

Greenberg, J., Vail, K., & Pyszczynski, T. (2014). Terror management theory and research: How the desire for death transcendence drives our strivings for meaning and significance. *Advances in Motivation Science, 1*, 85–134.

Haidt, J. (2010). Moral psychology must not be based on faith and hope: Commentary on Narvaez (2010). *Perspectives on Psychological Science, 5*, 182–184.

Haidt, J., & Joseph, C. (2004). Intuitive ethics: How innately prepared intuitions generate culturally variable virtues. *Daedalus, 133*, 55–66.

Haidt, J., Koller, S.H., & Dias, M.G. (1993). Affect, culture, and morality, or is it wrong to eat your dog? *Journal of Personality and Social Psychology, 65*, 613–628.

Hirschberger, G. (2006). Terror management and attributions of blame to innocent victims: reconciling compassionate and defensive responses. *Journal of Personality and Social Psychology, 91*, 832–844.

Hirschberger, G., Pyszczynski, T., Ein-Dor, T., Shani Sherman, T., Kadah, E., Kesebir, P., & Park, Y. C. (2015, September 7). Fear of death amplifies retributive justice motivations and encourages political violence. *Peace and Conflict: Journal of Peace Psychology*. Advance online publication.

Horberg, E.J., Oveis, C., Keltner, D., & Cohen, A.B. (2009). Disgust and the moralization of purity. *Journal of Personality and Social Psychology, 97*, 963–976.

Jonas, E., Schimel, J., Greenberg, J., & Pyszczynski, T. (2002). The Scrooge effect: Evidence that mortality salience increases prosocial attitudes and behavior. *Personality and Social Psychology Bulletin, 28*, 1342–1353.

Jong, J., Halberstadt, J., & Bluemke, M. (2012). Foxhole atheism, revisited: The effects of mortality salience on explicit and implicit religious belief. *Journal of Experimental Social Psychology, 48*, 983–989.

Kesebir, P., & Pyszczynski, T. (2011). A moral-existential account of the psychological factors fostering intergroup conflict. *Social and Personality Psychology Compass, 5*, 878–890.

Kesebir, P., & Pyszczynski, T. (2012). The role of death in life: Existential aspects of human motivation. In R. Ryan (Ed.), *The Oxford handbook of human motivation* (pp. 43–64). New York: Oxford University Press.

Kirkpatrick, L.A. (2005). *Attachment, evolution, and the psychology of religion*. New York: Guilford.

Kohlberg, L. (1969). Stage and sequence: The cognitive-developmental approach to socialization. In D.A. Goslin (Ed.), *Handbook of socialization theory and research* (pp. 347–480). Chicago: Rand McNally.

Koleva, S.P., Graham, J., Ditto, P., Iyer, R., & Haidt, J. (2012). Tracing the threads: How five moral concerns (especially purity) help explain culture war attitudes. *Journal of Research in Personality, 46*, 184–194.

Landau, M.J., Goldenberg, J.L., Greenberg, J., Gillath, O., Solomon, S., Cox, C., . . . Pyszczynski, T. (2006). The siren's call: Terror management and the threat of men's sexual attraction to women. *Journal of Personality and Social Psychology, 90*, 129–146.

Landau, M.J., Greenberg, J., & Solomon, S. (2004). The motivational underpinnings of religion. *Behavioral and Brain Sciences, 27*, 743–744.

Norenzayan, A., Dar-Nimrod, I., Hansen, I., Proulx, T. (2009). Mortality salience and religion: divergent effects on the defense of cultural worldviews for the religious and the non-religious. *European Journal of Social Psychology, 39*(1), 101–113.

Norenzayan, A., Henrich, J, & Slingerland, E. (2013). Religious prosociality: A synthesis. In P.J. Richerson & M.H. Christiansen (Eds.), *Cultural evolution: Society, technology, language and religion* (pp. 365–379). Cambridge, MA: MIT Press.

Norenzayan, A., Shariff, A.F., Gervais, W.M., Willard, A.K., McNamara, R.A., Slingerland, E., & Henrich, J. (2014). The cultural evolution of prosocial religions. *Behavioral and Brain Sciences*, 1–86.

Ochsmann, R. (1984). Belief in afterlife as a moderator of fear of death? *European Journal of Social Psychology*, *14*, 53–67.

Osarchuk, M., & Tatz, S.J. (1973). Effect of induced fear of death on belief in afterlife. *Journal of Personality and Social Psychology*, *27*, 256–260.

Pyszczynski, T., Greenberg, J., Solomon, S., & Maxfield, M. (2006). On the unique psychological import of the human awareness of mortality: Theme and variations. *Psychological Inquiry*, *17*, 328–356.

Pyszczynski, T., Solomon, S., & Greenberg, J. (2015). Thirty years of terror management theory: From Genesis to Revelation. In M. Zanna & J. Olson (Eds.), *Advances in experimental social psychology* (pp. 1–70). Waltham, MA: Academic Press/Elsevier.

Rosenblatt, A., Greenberg, J., Solomon, S., Pyszczynski, T., & Lyon, D. (1989). Evidence for terror management theory: I. The effects of mortality salience on reactions to those who violate or uphold cultural values. *Journal of Personality and Social Psychology*, *57*, 681–690.

Rothschild, Z., Abdollahi, A., & Pyszczynski, T. (2009). Does peace have a prayer? The effect of mortality salience, compassionate values and religious fundamentalism on hostility toward out-groups. *Journal of Experimental Social Psychology*, *45*, 816–827.

Rozin, P., Haidt, J., & McCauley, C.R. (1999). Disgust: The body and soul emotion. In T. Dalgleish & M.J. Power (Eds.), *Handbook of cognition and emotion* (pp. 429–445). New York: Wiley.

Shariff, A.F., & Norenzayan, A. (2011). Mean gods make good people: Different views of God predict cheating behavior. *International Journal for the Psychology of Religion*, *21*, 85–96.

Schimel, J., Hayes, J., Williams, T., & Jahrig, J. (2007). Is death really the worm at the core? Converging evidence that worldview threat increases death-thought accessibility. *Journal of Personality and Social Psychology*, *92*, 789–803.

Schmidt, K. (2009). Göbekli Tepe—Eine Beschreibung der wichtigsten Befunde erstellt nach den Arbeiten der Grabungsteams der Jahre 1995–2007. In *Erste Tempel—Frühe Siedlungen. 12000 Jahre Kunst und Kultur* (pp. 187–223). Oldenburg.

Shweder, R.A., Much, N.C., Mahapatra, M., & Park, L. (1997). The "big three" of morality (autonomy, community, divinity) and the "big three" explanations of suffering. In A.M. Brandt & P. Rozin (Eds.), *Morality and health* (pp. 119–169). New York: Routledge.

Skitka, L.J., Bauman, C.W., & Sargis, E.G. (2005). Moral conviction: Another contributor to attitude strength or something more? *Journal of Personality and Social Psychology*, *88*, 895–917.

Solomon, S., Greenberg, J., & Pyszczynski, T. (1991). A terror management theory of social behavior: The psychological functions of self-esteem and cultural worldviews. *Advances in Experimental Social Psychology*, *24*, 93–159.

Solomon, S., Greenberg, J., & Pyszczynski, T. (2015). *The worm at the core: The role of death in life*. New York: Random House.

Wheatley, T., & Haidt, J. (2005). Hypnotic disgust makes moral judgments more severe. *Psychological Science, 16,* 780–784.

Willer, R. (2009). No atheists in foxholes: Motivated reasoning and religious ideology. In J. Jost, A. Kay, & H. Thorisdottir (Eds.), *Social and psychological bases of ideology and system justification* (pp. 241–264). Oxford: Oxford University Press.

Wright, R. (2009). *The evolution of God.* New York: Little, Brown.

# 3

# MORAL OPPORTUNITIES VERSUS MORAL TESTS

*Dale T. Miller and Benoît Monin*

A growing literature suggests that people are strongly motivated to see themselves and be seen by others as moral (Aquino & Reed, 2002; Dunning, 2007; Monin & Jordan, 2009; Nisan, 1991). This motivation leads people to act in ways that their culture deems moral and to avoid acting in ways that it deems immoral. One challenge in maintaining a moral identity is that perceptions of morally relevant situations cleave into two distinct types: those that provide potential for the enhancement of one's moral image and those that threaten to diminish that same image.

Situations we term *moral opportunities* provide individuals with at least one behavioral option that could potentially enhance their moral self-image. When faced with a moral opportunity, making the "moral" choice leaves one feeling better about one's moral standing, but making the "nonmoral" choice does not leave one feeling worse. In contrast, situations we term *moral tests* confront individuals with at least one behavioral option that has the potential to diminish their moral self-image. When faced with a moral test, making the "moral" choice does not leave one feeling better about one's moral standing, but making the "nonmoral" choice leaves one feeling worse. To successfully maintain a positive moral self-image people must both embrace moral opportunities when their self-images have been threatened and avoid failing moral tests.

In this chapter we delineate and illustrate the two categories of moral situations. In applying the term "moral" to situations we imply only that people perceive their actions in those situations to have the potential to increase or decrease their sense of being a good, virtuous person. Further, our analysis assumes that people are concerned with both their moral public image and their moral self-image. In the service of expository simplicity we restrict our focus here to moral self-image, but we acknowledge that in many of the depicted situations it is difficult to determine whether the primary driver of the phenomenon is moral self-image or moral public image.

## Defining Moral Opportunities and Moral Tests

Moral opportunities and moral tests confront actors with the behavioral means of substantiating or undermining, respectively, an identity claim that they are a moral person. Kant's (1785) distinction between perfect and imperfect duties bears instructive similarities to the difference between moral tests and moral opportunities. Kant viewed failing to perform a perfect duty as a moral transgression, for according to him performing perfect duties is a basic obligation for a human being. In our language, to fail to perform a perfect duty is to fail a moral test. Kant's imperfect duties and what we term moral opportunities do not have the same moral force: they do not merit blame when they are not enacted, but do merit praise when they are completed.

Our distinction between moral opportunities and moral tests also bears similarities to the distinction that Janoff-Bulman, Sheikh, and Hepp (2009) make between proscriptive and prescriptive morality. Proscriptive morality focuses on negative outcomes and on what one should not do, with the threat of moral blame; prescriptive morality focuses on positive outcomes and on what one should do, with the promise of moral credit. However, moral tests are neither simply instances of proscriptive morality nor moral opportunities; simply instances of prescriptive morality. Moral tests and moral opportunities can both involve either prescriptive or proscriptive elements. The moral test that is failed by the act of cheating on an exam involves a proscriptive morality, whereas the moral test that is failed by letting a colleague's racist joke go unchallenged involves a prescriptive morality. In a parallel fashion, the moral opportunity afforded by the decision to discontinue buying products from countries with poor labor conditions involves a proscriptive morality, whereas the moral opportunity afforded by the decision to seek out a charity to donate a windfall to involves a prescriptive morality. It may be true that proscriptive morality more often leads to tests, and prescriptive morality to opportunities, but the examples just provided show that the concepts can be meaningfully distinguished.

We assume that virtually all people construe some situations as moral opportunities and some as moral tests, but vary considerably in which situations they construe as moral tests and which as moral opportunities. Consider the request to donate blood. Theoretically, this request could be construed as either a moral test or a moral opportunity, though it falls squarely within the realm of prescriptive morality. Those who consider this request a moral test would be expected to experience a "cold prickle" (Andreoni, 1995) if they refused to donate, but not to feel a "warm glow" if they did. On the other hand, those who experience this request as a moral opportunity would be expected to experience a "warm glow" if they complied but not a "cold prickle" if they did not. The more of an opportunity a situation provides, the less of a test it represents, and vice versa.

## Distinctive Reactions to Moral Tests and Moral Opportunities

If the distinction between moral tests and moral opportunities is to prove useful, it is important to show that people react differently to the two situations. Thus, we begin by showing that people's reactions to morally relevant situations vary in ways that are consistent with the logic underlying our conceptualization of this distinction.

### *Avoiding Moral Tests*

People have little incentive to seek out moral tests: they present no promise of enhancing people's moral self-images yet present considerable risk. When confronted with a moral test people must choose either to pay the material or psychological price required to pass the test, or to fail the test and incur damage to their public and private image. Given the no-win nature of moral tests, people should be motivated to take actions that preemptively reduce their exposure to them.

One example of the strategic avoidance of a moral test is found in Gaertner's (1973) telephone study of racial discrimination among registered White conservatives and liberals in New York City. The study involved the willingness of the randomly dialed respondents to help a Black or White caller (identifiable on the basis of their dialects) who claimed that their car had broken down on a local highway and that they had just used their last quarter to try to call their mechanic from a public phone booth. The Black and White callers explained that they had misdialed and that they now needed the respondent to help to call the mechanic for them. White conservative participants helped Black callers less than White callers, whereas White liberals did not discriminate. More relevant to our analysis, although liberals helped without regard to race when the need for their assistance was articulated, they, unlike conservatives, were more likely to hang up prior to learning fully of the caller's need for help when the caller was Black than White. One interpretation of this is that for White liberals the request to help a Black person provided more of a moral test than it did for White conservatives and this led the former to be more likely to help Blacks (thereby passing a moral test when faced with it), but it also led them to be more likely to escape the situation prior to the request for help (thereby avoiding being confronted with a moral test that would be costly to either pass or fail).

The desire to avoid a moral test may similarly underlie the finding that when ultimatum game players are given a choice between (1) freely allocating $10 between themselves and an anonymous participant and (2) walking away from this choice with only $9, many participants do the latter (Dana, Cain, & Dawes,

2006; see also Forgas, this volume). This result is striking because the participants' choice is potentially costing them money—they are opting for $9 when they could have kept all $10 in the first situation. This behavior makes sense, however, if we assume that those who opt out anticipate that moral image concern would not let them keep more than $9 were they free to choose the amount to allocate. That "opt-outers" are trying to escape what they perceive to be a costly moral test is supported by the fact that they are the ones who share the most when no opt-out response is available.

The reluctance to take actions that would benefit the self in the short term because of imbedded moral tests may also explain why people are often surprisingly reluctant to accept gifts or favors from others (Greenberg & Shapiro, 1971). Once people accept a gift the pressures of the reciprocity norm insures they will later face a moral test that they might not be able or willing to pass. Thus, whatever value a gift may have, it may be refused if it does not come with a clear understanding of what would constitute repayment and the belief this would be a reasonable exchange.

The desire to avoid future moral tests can even lead people to shun moral opportunities if embracing them will sow the seeds for future moral tests. For this reason, the most effective framings of moral opportunities are often those that address people's fear that availing themselves of such opportunities would expose them to future moral tests. One example of this logic at work may be the greater effectiveness of offering products in exchange for donations (the "exchange fiction," see Holmes, Miller, & Lerner, 2002). Receiving a token gift in return for a donation may diminish somewhat the identity enhancement potential from the donation (making it less of an opportunity) but it may nevertheless increase its overall attractiveness by minimizing the potential of future tests. Specifically, if you receive something in exchange for your donation, you are not claiming to be an unconditional donor, and thus a subsequent request to donate without the offer of a gift is not a test of such a claim, and less likely to lead to consistency-induced compliance (Freedman & Fraser, 1966). As a general rule, we predict that the less a helping opportunity carries with it the potential of future moral tests, the more likely people will be to take it.

## Seeking Moral Opportunities

If moral tests are to be avoided, moral opportunities are to be embraced, especially when one's moral image has been threatened. Seizing a moral opportunity, unlike passing a moral test, has the potential to restore a tarnished moral self-image. Thus, experiences that lower a person's current moral self-evaluation should increase the appeal of an opportunity to restore that evaluation. The transgression–compliance paradigm (Freedman, Wallington, & Bless, 1967; McMillen, 1971) illustrates how this fact can be leveraged to increase compliance.

In this paradigm participants are first led to believe that their actions have accidentally caused someone (generally the experimenter or another participant) unjust harm. They next are provided with a request for help supposedly unrelated to the experiment. Compared with those who committed no "transgression," these participants are found to comply more readily with the request to help. According to our analysis, inducing participants to commit a harmful act lowers their moral self-evaluation, thereby increasing the appeal of a chance to redeem their self-image, which moral opportunities but not moral tests provide. (For evidence that availing oneself of moral opportunities may be a strategy people use to comfort themselves even when experiencing a diffuse negative mood, see the chapters by Crockett and Forgas in this volume.)

What evidence is there that the typical request in a transgression–compliance study (see O'Keefe, 2000, for a review) constitutes a moral opportunity rather than a moral test? For one thing, these measures typically elicit helping responses from fewer (often far fewer) than 50% of the participants in the control group. This level of response is more characteristic of what we would assume an opportunity rather than a test would elicit. Of course, one could claim that people who have transgressed would be more eager to avoid failing subsequent moral tests, too, and this may be true. However, the fact that those who have transgressed are as likely to help someone unrelated to their transgression as its victim (O'Keefe, 2000) suggests that the requests for help are viewed as opportunities rather than tests. If the request to help was viewed as a test, one would expect that it would be stronger, and hence more likely to be complied with, when it came from the victim of the transgression. On the other hand, this would not be expected to be the case were it viewed as a moral opportunity; indeed, a request from someone unrelated to the transgression would, if anything, provide a greater moral opportunity.

Another means to increase the appeal of moral opportunities is to make people feel that they have been hypocritical. To act hypocritically is to fail a moral test and it will leave people desirous of redeeming their self-images. One demonstration of this relationship is provided by Stone et al.'s (1994) experiment in which half of their college participants were made mindful of their unsafe sexual practices, while the other half were made mindful of the unsafe sexual practices of their friends. Additionally, half the participants had first videotaped a speech for local high schools in which they advocated for safe sex. Those participants who were both mindful of their past failures and had made the speech were deemed to have acted hypocritically.

Following these manipulations, some participants were given the option either to donate some of the money they had earned to a homeless organization or to buy condoms and take informational pamphlets about AIDS, whereas other participants were given only the first option. Participants in the hypocrisy condition who had the option of doing either bought significantly more condoms than other participants, but did not donate more to the homeless. However, participants in the hypocrisy condition who were not given the option to buy condoms did donate more to the homeless than other participants. For participants whose moral identities were threatened by reminding them of their past unsafe sexual behavior, it appears the opportunity to buy condoms had more redemptive potential than the opportunity to donate to the homeless. Nevertheless, it was still possible for these participants to imbue the latter opportunity with such potential when that was the only moral opportunity available. The fact that participants seized the chance to donate to the homeless when that was the only option available clearly demonstrates its status as a moral opportunity, as they did not feel compelled to donate (as they would in a test) when they had had the opportunity to buy condoms instead.

## The Creation and Negation of Moral Opportunities and Tests

Our discussion has demonstrated that whether a behavioral choice is construed as a moral test or a moral opportunity is not fixed. Context matters. What constitutes a test for one person in one context may not for another person or for the same person in another context. The same is true of opportunities. One reason for this is that individuals by virtue of their previous actions are architects of their own tests and opportunities. Another reason is that the methods employed by those who seek to change the behavior of others powerfully shape whether actions are experienced as moral tests, moral opportunities, or neither.

### The Role of the Self in Defining and Nullifying Tests and Opportunities

People's individual histories and values determine whether they construe a situation as a moral test, a moral opportunity, or as not morally relevant at all. When Colby and Damon (1992) interviewed exceptional moral exemplars, the most noteworthy common feature in these narratives was that these individuals reported embracing their causes not because of their desire to "do good" but because of their sense that the alternative was inconceivable—they had to do something given the pressing need they perceived. In our language, this means that what could appear to observers as the pursuit of a moral opportunity was experienced by these individuals as a clear moral test. In such circumstances, many people instead diffuse responsibility or claim helplessness, thereby transforming potential (failed) moral tests into mere (missed) moral opportunities. Philosopher Peter Singer tries to short-circuit precisely this means of psychological escape with the very title of his book *The Life You Can Save* (2009)—It is just one life and you can save it: Now will you?

People's past actions also play an important role in defining whether they will see their present circumstances as affording moral tests or moral opportunities.

On one hand, past actions can increase the likelihood that a particular action will be seen as a moral test. As discussed earlier, having previously accepted a favor from someone makes any future request by that person a much greater moral test than it otherwise would be. Similarly, failing to practice a prescribed act (e.g., safe sex) constitutes a much greater failed moral test for someone who has made a previous commitment to do so. On the other hand, past actions can also reduce what otherwise would seem a moral test from feeling so. For example, when people's past actions provide them with moral credentials that make them secure in their moral self-image, they will be less likely to see potentially problematic situations as tests of their moral identity (Miller & Effron, 2010; Monin & Miller, 2001).

One's past actions also affect how much of a moral opportunity situations are perceived to afford. Earlier we saw how past actions (e.g., transgressions) affect the likelihood that people will avail themselves of moral opportunities. But they also can affect what people define as a moral opportunity. For example, the motivation of "transgressors" to redeem their temporarily diminished moral self-evaluations can even lead them to imbue requests of dubious merit with redemptive moral potential. One example of this is Brock and Becker's (1966) finding that Ohio State University (OSU) undergraduates induced to break a piece of experimental equipment were more likely than their "nontransgressing" peers to subsequently sign a petition advocating an increase in OSU tuition. It is difficult to imagine that refusing to support the tuition hike would be seen as a failed moral test to an undergraduate (indeed, no students in the control condition signed the petition). It may also seem surprising that undergraduates seeking to enhance their threatened moral image would see any great redemptive potential in this act, but apparently they were able to convince themselves that it was at least above the bar on this score.

## The Role of Others in Defining and Nullifying Tests and Opportunities

Third parties also play an important role in defining what circumstances are defined as moral opportunities and moral tests. Sometimes the influence of third parties comes via rhetoric and sometimes via "carrots" and "sticks."

### Using Rhetoric to Create Tests and Opportunities

When social planners or others wish to increase or decrease the frequency of a behavior, they frequently attempt to leverage the moral opportunity or moral test potential of the behavior. For example, one obvious way to increase the likelihood that a person will avail herself of a moral opportunity is to emphasize the "warm glow" potential that taking that action has (Aquino, McFerran, & Laven, 2011)—in effect, labeling the behavior a moral opportunity. Pointing out to people that they can feel virtuous without incurring much cost can be especially effective.

Thus, having citizens contemplate the "voter" identity is more likely to get them to the voting booth the next day than simply having them consider "voting" (Bryan, Walton, Rogers, & Dweck, 2011)—it makes a moral opportunity salient by placing a desired identity within reach.

Marketers commonly use identity pitches to show how purchasing their products provides the opportunity for a warm glow, as in Target's claim that "When you shop at Target, you become a do-gooder in your community." Similarly, HP's instruction handouts accompanying their printer cartridges promise a warm glow by encouraging users to "feel good about recycling."

Rhetoric can also serve to encourage people to see performing undesirable behaviors as failing moral tests. Public service campaigns, for example, often seek to change behavior by marketing an undesired behavior as a failed moral test (Miller & Prentice, 2013). For example, the Vancouver Police Department's 2011 campaign against sexual assault used the tagline "Don't be that guy," which was credited with a 10% drop in reported assaults (Matas, 2012). This ad presumably was successful because it framed dating misconduct as a failed moral test, thereby making salient an identity to be avoided (you know that guy and you don't want to be him).

Experimental work also illustrates the powerful role that priming negative identities can play in framing a choice as a moral test. Earlier we saw that the positive identity prompted by the label "voter" made voting more attractive by framing this act as a moral opportunity. Negative identity prompts appear to function similarly, as suggested by the finding that the admonition "Don't be a cheater" was more effective at reducing unethical behavior than the admonition "Don't cheat" (Bryan, Adams, & Monin, 2013), presumably because it unambiguously framed the situation as a test of one's moral character.

## Using Rewards and Punishments to Augment the Power of Tests and Opportunities

Third parties interested in changing social behavior often employ rewards and punishment, sometimes with surprising results. Distinguishing between moral tests and moral opportunities helps illuminate when and why these strategies sometimes are effective and sometimes are not.

When social planners decide it is desirable to either increase some behavior (e.g., blood donation) or decrease it (e.g., energy consumption), they frequently follow price theory (Stigler, 1987) and employ the economic levers of subsidies and taxes.

In theory, social planners seeking to produce a behavioral change could either subsidize the desirable behavior or tax the undesirable behavior. However, assuming that the targeted population agrees that the outcome sought by the social planners (e.g., adequate blood supply, economic sustainability) is socially desirable, we propose that the favored economic lever will depend on whether the targeted moral action is socially represented as an opportunity or a test. For opportunities, subsidizing the desired behavior will seem most appropriate; for tests, taxing the undesired behavior will seem most appropriate.

Fining people for failing to do something they should feel good about doing seems wrong, as does compensating people for doing something they should feel bad about not doing, and attempting either is likely to prove politically unpopular. For example, jurisdictions that incentivize voting (Funk, 2010) tend to do so by fining people for not voting (rather than paying people for voting), suggesting that voting is seen as a moral test, something to feel bad about not doing, not to feel good about for doing. On the other hand, jurisdictions that incentivize blood donation (Niza, Tung, & Marteau, 2013) do so by compensating people for donating blood (rather than fining those who do not), suggesting that this act is seen as a moral opportunity, something to feel good about doing, not to feel bad about for not doing. When authorities change the lever they use over time, it likely reflects a consensual change in the moral status of the act. For example, the shift in lever preference from incentives to fines in the case of home recycling in many American towns suggests that the social representation of recycling in these communities has transformed from a moral opportunity to a moral test.

## How Employing Carrots and Sticks Changes the Perception of Tests and Opportunities

Which economic lever social planners choose in their effort to increase certain behaviors and decrease others not only reflects whether those behaviors are seen as moral opportunities or moral tests but also helps define the status of those actions as moral opportunities or tests. Sometimes the choice of lever strengthens the existing framing; sometimes it undermines it.

### *The Potential Costs of Subsidizing Behavior*

If the moral opportunity provided by a behavior (e.g., blood donation) is insufficient to prompt enough people to engage in the behavior, it might seem reasonable to augment the existing psychological incentive with an economic one. The expectation would be that this would increase the frequency of the desired behavior among both those who previously saw the situation as a moral opportunity (they now would have two motives for undertaking the behavior) and those who previously did not see the situation as a moral opportunity (they now would at least have an economic motive for undertaking the action).

The reality appears more complicated than this, however, as suggested first by Richard Titmuss (1971) in his analysis of the British government's decision to increase the supply of blood by compensating blood donors. Titmuss argued that rather than supplement the civic-mindedness that already motivated blood donation, the offer of a financial incentive would backfire and actually reduce the likelihood that people would donate. Economists initially resisted the suggestion that subsidies would "crowd out" prosocial motivation in the realm of blood donation (Arrow, 1972; Solow, 1971), but recent empirical evidence supports this prediction (Mellstrom & Johannesson, 2008; Niza et al., 2013).

The so-called crowding-out effect is similar but importantly different from the overjustification effect documented by psychologists (Deci, 1975; Lepper & Greene, 1980). The latter refers to the effect wherein accepting an external incentive for an activity that you are initially intrinsically motivated to perform diminishes your willingness to perform that activity once the incentive is removed. For example, the overjustification effect describes the situation wherein people induced to donate blood for a financial consideration would be less so inclined in the future if the reward were removed. The crowding-out effect (Frey & Jegen, 2001) most commonly refers to people's diminished willingness to undertake a potentially morally satisfying action (e.g., donate blood) when an extrinsic incentive is offered, yielding less of the behavior even with the external incentive still in place. In this latter case the question is how the offer of an incentive changes the appeal of an activity you have not yet performed rather than the appeal of one you have already performed (Bruno, 2013).

There are two reasons why the offer of compensation for blood donation could make it less of a moral opportunity for people. First, it could lead people to see blood donation not as an act of community service but as a commercial activity (Healy, 2006) and thus devoid of moral significance. Second, even if the introduction of remuneration did not strip blood donation of its moral significance for actors, it could diminish its appeal to them by obscuring the signal that it sent to observers about the actors' moral virtue (Bénabou & Tirole, 2006; Kelley, 1972; Seabright, 2009). The act of blood donation, once remunerated, would no longer unambiguously signal that the donors' motives were moral even if they were. Indeed, observers are reluctant to extract any positive signal about a person's moral motivation from behavior in situations that could be explained by self-interest (Hilton, Fein, & Miller, 1990).

It is noteworthy that offering nonfinancial incentives has proven more effective in increasing blood donation than the offer of cash (Kamenica, 2012). In one relevant study, Glynn et al. (2003) surveyed over 45,000 US blood donors on their attitudes toward incentives for blood donation. Their respondents indicated that offering them cholesterol screening and prostate-specific antigen screening for donation would increase their willingness to donate but that offering financial incentives would have the opposite effect. This finding suggests that the opportunity to affirm one's identity as a good citizen and moral person may not be removed or compromised by the offer of nonmonetary rewards, perhaps because the offer of this form of compensation does not "commercialize" the transaction or "commodify" the gift. Supporting this possibility, a 15-country representative survey of potential blood donors (Costa-Font, Jofre-Bonet, & Yen, 2013) found that the appeal of the different forms of compensation depended on the respondents' experience with blood donation. Those most in favor of nonmonetary (social) rewards tended to have previously donated blood and therefore presumably were most desirous of maintaining its status as a moral opportunity. On the other hand, those most in favor of monetary rewards for blood donation tended to be people who had not donated in the past.

Our interpretation of the blood donation findings is that those who view it in moral terms tend to see it as a moral opportunity rather than a moral test. It is nevertheless possible that some people could view the request to give blood as a moral test, something they feel an obligation to do. For these people we also predict that compensation would diminish their likelihood donating blood because it would liberate them from feelings of obligation. Specifically, the offer of compensation would signal that although blood donation may be socially valuable, it is not obligatory; it is simply an action that people are free to do or not to do.

One example of how the offer of compensation can undermine the status of a behavior as a moral test is provided by Sudarshan (2012). This field experiment found that telling homeowners about their neighbors' lower energy usage had a positive (downward) effect on their own usage, as one would expect to the extent that this information was revealing to people that they were failing the moral test of not being as socially responsible as their neighbors.[1]

In contrast, no positive effect on energy use was found when the peer information was accompanied by a financial incentive for conserving. Homeowners apparently were not made uncomfortable by the information that they were performing below their peers in energy conservation when authorities were using subsidies to close the gap. They presumably reasoned that if their high energy use was really a moral failure they would be punished (taxed) for deviating from neighborhood norms rather than simply not being compensated for complying with those norms. Offering compensation for undertaking an action signals that the action is optional, not morally mandated.

In conclusion, the offer of a subsidy for performing an action will diminish the capacity of that action to function as either a moral opportunity or a moral test. We identified two reasons that compensation undermines the moral opportunity value of an action. First, by commercializing the action it defines it as a market activity rather than a moral one (Fiske, 1992; Healy, 2006). Second, even if moral value remains attached to the action, the presence of compensation renders ambiguous what performing that action signals about the person's moral motivation (Bénabou & Tirole, 2006; Kelley, 1972). Did the person perform it because she was a socially responsible person or because she wanted the compensation? And it is not just moral opportunities that are undermined by compensation:

moral tests are as well. Compensation diminishes the potential of an action to be a moral test because it signals that the behavior is not collectively viewed as a test, because authorities typically discourage the failure of tests by employing taxes not subsidies. Of course, none of this guarantees that the offer of compensation will diminish the supply of a particular behavior, because (1) it may not currently be moralized as either an opportunity or a test, or (2) the compensation could provide enough external incentive to make up for any diminished internal motivation that results from the offer of compensation.

## The Potential Costs of Taxing Behavior

That increasing the cost of something diminishes its demand is axiomatic in economics, so one might expect that when the framing of an undesirable behavior as a failed moral test (a psychological tax) is insufficient to deter it, adding an economic tax could only help. Not only would the material cost be expected to act as a deterrent, but imposing an economic tax would provide a further signal that the action is socially disapproved of. Indeed, the expressive theory of law (McAdams, 2015) explicitly assumes that an important function of making an action illegal is that it signals consensual disapproval of the act. In short, one can predict that adding economic penalties to failed moral tests will diminish their frequency, and we suspect that they generally do—but not always.

An instructive example of how the application of a fine designed to reinforce a moral test can backfire is provided by an intervention study (Gneezy & Rustichini, 2000) conducted in 10 private Israeli daycare centers, where many parents routinely were tardy to pick up their children. The intervention strategy was one of traditional deterrence: the investigators fined late-coming behavior. At six of the daycare centers, parents were informed that they would pay a fine (approximately $4) every time they picked their child up after 4:15 p.m. The remaining four daycare centers served as a control group.

The results were striking. The number of late pickups *increased* significantly with the imposition of a fine and remained at the increased level even after the fine was removed. One interpretation of this finding is that before the fine, tardy parents were failing a moral test as their behavior was inflicting costs on the other parents and on the daycare center staff. Some parents obviously were willing to fail this test, but many were not. With the introduction of the fine, what had been a moral test became a commercial transaction. Now, late-comers were no longer free-riding; they were simply choosing to pay a material price for their lateness.

Further evidence that specifying economic taxes for socially disapproved behavior can sometimes actually license that behavior is provided by Wilkinson-Ryan's (2010) experiments on the impact of economic sanctions on breach of legal contracts. In a series of experiments she finds that people are less likely to perform their contractual obligations when the contract includes a liquidated damages clause specifying the penalty for nonperformance than when it does not. It appears that without specifying the penalty people see their nonperformance of a contract as reflecting negatively on their moral identity (a failed moral test), but this is not the case when there is an economic price associated with nonperformance (see also Holmas, Kjerstad, Luras, & Straume, 2010).

The risk of an economic tax undermining the psychological tax associated with a failed moral test is higher when the fine is perceived to be equity based rather than deterrence based (Brickman, 1977). Equity-based fines have two required properties. First, they must be easily tied to the undesirable action—that is, the fine must be imposed every time the action is performed. This was the case in the daycare center, where the failure of parents to pick up their kids at the scheduled time automatically resulted in them being charged a late fee. In the case of deterrence-based fines (e.g., "pooper scooper" laws), the connection between the fine and the infraction is far from automatic and requires the violator to be "caught," which is often a low probability event. Second, in the case of equity-based fines there exists the perception that the fine will be used to compensate those who bear the burden of the target's problematic behavior (e.g., the daycare staff who have to stay late in the case of late pickups). In contrast, the size of deterrent-based fines is typically prorated not to the cost of the infraction but to the likelihood of catching perpetrators. Fines should only undermine moral tests, then, when they are seen as equitable compensation for the infraction and not as a deterrent.

What if people are fined for failing to undertake what previously had been perceived as a moral opportunity? This will surely undermine the behavior's status as a moral opportunity but it is unlikely to decrease its supply. For example, when fines are imposed on people for not recycling, those who previously recycled and derived moral satisfaction from doing so are unlikely to slacken off in their recycling efforts. They will still see it as the right thing to do (and the wrong thing not to do), and for this reason they will likely continue to do it, though they are not likely to continue to experience a warm glow when they do it. In other words, it will become a moral test, but one that the individuals who once were eager to take advantage of the moral opportunity it previously provided should also be eager not to fail.

## Conclusion

Maintaining a moral self-image requires regulating one's behavior. On the one hand, it requires seizing moral opportunities that have the potential to enhance one's moral image. On the other hand, it requires not failing moral tests that have the potential to diminish one's moral image. It is not enough to observe that someone took or did not take the moral action in a situation to know whether they enhanced or diminished their moral image. The distinction between moral opportunities and moral tests deepens our understanding of moral self-regulation and social behavior more broadly.

## Note

1 Note that learning of a moral norm in advance of one's own choice generally is likely to create a moral test if one expects to perform below the norm, but an opportunity if one expects to perform above it.

## References

Andreoni, J. (1995). Warm-glow versus cold prickle: The effects of positive and negative framing on cooperation in experiments. *Quarterly Journal of Economics, 110*, 1–21.

Aquino, K., McFerran, B., & Laven, M. (2011). Moral identity and the experience of elevation in response to acts of uncommon goodness. *Journal of Personality and Social Psychology, 100*(4), 703–718.

Aquino, K., & Reed, A. (2002). The self-importance of moral identity. *Journal of Personality and Social Psychology, 83*, 1423–1440.

Arrow, K.J. (1972). Gifts and exchanges. *Philosophy and Public Affairs, 1*(4), 343–362.

Bénabou, R., & Tirole, J. (2006). Incentives and prosocial behavior. *American Economic Review, 96*(5), 1652–1678.

Brickman, P. (1977). Crime and punishment in sports and society. *Journal of Social Issues, 33*(1), 140–164.

Brock, T.C., & Becker, L.A. (1966). "Debriefing" and susceptibility to subsequent experimental manipulations. *Journal of Experimental Social Psychology, 2*, 314–323.

Bruno, B. (2013). Reconciling economics and psychology on intrinsic motivation. *Journal of Neuroscience, Psychology, and Economics, 6*(2), 136–149.

Bryan, C.J., Adams, G.S., & Monin, B. (2013). When cheating would make you a cheater: Implicating the self prevents unethical behavior. *Journal of Experimental Psychology: General, 142*(4), 1001–1005.

Bryan, C., Walton, G.M., Rogers, T., & Dweck, C.S. (2011). Motivating voter turnout by invoking the self. *Proceedings of the National Academy of Sciences, 108*(31), 12653–12656.

Colby, A., & Damon, W. (1992). *Some do care: Contemporary lives of moral commitment.* New York: Simon and Schuster.

Costa-Font, J., Jofre-Bonet, M., & Yen, S.T. (2013). Not all incentives wash out the warm glow: The case of blood donation revisited. *Kyklos, 66*(4), 529–551.

Dana, J., Cain, D.M., & Dawes, R. (2006). What you don't know won't hurt me: Costly (but quiet) exit in dictator games. *Organizational Behavior and Human Decision Processes, 100*, 193–201.

Deci, E.L. (1975). *Intrinsic motivation.* New York: Plenum.

Dunning, D. (2007). Self-image motives and consumer behavior: How sacrosanct self-beliefs sway preferences in the marketplace. *Journal of Consumer Psychology, 17*(4), 237–249.

Fiske, A.P. (1992). The four elementary forms of sociality: Framework for a unified theory of social relations. *Psychological Review, 99*(4), 689–723.

Freedman, J.L., & Fraser. S.C. (1966). Compliance without pressure: The foot-in-the-door technique. *Journal of Personality and Social Psychology, 4*, 196–202.

Freedman, J.L., Wallington, S.A., & Bless, E. (1967). Compliance without pressure: The effect of guilt. *Journal of Personality and Social Psychology*, 7, 117–124.

Frey, B., & Jegen, R. (2001). Motivation crowding theory: A survey of empirical evidence. *Journal of Economic Surveys*, 15(5), 589–611.

Funk, P. (2010). Social incentives and voter turnout: Evidence from the Swiss mail ballot system. *Journal of the European Economic Association*, 8(5), 1077–1103.

Gaertner, S.L. (1973). Helping behavior and racial discrimination among Liberals and Conservatives. *Journal of Personality and Social Psychology*, 25, 335–341.

Glynn, S.A., Williams, A.E., Nass, C.C., Bethel, J., Kessler, D., Scott, E.P., ... Schreiber, G.B. (2003). Attitudes toward blood donation incentives in the United States: Implications for donor recruitment. *Transfusion*, 43, 7–16.

Gneezy, U., & Rustichini, A. (2000). A fine is a price, *Journal of Legal Studies*, 29(1), 1–17.

Greenberg, M., & Shapiro, S. (1971). Indebtedness: An adverse aspect of asking for and receiving help. *Sociometry*, 34(2), 290–301.

Healy, K. (2006). *Last best gifts: Altruism and the markets for human blood and organs*. Chicago: University of Chicago Press.

Hilton, J., Fein, S., & Miller, D.T. (1990). Suspicion and dispositional inference. *Personality and Social Psychology Bulletin*, 19, 501–512.

Holmas, T.H., Kjerstad, E., Luras, H., & Straume, O.R. (2010). Does monetary punishment crowd out pro-social motivation? *Journal of Economic Behavior and Organization*, 75(2), 261–267.

Holmes, J.G., Miller, D.T., & Lerner, M.J. (2002). Committing altruism under the cloak of self-interest: The exchange fiction. *Journal of Experimental Social Psychology*, 38, 144–151.

Janoff-Bulman, R., Sheikh, S., & Hepp, S. (2009). Proscriptive versus prescriptive morality: Two faces of moral regulation. *Journal of Personality and Social Psychology*, 96, 521–537.

Kamenica, E. (2012). Behavioral economics and psychology of incentives. *Annual Review of Economics*, 4, 427–452.

Kant, I. (1785). *Groundwork for the metaphysics of morals*. Translated by J.W. Ellington (3rd ed., 1981). Indianapolis, IN: Hackett.

Kelley, H.H. (1972). *Causal schemata and the attribution process*. Morristown, NJ: General Learning Press.

Lepper, M., & Greene, D. (1980). *The hidden cost of rewards*: New York: Lawrence Erlbaum.

Matas, R. (2012, January 21). "Don't be that guy" ad campaign cuts Vancouver sex assaults by 10 per cent in 2011. *Globe and Mail*. Retrieved from http://www.theglobeand mail.com/news/british-columbia/dont-be-that-guy-ad-campaign-cuts-vancouver-sex-assaults-by-10-per-cent-in-2011/article1359241/

McAdams, R. (2015). *The expressive powers of law: Theories and limits*. Cambridge, MA: Harvard University Press.

McMillen, D.L. (1971). Transgression, self-image, and compliant behavior. *Journal of Personality and Social Psychology*, 20, 176–179.

Mellstrom, C., & Johannesson, M. (2008). Crowding out in blood donation: Was Titmuss right? *Journal of the European Economic Association*, 6(4), 845–863.

Miller, D.T., & Effron, D.A. (2010). Psychological license: When it is needed and how it functions. In M.P. Zanna & J.M. Olson (Eds.), *Advances in experimental social psychology* (Vol. 43, pp. 117–158). San Diego, CA: Academic Press/Elsevier.

Miller, D.T., & Prentice, D.A. (2013). Psychological levers of behavior change. In E. Shafir (Ed.), *Behavioral foundations of policy* (pp. 301–309). Princeton, NJ: Princeton University Press.

Monin, B., & Jordan, A.H. (2009). The dynamic moral self: A social psychological perspective. In D. Narvaez & D.K. Lapsley (Eds.), *Personality, identity, and character: Explorations in moral psychology* (pp. 341–354). New York: Cambridge University Press.

Monin, B., & Miller, D.T. (2001). Moral credentials and the expression of prejudice. *Journal of Personality and Social Psychology, 81*, 33–43.

Nisan, M. (1991). The moral balance model: Theory and research extending our understanding of choice and deviation. In W.M. Kurtines & J.L. Gerwitz (Eds.), *Handbook of moral behavior and development* (Vol. 3, pp. 213–249). Hillsdale, NJ: Lawrence Erlbaum.

Niza, C., Tung, B., & Marteau, T.M. (2013). Incentivizing blood donation: Systematic review and meta-analysis to test Titmuss' hypotheses. *Health Psychology, 32*(9), 941–949.

O'Keefe, D.J. (2000). Guilt and social influence. *Communication Yearbook, 23*, 67–101.

Seabright, P. (2009). Continuous preferences and discontinuous choices: How altruists respond to incentives. *B.E. Journal of Theoretical Economics, 9*, 14.

Singer, P. (2009). *The life you can save: Acting now to end world poverty.* New York: Random House.

Solow, R. (1971). Blood and thunder: Review of *The gift relationship: From human blood to social policy* by Richard Titmuss. *Yale Law Journal, 80*(8), 1696–1711.

Stigler, G. (1987). *The theory of price* (4th ed.). New York: Macmillan.

Stone, J., Aronson, E., Crain, A.L., Winslow, M.P., & Fried, C.B. (1994). Inducing hypocrisy as a means of encouraging young adults to use condoms. *Personality and Social Psychology Bulletin, 20*, 116–128.

Sudarshan, A. (2012). Money for nothing: Using peer comparisons and financial incentives to reduce electricity demand in urban Indian households. North-East Universities Development Consortium Conference, Dartmouth, November 3–4.

Titmuss, R.M. (1971). *The gift relationship: From human blood to social policy.* New York: Pantheon Books.

Wilkinson-Ryan, T. (2010). Do liquidated damages encourage efficient breach: A psychological experiment? *Michigan Law Review, 108*, 633–671.

# 4

# THREAT, MORALITY AND POLITICS

## A Differentiated Threat Account of Moral and Political Values

*Simon M. Laham and Chelsea Corless*

### Introduction

Psychological and social scientists have long attempted to ground political orientation and related moral values in basic cognitive, affective and behavioural processes (see Carney, Jost, Gosling, & Potter, 2008; Jost, Glaser, Kruglanski, & Sulloway, 2003, for reviews; see also Brandt, Wetherell, & Crawford; and Frimer, this volume). Prominent recent accounts have structured explanations of morality and politics around individual differences in threat sensitivity and related constructs (e.g., Duckitt, 2001; Hibbing, Smith, & Alford, 2014; Janoff-Bulman, 2009; Jost et al., 2003; see also Pyszczynski, this volume). The broad claim of such accounts is that heightened sensitivity to threat is positively associated with political conservatism.

In this chapter we argue that there is utility in differentiating among sensitivities to different kinds of threats. With Neuberg, Kenrick and Schaller (2011) we agree that '[t]he psychology of threat is most aptly characterized as the evolved psycholog*ies* of threats (plural)' (p. 1043, italics in original). Moreover, we claim that sensitivities to different kinds of threats are associated with different political orientations and moral values; while sensitivities to some threats may very well be associated with conservatism, sensitivities to other threats may be associated with liberalism (see Brandt et al., this volume, for a different approach to threat and political values).

After considering the details of extant accounts of threat, politics and morality, we provide a theoretical justification for differentiating amongst kinds of threats (grounded in evolutionary and clinical psychology). We then review work that shows that while sensitivities to some kinds of threats (especially disgust-related threats) are associated with conservative moral values, sensitivities to other kinds of threats (especially social evaluation threats) are associated with a liberal worldview. We end by considering other loci of differentiation in the work on threat, morality and politics.

## Threat, Politics and Morality

The most influential recent account of the relationship between threat sensitivity and political orientation is by Jost et al. (2003). According to Jost and colleagues, political conservatism is the ideological expression of psychological attempts to manage fear and uncertainty. Existential and epistemic threats activate goals to reduce those threats, goals which are fulfilled by resisting change and endorsement or acceptance of inequality (two key planks of the conservative platform). One key tenet of this account is that people who are dispositionally prone to experience fear and related threat-based affects should be inclined towards political conservatism as a coping strategy. In a meta-analytic survey, Jost and colleagues found positive associations between various measures of dispositional threat sensitivity and political conservatism, although the size of the associations varied across measures.

More recent accounts of the threat–politics link tell similar stories. Janoff-Bulman (2009) singles out the behavioural inhibition system as especially relevant in understanding political conservatism. On Janoff-Bulman's account, the behavioural immune system, which is the neurobehavioural system that mediates reactivity to threat and punishment, underpins conservatives' motivations to maintain social order and protect the larger community.

Hibbing et al. (2014) ground political orientation in an even broader cognitive-affective individual difference: the negativity bias. Hibbing and colleagues suggest that conservatives are more sensitive to *all classes* of negative stimuli (not only threatening stimuli) than are liberals (although Hibbing et al. do briefly acknowledge possible exceptions to this overall pattern).

Other work, which focuses more specifically on moral values, shows a broadly similar pattern of results. Much of this work is done within the framework of Moral Foundations Theory (Haidt, 2012; Haidt & Joseph, 2004), which posits that the moral universe is composed of five (or six) moral foundations: Care/Harm, Fairness/Cheating, Loyalty/Betrayal, Authority/Subversion, Sanctity/Degradation and (Liberty/Oppression). The *care* foundation emphasizes compassion, empathy and absence of suffering. Actions are deemed morally good in this foundation to the extent that they uphold one or more of these concerns, and morally bad to the extent that they violate them. The *fairness* foundation is structured around equality, proportionality, reciprocity and justice and serves to regulate cooperative activity and condemn cheating and defection. *Loyalty* involves a moral duty to favor, support and protect the ingroup, while *authority* centers on the morality of dominance and submission and respect for hierarchy. *Sanctity* emphasizes the dignity, purity and nobility of humankind (see Pyszczynski, this volume, for an exploration of mortality salience and the moral foundations).

The first two foundations, *care* and *fairness*, have been termed the *individualizing* foundations, given their emphasis on the preservation and protection of individual rights. The *loyalty, authority* and *sanctity* foundations have been dubbed the *binding* foundations, as it is argued that endorsement of these foundations serves primarily to protect and bind the group, to foster social cohesion and solidarity. These higher-order foundation clusters are of particular relevance here because research has shown that whereas political liberals tend to moralize the individualizing foundations, political conservatives tend to moralize all five foundations (e.g., Graham, Haidt, & Nosek, 2009; a more nuanced discussion of the complexities of political orientation and moral value endorsement follows later; see also Brandt et al., this volume). Thus, patterns of moral foundation endorsement can be used as a rough proxy for political orientation.

Broadly speaking, work linking threat sensitivity to moral foundation endorsement has found that some measures of threat sensitivity are associated with a pattern of moral values indicative of a conservative worldview (specifically with increased endorsement of the *binding* foundations). Van Leeuwen and Park (2009), for example, showed that *belief in a dangerous world* negatively predicted the moral foundations *progressivism* score (*individualizing* minus *binding*). Further, Wright and Baril (2013) found that belief in a dangerous world positively predicted *binding* endorsement.

Although all this work suggests that threat sensitivity is associated with conservatism and binding endorsement, there is reason to believe that the story may be a little more complicated. Common to the earlier accounts of political orientation and moral values is theorizing at a rather molar level, a level at which important theoretical distinctions are not made among threat-related constructs. Yet even within extant work there is reason to suspect that not all threat-related constructs show the same pattern of associations with moral and political values. As previously mentioned, Jost et al. (2003) report that while certain threat-related variables predict conservatism (e.g., belief in a dangerous world), others do not.

This latter finding is consistent with more recent meta-analyses that demonstrate null or even *negative* associations between neuroticism, the personality trait most closely associated with threat sensitivity, and political conservatism (Gerber, Huber, Doherty, Dowling, & Ha, 2010; Hirsh, DeYoung, Xu, & Peterson, 2010; Sibley, Osborne, & Duckitt, 2012). In addition, empirical work that has examined the role of the behavioural inhibition system in the political domain has yielded null findings (Amass, 2004; Sheikh, 2007) or has shown that liberals score higher than conservatives (Iyer's study as cited in Inbar & Pizarro, 2014a). And work on moral foundation endorsement (e.g., Hirsh et al., 2010) has found no evidence that neuroticism in general, or its two aspects (withdrawal and volatility), show any clear associations with moral foundations. This variation in findings suggests that it may be worth explicitly considering distinctions among threat-related constructs when it comes to understanding moral values and political orientations. We argue, in what follows, that while some threat-related constructs may indeed relate to a conservative worldview, others may in fact relate to a liberal worldview.

## A Differentiated Threat Account of Moral Values and Political Orientation

A *threat* is anything (sentient or not) likely to cause damage or danger. On this definition, many different kinds of things may be threats: other people, animals, moving vehicles, microbes, guns. While some threats may be unique to recent historical times (e.g., plane crashes), others may have posed long-standing and recurrent evolutionary challenges and may thus have played a role in shaping our evolved psychology (Neuberg et al., 2011; see Frimer; and von Hippel, Ronay, & Maddux, this volume, for more on evolutionary approaches to morality). Evolutionary theorizing about threat-related psychology posits the existence of a suite of domain-specific threat-detection modules, each attuned to a different class of evolutionarily relevant threats (e.g., Boyer & Bergstrom, 2010).

Although different threat-detection systems may share some attributes, in terms of an evolutionary account, each module is likely to be domain specific and somewhat distinct functionally. Thus each module will not only be sensitive to cues relevant to a specific class of threat, but also will likely involve rather different computations and outputs because both the cues relevant to, and the responses pertinent to, different kinds of threat differ. As Boyer and Bergstrom (2010) argue, cues relevant to the detection of predators may not be the same as those that indicate infection. Moreover, the behaviours required to avoid mobile predators are likely to be different to those required to avoid a static source of contamination (e.g., putrefied meat).

What kinds of threats does it make sense to distinguish between? To answer this question, one can turn to work in clinical psychology. Some theorists (e.g., Marks & Nesse, 1994; Sloman, 2008; Stein & Bouwer, 1997) suggest that psychopathologies are instances of otherwise functional psychological systems gone to extremes. Öhman, for example, has suggested that adaptive systems pertinent to the detection and avoidance of evolutionarily relevant threats may be implicated in the case of certain phobias (e.g., Öhman, 1986, 2000). If this were true, one would expect the kinds of stimuli around which phobias are structured to be the very same for which we have dedicated threat-detection modules.

Consistent with this notion, the classes of threat stimuli that emerge when considering variants of anxiety-related disorders in clinical work mirror those posited as recurrent evolutionary hazards. In an influential review of factor analytic studies on fears, Arindell, Pickersgill, Merckelbach, Ardon and Cornet (1991) found that over 90% of all fear dimensions could be summarized using four factors. One factor was loaded on by items relating to *fear of social evaluation*, including fear of criticism and rejection. The second factor related to *agoraphobic fears*, which was indicated by items assessing discomfort with crowds, crossing streets and being in public places. The third factor tapped *fear of animals*, including small animals (e.g., mice) and creepy-crawlies (e.g., insects). The fourth factor was a heterogeneous collection of items reflecting *blood-injection-injury fears*, such as fear of injection/ blood, fear of disease, contamination and death. As Öhman (2000) argues, these four factors not only reflect four prominent types of phobias (social, agoraphobic, animal and blood-injection-injury), but also represent recurrent evolutionary threats: fear of social interaction, abandonment, predation, contamination and injury—threat classes also posited by other theorists as likely evolutionarily relevant threat classes (Boyer & Bergstrom, 2010; Boyer & Lienard, 2006).

Not only do threatening stimuli cluster into evolutionarily and clinically meaningful groupings, sensitivity to different clusters of stimuli may differentially predict outcomes of moral relevance. In one study, Perkins, Kemp, and Corr (2007) showed that only fears related to tissue damage (part of the blood-injection-injury grouping) were a unique predictor of performance in a task requiring participants to consider an extraction plan for a military operation, a plan involving the weighing of combatant lives. Other fear factors did not uniquely predict performance on this task.

Taken together, this work suggests that there might be utility in distinguishing among kinds of threats when predicting various outcomes and even political ideologies. But how might these different threat sensitivities relate to moral and political values? Given that both animal and blood-injection-injury phobias have been shown to have a common disgust-related affective base (see Cisler, Olatunji, & Lohr, 2009, for a review) and that disgust-sensitivity has been associated with political conservatism and related moral values (e.g., Inbar & Pizarro, 2014b), we suggest that sensitivities to these kinds of threats will be positively associated with endorsement of the binding foundations and with political conservatism.

What associations will manifest between social evaluation and agoraphobic threat sensitivities and moral values? On the one hand, it is possible that heightened sensitivity to social threats and fear of abandonment and neglect when in need will be associated with more conservative values. On Öhman's (2000) account, social fears are part of the dominance–submissiveness system, which should be attuned to regulating the authority/subversion foundation, a central concern for political conservatives. Social rank models also implicate threat-related affect in the maintenance of social hierarchies (see Sloman, 2008, for a review).

On the other hand, however, work in clinical psychology suggests that people with hyperactive social threat-detection systems (i.e., those suffering from social anxiety disorders) may be more focused on the moral concerns of the individualizing foundations of care and fairness. Evidence from retrospective studies shows that social-phobic adults recall childhoods replete with bullying, humiliation and criticism (Hackmann, Clark, & McManus, 2000; Hackmann, Surawy, & Clark, 1998; Hope, Heimberg, & Klein, 1990). In addition, Rapee and Heimberg (1997) showed that while people with social phobia assume that others are inherently critical, they also place high value on the importance of being positively valued by others (see Rapee & Spence, 2004, for a review). This suggests a set of preferences and beliefs surrounding *interpersonal* interaction that prioritizes positive regard as an end, but assumes that others will not naturally seek such an end. In a world perceived as full of critical and bullying others, one might value moral rules that promote care and fair treatment and inhibit harm and unfairness. Consistent with this, people who fear rejection by intimate others or the social group have been found to be particularly concerned with reciprocity and fairness (Bartz & Lydon, 2008; Erwin, Heimberg, Schneier, & Liebowitz, 2003; Koleva, Selterman, Iyer, Ditto, & Graham, 2014).

## Social Threat, Disgust-Related Threat and Moral Values

To test these possibilities, we (Laham & Corless, 2014a) conducted a large online survey assessing people's sensitivities to various kinds of threatening stimuli and their moral values. Eight hundred and fifty-one US citizens participated via Amazon Mechanical Turk. They completed the Fear Survey Schedule-III (Wolpe & Lang, 1964) as a measure of differentiated threat. This is a 52-item measure that asks people to rate the extent to which each of 52 stimuli (e.g., snakes, failure, bats, journeys by car, human blood) causes fear and disturbance. The Moral Foundations Questionnaire (Graham et al., 2011) was used to assess the extent to which people endorse the five moral foundations identified by Haidt.

Exploratory factor analysis of the Fear Survey Schedule-III yielded a three-factor solution which provided initial measurement evidence for distinguishing between at least three kinds of threat sensitivity. These were labelled *social evaluation threat*, *agoraphobic threat*, and *disgust-related threat*. This last factor was a combination of blood-injection-injury, contamination and animal threats. It was labelled *disgust-related threat* as recent work suggests a role for disgust in specific phobias such as spider and blood-injection-injury and in contamination-related obsessive-compulsive disorder (Cisler et al., 2009).

A similar factor analysis of the Moral Foundations Questionnaire yielded a two-factor solution: *individualizing* (loaded on by items relating to sensitivity to suffering and discrimination) and *binding* (loaded on by items relating to respect, loyalty to family and country and concerns for purity). These higher order foundation clusters often emerge when this questionnaire is factor analyzed (e.g., Hirsh et al., 2010).

Consistent with the differentiated threat account, while disgust-related threat was positively associated with binding values, social evaluation threat was positively associated with individualizing values. A similar pattern emerged when each of the moral foundations clusters was regressed onto the set of three threat variables: disgust-related threat was the only unique predictor of *binding*, whereas social evaluation threat uniquely and positively predicted *individualizing*.

To assess the generalizability of these effects, we conducted a similar study with a sample of Australian undergraduate students. Much work on the relationships between threat, morality and politics has been conducted in the US, so it is worth considering whether there is even minimal generalizability of the current findings across political contexts. Two hundred and nineteen participants completed the Fear Survey Schedule-III and the Moral Foundations Questionnaire. Factor analyses of these scales yielded largely similar three- and two-factor solutions, respectively, suggesting that the structures of threat sensitivity and moral foundations are generalizable to the Australian context. Correlation and regression analyses also gave results similar to the US sample: social evaluation threat was positively associated with *individualizing* and disgust-related threat with *binding*. These patterns held both for zero-order associations and in multiple regression contexts.

To get a more fine-grained sense of the role of these different threats, we decomposed the foundation clusters into individual moral foundations. When regression analyses were rerun using each individual foundation as a dependent variable (i.e., separate regressions for care, fairness, loyalty, authority and sanctity), results largely replicated analyses using the foundation clusters of individualizing and binding. That is, social evaluation threat uniquely predicted both care and fairness, whereas disgust-related threat uniquely predicted loyalty, authority and sanctity. This broad pattern of results held across both samples (except for the effect of social evaluation threat on care, which had $p = .11$ in the Australian sample).

Having thus established the utility of a differentiated threat account in explaining variation in moral values, we next sought to explore the role of social evaluation and disgust-related threat sensitivities in the relationship between personality and political orientation.

## Threat Sensitivities, Political Orientation and the Neuroticism–Conservatism Paradox

Social scientists have long attempted to ground political orientation in personality processes (see Carney, Jost, Gosling, & Potter, 2008, and Jost et al., 2003, for reviews). Two of the most consistent findings are that openness/intellect positively predicts a liberal orientation (in the US sense of the term), whereas conscientiousness positively predicts a conservative orientation (e.g., Gerber et al., 2010; Hirsh et al., 2010; Sibley et al., 2012).

Another remarkably consistent finding is the null or small *negative* association between neuroticism and political conservatism (e.g., Gerber et al., 2010; Hirsh et al., 2010; Sibley et al., 2012). In addition, neither neuroticism in general nor its aspects (withdrawal or volatility) show associations with moral foundation endorsement (Hirsh et al., 2010). This pattern of results may seem surprising given that neuroticism is the personality domain most closely associated with threat sensitivity. A differentiated threat account of moral values may help explain this apparent anomaly.

To test this possibility, we (Laham & Corless, 2014b) conducted another MTurk study in which we measured the Big Five domains of personality, as well as their aspects, using the Big Five Aspects Scale (DeYoung, Quilty, & Peterson, 2007). We also administered the Fear Survey Schedule-III, the Moral Foundations Questionnaire and multiple measures of political orientation, including ideological self-placement on the political spectrum (general, social, economic) and an issue-based measure of political conservatism (Social and Economic Conservatism Scale; Everett, 2013). In a sample of 372 US citizens, we replicated the Fear Survey Schedule-III and Moral Foundations Questionnaire factor structures. Replicating previous work, neuroticism (especially the withdrawal aspect) had small, negative associations with various measures of political conservatism.

We also showed, consistent with previous work, that neuroticism (measured at the domain and aspect levels) was positively associated with sensitivities to different threats, both at the zero-order level and when controlling for the other four domains of personality. Importantly, we replicated Laham and Corless (2014a) in showing that while disgust-related threat was positively (and uniquely) associated with *binding* (i.e., concerns relating to loyalty to the ingroup, purity and respect for authority), social evaluation threat was positively (and uniquely) associated with *individualizing* (i.e., concerns with care, sensitivity to others' suffering and fair treatment). We also showed that *binding* was positively associated, and *individualizing* was negatively associated, with political conservatism as indexed by ideological self-placement and scores on the Social and Economic Conservatism Scale.

Can the association between neuroticism and political orientation be made sense of in light of the differentiated threat account? To answer this question, we specified a structural equation model using the following causal hierarchy: Neuroticism → Threat Sensitivities → Moral Values → Political Orientation (a more nuanced discussion of causality follows). More specifically, we assessed the indirect effects of withdrawal and volatility on a political conservatism composite (average of ideological self-placement and Social and Economic Conservatism Scale measures) via threats and moral foundations (see Figure 4.1 for a schematic of this model). The total indirect effect of withdrawal on political conservatism is, as expected, small and negative. When this effect is decomposed into its constituent, specific indirect effects, one can see that the resultant total is comprised, primarily, of positive effects of withdrawal on conservatism via disgust-related threat sensitivity, but negative effects of withdrawal on conservatism via social evaluation threat and the foundation clusters. The negative indirect effects of this aspect of neuroticism on conservatism via social evaluation threat outweigh the positive effects via disgust-related threat, which biases the overall effect in a negative direction.

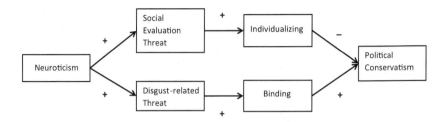

**FIGURE 4.1** Schematic of the associations between neuroticism, threat sensitivities, moral values and political orientation.

It is not surprising that it is the *withdrawal* aspect of neuroticism (as opposed to *volatility*) that best accounts for this pattern of results. *Withdrawal* has been described as reflecting susceptibility to withdrawal-related negative emotions (sample items: 'Am filled with doubts about myself', 'Worry about many things'), whereas *volatility* reflects irritability and impulsiveness (sample items: 'Get angry easily', 'Change my mood a lot'; DeYoung et al., 2007).

## Additional Loci of Differentiation

Our focus thus far has been on distinguishing among kinds of threatening stimuli and exploring their differential associations with moral and political values. There is at least one other locus of differentiation that is worth discussing when it comes to the literature on threat, morality and political orientation: that between different measures of political orientation. First, however, let us consider another kind of distinction among predictors.

### *Further Differentiation Among Predictors*

We have focused on *horizontal* distinctions among different kinds of threat stimuli. Another important distinction is between constructs in the *vertical* dimension— across levels of generality. Sensitivity to narrow classes of specific threats (e.g., social, disgust-based) can be thought of as being nested within broader, more general threat-related constructs (e.g., neuroticism). It is important to consider distinctions among constructs of different bandwidths (Cronbach & Gleser, 1957; John & Benet-Martinez, 2014) in work on threat, morality and politics. Using broad versus narrow measures of threat-sensitivity may lead to different results. Broadband constructs, such as neuroticism or behavioural inhibition, seem to yield small to null effects (e.g., Hirsh et al., 2010), whereas narrower constructs, such as belief in a dangerous world, yield much larger effects (e.g., van Leeuwen & Park, 2009; although the size of these latter effects may be due to factors other than narrow bandwidth).

One danger in operationalizing 'threat-sensitivity' at different levels of breadth or generality is that inferences about constructs at one level may be (mis)taken as inferences about constructs at another. For example, showing that belief in a dangerous world is positively (and strongly) associated with political conservatism and claiming, as a result, that general *threat sensitivity* is associated with political conservatism (as do van Leeuwen & Park, 2009, for example), is to move (perhaps unjustifiably) from an inference about a narrow construct (belief in a dangerous world) to an inference about a broad construct (threat sensitivity). Researchers should be careful when making claims about broad-bandwidth constructs, such as threat-sensitivity, based on narrowly-defined constructs, such as belief in a dangerous world.

## *Differentiating Among Political Orientation Variables*

Much has been written about the appropriate way to measure political orientation; there are many measures and just as many critiques (see Everett, 2013, for a review). Not only is there a need to demonstrate findings with multiple measures of conservatism (as we have done), but there is also a need to distinguish among different dimensions of political orientation. Economic and social conservatism have been argued to be distinct dimensions of the conservative ideology and resultant of different underlying processes (Feldman, 2013). Social (or sometimes *moral*) conservatism describes preferences for tradition and order and resistance to change. Economic conservatism describes attitudes opposed to resource redistribution. Duckitt (2001) has similarly suggested that right-wing authoritarianism (which is associated with social conservatism) and social dominance orientation (which is associated with economic conservativism) constitute two dimensions of the conservative ideology and are associated with different underlying psychological causes, namely perceptions of the world as a dangerous place and perceptions of the world as a competitive jungle, respectively.

Indeed, some work on threat sensitivity and political orientation has found effects of threat on only one or the other of these two dimensions, suggesting that it is worth treating them separately. Wright and Baril (2013), for example, found that belief in a dangerous world is positively associated with social (as opposed to economic) conservatism. Verhulst, Eaves, and Hatemi (2012), on the other hand, showed that neuroticism is positively associated with liberal economic attitudes.

In our data (Laham & Corless, 2014b) a factor analysis of the Social and Economic Conservatism Scale did not suggest such a two-factor solution. However, computing separate indices for economic and social conservativism, based on Everett (2013), we found that the correlations between both social evaluation and disgust-related threats and political conservatism were stronger for the social dimension. The disgust-related threat finding is consistent with work showing that disgust-sensitivity is more strongly associated with social than economic conservatism (e.g., Inbar, Pizarro, Iyer, & Haidt, 2012). The social evaluation threat finding suggests that sensitivity to such threats is associated with decreased acceptance of tradition and authority and with acceptance of change, rather than with a rejection of economic inequality. The prioritizing of individual rights and fairness concerns over respect for tradition and the group may account for this association between social evaluation threat sensitivity and social liberalism.

## Caveats and Future Directions

Given that the work covered in this chapter is the first on the differentiated threat account of moral values, numerous questions and ambiguities remain. One important issue is that of causality. Although we have adopted an implicit causal ordering of variables in our modelling work (Neuroticism → Threat Sensitivities → Moral Values → Political Orientation), we remain agnostic about the causal hierarchy underpinning the effects noted earlier. Whereas Jost and colleagues' (2003) motivated cognition account suggests that conservatism is a coping reaction to threat and thus caused by threat, other accounts suggest that both threat sensitivity and conservatism may share a common cause (e.g., Verhulst et al., 2012). Future work should adopt both experimental and longitudinal/developmental approaches to clarify issues of cause.

Moreover, such work would benefit from adopting a differentiated threat approach. Although some experimental work has shown "conservative shift" after threat (e.g., Inbar, Pizarro, Knobe, & Bloom, 2009), this work has not distinguished between different kinds of threat. On the differentiated threat account, one might predict a conservative shift after a disgust-related threat and a liberal shift after a social evaluation threat.

While experimental research is important to establish the *possibility* that threat may causally affect moral and political values, any such demonstration does not guarantee the causal role of threat sensitivity in the ontogenetic development of moral values or political orientation. Thus, experimental work should be complemented with longitudinal work which can assess the causal ordering of variables during development (e.g., Block & Block, 2006).

Another shortcoming of the current work is the exclusive reliance on self-report measures of threat sensitivity. Although some extant work which has gone beyond self-report has shown that attentional biases towards negative stimuli are associated with political conservatism (e.g., Carraro, Castelli, & Macchiella, 2011; Dodd et al., 2012), this work has not explicitly distinguished among kinds of threat. Future work could use paradigms such as the dot-probe task, the emotional Stroop, the flanker task and eye-tracking to assess cognitive processes associated with the processing of different kinds of threats, with a specific focus on distinguishing between sensitivities to social versus disgust-related threats.

## Conclusion

The work reviewed in this chapter provides initial support for the utility of differentiating among kinds of threats in developing threat-sensitivity accounts of moral values and political orientation. Distinguishing between disgust-grounded specific phobic threats and social evaluation threats revealed that sensitivities to these different kinds of threats had opposing relationships with moral values and political orientation. Disgust-related threat sensitivity behaves much like extant theories would predict (being positively associated with conservatism and binding endorsement). The more sensitive one is to threats of injury and potential sources of contamination (e.g., blood, small animals), the more one moralizes loyalty, authority and sanctity and the more one endorses a politically conservative worldview. Social evaluation threat sensitivity, on the other hand, behaves in a way opposite to that predicted by extant accounts of threat, morality and politics. The more sensitive one is to failure and making mistakes, the more one is likely to be concerned about fairness and the suffering of others, and the more politically liberal one is inclined to be.

Distinguishing between these two kinds of threats also provides some insight into the somewhat puzzling association between neuroticism and political conservatism. The reason why one consistently observes small, negative associations between neuroticism and conservatism is because this personality trait has indirect effects of opposing sign (positive via disgust-related threat, and negative via social evaluation threat) on conservatism, which to some extent cancel each other out, yielding the overall, small association. More broadly, this approach reiterates the importance of looking to evolutionary and clinical research in developing both theory and measurement for the psychology of morality.

## References

Amass, T. (2004). *Empirical evaluation of political ideology as motivated social cognition.* Unpublished honors thesis, New York University.

Arindell, W.A., Pickersgill, M.J., Merckelbach, H., Ardon, M.A., & Cornet, F.C. (1991). Phobic dimensions: III. Factor analytic approaches to the study of common phobic fears: An updated review of findings obtained with adult subjects. *Advances in Behavior Research and Therapy, 13,* 73–130.

Bartz, J.A., & Lydon, J.E. (2008). Relationship-specific attachment, risk regulation, and communal norm adherence in close relationships. *Journal of Experimental Social Psychology, 44,* 655–663.

Block, J., & Block, J.J. (2006). Nursery school personality and political orientation two decades later. *Journal of Research in Personality, 40,* 734–749.

Boyer, P., & Bergstrom, B. (2010). Threat-detection in child development: An evolutionary perspective. *Neuroscience & Biobehavioral Reviews, 35,* 1034–1041.

Boyer, P., & Lienard, P. (2006). Why ritualized behaviour? Precaution systems and action parsing in developmental, pathological and cultural rituals. *Behavioral and Brain Sciences, 29,* 1–56.

Carney, D.R., Jost, J.T., Gosling, S.D., & Potter, J. (2008). The secret lives of liberals and conservatives: Personality profiles, interaction styles, and the things they leave behind. *Political Psychology, 29*, 807–840.

Carraro, L., Castelli, L., & Macchiella, C. (2011). The automatic conservative: Ideology-based attentional asymmetries in the processing of valenced information. *PLOS ONE 6*, e26456.

Cisler, J.M., Olatunji, B.O., & Lohr, J.M. (2009). Disgust, fear and the anxiety disorders: A critical review. *Clinical Psychology Review, 29*, 34–46.

Cronbach, L.J., & Gleser, G.C. (1957). *Psychological tests and personnel decisions*. Urbana: University of Illinois Press.

DeYoung, C.G., Quilty, L.C., & Peterson, J.B. (2007). Between facets and domains: 10 aspects of the Big Five. *Journal of Personality and Social Psychology, 93*, 880–896.

Dodd, M.D., Balzer, A., Jacobs, C.M., Gruszczynski, M.W., Smith, K.B., & Hibbing, J.R. (2012). The political left rolls with the good; the political right confronts the bad. *Philosophical Transactions of the Royal Society of London, Biological Sciences, 367*, 640–649.

Duckitt, J. (2001). A dual process cognitive-motivational theory of ideology and prejudice. *Advances in Experimental Social Psychology, 22*, 41–113.

Erwin, B.A., Heimberg, R.G., Schneier, F.R., Liebowitz, M.R. (2003). Anger experience and expression in social anxiety disorder: Pretreatment profile and predictors of attrition and response to cognitive-behavioral treatment. *Behavior Therapy, 32*, 331–350.

Everett, J.A.C. (2013). The 12-item social and economic conservatism scale (SECS). *PLOS ONE, 8*, e82131.

Feldman, S. (2013). Political ideology. In L. Huddy, D.O. Sears, & J.S. Levy (Eds.), *Oxford handbook of political psychology* (pp. 591–626). Oxford: Oxford University Press.

Gerber, A.S., Huber, G.A., Doherty, D., Dowling, C.M., & Ha, S.E. (2010). Personality and political attitudes: Relationships across issue domains and political contexts. *American Political Science Review, 104*, 111–133.

Graham, J., Haidt, J., & Nosek, B.A. (2009). Liberals and conservatives rely on different sets of moral foundations. *Journal of Personality and Social Psychology, 96*, 1029–1046.

Graham, J., Nosek, B.A., Haidt, J., Iyer, R., Koleva, S., & Ditto, P.H. (2011). Mapping the moral domain. *Journal of Personality and Social Psychology, 101*, 366–385.

Hackmann, A., Clark, D.M., & McManus, F. (2000). Recurrent images and early memories in social phobia. *Behaviour Research and Therapy, 38*, 601–610.

Hackmann, A., Surawy, C., & Clark, D.M. (1998). Seeing yourself through others' eyes: A study of spontaneously occurring images in social phobia. *Behavioural and Cognitive Psychotherapy, 26*, 3–12.

Haidt, J. (2012). *The righteous mind: Why good people are divided by politics and religion*. New York: Pantheon.

Haidt, J., & Joseph, C. (2004). Intuitive ethics: How innately prepared intuitions generate culturally variable virtues. *Daedalus, 133*, 55–66.

Hibbing, J.R., Smith, K.B., & Alford, J.R. (2014). Differences in negativity bias underlie variations in political ideology. *Behavioral and Brain Sciences, 37*, 297–350.

Hirsh, J.B., DeYoung, C.G., Xu, X., & Peterson, J.B. (2010). Compassionate liberals and polite conservatives: Associations of agreeableness with political ideology and moral values. *Personality and Social Psychology Bulletin, 36*, 655–664.

Hope, D.A., Heimberg, R.G., & Klein, J.F. (1990). Social anxiety and the recall of interpersonal information. *Journal of Cognitive Psychotherapy, 4*, 185–195.

Inbar, Y., & Pizarro, D. (2014a). Disgust, politics and responses to threat. *Behavioral and Brain Sciences, 37*, 315–316.

Inbar, Y., & Pizarro, D.A. (2014b). Pollution and purity in moral and political judgment. In J. Wright & H. Sarkissian (Eds.), *Advances in experimental moral psychology: Affect, character, and commitments* (pp. 111–129). London: Continuum Press.

Inbar, Y., Pizarro, D.A., Iyer, R., & Haidt, J. (2012). Disgust sensitivity, political conservatism, and voting. *Social Psychological and Personality Science, 3*, 537–544.

Inbar, Y., Pizarro, D.A., Knobe, J., & Bloom, P. (2009). Disgust sensitivity predicts intuitive disapproval of gays. *Emotion, 9*, 435–439.

Janoff-Bulman, R. (2009). To provide or protect: Motivational bases of political liberalism and conservatism. *Psychological Inquiry, 20*, 120–128.

John, O.P., & Benet-Martinez, V. (2014). Measurement: Reliability, construct validation, and scale construction. In H.T. Reis & C.M. Judd (Eds.), *Handbook of research methods in social and personality psychology* (2nd ed., pp. 473–503). Cambridge: Cambridge University Press.

Jost, J.T., Glaser, J., Kruglanski, A.W., & Sulloway, F. (2003). Political conservatism as motivated social cognition. *Psychological Bulletin, 129*, 339–375.

Koleva, S., Selterman, D., Iyer, R., Ditto, P., & Graham, J. (2014). The moral compass of insecurity: Anxious and avoidant attachment predict moral judgment. *Social Psychological and Personality Science, 5*, 185–194.

Laham, S.M., & Corless, C. (2014a). *A differentiated threat account of moral values.* Manuscript in preparation.

Laham, S.M., & Corless, C. (2014b). *Neuroticism and political orientation: A differentiated threat account of the role of neuroticism in moral and political values.* Manuscript in preparation.

Marks, I.M., & Nesse, R.M. (1994). Fear and fitness: An evolutionary analysis of anxiety disorders. *Ethology and Sociobiology, 15*, 247–261.

Neuberg, S.L., Kenrick D.T., & Schaller, M. (2011). Human threat management systems: Self-protection and disease avoidance. *Neuroscience and Biobehavioral Review, 35*, 1042–1051.

Öhman, A. (1986). Face the beast and fear the face: Animal and social fears as prototypes for evolutionary analyses of emotion. *Psychophysiology, 23*, 123–145.

Öhman, A. (2000). Fear and anxiety: Evolutionary, cognitive and clinical perspectives. In M. Lewis & J.M. Haviland-Jones (Eds.), *Handbook of emotions* (3rd ed., pp. 573–593). London: Guilford Press.

Perkins, A.M., Kemp, S.E., & Corr, P.J. (2007). Fear and anxiety as separable emotions: An investigation of the revised reinforcement sensitivity theory of personality. *Emotion, 7*, 252–261.

Rapee, R.M., & Heimberg, R.G. (1997). A cognitive-behavioral model of anxiety in social phobia. *Behaviour Research and Therapy, 35*, 741–756.

Rapee, R.M., & Spence, S.H. (2004). The etiology of social phobia: Empirical evidence and an initial model. *Clinical Psychology Review, 24*, 737–767.

Sheikh, S. (2007). *Moral motivations: The relationship between self-regulation and morality.* Unpublished master's thesis, University of Massachusetts, Amherst.

Sibley, C.G., Osborne, D., & Duckitt, J. (2012). Personality and political orientation: Meta-analysis and test of a threat-constraint model. *Journal of Research in Personality, 46*, 664–677.

Sloman, L. (2008). A new comprehensive evolutionary model of depression and anxiety. *Journal of Affective Disorders, 106*, 219–228.

Stein, D.J., & Bouwer, C. (1997). A neuro-evolutionary approach to the anxiety disorders. *Journal of Anxiety Disorders, 11*, 409–429.

Van Leeuwen, F., & Park, J.H. (2009). Perceptions of social dangers, moral foundations, and political orientation. *Personality and Individual Differences, 42*, 169–173.

Verhulst, B., Eaves, L.J., Hatemi, P.K. (2012). Correlation not causation: The relationship between personality traits and political ideologies. *American Journal of Political Science, 56*, 34–51.

Wolpe, J., & Lang, P.J. (1964). A fear survey schedule for use in behavior therapy. *Behavior Research and Therapy, 2*, 27–30.

Wright, J.C., & Baril, G.L. (2013). Understanding the role of dispositional and situational threat sensitivity in our moral judgments. *Journal of Moral Education, 42*, 383–397.

# 5

# COMPUTATIONAL MODELING OF MORAL DECISIONS

*Molly J. Crockett*

*The cognitive processes that give rise to moral decisions have long been the focus of intense study. Here I illustrate how computational approaches to studying moral decision-making can advance this endeavor. Computational methods have traditionally been employed in the domains of perceptual and reward-based learning and decision-making, but until recently had not been applied to the study of moral cognition. Using examples from recent studies I show how computational properties of choices can provide novel insights into moral decision-making. I conclude with an exploration of new research avenues that arise from these insights, such as how uncertainty in choice shapes morality, and how moral decision-making can be viewed as a learning process.*

## Introduction

Moral decisions often involve tradeoffs between personal benefits and preventing harm to others. How do we decide when faced with such dilemmas? And how do we judge the moral decisions of others? These questions have long been the focus of intense study in philosophy, psychology, and more recently neuroscience. To investigate these questions, researchers have employed a variety of methods, ranging from hypothetical thought experiments (Cushman, Young, & Hauser, 2006; Greene, Sommerville, Nystrom, Darley, & Cohen, 2001; Haidt, 2001) to virtual reality environments (David, McDonald, Mott, & Asher, 2012; Slater et al., 2006) to real moral decisions (Batson, Duncan, Ackerman, Buckley, & Birch, 1981; Crockett, Kurth-Nelson, Siegel, Dayan, & Dolan, 2014; FeldmanHall, Mobbs et al., 2012; Hein, Silani, Preuschoff, Batson, & Singer, 2010; Valdesolo & DeSteno,

2008). In this chapter I will review recent work illustrating new approaches to investigating moral cognition that borrow from methods traditionally employed in the domains of perceptual and reward-based decision-making (see also Gawronski, Conway, Armstrong, Friesdorf, & Hütter, this volume). Throughout, I will focus on moral cognition concerned with harm and care toward others (see also Forgas, Jussim, & Van Lange; and Haslam, this volume).[1]

Early studies in this area examined the extent to which people would invest effort in helping others in need, and how features of social situations influenced helping behavior. These experiments often involved elaborately staged situations, for example with confederates trapped by falling bookcases (Ashton & Severy, 1976), having epileptic seizures (Darley & Latané, 1968), or collapsing in subway cars (Piliavin & Piliavin, 1972). In classic studies by Batson et al. (1981) subjects were given the opportunity to reduce the number of electric shocks delivered to a confederate by taking on some of the shocks themselves. These studies laid the groundwork for much of what we know about altruism and moral behavior, and they have high ecological validity. However, because these procedures generally gather only a single data point per subject, they provide rather sparse data sets that do not allow for interrogation of the computations underlying choices. These methods are also impractical for investigating the neural mechanisms of decision-making.

Perhaps the most widely used method for studying moral cognition is examining how people respond to hypothetical scenarios. For example, in the classic "trolley problem" (Foot, 1967; Thomson, 1976), a trolley is hurtling out of control down the tracks toward five workers, who will die if you do nothing. You and a large man are standing on a footbridge above the tracks. You realize that you can push the large man off the footbridge onto the tracks, where his body will stop the trolley and prevent it from killing the workers. Is it morally permissible to push the man, killing him but saving the five workers? By systematically varying features of these scenarios, researchers have uncovered a trove of insights into the mechanics of moral judgment, illuminating important influences of factors such as intentionality (Young, Camprodon, Hauser, Pascual-Leone, & Saxe, 2010; Young, Cushman, Hauser, & Saxe, 2007), actions (Cushman, 2013; Cushman et al., 2006; Spranca, Minsk, & Baron, 1991), physical contact (Cushman et al., 2006; Greene et al., 2009), and incidental emotions (Eskine, Kacinik, & Prinz, 2011; Horberg, Oveis, & Keltner, 2011; Ugazio, Lamm, & Singer, 2012), among others.

However, hypothetical scenarios may be less useful for investigating moral *decisions*, as it is unclear to what extent judgments in these scenarios reflect how people would actually behave when faced with a real moral decision. This question was addressed directly in a recent study (FeldmanHall, Mobbs et al., 2012). Subjects were given the opportunity to spend up to £1 to reduce the intensity of an electric shock delivered to a confederate sitting in the next room, whom they had recently met. Decisions were probed in two conditions. In the "real" condition, subjects were led to believe they would be making decisions with real consequences for themselves and the confederate. In the "hypothetical" condition, subjects were explicitly instructed that their decisions were hypothetical and would not have consequences for themselves or the confederate. Subjects behaved differently in the real versus hypothetical conditions, and real versus hypothetical decisions engaged overlapping but distinct neural networks (FeldmanHall, Dalgleish et al., 2012). Another similarly motivated recent study showed that decisions about whether to cooperate with an anonymous other differed in real versus hypothetical situations (Vlaev, 2012). Collectively this work suggests that moral decisions as probed by hypothetical scenarios may not necessarily be reflective of true moral preferences.

How, then, might we investigate the psychological (and neural) processes governing moral decisions? Behavioral economic games offer a tool for probing social preferences by measuring how people make decisions that have real monetary consequences for themselves and anonymous others, as well as the neural processes underlying such decisions (Camerer, 2003; Glimcher & Fehr, 2013). For instance, in the dictator game, participants are given some money and can share none, some, or all of it with an anonymous other person. The amount shared is reflective of the value people place on rewards to others, as well as attitudes toward inequality: the more people value rewards to others, and the more they dislike being in an advantageous position relative to someone else, the more money they will transfer to the other person (Camerer, 2003; Glimcher & Fehr, 2013).

There are several features of economic games that make them well suited for probing moral decision-making. Because they are incentivized, choices in these paradigms are faithful reflections of people's actual preferences. This is especially critical in the case of moral decision-making. Self-report questionnaires aimed at measuring moral preferences suffer from the obvious limitation that social desirability is likely to have a strong influence on people's answers. When there is no cost to answering "no" to the question of whether you would harm someone else for personal gain, most people would do so to preserve their reputation, regardless of their actual preferences. Subject anonymity is important for similar reasons. If subjects interact face-to-face with one another, then prosocial decisions could be reflective of people's selfish desire to preserve their own reputation, rather than their true preferences with regard to the welfare of others.

Perhaps even more importantly, economic games are also amenable to building computational models of choice processes and linking these models to neural activity. Despite progress in mapping the facets of moral cognition, still very little is known about the computational mechanisms that underlie moral decisions and indeed social cognition more broadly (Korman, Voiklis, & Malle, 2015). Formalizing the components of cognitive processes and how these components interact using a mathematical, model-based approach has advanced our understanding of many other aspects of cognition, including perception, reasoning, learning, language, and reward-based decision-making. Applying a similar model-based approach to moral cognition will yield similar progress and generate novel predictions about the nature of moral decision-making and its neural basis. This approach shares many features with formal models of social preferences that have been widely used in behavioral economics and psychology to describe social behavior (Fehr & Schmidt, 1999; Messick & Schell, 1992; Van Lange, 1999). A central aim of computational work that goes beyond these approaches is to provide more insight into the decision *process*, for example by investigating how noise in the decision process can influence moral choices.

Decades of research on social preferences using economic games has demonstrated that when it comes to monetary exchanges, people do value others' outcomes to a certain extent—although they care about their own outcomes far more (Charness & Rabin, 2002; Engel, 2011; Fehr & Schmidt, 1999). This work provides proof-of-principle that even complex social behaviors can be accurately described using formal mathematical models. However, it is unclear to what extent these paradigms probe *moral* preferences. Gray, Young, and Waytz argue that the essence of a moral transgression is an intentional agent causing harm to a suffering moral patient (Gray, Waytz, & Young, 2012; Gray, Young, & Waytz, 2012). Although economic games certainly capture intentional decisions, whether they induce suffering is debatable. Given that the worst possible outcome for a recipient in a dictator game is to receive nothing, and even putatively "unfair" transfers in the dictator game (i.e., < 50%) yield benefits for the recipient, it seems inappropriate to construe the dictator game as a moral decision.

Computing the costs of others' suffering is central to the process of making moral decisions. Although the bulk of research on value-based decision-making has investigated decisions involving only oneself, several studies have examined the neural basis of decisions that affect others. There is growing evidence that computing the value of outcomes to others engages neural mechanisms similar to those used to compute the value of one's own outcomes. At the heart of this process is a value-based decision-making circuitry that includes the striatum and the ventromedial prefrontal cortex (vmPFC). The current consensus is that the vmPFC computes the subjective value of the chosen option when a choice is made, as well as the experienced value of the outcome when it is received (Clithero & Rangel, 2013). Meanwhile, the striatum computes value differences between expectations and experiences, that is, *prediction errors* (Clithero & Rangel, 2013). Decisions affecting others engage the striatum and vmPFC in a similar manner to decisions that affect only oneself (Fehr & Krajbich, 2013). For example, choosing to donate money to anonymous others or charities activates the vmPFC and striatum in a similar manner to choices that reap rewards for oneself

(Harbaugh, Mayr, & Burghart, 2007; Hare, Camerer, Knoepfle, O'Doherty, & Rangel, 2010; Zaki & Mitchell, 2011). A recent meta-analysis comparing the neural correlates of rewards to self and rewards to others (i.e., vicarious rewards) showed that self and vicarious rewards engage overlapping regions of vmPFC (Morelli, Sacchet, & Zaki, 2015).

Thus far the majority of studies investigating social preferences have examined decisions involving rewarding outcomes to others. How people value aversive outcomes to others is less well understood. Recently my colleagues and I developed new methods for measuring how people compute the value of painful outcomes to others, relative to themselves (Crockett et al., 2014). In the following sections I will describe these methods and the questions that have arisen out of studies employing it.

## Quantifying the Costs of Harm to Self and Others

We are able to quantify how much people value harm to self versus others by inviting them to trade profits for themselves against pain to either themselves or others. In essence, this involves measuring how much people are willing to pay to prevent pain to themselves and others, as well as how much compensation people require to increase pain to themselves and others. By combining questions such as these with computational models of choice, we are able to extract the precise values people ascribe to their own negative outcomes as well as those of others.

Two participants visit the lab in each experimental session. They arrive at staggered times and are led to different rooms to ensure they do not see or interact with one another. Next, each participant is led through a well-validated pain thresholding procedure in which we use an electric stimulation device (Digitimer DS5) to deliver electric shocks to the left wrist of our volunteers (Story et al., 2013; Vlaev, Seymour, Dolan, & Chater, 2009). Shocks delivered by this device can range from imperceptible to intolerably painful, depending on the electric current level. Importantly, the shocks are safe and don't cause any damage to the skin.

In the thresholding procedure, we start by delivering a shock at a very low current level—0.1 milliamps (mA)—that is almost imperceptible. We then gradually increase the current level, shock by shock, and the volunteer rates each shock on a scale from 0 (imperceptible) to 10 (intolerable). We stop increasing the current once the volunteer's rating reaches a 10. For the shocks used in the experiment we use a current level that corresponds to a rating of 8 out of 10, so the shocks are unpleasant, but not intolerable.

Critically, this procedure allows us to ensure that (1) the stimuli delivered in our experiment are in fact painful, (2) the stimuli are subjectively matched for the two participants, which is a necessary precondition for comparing the valuation of pain to self and others, and (3) subjects experience the stimuli about which they will later be making decisions, and are also told that the other participant has experienced the same stimuli, which is important for minimizing ambiguity in those decisions.

Next, the participants are randomly assigned to the roles of "decider" and "receiver." We used a randomization procedure that preserved subjects' anonymity, while at the same time confirmed the existence of another participant in the experiment and transparently provided a fair allocation of roles. Anonymity here is essential because we want to isolate the contribution of moral *preferences* for avoiding harm to others, independently from the influence of selfish concerns about preserving one's own reputation and avoiding retaliation, both of which could readily explain altruistic behavior in the context of a face-to-face interaction where identities are common knowledge (Fehr & Krajbich, 2013). In addition, anonymity is important for establishing a baseline level of moral preferences. It is well known that characteristics of the victim influence helping behavior (Penner, Dovidio, Piliavin, & Schroeder, 2005; Piliavin, Piliavin, & Rodin, 1975; Stürmer, Snyder, Kropp, & Siem, 2006), but the influences of these factors can only be fully understood relative to baseline (Fehr & Krajbich, 2013).

Following this, the decider completes a decision task (Figure 5.1). In this task they make a series of approximately 160 decisions involving tradeoffs between

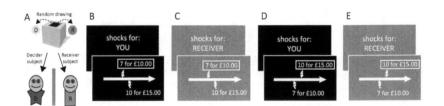

**FIGURE 5.1** A paradigm for extracting the subjective value of harm to self and others. (A) Subjects remained in separate testing rooms at all times and were randomly assigned to roles of decider and receiver. (B–E) In each trial the decider chose between less money and fewer shocks, and more money and more shocks. The money was always for the decider, but in half the trials the shocks were for the decider (B and D) and in the other half the shocks were for the receiver (C and E). In all trials, if the decider failed to press a key within 6 s the highlighted default (top) option was registered; if the decider pressed the key, the alternative (bottom) option was highlighted and registered instead. In half the trials, the alternative option contained more money and shocks than the default (B and C), and in the other half the alternative option contained less money and fewer shocks than the default (D and E).

*Note:* Adapted from Crockett, M.J., Kurth-Nelson, Z., Siegel, J.Z., Dayan, P., & Dolan, R.J. (2014). Harm to others outweighs harm to self in moral decision making. *Proceedings of the National Academy of Sciences, 111*(48), 17320–17325.

profits for themselves against pain for either themselves or the receiver. In each trial deciders choose between less money and fewer shocks, and more money and more shocks. The money is always for the decider, but in half the trials the shocks are for the decider (Figure 5.1A and 5.1C) and in the other half the shocks are for the receiver (Figure 5.1B and 5.1D). In all trials, if the decider fails to press a key within 6 s the highlighted default (top) option is registered; if the decider presses the key, the alternative (bottom) option is highlighted and registered instead. In half the trials, the alternative option contains more money and shocks than the default (Figure 5.1A and 5.1B), and in the other half the alternative option contains less money and fewer shocks than the default (Figure 5.1C and 5.1D). To avoid habituation and preserve choice independence, no money or shocks are delivered during the task. Instead, one trial is selected by the computer and implemented at the end of the experiment, and subjects are made aware of this. Subjects are also instructed that their decisions will be completely anonymous and confidential with respect to both the receiver and the experimenters.

The key dependent measure that can be extracted from this paradigm is a pair of subject-specific *harm aversion* parameters that are derived from a computational model of subjects' choices. These parameters capture the subjective costs of harm to self and others and are proportional to the amount of money subjects are willing to pay to prevent an additional shock to themselves and the receiver; in other words, harm aversion represents an "exchange rate" between money and pain. When we began this research we had very little basis for predicting what these exchange rates would look like. So in our first study we used a staircasing procedure that homes in on subjects' exchange rates by estimating the exchange rate after each choice and then generating subsequent choices that will provide the most new information about the exchange rates. One obvious drawback of this approach is that subjects' preferences influence the choice set they see in the task, and if this is discovered there is the possibility that subjects could consciously "game" the task. There is also the issue that the context in which choices are made can influence the choices themselves; for example, people are willing to pay more to avoid a medium-intensity shock when it is presented alongside low-intensity shocks than when it is presented in the context of high-intensity shocks (Vlaev et al., 2009). Thus, it is preferable to present all subjects with the same set of choices that are predetermined to be able to detect exchange rates within the range expected in the population. We did this in our second study once having determined the range of exchange rates expected in the population, which were recovered using the staircasing procedure described earlier.

One of the most common methods for modeling decision-making involves two steps (Daw, 2011). In the first step, a *value model* is specified that relates features of the choice options to their underlying subjective values. For instance, a very basic value model for a dictator game might simply state that the subjective value of a given choice in the dictator game consists of the amount of money kept for oneself, multiplied by a self-weight parameter that indicates how much one cares for their own outcome, plus the amount of money transferred, multiplied by an other-weight parameter that indicates how much one cares for the other's outcome. In the second step, a *choice model* is specified that passes the subjective values (coming from the value model) through a stochastic decision process whereby choice options with higher subjective values are more likely to be selected. Critically, there is noise in the selection process, and the amount of noise is modulated by additional parameters. Here I will describe the findings that arise from the value model; in the next section I will discuss the choice model.

In our studies we fit a series of value models to subjects' choices and used Bayesian model comparison to identify the one that explained their choices the best (Burnham & Anderson, 2002). The best value model turned out to be quite simple. Essentially, the value model indicates that differences in subjective value between the choice options depend on the following parameters:

- A *self harm aversion* parameter that captures how much one prefers to avoid shocks to oneself
- An *other harm aversion* parameter that captures how much one prefers to avoid shocks to others
- A *loss aversion* parameter that weights negative outcomes (i.e., monetary losses and increases in shocks) more strongly than positive ones (i.e., monetary gains and decreases in shocks).

Strikingly, when we examined these estimates we found in both studies that harm aversion for others was greater on average than harm aversion for self (Figure 5.2A and 5.2B). In other words, people were willing to pay more to prevent shocks to others than the same shocks to themselves, and likewise they required greater compensation to increase shocks to others than to increase shocks to themselves. This "hyperaltruistic" disposition was present in the majority of subjects (Figure 5.2C and 5.2D). Notably, hyperaltruism is not predicted by existing economic models of social preferences (Charness & Rabin, 2002; Fehr & Schmidt, 1999), and even more recent research linking empathy and altruism would not predict that people would care about avoiding others' pain *more* than their own (Batson et al., 1981; Bernhardt & Singer, 2012; Hein et al., 2010).

What, then, could explain hyperaltruistic harm aversion? We suggested two potential explanations that are not mutually exclusive (Crockett et al., 2014). First, harming others carries a cost of moral responsibility that harming oneself does not, and this cost could explain why people are willing to pay more to avoid

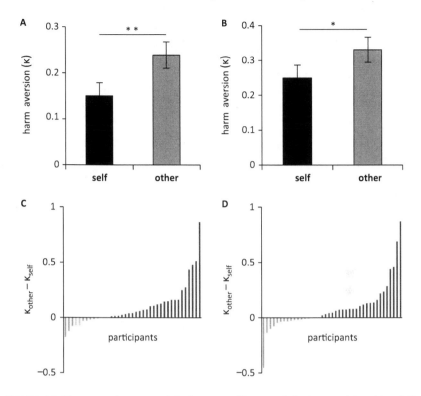

**FIGURE 5.2** Harm to others outweighs harm to self in moral decision-making. (A and B) Estimates of harm aversion for self and other in study 1 (A) and 2 (B). Error bars represent SEM difference between $\kappa_{self}$ and $\kappa_{other}$. (C and D) Distribution of hyperaltruism ($\kappa_{other} - \kappa_{self}$) across subjects in study 1 (C) and 2 (D).

*Note:* $*p < 0.05$, $**p < 0.01$.

harming others than themselves. This account gels with work showing that in hypothetical scenarios people dislike being responsible for bad outcomes (Leonhardt, Keller, & Pechmann, 2011).

The second explanation stems from the fact that decisions affecting other people are necessarily uncertain because we can never truly know what another person's subjective experience is like (Harsanyi, 1955; Nagel, 1974). In the case of pain, there is a risk that what is tolerably painful for oneself might be intolerably painful for another. Because we want to avoid imposing intolerable costs on another person, we may adopt a risk-averse choice strategy, erring on the side of caution when it comes to actions that could potentially harm others. Indeed, many of our subjects expressed this logic when explaining their choices post hoc. One typical subject reported, "I knew what I could handle, but I wasn't sure about the other person and didn't want to be cruel." In this way, uncertainty about others' subjective experience in the presence of social norms that strongly proscribe harming others could naturally lead to the pattern of hyperaltruistic choices that we observe. Intriguingly, empirical support for the uncertainty explanation comes directly from the choice model.

## The Role of Uncertainty in Moral Decisions

As described earlier, the choice model translates information about the subjective value of choice options into actual decisions. Typically this model takes the form of a softmax equation (Daw, 2011). Our choice model contained two parameters—a *choice accuracy* parameter[2] and an *irreducible noise* parameter—that respectively capture the noisiness of "difficult" choices (where the choice options are similarly attractive) and "easy" choices (where one of the choice options is substantially more attractive than the other). When choice accuracy is high, the more highly valued option will be deterministically chosen even if there is only a tiny difference in subjective value between the best and worst options; when it is low, choices will seem random. Meanwhile when irreducible noise is high, subjects may occasionally make "irrational" choices where a very unattractive option is selected over a very attractive one.

Previous work has linked the choice accuracy parameter to subjective confidence in choice. Subjects were asked to make decisions between pairs of food items that differed in attractiveness. After each choice they were asked to rate how confident they felt about their choice. Comparing the choice accuracy parameter for low-confidence and high-confidence choices indicated that low-confidence choices were significantly noisier than high-confidence choices (De Martino, Fleming, Garrett, & Dolan, 2013). This suggests that subjective feelings of confidence in choice are related to objectively quantifiable aspects of decisions that are captured in the choice model.

In our experiments we investigated whether hyperaltruism was related to the noisiness of choices for self and others. If people are hyperaltruistic because they are more uncertain when deciding for others relative to themselves, we should see that the degree of hyperaltruism correlates with the extent to which choices are noisier for others than self, as indicated by either the choice accuracy parameter or the irreducible noise parameter. We indeed observed this effect for the choice accuracy parameter (Figure 5.3A). Hyperaltruistic subjects had noisier choices for others than for self. Although we did not measure subjective confidence in our studies, the findings of De Martino et al. (2013) would suggest that hyperaltruism is related to less confidence when choosing for others than for self.

Another interesting observation is that two distinct groups of subjects could be segregated with respect to choice accuracy in both studies (Figure 5.3B and 5.3C). When we pooled this data and examined group differences it became evident that

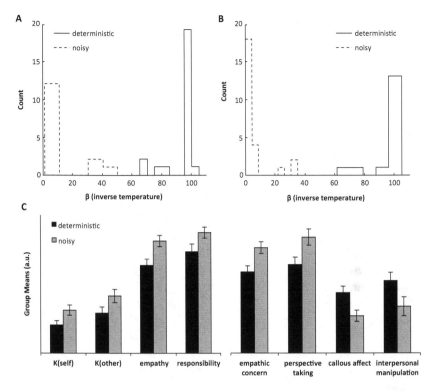

**FIGURE 5.3** Choice noisiness is associated with prosocial traits and behavior. (A and B) In both studies we observed a bimodal distribution of the choice accuracy parameter. We split subjects into groups with high parameter estimates ("deterministic") and low parameter estimates ("noisy"). (C) The noisy and deterministic groups differed on task performance (left panel) and personality traits (right panel).

*Note:* a.u. = arbitrary units.

the group with noisier choices displayed more prosocial characteristics than those whose choices were deterministic (Figure 5.3D). Noisier subjects were more harm averse than the deterministic subjects, both for themselves and others. Noisier subjects also reported feeling more empathy and responsibility for the receiver than did the deterministic subjects. Finally, noisier subjects possessed more empathic traits (perspective taking and empathic concern) and fewer psychopathic traits (callous affect and interpersonal manipulation) than the deterministic subjects.

Together these data provide further evidence that moral preferences are associated with uncertainty when decisions impact others. Intriguingly, however, this perspective is inconsistent with a separate line of research demonstrating increased selfish behavior in the face of uncertainty. In one study, Dana and colleagues compared choices in a standard dictator game with those in a modified dictator game where the outcome for the recipient was uncertain (Dana, Weber, & Kuang, 2007). Across all conditions dictators chose between two options ("A" and "B"). In a baseline treatment, 74% of dictators preferred option B ($5–$5) to option A ($6–$1). In a "hidden information" treatment, dictators could again receive $6 for choosing A and $5 for choosing B. However, they did not know initially whether choosing A or B would yield $1 or $5 for the receiver. In fact the payoffs could be (A: $6, $1; B: $5, $5), as in the baseline treatment, or instead (A: $6, $5; B: $5, $1). The actual outcomes were determined by a coin flip and could be cost-lessly revealed before the dictators made their decision. Here, only 47% of dicta-tors revealed the true payoffs and selected the fair option—a significantly lower proportion than in the baseline treatment. This suggests that fair choices in the baseline treatment are at least partially motivated by a desire to appear fair rather than a true preference for fair outcomes. A second study showed similar results when the outcome for the recipient was determined jointly by two dictators. In this study, a selfish choice by one dictator could not guarantee a bad outcome for the recipient, as the other dictator could still ensure a fair outcome. Thus, when uncertainty about outcomes obscures the relationship between choices and consequences, more people choose selfishly. In other words, uncertainty provides a smokescreen behind which selfishness can hide.

Another study suggests that not only does uncertainty promote selfishness, but people actually prefer more uncertainty rather than less in the context of social dilemmas. Haisley and Weber (2010) compared choices in a "risky" dictator game with those in a more uncertain "ambiguous" dictator game. In the risky game, the prosocial choice yielded $2 for self and $1.75 for the receiver, and the selfish choice yielded $3 for self and either $0 or $0.50 for the receiver (each occurring with 50% probability). In the ambiguous game, the prosocial choice again yielded $2 for self and $1.75 for the receiver, and the selfish choice yielded $3 for self and either $0 or $0.50 for the receiver, each occurring with an *unknown* probability. Thus the ambiguous game contained more uncertainty about the outcome of the receiver. Dictators were more likely to choose the selfish option in the ambigu-ous game, and this was driven by self-serving beliefs about the likely outcome for the receiver. In other words, the increased uncertainty about outcomes in the ambiguous game allowed room for dictators to convince themselves that the self-ish choice would not be too harmful for the receiver, and these self-serving beliefs led them to prefer more uncertainty rather than less (Haisley & Weber, 2010).

How can these findings be reconciled with our recent observation that hyper-altruism relates positively to uncertainty in choice? One possibility concerns the nature of the outcome for the receiver. Thus far all of the studies demonstrating increased selfishness in the face of uncertainty have investigated choices about monetary outcomes. However, as outlined earlier it is not clear whether selfish choices in these paradigms cause suffering for the receiver. It may be the case that uncertainty only increases altruism for truly *moral* decisions that concern the suffering of another person. In these kinds of decisions, moral risk aversion may drive increased altruism under uncertainty, whereas in monetary exchange decisions the desire to appear fair may primarily drive altruistic choices, and when appearances can be preserved under uncertain conditions, selfishness may prevail.

Alternatively, it may be that different kinds of uncertainty have different effects on altruism. People may be uncertain about *whether self-serving actions produce harmful consequences*, or about *how a harmful outcome will be experienced*. The studies with monetary outcomes involved the first kind of uncertainty, whereas our recent studies with painful outcomes involved the second kind. When the consequences of self-serving actions are uncertain, the link between actions and outcomes is obscured, and this may degrade the sense of moral responsibility, enabling selfish behavior. However, when outcomes are certain and responsibility is thus preserved, uncertainty about how those outcomes will be experienced may lead to moral risk aversion. Teasing apart how different types of uncertainty affect moral decisions is an intriguing avenue for future research. One important question is how these different types of uncertainty are reflected in the parameters of the choice model. It may be that the choice accuracy parameter is differentially sensitive to uncertainty about consequences, which can in principle be resolved with more information, versus uncertainty about experiences, which can never be resolved because the subjective experience of others is fundamentally unknowable (Harsanyi, 1955; Nagel, 1974).

## Moral Decision-Making as a Learning Process

In the previous section I discussed how uncertainty about outcomes and the experiences of others affects moral decision-making. What if people are also uncertain about their own moral preferences? Thus far we have treated preferences as fixed quantities that are fully known to the decision-maker. From this perspective, decision-making simply involves translating the underlying subjective values into active choices. But if people are uncertain about their own preferences, the process of decision-making could be a form of learning whereby people discover their preferences by making choices and then observing their reactions to those choices. From this perspective, preferences are not fixed quantities but rather take the form of probabilistic belief distributions. This idea emerges from an "active inference" framework for decision-making that characterizes decision-making as a (Bayesian) inference problem (Friston et al., 2013, 2014). Inferred representations of self and others may serve the function of predicting and optimizing the potential outcomes of social interactions (Moutoussis, Fearon, El-Deredy, Dolan, & Friston, 2014). This idea is also related to economic models of self-signaling and social psychological theories of self-perception, in which actions provide signals to ourselves that indicate what kind of people we are (Bem, 1972; Bodner & Prelec, 2003).

This perspective may shed light on various well-documented yet conflicting aspects of moral decision-making: moral licensing, conscience accounting, and moral consistency. Moral licensing describes the process whereby morally good behavior "licenses" subsequent immoral behavior (Merritt, Effron, & Monin, 2010). For example, laboratory studies have shown that subjects who purchase environmentally friendly products are subsequently more likely to cheat for personal gain (Mazar & Zhong, 2010), and subjects who demonstrate nonracist attitudes are more likely to subsequently show racist behavior (Monin & Miller, 2001). Moral licensing was also evident in a recent study of real-world moral behavior using ecological momentary assessment (Hofmann, Wisneski, Brandt, & Skitka, 2014). Conscience accounting describes the reverse process, whereby people who initially behave immorally are more likely to compensate for their bad behavior by doing a good deed. For instance, subjects who initially told a lie were more likely to donate to charity than those who did not lie (Gneezy, Imas, & Madarasz, 2014). Finally, moral consistency describes a tendency to make moral choices that are similar to previous ones. It is well known from work on cognitive dissonance that behaving inconsistently is uncomfortable (Festinger, 1962; Higgins, 1987); the "foot-in-the-door" persuasion technique capitalizes on this, making people more likely to help in the future if they have helped in the past (Freedman & Fraser, 1966). Related work on moral identity has shown that inducing people to recall past moral behavior increases the likelihood of future moral deeds (Shao, Aquino, & Freeman, 2008). Moral licensing and conscience accounting seem to contradict moral consistency, as the former involve inconsistent patterns of choice. What could explain this contradiction?

If moral preferences are not fixed known quantities but rather belief distributions whose precision can be improved with experience, we might expect moral choices to initially be rather noisy in the absence of experience. This noise could manifest in the form of moral licensing and conscience accounting. With increased experience in the choice context, however, people should learn about their own preferences and choices should become less noisy, resulting in moral consistency. Treating moral decision-making as an inference problem leads to a prediction that moral licensing and conscience accounting should manifest in new contexts where decision-makers have limited experience, while moral consistency should appear in situations where decision-makers have extensive experience. Furthermore, computational models of choice should reflect a quantitative relationship between the precision of beliefs about one's own preferences and the noisiness of choices—with choices becoming less noisy over time as beliefs become more precise.

Considering moral decision-making as a learning process also highlights a possible role for prediction errors in guiding moral decisions. In standard reinforcement learning models, prediction errors represent discrepancies between expected and experienced outcomes, and guide learning by adjusting expectations. In the context of moral decisions, choices that are inconsistent with one's self-concept may similarly generate prediction errors. For example, if someone is uncertain about how much he dislikes cheating, and he predicts that he won't mind it much, but then after cheating he feels very guilty, the resulting prediction error teaches him something about his own preferences—he now knows he dislikes cheating with greater certainty than before. There is indeed evidence for prediction error–like signals during social decision-making (Chang, Smith, Dufwenberg, & Sanfey, 2011; Kishida & Montague, 2012; Xiang, Lohrenz, & Montague, 2013). Whether similar signals are present during moral decisions and play a role in dynamic aspects of moral choices like licensing and consistency is unknown.

The concept of prediction errors may also provide a computational account of the phenomenon of moral hypocrisy, where people view themselves as moral while failing to act morally (Batson, Kobrynowicz, Dinnerstein, Kampf, & Wilson, 1997). Batson et al. (1999) showed that moral hypocrisy can be reduced by heightening self-awareness, suggesting that moral hypocrisy arises when people fail to compare their behavior with their own moral standards (Batson, Thompson, Seuferling, Whitney, & Strongman, 1999). On a computational level, this might correspond to a suppression of prediction errors resulting from discrepancies between personal moral values and immoral behavior—a hypothesis that could be tested with neuroimaging.

## Concluding Remarks

Research on value-based decision-making has shown that it is informative to examine not just the choices people make, but also the computational mechanisms that underlie *how* those decisions are made (De Martino et al., 2013; Krajbich, Armel, & Rangel, 2010). Recent work has extended this approach to investigating social and also moral decision-making (Crockett et al., 2014; Kishida & Montague, 2012). A model-based approach can provide additional insight into human morality by describing how cognitive processes such as uncertainty and learning interact with and influence preferences. Another advantage of this approach is that it can generate novel and testable predictions about the dynamics of moral decision-making, such as how they unfold over time and how past decisions can influence future ones. Finally, computational models advance theory by forcing researchers to formalize the components of cognition and how they operate at an algorithmic level. This approach thus holds promise for addressing long-standing unanswered questions about human moral cognition and behavior.

## Acknowledgments

This work was supported by a Sir Henry Wellcome Postdoctoral Fellowship awarded to M.J.C. (092217/Z/10/Z). The author would like to thank Paul Van Lange for helpful comments.

## Notes

1 Although there is ample evidence suggesting morality is about more than harm and care (Graham et al., 2011; Haidt, 2007), I focus on this domain here because the bulk of research on moral cognition has investigated this particular aspect of morality, and because harm and care toward others has obvious parallels with behavioral economic studies of social preferences and work in computational neuroscience about the valuation of outcomes.

2 This is sometimes referred to as the *inverse temperature* or *softmax slope*.

## References

Ashton, N.L., & Severy, L.J. (1976). Arousal and costs in bystander intervention. *Personality and Social Psychology Bulletin*, 2(3), 268–272.

Batson, C.D., Duncan, B.D., Ackerman, P., Buckley, T., & Birch, K. (1981). Is empathic emotion a source of altruistic motivation? *Journal of Personality and Social Psychology*, 40(2), 290–302.

Batson, C.D., Kobrynowicz, D., Dinnerstein, J.L., Kampf, H.C., & Wilson, A.D. (1997). In a very different voice: Unmasking moral hypocrisy. *Journal of Personality and Social Psychology*, 72(6), 1335–1348.

Batson, C.D., Thompson, E.R., Seuferling, G., Whitney, H., & Strongman, J.A. (1999). Moral hypocrisy: Appearing moral to oneself without being so. *Journal of Personality and Social Psychology*, 77(3), 525–537.

Bem, D.J. (1972). Self-perception theory. In L. Berkowitz (Ed.), *Advances in experimental social psychology* (Vol. 6, pp. 1–62). San Diego, CA: Academic Press. Retrieved from http://www.sciencedirect.com/science/article/pii/S0065260108600246

Bernhardt, B.C., & Singer, T. (2012). The neural basis of empathy. *Annual Review of Neuroscience*, 35(1), 1–23.

Bodner, R., & Prelec, D. (2003). Self-signaling and diagnostic utility in everyday decision making. In I. Brocas & J. Carillo (Eds.), *The psychology of economic decisions* (Vol. 1, pp. 105–26). Oxford: Oxford University Press.

Burnham, K.P., & Anderson, D.R. (2002). *Model selection and multimodel inference: A practical information-theoretic approach.* New York: Springer.

Camerer, C. (2003). *Behavioral game theory: Experiments in strategic interaction.* Princeton, NJ: Princeton University Press.

Chang, L.J., Smith, A., Dufwenberg, M., & Sanfey, A.G. (2011). Triangulating the neural, psychological, and economic bases of guilt aversion. *Neuron*, 70(3), 560–572.

Charness, G., & Rabin, M. (2002). Understanding social preferences with simple tests. *Quarterly Journal of Economics*, 117(3), 817–869.

Clithero, J.A., & Rangel, A. (2013). The computation of stimulus values in simple choice. In P.W. Glimscher & E. Fehr (Eds.), *Neuroeconomics: Decision making and the brain* (2nd ed., pp. 125–147). San Diego, CA: Academic Press.

Crockett, M.J., Kurth-Nelson, Z., Siegel, J.Z., Dayan, P., & Dolan, R.J. (2014). Harm to others outweighs harm to self in moral decision making. *Proceedings of the National Academy of Sciences, 111*(48), 17320–17325.

Cushman, F. (2013). Action, outcome, and value: A dual-system framework for morality. *Personality and Social Psychology Review, 17*(3), 273–292.

Cushman, F., Young, L., & Hauser, M. (2006). The role of conscious reasoning and intuition in moral judgment: Testing three principles of harm. *Psychological Science, 17*(12), 1082–1089.

Dana, J., Weber, R.A., & Kuang, J.X. (2007). Exploiting moral wiggle room: Experiments demonstrating an illusory preference for fairness. *Economic Theory, 33*(1), 67–80.

Darley, J.M., & Latané, B. (1968). Bystander intervention in emergencies: Diffusion of responsibility. *Journal of Personality and Social Psychology, 8*(4, Pt. 1), 377–383.

David, C., McDonald, M.M., Mott, M.L., & Asher, B. (2012). Virtual morality: Emotion and action in a simulated three-dimensional "trolley problem." *Emotion, 12*(2), 364–370.

Daw, N.D. (2011). Trial-by-trial data analysis using computational models. In M.R. Delgado, E.A. Phelps, & T.W. Robbins (Eds.), *Decision making, affect, and learning: Attention and performance XXIII* (pp. 3–38). Oxford: Oxford University Press.

De Martino, B., Fleming, S.M., Garrett, N., & Dolan, R.J. (2013). Confidence in value-based choice. *Nature Neuroscience, 16*(1), 105–110.

Engel, C. (2011). Dictator games: A meta study. *Experimental Economics, 14*(4), 583–610.

Eskine, K.J., Kacinik, N.A., & Prinz, J.J. (2011). A bad taste in the mouth: gustatory disgust influences moral judgment. *Psychological Science, 22*(3), 295–299.

Fehr, E., & Krajbich, I. (2013). Social preferences and the brain. In P.W. Glimscher & E. Fehr (Eds.), *Neuroeconomics: Decision making and the brain* (2nd ed., pp. 193–218). San Diego, CA: Academic Press.

Fehr, E., & Schmidt, K.M. (1999). A theory of fairness, competition, and cooperation. *Quarterly Journal of Economics, 114*(3), 817–868.

FeldmanHall, O., Dalgleish, T., Thompson, R., Evans, D., Schweizer, S., & Mobbs, D. (2012). Differential neural circuitry and self-interest in real vs hypothetical moral decisions. *Social Cognitive and Affective Neuroscience, 7*(7), 743–751.

FeldmanHall, O., Mobbs, D., Evans, D., Hiscox, L., Navrady, L., & Dalgleish, T. (2012). What we say and what we do: The relationship between real and hypothetical moral choices. *Cognition, 123*(3), 434–441.

Festinger, L. (1962). *A theory of cognitive dissonance.* Stanford, CA: Stanford University Press.

Foot, P. (1967). The problem of abortion and the doctrine of double effect. *Oxford Review, 5*, 5–15.

Freedman, J.L., & Fraser, S.C. (1966). Compliance without pressure: The foot-in-the-door technique. *Journal of Personality and Social Psychology, 4*(2), 195–202.

Friston, K., Schwartenbeck, P., FitzGerald, T., Moutoussis, M., Behrens, T., & Dolan, R.J. (2013). The anatomy of choice: active inference and agency. *Frontiers in Human Neuroscience, 7*, 598.

Friston, K., Schwartenbeck, P., FitzGerald, T., Moutoussis, M., Behrens, T., & Dolan, R.J. (2014). The anatomy of choice: dopamine and decision-making. *Philosophical Transactions of the Royal Society of London B: Biological Sciences, 369*(1655), 20130481.

Glimscher, P.W., & Fehr, E. (2013). *Neuroeconomics: Decision making and the brain.* San Diego, CA: Academic Press.

Gneezy, U., Imas, A., & Madarász, K. (2014). Conscience accounting: Emotion dynamics and social behavior. *Management Science*, *60*(11), 2645–2658.

Graham, J., Nosek, B.A., Haidt, J., Iyer, R., Koleva, S., & Ditto, P.H. (2011). Mapping the moral domain. *Journal of Personality and Social Psychology*, *101*(2), 366–385.

Gray, K., Waytz, A., & Young, L. (2012). The moral dyad: A fundamental template unifying moral judgment. *Psychological Inquiry*, *23*(2), 206–215.

Gray, K., Young, L., & Waytz, A. (2012). Mind perception is the essence of morality. *Psychological Inquiry*, *23*(2), 101–124.

Greene, J.D., Cushman, F.A., Stewart, L.E., Lowenberg, K., Nystrom, L.E., & Cohen, J.D. (2009). Pushing moral buttons: The interaction between personal force and intention in moral judgment. *Cognition*, *111*(3), 364–371.

Greene, J.D., Sommerville, R.B., Nystrom, L.E., Darley, J.M., & Cohen, J.D. (2001). An fMRI investigation of emotional engagement in moral judgment. *Science*, *293*(5537), 2105–2108.

Haidt, J. (2001). The emotional dog and its rational tail: A social intuitionist approach to moral judgment. *Psychological Review*, *108*(4), 814–834.

Haidt, J. (2007). The new synthesis in moral psychology. *Science*, *316*(5827), 998–1002.

Haisley, E.C., & Weber, R.A. (2010). Self-serving interpretations of ambiguity in other-regarding behavior. *Games and Economic Behavior*, *68*(2), 614–625.

Harbaugh, W.T., Mayr, U., & Burghart, D.R. (2007). Neural responses to taxation and voluntary giving reveal motives for charitable donations. *Science*, *316*(5831), 1622–1625.

Hare, T.A., Camerer, C.F., Knoepfle, D.T., O'Doherty, J.P., & Rangel, A. (2010). Value computations in ventral medial prefrontal cortex during charitable decision making incorporate input from regions involved in social cognition. *Journal of Neuroscience*, *30*(2), 583–590.

Harsanyi, J.C. (1955). Cardinal welfare, individualistic ethics, and interpersonal comparisons of utility. *Journal of Political Economy*, *63*(4), 309–321. Retrieved from http://econpapers.repec.org/article/ucpjpolec/v_3A63_3Ay_3A1955_3Ap_3A309.htm

Hein, G., Silani, G., Preuschoff, K., Batson, C.D., & Singer, T. (2010). Neural responses to ingroup and outgroup members' suffering predict individual differences in costly helping. *Neuron*, *68*(1), 149–160.

Higgins, E.T. (1987). Self-discrepancy: A theory relating self and affect. *Psychological Review*, *94*(3), 319–340.

Hofmann, W., Wisneski, D.C., Brandt, M.J., & Skitka, L.J. (2014). Morality in everyday life. *Science*, *345*(6202), 1340–1343.

Horberg, E.J., Oveis, C., & Keltner, D. (2011). Emotions as moral amplifiers: An appraisal tendency approach to the influences of distinct emotions upon moral judgment. *Emotion Review*, *3*(3), 237–244.

Kishida, K.T., & Montague, P.R. (2012). Imaging models of valuation during social interaction in humans. *Biological Psychiatry*, *72*(2), 93–100.

Korman, J., Voiklis, J., & Malle, B.F. (2015). The social life of cognition. *Cognition*, *135*, 30–35.

Krajbich, I., Armel, C., & Rangel, A. (2010). Visual fixations and the computation and comparison of value in simple choice. *Nature Neuroscience*, *13*(10), 1292–1298.

Leonhardt, J.M., Keller, L.R., & Pechmann, C. (2011). Avoiding the risk of responsibility by seeking uncertainty: Responsibility aversion and preference for indirect agency when choosing for others. *Journal of Consumer Psychology*, *21*(4), 405–413.

Mazar, N., & Zhong, C.-B. (2010). Do green products make us better people? *Psychological Science*, *21*(4), 494–498.

Merritt, A.C., Effron, D.A., & Monin, B. (2010). Moral self-licensing: When being good frees us to be bad. *Social and Personality Psychology Compass*, *4*(5), 344–357.

Messick, D.M., & Schell, T. (1992). Evidence for an equality heuristic in social decision making. *Acta Psychologica*, *80*(1), 311–323.

Monin, B., & Miller, D.T. (2001). Moral credentials and the expression of prejudice. *Journal of Personality and Social Psychology*, *81*(1), 33–43.

Morelli, S.A., Sacchet, M.D., & Zaki, J. (2015). Common and distinct neural correlates of personal and vicarious reward: A quantitative meta-analysis. *NeuroImage*, *112*, 244–253.

Moutoussis, M., Fearon, P., El-Deredy, W., Dolan, R.J., & Friston, K.J. (2014). Bayesian inferences about the self (and others): A review. *Consciousness and Cognition*, *25*, 67–76.

Nagel, T. (1974). What is it like to be a bat? *Philosophical Review*, *83*(4), 435.

Penner, L.A., Dovidio, J.F., Piliavin, J.A., & Schroeder, D.A. (2005). Prosocial behavior: Multilevel perspectives. *Annual Review of Psychology*, *56*(1), 365–392.

Piliavin, I.M., Piliavin, J.A., & Rodin, J. (1975). Costs, diffusion, and the stigmatized victim. *Journal of Personality and Social Psychology*, *32*(3), 429–438.

Piliavin, J.A., & Piliavin, I.M. (1972). Effect of blood on reactions to a victim. *Journal of Personality and Social Psychology*, *23*(3), 353–361.

Shao, R., Aquino, K., & Freeman, D. (2008). Beyond moral reasoning: A review of moral identity research and its implications for business ethics. *Business Ethics Quarterly*, *18*(4), 513–540.

Slater, M., Antley, A., Davison, A., Swapp, D., Guger, C., Barker, C., . . . Sanchez-Vives, M.V. (2006). A virtual reprise of the Stanley Milgram obedience experiments. *PLOS ONE*, *1*(1), e39.

Spranca, M., Minsk, E., & Baron, J. (1991). Omission and commission in judgment and choice. *Journal of Experimental Social Psychology*, *27*(1), 76–105.

Story, G.W., Vlaev, I., Seymour, B., Winston, J.S., Darzi, A., & Dolan, R.J. (2013). Dread and the disvalue of future pain. *PLOS Computational Biology*, *9*(11), e1003335.

Stürmer, S., Snyder, M., Kropp, A., & Siem, B. (2006). Empathy-motivated helping: The moderating role of group membership. *Personality and Social Psychology Bulletin*, *32*(7), 943–956.

Thomson, J.J. (1976). Killing, letting die, and the trolley problem. *Monist*, *59*(2), 204–217.

Ugazio, G., Lamm, C., & Singer, T. (2012). The role of emotions for moral judgments depends on the type of emotion and moral scenario. *Emotion*, *12*(3), 579–590.

Valdesolo, P., & DeSteno, D. (2008). The duality of virtue: Deconstructing the moral hypocrite. *Journal of Experimental Social Psychology*, *44*(5), 1334–1338.

Van Lange, P.A.M. (1999). The pursuit of joint outcomes and equality in outcomes: An integrative model of social value orientation. *Journal of Personality and Social Psychology*, *77*(2), 337–349.

Vlaev, I. (2012). How different are real and hypothetical decisions? Overestimation, contrast and assimilation in social interaction. *Journal of Economic Psychology*, *33*(5), 963–972.

Vlaev, I., Seymour, B., Dolan, R.J., & Chater, N. (2009). The price of pain and the value of suffering. *Psychological Science*, *20*(3), 309–317.

Xiang, T., Lohrenz, T., & Montague, P.R. (2013). Computational substrates of norms and their violations during social exchange. *Journal of Neuroscience*, *33*(3), 1099–1108.

Young, L., Camprodon, J.A., Hauser, M., Pascual-Leone, A., & Saxe, R. (2010). Disruption of the right temporoparietal junction with transcranial magnetic stimulation reduces the role of beliefs in moral judgments. *Proceedings of the National Academy of Sciences, 107*(15), 6753–6758.

Young, L., Cushman, F., Hauser, M., & Saxe, R. (2007). The neural basis of the interaction between theory of mind and moral judgment. *Proceedings of the National Academy of Sciences, 104*(20), 8235–8240.

Zaki, J., & Mitchell, J.P. (2011). Equitable decision making is associated with neural markers of intrinsic value. *Proceedings of the National Academy of Sciences, 108*(49), 19761–19766.

# 6

# UNDERSTANDING RESPONSES TO MORAL DILEMMAS

## Deontological Inclinations, Utilitarian Inclinations, and General Action Tendencies

*Bertram Gawronski, Paul Conway, Joel B. Armstrong, Rebecca Friesdorf, and Mandy Hütter*

## Introduction

For centuries, societies have wrestled with the question of how to balance the rights of the individual versus the greater good (see Forgas, Jussim, & Van Lange, this volume); is it acceptable to ignore a person's rights in order to increase the overall well-being of a larger number of people? The contentious nature of this issue is reflected in many contemporary examples, including debates about whether it is legitimate to cause harm in order to protect societies against threats (e.g., shooting an abducted passenger plane to prevent a terrorist attack) and whether it is acceptable to refuse life-saving support for some people in order to protect the well-being of many others (e.g., refusing the return of American citizens who became infected with Ebola in Africa for treatment in the US). These issues have captured the attention of social scientists, politicians, philosophers, lawmakers, and citizens alike, partly because they involve a conflict between two moral principles.

The first principle, often associated with the moral philosophy of Immanuel Kant, emphasizes the irrevocable universality of rights and duties. According to the principle of *deontology*, the moral status of an action is derived from its consistency with context-independent norms (*norm-based morality*). From this perspective, violations of moral norms are unacceptable irrespective of the anticipated outcomes (e.g., shooting an abducted passenger plane is always immoral because it violates the moral norm not to kill others). The second principle, often associated with the moral philosophy of John Stuart Mill, emphasizes the greater good. According to the principle of *utilitarianism*, the moral status of an action depends on its outcomes, more specifically its consequences for overall well-being (*outcome-based morality*). From this perspective, violations of moral norms can be acceptable if they increase the well-being of a larger number of people (e.g., shooting an abducted passenger plane is morally acceptable if it safeguards the well-being of many others). Although both principles are intuitively plausible, their simultaneous consideration can cause feelings of moral conflict when they suggest different conclusions in a particular situation. Over the past decade, research in moral psychology has identified numerous determinants of deontological and utilitarian judgments, thereby providing valuable insights into the psychological processes underlying moral decision making.

Despite the exponentially growing body of research on deontological and utilitarian judgments, a deeper understanding of their underlying processes has been undermined by two fundamental problems: (1) the treatment of deontological and utilitarian inclinations as opposite ends of a single bipolar continuum rather than independent dimensions, and (2) the conflation of the two moral inclinations with general action tendencies. In the current chapter, we review our ongoing work on a mathematical model that resolves these problems by disentangling and quantifying the unique contributions of (1) deontological inclinations, (2) utilitarian inclinations, and (3) general action tendencies. We argue that this model offers a more fine-grained analysis of the psychological underpinnings of moral judgments, thereby imposing tighter constraints on current theories of moral psychology (see also Crockett, this volume).

## Moral Principles, Moral Judgments, and Psychological Processes

Although research in moral psychology has sometimes conflated normative, empirical, and theoretical aspects of morality (e.g., Kohlberg, 1969), contemporary approaches draw a sharp distinction between (1) moral principles, (2) moral judgments, and (3) underlying psychological processes. Moral principles are abstract philosophical propositions that specify the general characteristics that make an action moral or immoral. According to the principle of deontology, the moral status of an action depends on its consistency with moral norms (e.g., do not inflict harm upon others). A central aspect of deontology is that the validity of these norms is context-independent; they always apply regardless of the circumstances. In contrast, the principle of utilitarianism states that the morality of an action depends on its outcomes, in particular its consequences for overall well-being. According to this principle, the context surrounding an action is essential, because the same action may increase well-being in some situations and decrease well-being in others. Thus, unlike the emphasis of context-independent norms in the principle of deontology, the principle of utilitarianism emphasizes the significance of the particular situation. Although the two moral principles often suggest the same conclusion regarding the moral status of an action (e.g., harming a person is immoral because it violates the moral norm not to inflict harm onto others and usually reduces overall well-being), the two principles can lead to conflicting conclusions when an action violates a moral norm, but increases overall well-being (e.g., harming a person is morally acceptable by utilitarian standards, but not by deontological standards, if it protects the lives of many others).

Moral principles have to be distinguished from moral judgments, which may be consistent or inconsistent with a particular principle. For example, to the extent that an empirically observed judgment is consistent with the principle of deontology, it may be described as deontological judgment. Similarly, empirically observed judgments that are consistent with the principle of utilitarianism are often described as utilitarian judgments. A well-known example is Foot's (1967) trolley dilemma, in which a runaway trolley will kill five people unless the trolley is redirected to a different track, causing the death of only one person instead of five. In research using the trolley dilemma, the decision to redirect the trolley is often described as utilitarian, because it maximizes the well-being of a larger number of people. Conversely, the decision not to redirect the trolley is often described as deontological, because it conforms to the moral norm not to inflict harm upon others (e.g., Greene, Sommerville, Nystrom, Darley, & Cohen, 2001).

Importantly, the mere consistency of a judgment with a particular moral principle does not imply that the psychological processes underlying the judgment involved the actual use of that principle (Cushman, Young, & Hauser, 2006). In the philosophical literature, this issue is known as the difference between *rule-following* and *rule-conforming* judgments (Wittgenstein, 1953). Whereas rule-following judgments are overt responses that result from the actual application of the relevant rule, rule-conforming judgments are overt responses that are consistent with the rule, but may or may not involve an actual application of this rule in the production of the response. For example, although deontological decisions in the trolley dilemma may stem from the deliberate application of the moral norm not to inflict harm upon others, the mere consistency of the decision with that norm does not imply its actual use in the decision-making process. Over the past decade, the distinction between *rule-following* and *rule-conforming* judgments has become a central theme in moral psychology, in that many theories explain moral judgments in terms of psychological processes that do not involve a reasoned application of moral principles (Greene & Haidt, 2002).

## A Dual-Process Theory of Moral Judgment

One of the most prominent examples of such theories is Greene's dual-process theory of moral judgment (Greene et al., 2001). The central assumption of the theory is that deontological and utilitarian judgments have their roots in two distinct psychological processes. Whereas utilitarian judgments are assumed to be the product of controlled cognitive evaluations of outcomes, deontological judgments are assumed to stem from automatic emotional responses to the idea of causing harm. To test these assumptions, moral psychologists have examined responses to moral dilemmas designed to pit deontology against utilitarianism, such as the trolley dilemma and various structurally similar scenarios (for a review, see Christensen, Flexas, Calabrese, Gut, & Gomila, 2014). Although the unrealistic, comical scenario of the trolley dilemma has raised concerns about its suitability to investigate moral judgments about real-world issues (Bauman, McGraw, Bartels, & Warren, 2014), the evidence obtained with this and structurally similar dilemmas is largely consistent with Greene's dual-process theory.

The hypothesized link between deontological judgments and automatic emotional responses is supported by studies showing increased activation of brain areas associated with emotional processes when participants considered personal moral dilemmas involving direct contact with the victim (Greene et al., 2001) and when participants made deontological judgments on difficult moral dilemmas (Greene, Nystrom, Engell, Darley, & Cohen, 2004). Participants made fewer deontological judgments when emotional distance from victims was increased (Petrinovich, O'Neill, & Jorgensen, 1993), after a humorous video clip that presumably reduced negative affect by trivializing the harm dealt to victims (Valdesolo & DeSteno, 2006), or when they suffered damage to brain regions associated with emotional processing (Ciaramelli, Muccioli, Ladavas, & di Pellegrino, 2007; Koenigs et al., 2007; Mendez, Anderson, & Shapira, 2005). Conversely, participants made more deontological judgments when imagining harm in vivid detail (Bartels, 2008; Petrinovich & O'Neill, 1996), while experiencing physiological stress (Starcke, Ludwig, & Brand, 2012), and after listening to a morally uplifting story that evoked warm feelings (Strohminger, Lewis, & Meyer, 2011).

The hypothesized link between utilitarian judgments and controlled cognitive processes is supported by studies showing increased activation in brain areas associated with working memory when participants considered impersonal moral dilemmas in which victims are distant (Greene et al., 2001) and when participants made utilitarian judgments on difficult dilemmas (Greene et al., 2004). Facilitating rational decision making increased utilitarian judgments (Bartels, 2008; Nichols & Mallon, 2006), whereas introducing time pressure (Suter & Hertwig, 2011) reduced utilitarian judgments, and cognitive load impaired reaction times for utilitarian but not deontological judgments (Greene, Morelli, Lowenberg, Nystrom, & Cohen, 2008). Participants with greater working memory capacity were more likely to make utilitarian judgments (Moore, Clark, & Kane, 2008), as were participants higher in deliberative, as opposed to intuitive, thinking styles (Bartels, 2008). Together, these findings are consistent with the view that deontological judgments stem from automatic affective response to the idea of causing harm, whereas utilitarian judgments stem from controlled cognitive evaluations of outcomes (Greene et al., 2001).

## Two Conceptual Problems

Although moral dilemma research has provided many interesting insights into the determinants of utilitarian versus deontological judgments, the traditional dilemma approach suffers from two important drawbacks that undermine its suitability for understanding the psychological underpinnings of moral judgments. The first problem is the treatment of deontological and utilitarian judgments as opposite ends of a bipolar continuum, which stands in contrast to the assumption that they are rooted in functionally independent processes (see Conway & Gawronski, 2013). In the traditional dilemma approach, participants must categorize harmful action as either acceptable or unacceptable, thereby making a judgment that conforms to either the deontological or the utilitarian principle. To behave in line with the deontological principle is to simultaneously behave in opposition to the utilitarian principle, and vice versa. Thus, the traditional approach confounds *selecting* one option with *rejecting* the other.

This confound would be acceptable if the moral inclinations underlying overt judgments were themselves inversely related (i.e., stronger inclinations of one kind are associated with weaker inclinations of the other kind). However, a central assumption of Greene's dual-process theory is that deontological and utilitarian judgments stem from two functionally independent processes, thereby allowing for the possibility that the two moral inclinations are active at the same time. Indeed, the entire field of moral dilemma research is predicated on the assumption that people experience a psychological conflict when the two moral inclinations suggest different courses of action. Such conflict would not occur if the two inclinations were inversely related.

The significance of this problem is illustrated by the fact that any empirical finding (e.g., difference in moral judgments across conditions) can be attributed to either (1) differences in deontological inclinations, (2) differences in utilitarian inclinations, or (3) differences in both. An illustrative example is a study by Bartels and Pizarro (2011) showing that psychopaths tend to make more utilitarian judgments compared to nonpsychopathic participants. However, counter to interpretations of this effect as reflecting stronger utilitarian inclinations among psychopaths, it seems more plausible that psychopaths have no concerns about violating moral norms, rather than strong concerns with maximizing the well-being of others. Such ambiguities in the interpretation of empirical findings undermine not only the possibility of drawing strong theoretical conclusions regarding the psychological underpinnings of moral judgments; they also diminish the value of these findings for practical applications outside of the lab.

A second major problem of the traditional dilemma approach is that it conflates the two moral inclinations with general preferences for action versus inaction (van den Bos, Müller, & Damen, 2011). In the classic dilemma approach, the utilitarian choice always involves action, whereas the deontological choice always involves inaction. However, preferences for action versus inaction may differ for various reasons that are unrelated to deontological and utilitarian inclinations (Albarracin, Hepler, & Tannenbaum, 2011; Carver & Scheier, 1998; Kuhl, 1985). Distinguishing between genuine deontological inclinations and a general preference for inaction is important, because deontological concerns can sometimes suggest action rather than inaction (e.g., bringing an American citizen who became infected with Ebola in Africa to the US for treatment). Although this possibility has been largely ignored in moral dilemma research, it plays a central role in research on proscriptive versus prescriptive morality (e.g., Janoff-Bulman, Sheikh, & Hepp, 2009). Whereas *proscriptive norms* specify what people should not do, *prescriptive norms* specify what people should do. Although harm caused by action is often perceived as more immoral than equivalent harm caused by inaction (e.g., Cushman et al., 2006; Spranca, Minsk, & Baron, 1991; see also Miller & Monin, this volume), the principle of deontology—defined as norm-based morality—implies that both actions and inactions can be immoral if they conflict with a moral norm. Whereas actions are immoral if they conflict with a proscriptive norm (e.g., pushing someone in front of a car), inactions are immoral if they conflict with a prescriptive norm (e.g., not helping the victim of a car accident).

Similar concerns apply to the confound between utilitarianism and action, because a general preference for action can produce a "utilitarian" judgment in situations where the utilitarian principle suggests action (i.e., moral dilemmas involving proscriptive norms) and a "deontological" judgment in situations where the deontological principle suggests action (i.e., moral dilemmas involving prescriptive norms). Such action tendencies have to be distinguished from utilitarian inclinations, which involve a genuine concern for maximizing well-being (Kahane, 2015). An illustrative example is the finding that people with high levels of testosterone show a greater willingness to inflict harm upon one person to increase the well-being of several others (Carney & Mason, 2010), which may be due to stronger utilitarian inclinations, weaker deontological inclinations, or both. Yet, an alternative interpretation is that individuals with high levels of testosterone simply have a stronger tendency to act regardless of whether action is consistent with the principle of deontology or utilitarianism (see Andrew & Rogers, 1972; Joly et al., 2006; Lynn, Houtman, Weathers, Ketterson, & Nolan, 2000). Thus, similar to the nonindependence of deontological and utilitarian inclinations in the traditional dilemma approach, the confound between the two moral inclinations and general action tendencies poses a major challenge for unambiguous interpretations of empirical results, thereby undermining the possibility of drawing strong theoretical and practical conclusions.

## Process Dissociation as a Solution to the Nonindependence Problem

To overcome the first problem—the nonindependence of deontological and utilitarian judgments—Conway and Gawronski (2013) developed a process dissociation (PD) model to disentangle the independent contributions of deontological and utilitarian inclinations to overt moral judgments. Although originally designed to examine memory (Jacoby, 1991), PD is a content-agnostic procedure that can be applied to any domain where traditional methods conflate the measurement of two psychological processes (for a review, see Payne & Bishara, 2009). The key to PD is employing both *incongruent* trials where the two underlying processes lead to divergent responses, as well as *congruent* trials where they lead to the same response.

Applied to moral dilemma research, incongruent dilemmas pit the principle of deontology against the principle of utilitarianism, such that a given action is acceptable from a utilitarian view but unacceptable from a deontological view (or vice versa). Congruent dilemmas have structure and wording identical to incongruent dilemmas, except that deontological or utilitarian standards imply the same moral judgment. For example, in the incongruent version of the proscriptive vaccine dilemma (see first column of Table 6.1), a doctor must decide whether to administer a vaccine with potential deadly side effects in order to cure an even deadlier disease, thereby saving many lives. In the congruent version of the proscriptive vaccine dilemma (see second column of Table 6.1), a doctor must decide whether to administer a vaccine with potential deadly side effects to cure the common flu, thereby reducing discomfort but not saving lives. According to the principle of deontology, administering the vaccine is unacceptable in both versions of the moral dilemma, because it conflicts with the moral norm not to inflict harm upon others. In contrast, from a utilitarian view administering the vaccine is acceptable in the incongruent, but not the congruent, version of the moral dilemma, because it maximizes well-being in the former, but not in the latter, case.

Conway and Gawronski's (2013) PD model disentangles the independent contribution of deontological and utilitarian inclinations to responses in proscriptive dilemmas involving harmful actions. To illustrate the logic of their model, participants' judgments in congruent and incongruent dilemmas can be illustrated by means of a processing tree (see Figure 6.1). Each of the three paths from left to right depicts judgment outcomes on the two kinds of dilemmas as a function of distinct underlying processes. The three paths in the figure capture the cases that (1) utilitarianism drives the response on a given dilemma (top path), (2) deontology drives the response (middle path), and (3) neither utilitarianism nor deontology drives the response (bottom path). $U$ depicts the case that utilitarianism drives the response, and $D$ depicts the case that deontology drives the response. Conversely, $1 - U$ depicts the case that utilitarianism does not drive the response, and $1 - D$ depicts the case that deontology does not drive the response.

Using the two columns on the right side of Figure 6.1, it is possible to go backward and identify the processing paths that lead participants to judge harmful action as acceptable or unacceptable for congruent and incongruent dilemmas. For example, on congruent dilemmas, harmful action will be judged as

**TABLE 6.1** Example of a moral dilemma involving either a proscriptive or a prescriptive norm, suggesting deontological decisions that are either congruent or incongruent with utilitarian assessments of outcomes.

| Proscriptive Dilemma | | Prescriptive Dilemma | |
|---|---|---|---|
| *Incongruent* | *Congruent* | *Incongruent* | *Congruent* |
| You are a doctor in an area that suffers from an outbreak of a highly contagious disease. Preliminary tests have shown the success of a new vaccine that is not approved by the health department of your country because of its severe side effects. The side effects of the vaccine will likely cause the death of dozens of people who are not infected, but the vaccine will save hundreds of lives by preventing spread of the virus. Is it acceptable in this case to use the vaccine? | You are a doctor in an area that suffers from an outbreak of a highly contagious disease. Preliminary tests have shown the success of a new vaccine that is not approved by the health department of your country because of its severe side effects. The side effects of the vaccine will likely cause the death of dozens of people who are not infected, but the vaccine will save about the same number of lives by preventing spread of the virus. Is it acceptable in this case to use the vaccine? | You are a doctor in an area that suffers from an outbreak of a highly contagious disease. Preliminary tests have shown the success of a new vaccine that is not approved by the health department of your country because of its severe side effects. The side effects of the vaccine will likely cause the death of dozens of people who are not infected, but the vaccine will save hundreds of lives by preventing spread of the virus. One of your colleagues plans to use the vaccine, but you could stop him by reporting his plans to the health department. Is it acceptable in this case to report your colleague to the health department? | You are a doctor in an area that suffers from an outbreak of a highly contagious disease. Preliminary tests have shown the success of a new vaccine that is not approved by the health department of your country because of its severe side effects. The side effects of the vaccine will likely cause the death of dozens of people who are not infected, but the vaccine will save about the same number of lives by preventing spread of the virus. One of your colleagues plans to use the vaccine, but you could stop him by reporting his plans to the health department. Is it acceptable in this case to report your colleague to the health department? |

unacceptable when utilitarianism drives the response (*U*). Alternatively, harmful action will be judged as unacceptable on congruent dilemmas when utilitarianism does not drive the response (*1 − U*) and, at the same time, deontology does drive the response (*D*). Harmful action will be judged as acceptable in congruent

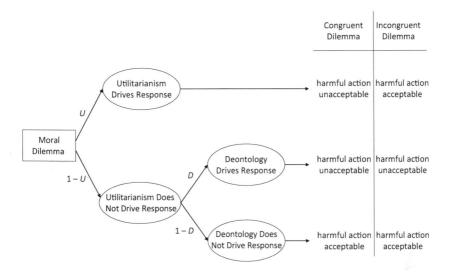

**FIGURE 6.1** Processing tree illustrating the underlying components leading to judgments that harmful action is either acceptable or unacceptable in congruent and incongruent moral dilemmas involving proscriptive norms.

*Note:* Copyright © 2013 by the American Psychological Association. Reproduced with permission. Figure adapted from Conway, P., & Gawronski, B. (2013). Deontological and utilitarian inclinations in moral decision-making: A process dissociation approach. *Journal of Personality and Social Psychology*, *104*, 216–235. The use of APA information does not imply endorsement by APA.

dilemmas only when neither utilitarianism $(1 - U)$ nor deontology $(1 - D)$ drives the response. Similarly, on incongruent dilemmas, participants will judge harmful action as unacceptable when utilitarianism does not drive the response $(1 - U)$ and, at the same time, deontology does drive the response $(D)$. However, harmful action will be judged as acceptable either when utilitarianism drives the response $(U)$, or alternatively when neither utilitarianism $(1 - U)$ nor deontology $(1 - D)$ drives the response.

By means of the processing paths depicted in Figure 6.1, it is now possible to create mathematical equations that delineate the probability of a particular judgment on congruent and incongruent dilemmas as a function of the two underlying inclinations. For example, the probability of judging harmful action as unacceptable on congruent dilemmas is represented by the cases where (1) utilitarianism drives the response, and (2) deontology drives the response when utilitarianism fails to drive the response. In algebraic terms, this probability is represented by the equation:

$$p(\text{unacceptable} \mid \text{congruent}) = U + [D \times (1 - U)] \tag{1}$$

Conversely, the probability of judging harmful action as acceptable on congruent dilemmas is represented by the case that neither utilitarianism nor deontology drives the response, which can be represented algebraically as:

$$p(\text{acceptable} \mid \text{congruent}) = (1 - U) \times (1 - D) \qquad (2)$$

The same logic can be applied to incongruent dilemmas. For example, the probability of judging harmful action as unacceptable on incongruent dilemmas is represented by the case that deontology drives the response when utilitarianism does not drive the response. Algebraically, this likelihood is represented by the equation:

$$p(\text{unacceptable} \mid \text{incongruent}) = D \times (1 - U) \qquad (3)$$

Conversely, the probability of judging harmful action as acceptable on incongruent dilemmas is represented by the cases that (1) utilitarianism drives the response, and (2) neither deontology nor utilitarianism drives the response. In algebraic terms, this probability is represented as:

$$p(\text{acceptable} \mid \text{incongruent}) = U + [(1 - U) \times (1 - D)] \qquad (4)$$

Using the empirically observed probabilities of participants' *acceptable* and *unacceptable* responses on congruent and incongruent dilemmas, these equations can be used to calculate numerical estimates for the two kinds of moral tendencies by solving them algebraically for the two parameters representing deontology ($D$) and utilitarianism ($U$).[1] Specifically, by including Equation 3 into Equation 1, the latter can be solved for $U$, leading to the following formula:

$$U = p(\text{unacceptable} \mid \text{congruent}) - p(\text{unacceptable} \mid \text{incongruent}) \qquad (5)$$

Moreover, by including the calculated value for $U$ in Equation 3, this equation can be solved for $D$, leading to the following formula:

$$D = p(\text{unacceptable} \mid \text{incongruent}) / (1 - U) \qquad (6)$$

These two formulas allow researchers to quantify the strength of deontological and utilitarian inclinations within participants by using their individual probabilities of showing a particular response on the two kinds of moral dilemmas. The resulting parameter values can then be used as measurement scores in experimental designs to investigate differences across conditions and in correlational designs to investigate relations to individual difference or criterion measures (for a more detailed discussion of technical details of PD, see Appendix B of Conway & Gawronski, 2013).

In their original application of PD to moral dilemma responses, Conway and Gawronski (2013) found that individual differences in perspective taking and empathic concern were positively related to $D$, but not $U$. Conversely, individual differences in need for cognition were positively related to $U$, but not $D$. Moreover, individual differences in moral identity were positively related to both $D$ and $U$, a pattern that was concealed in the traditional approach due to the treatment of the two moral inclinations as opposite ends of a bipolar continuum. Two experimental studies further showed that cognitive load reduced $U$ without affecting $D$, whereas increased salience of harm increased $D$ without affecting $U$. Together, these results demonstrate the usefulness of PD to disentangle and quantify the functionally independent contributions of deontological and utilitarian inclinations to moral dilemma judgments (for additional examples, see Friesdorf, Conway, & Gawronski, 2015; Lee & Gino, 2015).

## A Multinomial Model of Moral Judgment

Although Conway and Gawronski's (2013) PD model provides a solution to the first problem—the nonindependence of deontological and utilitarian judgments—it does not resolve the second problem because it retains the confound between the two moral inclinations and general action tendencies. $D$ scores still conflate deontological inclinations with a general preference for inaction, and $U$ scores still conflate utilitarian inclinations with a general preference for action. To simultaneously resolve both conceptual problems of traditional dilemma research, we recently developed an extended model that provides separate parameters for (1) deontological inclinations, (2) utilitarian inclinations, and (3) general preference for inaction (see Figure 6.2). To emphasize the conceptual and stochastic difference from the parameters of Conway and Gawronski's PD model, the three parameters are depicted with the two-digit acronyms $De$ (for deontology), $Ut$ (for utilitarianism), and $In$ (for inaction).

The central difference from Conway and Gawronski's PD model is that the extended model captures cases in which the deontological principle prohibits action (i.e., proscriptive dilemmas) as well as cases in which the deontological principle prescribes action (i.e., prescriptive dilemmas). For either type of dilemma, the moral implication of the utilitarian principle depends on the respective outcomes, such that action is acceptable in proscriptive dilemmas and inaction is acceptable in prescriptive dilemmas if either decision increases overall well-being. Thus, the parameter estimates of the extended model are based on participants' responses to four kinds of moral dilemmas that differ with regard to whether (1) the dilemma involves a proscriptive or prescriptive norm and (2) the outcomes of action versus inaction suggest utilitarian choices that are either congruent or incongruent with the deontological norm (for an example, see Table 6.1). Because the three processes lead to different outcomes on the four kinds of dilemmas (see Figure 6.2), the extended model allows us to disentangle and quantify their unique contributions to moral dilemma judgments, thereby resolving the two conceptual problems of the traditional approach.

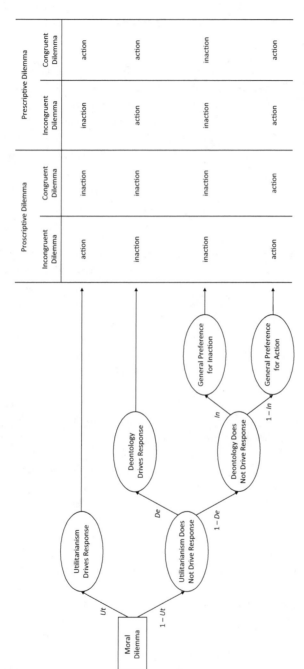

|  | Proscriptive Dilemma | | Prescriptive Dilemma | |
| --- | --- | --- | --- | --- |
|  | Incongruent Dilemma | Congruent Dilemma | Incongruent Dilemma | Congruent Dilemma |
| Utilitarianism Drives Response | action | inaction | inaction | action |
| Deontology Drives Response | inaction | inaction | action | action |
| General Preference for Inaction | inaction | inaction | inaction | inaction |
| General Preference for Action | action | action | action | action |

**FIGURE 6.2** Processing tree illustrating the underlying components leading to action or inaction in congruent and incongruent moral dilemmas involving either proscriptive or prescriptive norms.

*Source:* Copyright © 2013 by the American Psychological Association. Reproduced with permission from Conway, P., & Gawronski, B. (2013). Deontological and utilitarian inclinations in moral decision-making: A process dissociation approach. *Journal of Personality and Social Psychology, 104,* 216–235. The use of APA information does not imply endorsement by APA.

Although the derivation of the model equations follows the same logic described for Conway and Gawronski's (2013) PD model, there are a few important differences in the mathematical underpinnings of the two models. Different from the use of linear algebra in the calculation of the two PD scores, our extended model uses multinomial modeling to estimate parameter values for the three processes (see Batchelder & Riefer, 1999). Whereas PD is based on two (nonredundant) equations with two unknowns, multinomial modeling involves a higher number of equations than unknowns. Thus, whereas PD scores can be calculated directly by means of linear algebra, parameter estimations in multinomial modeling are based on maximum likelihood statistics. Specifically, multinomial modeling involves systematic adjustments in the parameter values to minimize the differences between the actual probabilities of observed responses and the probabilities predicted by the model. The deviation between actual and predicted probabilities serves as the basis for statistical tests of goodness-of-fit, which provides evidence regarding the validity of the model in describing the data. If the deviation between actual and predicted probabilities is small, fit statistics will reveal a nonsignificant deviation between the two, suggesting that the model accurately describes the data. If, however, the deviation between actual and predicted probabilities is large, fit statistics will reveal a significant deviation between the two, indicating that the model does not accurately describe the data. To the extent that the model fits the data, the parameter estimates can be used to investigate effects of experimental manipulations and correlations with individual difference or criterion measures, similar to the PD approach (for an example, see Conrey, Sherman, Gawronski, Hugenberg, & Groom, 2005).

## Preliminary Findings

To test the validity of our multinomial model, we conducted a pilot study in which participants were asked to indicate for a set of newly created moral dilemmas whether the decision suggested in the dilemma is acceptable or unacceptable. The dilemmas included four parallel versions of six scenarios that varied in terms of whether (1) the dilemma involved a proscriptive or prescriptive norm and (2) the outcomes of action versus inaction suggested utilitarian choices that were either congruent or incongruent with the deontological norm (for an example, see Table 6.1). The sample of our pilot study included 204 psychology undergraduates from the University of Texas at Austin. The model fit the data well, $G^2(1) = 1.56$, $p = .21$. Both the *De* and the *Ut* parameters differed significantly from zero, demonstrating that both processes contributed participants' responses to our moral dilemmas (see Table 6.2). The *In* parameter did not differ significantly from its reference point of 0.5, which reflects an equal distribution of *action* and *inaction* tendencies. The finding that the *In* parameter was slightly lower than

**TABLE 6.2** Parameter estimates for utilitarian inclinations (Ut), deontological inclinations (De), and action aversion (In).

| Parameter | Estimated Score | Standard Error | 95% Confidence Interval |
| --- | --- | --- | --- |
| Ut | 0.213 | 0.013 | 0.187–0.240 |
| De | 0.347 | 0.017 | 0.313–0.381 |
| In | 0.476 | 0.013 | 0.451–0.502 |

0.5 demonstrates that, on average, participants in the study showed a general preference for action regardless of the dilemma details (see Table 6.2).

To explore the usefulness of our model in providing deeper insights into the psychological underpinnings of moral judgments, we also investigated gender differences in the three parameters. A recent meta-analysis ($N = 6,100$) using Conway and Gawronski's (2013) PD model suggests that women show stronger deontological inclinations than men ($d = .57$), while men show only slightly stronger utilitarian inclinations than women ($d = .10$) (Friesdorf et al., 2015). Using our multinomial model, we replicated this pattern in a second pilot study with 94 women and 105 men from Amazon's Mechanical Turk.[2] Overall, the model fit the data well, $G^2(2) = 1.16, p = .56$. Whereas women showed significantly higher De scores than men, there were no significant gender differences on the Ut parameter (see Figure 6.3). Yet, our extended model also revealed a significant difference on the In parameter, in that women showed a significantly stronger preference for inaction than men. This result suggests that gender differences in moral dilemma judgments are due to differences in deontological inclinations and action aversion, but not utilitarian inclinations.

Expanding on the results of our pilot studies, two follow-up studies aimed to provide deeper insights into the psychological processes underlying deontological inclinations, utilitarian inclinations, and general action tendencies. A central assumption of Greene et al.'s (2001) dual-process theory is that deontological judgments stem from automatic emotional processes, whereas utilitarian judgments are the product of controlled cognitive processes. Although these assumptions are consistent with a considerable body of research, the available evidence remains ambiguous due to (1) the nonindependent measurement of the two moral inclinations in the traditional dilemma approach and (2) the conflation of the two moral inclinations with general action tendencies. For example, it is possible that automatic emotional processes contribute to the moral dilemma responses, not by increasing deontological concerns with norm violations but by increasing action aversion (Miller, Hannikainen, & Cushman, 2014). Similarly, one could argue that controlled cognitive processes contribute not only to utilitarian assessments of outcomes but also to deontological assessments of norm violations.

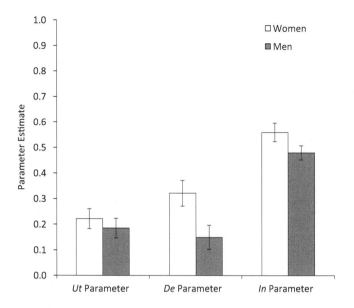

**FIGURE 6.3** Parameter estimates for utilitarian inclinations (*Ut*), deontological inclinations (*De*), and action aversion (*In*) for women and men (*N* = 199). Error bars depict 95% confidence intervals.

To provide deeper insights into the psychological underpinnings of deontological inclinations, utilitarian inclinations, and general action tendencies, we asked 190 participants on Amazon's Mechanical Turk to indicate for our new set of moral dilemmas whether the described action is acceptable or unacceptable.[3] To investigate the resource-dependence of the underlying psychological processes, half of the participants were asked to rehearse 8-digit letter strings while reading and responding to the dilemmas (high load). The remaining half were asked to rehearse 2-digit letter strings while reading and responding to the dilemmas (low load). As with our two pilot studies, our extended model fit the data, $G^2(2) = 4.79$, $p = .09$. Interestingly, cognitive load did not show any significant effects on the *Ut* parameter and the *De* parameter (see Figure 6.4). The only significant effect occurred for the *In* parameter, which showed a higher preference for inaction under high load compared to low load. These results suggest that limited cognitive resources influence moral judgments by inducing a general preference for inaction regardless of the particular situation rather than by disrupting utilitarian assessments of outcomes or deontological assessments of norm violations (see also Trémolière & Bonnefon, 2014).

Because the obtained effect of cognitive load challenges one of the most central assumptions in moral dilemma research, we aimed to replicate it in a

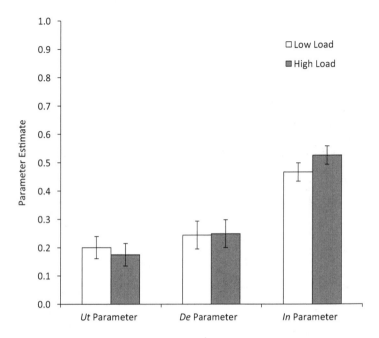

**FIGURE 6.4** Parameter estimates for utilitarian inclinations (*Ut*), deontological inclinations (*De*), and action aversion (*In*) as a function of cognitive load (*N* = 190). Error bars depict 95% confidence intervals.

follow-up study with 180 participants from Amazon's Mechanical Turk.[4] Again, our extended model fit the data very well, $G^2(2) = 1.07, p = .58$. Corroborating the validity of the obtained results, cognitive load did not show any significant effects on the *Ut* parameter and the *De* parameter. Yet, cognitive load did show a significant effect on the *In* parameter, in that participants in the high-load condition showed an enhanced preference for inaction compared to participants in the low-load condition (see Figure 6.5). Together, these results challenge earlier interpretations of cognitive load effects as being driven by a reduction in utilitarian assessments of outcomes (e.g., Greene et al., 2008). Instead, our findings suggest that cognitive load induces a general reluctance to act regardless of the specific situation.

In our ongoing research, we are exploring whether emotional processes influence moral judgments via deontological inclinations, utilitarian inclinations, or general action tendencies (see Miller et al., 2014). Although speculative at this point, emotional processes might influence moral judgments through various mechanisms that are unrelated to deontological inclinations (see also Forgas, this volume). Together with the identified effect of cognitive load on general action tendencies, emotional effects on utilitarian inclinations or general action

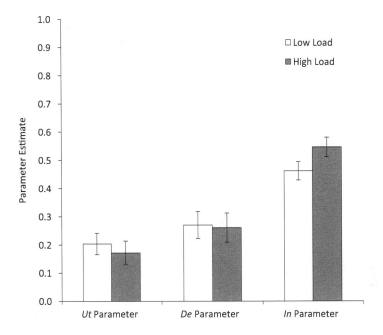

**FIGURE 6.5** Parameter estimates for utilitarian inclinations (*Ut*), deontological inclinations (*De*), and action aversion (*In*) as a function of cognitive load ($N = 180$). Error bars depict 95% confidence intervals.

tendencies may require significant revisions in the interpretation of previous findings, posing a major challenge to existing theories of moral judgment.

## Conclusion

The current chapter reviewed our ongoing pilot work on a multinomial model of moral judgment. Although previous research provided interesting insights into the determinants of deontological and utilitarian judgments, a deeper understanding of their underlying processes has been undermined by (1) the treatment of deontological and utilitarian inclinations as opposite ends of a single bipolar continuum rather than independent dimensions, and (2) the conflation of the two moral inclinations with general action tendencies. Our multinomial model resolves both conceptual problems by quantifying the unique contributions of (1) deontological inclinations, (2) utilitarian inclinations, and (3) general action tendencies. A major aspect of this endeavor is the integration of both proscriptive and prescriptive norms, the latter of which have been largely ignored in traditional moral dilemma research. By offering a more fine-grained analysis of the psychological underpinnings of moral judgment, our model not only imposes

tighter constraints on current theories of moral psychology, but it also offers valuable practical insights for the resolution of moral controversies in society.

## Acknowledgment

This chapter is based upon work supported by the National Science Foundation under Grant No. 1449620. Any opinions, findings, and conclusions or recommendations expressed in this material are those of the authors and do not necessarily reflect the views of the National Science Foundation.

## Notes

1 Note that Equation 1 and 2 are mathematically redundant, because $p$(acceptable | congruent) = $1 - $ p(unacceptable | congruent). Similarly, Equation 3 and 4 are mathematically redundant, because $p$(acceptable | incongruent) = $1 - $ p(unacceptable | incongruent). Thus, the basic logic of PD is to solve two (nonredundant) equations for two unknowns on the basis of observed data.

2 The original sample included 228 participants. Twenty-four participants started the study but did not complete it. Five participants failed to pass an instructional attention check, and were therefore excluded from the analysis (Oppenheimer, Meyvis, & Davidenko, 2009).

3 The original sample included 242 participants. Forty-three participants started the study but did not complete it. Nine participants failed to pass an instructional attention check, and were therefore excluded from the analysis (Oppenheimer et al., 2009).

4 The original sample included 233 participants. Thirty-nine participants started the study but did not complete it. Fourteen participants failed to pass an instructional attention check, and were therefore excluded from the analysis (Oppenheimer et al., 2009).

## References

Albarracin, D., Hepler, J., & Tannenbaum, M. (2011). General action and inaction goals: Their behavioral, cognitive, and affective origins and influences. *Current Directions in Psychological Science, 20*, 119–123.

Andrew, R.J., & Rogers, L.J. (1972). Testosterone, search behavior and persistence. *Nature, 237*, 343–345.

Bartels, D. (2008). Principled moral sentiment and the flexibility of moral judgment and decision making. *Cognition, 108*, 381–417.

Bartels, D.M., & Pizarro, D.A. (2011). The mismeasure of morals: Antisocial personality traits predict utilitarian responses to moral dilemmas. *Cognition, 121*, 154–161.

Batchelder, W.H., & Riefer, D.M. (1999). Theoretical and empirical review of multinomial process tree modeling. *Psychonomic Bulletin & Review, 6*, 57–86.

Bauman, C.W., McGraw, A.P., Bartels, D.M., & Warren, C. (2014). Revisiting external validity: Concerns about trolley problems and other sacrificial dilemmas in moral psychology. *Social and Personality Psychology Compass, 8*, 536–554.

Carney, D.R., & Mason, M.F. (2010). Moral decisions and testosterone: When the ends justify the means. *Journal of Experimental Social Psychology, 46*, 668–671.

Carver, C.S., & Scheier, M.F. (1998). *On the self-regulation of behavior.* New York: Cambridge University Press.

Christensen, J.F., Flexas, A., Calabrese, M., Gut, N.K., & Gomila, A. (2014). Moral judgment reloaded: A moral dilemma validation study. *Frontiers in Psychology, 5,* 607.

Ciaramelli, E., Muccioli, M., Ladavas, E., & di Pellegrino, G. (2007). Selective deficit in personal moral judgment following damage to ventromedial prefrontal cortex. *Social Cognitive and Affective Neuroscience, 2,* 84–92.

Conrey, F.R., Sherman, J.W., Gawronski, B., Hugenberg, K., & Groom, C. (2005). Separating multiple processes in implicit social cognition: The quad-model of implicit task performance. *Journal of Personality and Social Psychology, 89,* 469–487.

Conway, P., & Gawronski, B. (2013). Deontological and utilitarian inclinations in moral decision-making: A process dissociation approach. *Journal of Personality and Social Psychology, 104,* 216–235.

Cushman, F., Young, L., & Hauser, M. (2006). The role of conscious reasoning and intuition in moral judgment: Testing three principles of harm. *Psychological Science, 17,* 1082–1089.

Foot, P. (1967). The problem of abortion and the doctrine of double effect. *Oxford Review, 5,* 5–15.

Friesdorf, R., Conway, P., & Gawronski, B. (2015). Gender differences in responses to moral dilemmas: A process dissociation analysis. *Personality and Social Psychology Bulletin, 41,* 696–713.

Greene, J.D., & Haidt, J. (2002). How (and where) does moral judgment work? *Trends in Cognitive Sciences, 6,* 517–523.

Greene, J.D., Morelli, S.A., Lowenberg, K., Nystrom, L.E., & Cohen, J.D. (2008). Cognitive load selectively interferes with utilitarian moral judgment. *Cognition, 107,* 1144–1154.

Greene, J.D., Nystrom, L.E., Engell, A.D., Darley, J.M., & Cohen, J.D. (2004). The neural bases of cognitive conflict and control in moral judgment. *Neuron, 44,* 389–400.

Greene, J.D., Sommerville, R.B., Nystrom, L.E., Darley, J.M., & Cohen, J.D. (2001). An fMRI investigation of emotional engagement in moral judgment. *Science, 293,* 2105–2108.

Jacoby, L.L. (1991). A process dissociation framework: Separating automatic from intentional uses of memory. *Journal of Memory and Language, 30,* 513–541.

Janoff-Bulman, R., Sheikh, S., & Hepp, S. (2009). Proscriptive versus prescriptive morality: Two faces of moral regulation. *Journal of Personality and Social Psychology, 96,* 521–537.

Joly, F., Alibhai, S.M.H., Galica, J., Park, A., Yi, Q.L., Wagner, L., & Tannock, I.F. (2006). Impact of androgen deprivation therapy on physical and cognitive function, as well as quality of life of patients with nonmetastatic prostate cancer. *Journal of Urology, 176,* 2443–2447.

Kahane, G. (2015). Sidetracked by trolleys: Why sacrificial moral dilemmas tell us little (or nothing) about utilitarian judgment. *Social Neuroscience, 10,* 551–560.

Koenigs, M., Young, L., Adolphs, R., Tranel, D., Cushman, F., Hauser, M., & Damasio, A. (2007). Damage to the prefrontal cortex increases utilitarian moral judgments. *Nature, 446,* 908–911.

Kohlberg, L. (1969). Stage and sequence: The cognitive-developmental approach to socialization. In D.A. Goslin (Ed.), *Handbook of socialization theory and research* (pp. 347–480). Chicago: Rand McNally.

Kuhl, J. (1985). *Action control: From cognition to behavior.* Berlin: Springer.

Lee, J.J., & Gino, F. (2015). Poker-faced morality: Concealing emotions leads to utilitarian decision making. *Organizational Behavior and Human Decision Processes, 126,* 49–64.

Lynn, S.E., Houtman, A.M., Weathers, W.W., Ketterson, E.D., & Nolan, V., Jr. (2000). Testosterone increases activity but not daily energy expenditure in captive male dark-eyed juncos, *Junco hyemalis*. *Animal Behaviour*, *60*, 581–587.

Mendez, M.F., Anderson, E., & Shapira, J.S. (2005). An investigation of moral judgment in frontotemporal dementia. *Cognitive and Behavioral Neurology*, *18*, 193–197.

Miller, R.M., Hannikainen, I.A., & Cushman, F.A. (2014). Bad actions or bad outcomes? Differentiating affective contributions to the moral condemnation of harm. *Emotion*, *14*, 573–587.

Moore, A.B., Clark, B.A., & Kane, M.J. (2008). Who shalt not kill? Individual differences in working memory capacity, executive control, and moral judgment. *Psychological Science*, *19*, 549–557.

Nichols, S., & Mallon, R. (2006). Moral dilemmas and moral rules. *Cognition*, *100*, 530–542.

Oppenheimer, D.M., Meyvis, T., & Davidenko, N. (2009). Instructional manipulation checks: Detecting satisficing to increase statistical power. *Journal of Experimental Social Psychology*, *45*, 867–872.

Payne, B.K., & Bishara, A.J. (2009). An integrative review of process dissociation and related models in social cognition. *European Review of Social Psychology*, *20*, 272–314.

Petrinovich, L., & O'Neill, P. (1996). Influence of wording and framing effects on moral intuitions. *Ethology & Sociobiology*, *17*, 145–171.

Petrinovich, L., O'Neill, P., & Jorgensen, M. (1993). An empirical study of moral intuitions: Toward an evolutionary ethics. *Journal of Personality and Social Psychology*, *64*, 467–478.

Spranca, M., Minsk, E., & Baron, J. (1991). Omission and commission in judgment and choice. *Journal of Experimental Social Psychology*, *27*, 76–105.

Starcke, K., Ludwig, A., & Brand, M. (2012). Anticipatory stress interferes with utilitarian moral judgment. *Judgment and Decision Making*, *7*, 61–68.

Strohminger, N., Lewis, R.L., & Meyer, D.E. (2011). Divergent effects of different positive emotions on moral judgment. *Cognition*, *119*, 295–300.

Suter, R.S., & Hertwig, R. (2011). Time and moral judgment. *Cognition*, *119*, 454–458.

Trémolière, B., & Bonnefon, J.-F. (2014). Efficient kill–save ratios ease up the cognitive demands on counterintuitive moral utilitarianism. *Personality and Social Psychology Bulletin*, *40*, 923–930.

Valdesolo, P., & DeSteno, D. (2006). Manipulations of emotional context shape moral judgment. *Psychological Science*, *17*, 476–477.

van den Bos, K., Müller, P.A., & Damen, T. (2011). A behavioral disinhibition hypothesis of interventions in moral dilemmas. *Emotion Review*, *3*, 281–283.

Wittgenstein, L. (1953). *Philosophische Untersuchungen*. Oxford: Blackwell.

# PART II
# Moral Aspects of Interpersonal Behavior

# 7

# A RELATIONAL PERSPECTIVE OF SOCIAL INFLUENCE ON MORAL ISSUES

*Jeffry A. Simpson, Allison K. Farrell, and Emma Marshall*

*Making social judgments and deciding how to act on our deepest moral convictions and virtues rarely occurs in a vacuum; these events typically transpire within close relationships, especially those with romantic partners. In this chapter, we discuss why it is important—indeed essential—to adopt a relational perspective to fully comprehend when, how, and why individuals are (or are not) influenced by their romantic partners when moral issues tied to core moral virtues arise. Working with Haidt's (2001) social intuitionist model of moral judgment, we discuss a few of the relationship-relevant variables that may moderate the strength of influence between partners when such issues are discussed. We then focus on what should happen when romantic partners hold different amounts of power within their relationship. Our primary focus is on what Haidt calls "interpersonal effects"—instances in which an individual's intuition, judgment, and reasoning regarding a specific moral issue should be more versus less strongly influenced by his or her partner's intuition, judgment, and reasoning on that issue.*

Imagine the following event: You and your romantic partner are watching the nightly news on television. You see a story about people who may have indirect ties to Al Qaida being detained by the US government for very long periods of time in what appear to be harsh conditions without normal due process. You feel strongly that it is not fair for any government to detain anyone without good evidence and proper due process, and you also worry about the harm being done to the detainees. Your partner, however, thinks this is fine, particularly given the need to protect the US in light of current terrorist threats around the world. After the story ends, you and your partner discuss whether these people should continue to be detained under these conditions. You mention the importance of fairness, due process, and avoiding unnecessary harm, but your partner stands firm in her belief that legitimate governments must take a hard stance with respect to potential terrorists. At the end of the discussion, you begin to agree with your partner without really knowing why, and you slide your opinion on the matter closer to your partner's position.

Early psychological theorists on moral thinking and development, such as Piaget (1932) and Kohlberg (1969), conceptualized morality as an effortful cognitive process that, although shaped by cultural norms, tends to occur in the absence of immediate interpersonal influences. However, situations such as the one just described suggest that these processes do not occur in a vacuum, and that other people can influence our moral thinking without us engaging in elaborate thinking. The "new synthesis" in moral psychology, which has risen in prominence during the past two decades, adopts a different perspective: Much moral thinking is an automatic, emotionally driven process that often is biased by the social context in which judgments are taking place (Haidt, 2008). As Rai and Fiske (2011) assert, "moral intuitions are defined by the particular types of social relationships in which they occur" (p. 57).

Despite the theoretical importance of social relationships on moral intuitions, judgments, and thinking, little research has examined how interpersonal relationships actually impact these variables. Haidt's (2001) social intuitionist model proposes some interpersonal links through which interaction partners may directly or indirectly influence each other's moral judgments and reasoning, but little research has tested these links and what strengthens or weakens them. In this chapter, we use relationship science to suggest when, and to what extent, romantic partners are likely to influence one another when discussing moral issues.

The chapter is divided into three sections. In the first section, we describe Haidt's (2001) social intuitionist model (SIM) of moral judgment and the five "moral foundations" that constitute the major content areas underlying moral judgments. In addition, we briefly review the rather limited research that has tested the interpersonal links (social and reasoned persuasion) contained in Haidt's model. In the second section, we discuss what a relational perspective on this model—especially the interpersonal links—can contribute to the morality field. We focus on romantic relationships because they are a social context in which a great deal of important persuasion can and often does occur on a daily basis. In particular, we discuss how certain relationship-relevant variables might moderate the strength of influence that an "actor" (one partner in a relationship) has on his or her "partner" (the other partner in a relationship) within the social intuitionist model framework. We also showcase how one major relationship variable—the amount of power each partner has in a relationship—can be applied to extend our understanding of when, how, and why certain individuals are more versus less influenced by their partners. In the final section, we offer concluding comments and further ideas for future research.

## The Social Intuitionist Model and Moral Foundations

According to Haidt's (2001) social intuitionist model (SIM) of moral judgment, moral judgments and decisions frequently occur in interpersonal contexts. Thus, according to Haidt, moral judgment is an inherently interpersonal process. The SIM, which is shown in Figure 7.1, claims that *eliciting situations* (e.g., watching a TV news story about long detentions of suspected terrorists) evoke automatic *intuitions* akin to gut-level sentiments within an individual (Person A). These intuitions are experienced as diffuse feelings that fall somewhere on a good-to-bad dimension regarding the eliciting situation. Intuitions are perceived very quickly, automatically, and with little or no deliberate or rational thinking. Once activated, they affect the individual's *judgment* of the eliciting situation, which often is expressed in observable verbal or nonverbal behavior. Following the expression of the judgment, individuals often engage in post hoc reasoning to support their judgment. During this reasoning process, individuals attempt to explain, justify, or make sense of their intuition and judgment.[1]

What makes this model dyadic are the pathways that connect Person A's judgment and reasoning to Person B's intuition, judgment, and reasoning about the eliciting situation, and vice versa. There are two sets of interpersonal pathways through which social influence can occur. *Reasoned persuasion*, represented by paths $A_1$ and $A_2$ in Figure 7.1, runs from one individual's explicit reasoning to the other's intuition. Reasoned persuasion occurs when Persons A and B directly communicate the reason(s) for their judgments to one another, which may then

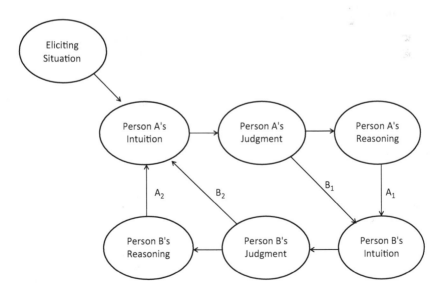

**FIGURE 7.1** Adapted version of Haidt's (2001) social intuitionist model of social judgment.

influence each other's intuitions. *Social persuasion*, represented by paths $B_1$ and $B_2$ in Figure 7.1, runs from one individual's judgment of the eliciting situation to the other's intuition. Social persuasion occurs when one person conforms to the other's judgment, even if there are no attempts to change opinions (or virtues) about the eliciting situation. Both sets of pathways (reasoned and social) suggest that individuals can and sometimes do influence each other's intuitions once an eliciting situation launches the process depicted in Figure 7.1.

Which variables are the wellspring of the intuitions, judgments, and reasoning that guide how partners perceive and evaluate specific moral issues? According to Haidt and Joseph (2004), there are six moral foundations, which are mental modules that reflect a person's core virtues: (1) *care/harm* (the extent to which an individual values cherishing and protecting other people); (2) *fairness/cheating* (the extent to which an individual values fair, equal, and just treatment of others); (3) *loyalty/ betrayal* (the extent to which an individual values standing up for his or her group, family, or nation [the ingroup]); (4) *authority/subversion* (the extent to which an individual values respect for legitimate authority and obeying social traditions); (5) *sanctity/degradation* (the extent to which an individual values decency and purity, and abhors disgusting things or actions); and (6) *liberty/oppression* (the extent to which an individual values freedom and loathes tyranny). Eliciting situations automatically activate one or more of these basic virtues in the minds of perceivers, which then rapidly and automatically affect their intuitions (see Figure 7.1).

## Research Testing the Reasoned and Social Persuasion Links in the Social Intuitionist Model

What has research revealed about the social intuitionist model, especially in the context of relationships? Although the SIM was published 14 years ago, there has been surprisingly little research examining the social components of the model (see the A and B paths in Figure 7.1). The literature still largely ignores the interpersonal contexts in which moral judgments and reasoning are made (Ellemers, Pagliaro, & Barreto, 2013; Haidt, 2013; Rai & Fiske, 2011). There is some support for these interpersonal effects in studies examining employee–employer/ organization and ingroup contexts (e.g., Ellemers et al., 2013; Hornsey, Majkut, Terry, & McKimmie, 2003; Kundu & Cummins, 2013). Kundu and Cummins (2013), for example, used the Asch conformity paradigm and found that moral judgments made by confederates influenced participants' own judgments. More specifically, when confederates judged an impermissible moral transgression as permissible, participants did as well, whereas those in the control group (who were not exposed to social influences) did not. Likewise, participants were more likely to judge a permissible moral judgment as impermissible if they were exposed to a confederate who did so. To the best of our knowledge, however, no research to date has tested for similar effects in intimate relationships.

## Expanding the Social Intuitionist Model: A Relational Perspective

The SIM has been highly influential in the field of morality, and it is especially appealing to social psychologists because of its inherently dyadic nature, given that the thoughts, feelings, and behaviors of one interaction partner can influence the other partner (and vice versa) at different specific stages of the model. However, the model says very little about whom the interaction partners are or what can and should affect the strength of the interpersonal paths. We believe that adopting a relational perspective can (1) provide deeper insights into when and how these interpersonal influences occur and (2) expand the SIM in some important ways.

To begin with, who are the interaction partners? Most individuals are unlikely to discuss moral issues with strangers or casual acquaintances on a regular basis. Instead, interaction partners are likely to be close relationship partners—family members, friends, and romantic partners. Closeness is defined as the frequency, diversity, duration, and strength of influence between two people (Berscheid, Snyder, & Omoto, 1989). In addition, self-disclosure of one's core beliefs and values is critical to the development and maintenance of close relationships (Reis & Shaver, 1988), so close relationship partners should be more inclined to discuss moral issues when eliciting situations arise, especially if they provide moral tests or moral opportunities for one or both partners (see Miller & Monin, this volume).

Research examining morally relevant behavior (as opposed to moral intuition, judgment, or reasoning outlined in the SIM) also suggests that close relationship partners should often play an important role in shaping moral judgments. Gino and Galinsky (2012), for example, found that when participants felt psychologically close to a person who acted in a selfish manner, they saw the behavior as less unethical or morally inappropriate (which, in turn, led them to behave in a similar manner). In sum, intimate partners—arguably those who are closest to us psychologically—should have the capacity to exert strong influence on our moral intuitions, judgments, and reasoning (see also Forgas, Jussim, & Van Lange, this volume).

## Relational Influences in the Social Intuitionist Model

To the extent that close relationship partners tend to be the most frequent and impactful interaction partners, we can expand the SIM by turning to relationship science for variables that are likely to govern whether and the degree to which partners influence one another once an eliciting situation has occurred.

Figure 7.2 shows how theories, models, and recent findings in relationship science can be incorporated into the social intuitionist model to clarify when interpersonal influences should—and should not—occur, depending on the perceptions and attributes of relationship partners (see the bottom half of Figure 7.2).

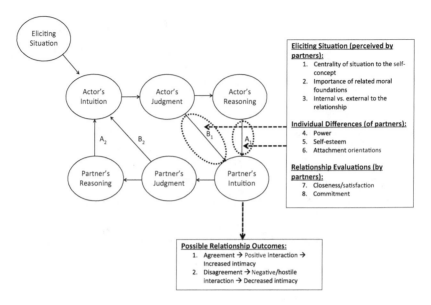

**FIGURE 7.2** Possible moderating factors of Haidt's (2001) interpersonal pathways in a relational context.

To keep the model and examples easier to follow, we focus on the perceptions/ attributes of *partners* (the person initially reacting to the judgments and reasoning of an actor following an eliciting situation) rather than both actors and partners, even though actor perceptions/attributes should also affect the interpersonal influence processes we discuss. In addition, we highlight only some of the possible moderating effects of certain relationship-relevant variables on only the actor-to-partner interpersonal pathways (Paths $A_1$ and $B_1$ in Figure 7.2) to keep the model and examples manageable.

As shown in Figure 7.2, certain perceptions and attributes of the partner should affect the strength of the *social persuasion path* (the actor's judgment to partner's intuition) and the *reasoned persuasion path* (the actor's reasoning to the partner's intuition), both of which appear on the right side of Figure 7.2. At the start of this process, the way in which partners perceive an eliciting situation (e.g., the terrorist detention news story) can affect how influential the actor is likely to be. If the eliciting situation is central to the identity or self-concept of the partner; if it is associated with important, self-defining virtues the partner cherishes (e.g., the paramount importance of fairness and harm-avoidance in all contexts); or if it stems from sources internal to the relationship (e.g., the actor aggravates the eliciting situation by denigrating the partner's concerns about fairness and harm-avoidance), the actor's judgment and reasoning should have a relatively weaker effect on the partner's intuition, judgment, and reasoning.

Certain personal attributes of the partner might also affect how persuasive the actor is. If, for instance, the partner has less power in the relationship, low self-esteem, or is insecurely attached, he or she may be more vulnerable to social or reasoned persuasion from the actor. As a rule, individuals who lack power (Galinsky, Rucker, & Magee, 2015), have lower self-esteem (Murray, Holmes, & Collins, 2006), or are more insecurely attached (Mikulincer & Shaver, 2007) should be more susceptible to influence from their partners given their "one-down" position in relationships, and this may be especially true when they are satisfied with or strongly committed to their partners/relationships. To illustrate, we expand on insecure attachment, which has received recent theoretical (Shaver & Mikulincer, 2012) and empirical (Koleva, Selterman, Iyer, Ditto, & Graham, 2014) coverage in the moral literature. Koleva et al. (2014) found that greater attachment avoidance (i.e., the tendency to value independence, autonomy, and control in close relationships) was associated with *weaker* moral concerns about the moral foundations of harm and unfairness, whereas greater attachment anxiety (i.e., the tendency to worry about relationship loss and seek greater security) was associated with *stronger* moral concerns about harm, unfairness, and impurity. Given these findings, it is likely that an actor's judgment or reasoning on moral issues related to harm, unfairness, and impurity should have a stronger impact on a partner's intuitions if the partner is anxiously attached, but the actor should have a weaker impact on a partner's intuitions if the partner is avoidantly attached.

Another possible set of relationship-relevant moderators is the partner's perceptions and evaluations of the relationship. To the extent that a partner feels very close to the actor, is highly satisfied with the relationship, or is strongly committed to it, actors should be able to exert greater influence on their partners. Gino and Galinsky (2012), for instance, found that individuals were more likely to adopt immoral behaviors and make lenient moral judgments about those behaviors when they were displayed by someone to whom they felt close. The relationship effectively "overrode" individuals' own moral compasses. Returning to our running example, if you feel very close to your mate, you should find his or her intuition, judgment, and reasoning about the long-term detention of possible terrorists relatively more compelling and influential, even if they go against your own virtues and values.

Furthermore, the way in which interpersonal influence is communicated and carried out may also affect relationship outcomes (see the bottom of Figure 7.2). If, for example, an actor and partner agree about how to view and evaluate an eliciting situation, they should have a more positive interaction, which may increase feelings of intimacy in both dyad members. According to Reis and Shaver (1988), feelings of intimacy are generated when one dyad member discloses a personally important or revealing piece of information; the "responding" partner then conveys understanding, validation, and caring toward the disclosing partner; and the disclosing partner then perceives these well-intentioned behaviors accurately.

Discussions that center on important moral issues ought to be good contexts in which these types of discussions often occur. If, however, the actor and partner sharply disagree about how to view or evaluate the eliciting situation, this may result in a highly negative interaction, which could decrease feelings of intimacy in both dyad members. Consistent with these ideas, Krebs and colleagues (2002) found that partners who had different moral perspectives were less likely to reach mutual resolutions during their interpersonal moral conflicts.

## Social Power Influences in the Social Intuitionist Model

We now explain in greater detail how one major relationship variable—differences in power within a relationship—may generate specific patterns of interpersonal influence effects within the social intuitionist model. One of the most fundamental concepts in relationship science is power (Huston, 1983; Simpson, Farrell, Oriña, & Rothman, 2015), which can be measured with the Relationship Power Inventory (Farrell, Simpson, & Rothman, in press). Stable differences in power can develop within a relationship for several reasons, such as one partner being perceived as having greater authority and the right to have more control, or when chronic asymmetries in dependence exist between partners (e.g., when one individual relies much more on the other than vice versa to obtain rewards or avoid punishments in the relationship; Rollins & Bahr, 1976; Thibaut & Kelley, 1959; see also Galinsky & Lee, this volume). Indeed, when one dyad member has greater control over the ultimate fate (i.e., good or bad outcomes) of the other across many situations, the more powerful person tends to adopt an agentic orientation and exert greater influence on the less powerful partner, especially when important decisions are being made in the relationship (Kirchler, 1995; Rucker, Galinsky, & Dubois, 2012). If, for instance, your partner has more power than you do, the strength of the interpersonal pathways leading from your mate to you should be greater than the corresponding pathways leading from you back to your mate. These predicted effects are shown in Figure 7.3 by the thicker lines running from the more powerful person's judgment and reasoning to the less powerful person's intuition (paths $A_1$ and $B_1$ on the right side) compared to the reverse paths (paths $A_2$ and $B_2$ on the left side).

The more powerful person should also have greater capacity to change the intuitions, judgments, and perhaps even the moral virtues of the less powerful person over time, especially if a couple has recurring discussions about the eliciting situation. Returning again to our example, to the extent that you have less power in the relationship and want to avoid conflicts with your higher-power partner, you may routinely comply with—and eventually come to agree with—the judgment and reasoning that your partner expresses about the government having legitimate authority to detain suspected terrorists without due process. Indeed, with the passage of time, you may gradually reduce the importance you place on the virtues of fairness and harm-avoidance, or you may increase the importance

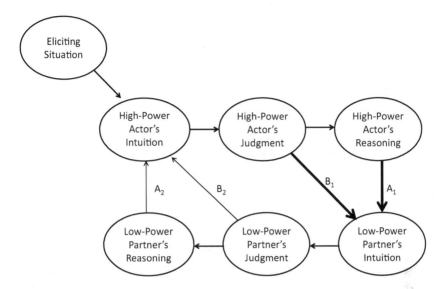

**FIGURE 7.3** Possible effects of within-relationship power differences on Haidt's (2001) social intuitionist model of social judgment.

of the virtues your partner deems most important: respect for authority and supporting the ingroup.

Differences in power may have some of the strongest effects on moral judgment and decision making when an outcome is important to the higher-power partner. Under these circumstances, the lower-power partner may habitually comply with—and eventually internalize—the intuitions, judgments, and reasoning of the higher-power partner with respect to the eliciting situation. There may be circumstances, however, when the higher-power partner considers and supports the intuitions, judgments, and virtues of the lower-power partner, even if the two partners disagree.

Unlike power differences between strangers or people who have clearly delineated role relationships (such as supervisor/supervisee and teacher/student), most romantic relationship partners are committed to each other for more than merely structural, role-governed reasons. Many partners are also committed for personal and/or moral reasons (Johnson, 1991). In addition, unlike relationships between total strangers or people involved in purely role or task-based relationships, romantic partners typically want to maintain their relationship over time. To do so, they establish some communal sharing rules (Fiske, 1992) and work to achieve long-term equity so their relationship will be happier and more stable in the long run (Walster, Berscheid, & Walster, 1973).

These unique aspects of romantic relationships give lower-power romantic partners somewhat greater potential to influence their higher-power partners than is true of lower-power partners in other types of relationships (Simpson et al., 2015). One circumstance in which higher-power relationship partners may be influenced by their less powerful partners is when the lower-power partner makes pleas to get their way on certain issues, perhaps by invoking the importance of fairness in the relationship or clarifying how important the relationship is to the higher-power partner (Oriña, Wood, & Simpson, 2002). Other circumstances may include situations in which the higher-power partner feels especially close to the lower-power partner, has low self-esteem, or truly relies on the lower-power partner for resources or outcomes that only he or she can provide.

Lower-power partners may also pay closer attention to the intuitions, judgments, reasoning, and virtues of their higher-power partners, given their greater outcome dependence in the relationship (Dépret & Fiske, 1993). If so, the lower-power partner may hold more accurate perceptions of the higher-power partner's intuitions, judgments, and reasoning, allowing the lower-power partner to behave more consistently with the intuitions, judgments, reasoning, or virtues held by the higher-power partner. One positive consequence of this is that interactions may go more smoothly. The higher-power partner, however, is likely to have less accurate perceptions of the lower-power partner's intuitions, judgments, reasoning, and virtues, which could lead higher-power partners to believe they are being "responsive" to their lower-power partner when, in fact, they are not. This could destabilize interactions and eventually harm the relationship.

In sum, patterns of social judgment and decision making on moral issues should depend on which partner in a relationship holds greater power, with the lower-power person often complying with—and perhaps eventually internalizing—the higher-power partner's intuitions, judgments, reasoning, and virtues with respect to certain moral issues, especially when a decision or outcome is important to the higher-power partner. That being said, many of the relational variables listed in Figure 7.2 are likely to moderate the strength of these interpersonal influence pathways.

## Conclusions

This chapter makes several contributions to the existing literature. First, it reveals how moral judgments can be informed by recent relationship theories, models, constructs, and findings, especially those pertaining to differences in power between partners in established romantic relationships. As we have shown, the application of these guiding principles permits one to generate novel predictions that cannot be derived without adopting a relational view of dyadic influence as it pertains to moral issues. For example, individuals who wield more power in a relationship should be less swayed by their partner's intuitions, judgments, and reasoning when discussing issues grounded in their core moral virtues. Conversely, those who have less power should be more susceptible to influence, which may be witnessed in changing their virtues to be more in line with those of their higher-power partner or avoiding eliciting situations where they may feel pressure to comply with their partner's desires, especially when they privately hold a different position on the issue.

Second, we suggest that the processes through which partners form and discuss moral judgments may have important consequences for the relationship. Growing more similar in moral judgments and beliefs about the importance of specific virtues may bring relationship partners closer and smooth their interactions. Conversely, continued disagreements about moral judgments and reasoning could elicit criticism, defensiveness, and heated interactions, all of which could destabilize the relationship. Moreover, if partners are unaware of each other's moral beliefs or virtues, they may inadvertently insult one another or be seen as being unresponsive. Focusing greater theoretical and empirical attention on how couples discuss important moral issues/dilemmas may also provide relationships researchers with new insights into when, how, and why relationships grow or fail.

In conclusion, few of our most important social judgments and decisions happen in social isolation; as Haidt (2001) and Rai and Fiske (2011) indicate, they almost always occur in interpersonal contexts. This makes the relative absence of empirical research on how relationship partners can and do affect one another on moral issues all the more surprising. A great deal can be learned by considering what we currently know about relationships, by measuring and modeling the intuitions, judgments, reasoning, and core virtues of *both* relationship partners as they actively make important judgments and decisions, and by measuring the *perceptions* that one partner has of the other on these key dimensions. Our hope is that this chapter will facilitate the integration of the morality and relationships literatures so we can better understand and generate new hypotheses with respect to these important topics.

## Note

1 Paxton and Greene (2010) claim that moral reasoning affects moral judgments by counteracting automatic processing tendencies that may bias judgments. Specifically, they suggest that judgments involving rights and duties occur primarily through intuition processes, whereas utilitarian judgments associated with promoting "the greater good" tend to be influenced by controlled reasoning. Similar patterns of relational thinking and modeling can also be applied to this alternative model.

## References

Berscheid, E., Snyder, M., & Omoto, A.M. (1989). The Relationship Closeness Inventory: Assessing the closeness of interpersonal relationships. *Journal of Personality and Social Psychology, 57*, 792.

Dépret, E.F., & Fiske, S.T. (1993). Social cognition and power: Some cognitive consequences of social structure as a source of control deprivation. In G. Weary, F. Gleicher, & K. Marsh (Eds.), *Control motivation and social cognition* (pp. 176–202). New York: Springer-Verlag.

Ellemers, N., Pagliaro, S., & Barreto, M. (2013). Morality and behavioural regulation in groups: A social identity approach. *European Review of Social Psychology, 24*, 160–193.

Farrell, A.K., Simpson, J.A., & Rothman, A.J. (in press). The Relationship Power Inventory (RPI): Development and validation. *Personal Relationships.*

Fiske, A.P. (1992). The four elementary forms of sociality: Framework for a unified theory of social relations. *Psychological Review, 99*, 689–723.

Galinsky, A.D., Rucker, D.D., & Magee, J.C. (2015). Power: Past findings, present considerations, and future directions. In M. Mikulincer, P.R. Shaver, J.A. Simpson, & J.F. Dovidio (Eds.), *APA handbook of personality and social psychology: Vol. 3. Interpersonal relations* (pp. 421–460). Washington, DC: American Psychological Association.

Gino, F., & Galinsky, A.D. (2012). Vicarious dishonesty: When psychological closeness creates distance from one's moral compass. *Organizational Behavior and Human Decision Processes, 119*, 15–26.

Haidt, J. (2001). The emotional dog and its rational tail: A social intuitionist approach to moral judgment. *Psychological Review, 108*, 814–834.

Haidt, J. (2008). Morality. *Perspectives on Psychological Science, 3*, 65–72.

Haidt, J. (2013). Moral psychology for the twenty-first century. *Journal of Moral Education, 42*, 281–297.

Haidt, J., & Joseph, C. (2004). Intuitive ethics: How innately prepared intuitions generate culturally variable virtues. *Daedalus, 133*, 55–66.

Hornsey, M., Majkut, L., Terry, D.J., & McKimmie, B.M. (2003). On being loud and proud: Non-conformity and counter-conformity to group norms. *British Journal of Social Psychology, 42*, 319–335.

Huston, T.L. (1983). Power. In H.H. Kelley et al. (Eds.), *Close relationships* (pp. 169–219). New York: W.H. Freeman.

Johnson, M.P. (1991). Commitment to personal relationships. In W.H. Jones & D. Perlman (Eds.), *Advances in personal relationships* (Vol. 3, pp. 117–143). London: Jessica Kingsley.

Kirchler, E. (1995). Studying economic decisions within private households: A critical review and design for a couple experiences diary. *Journal of Economic Psychology, 16*, 393–416.

Kohlberg, L. (1969). *Stage and sequence: The cognitive-developmental approach to socialization* (pp. 347–480). New York: Rand McNally.

Koleva, S., Selterman, D., Iyer, R., Ditto, P., & Graham, J. (2014). The moral compass of insecurity: Anxious and avoidant attachment predict moral judgment. *Social Psychology and Personality Science, 5*, 185–194.

Krebs, D.L., Denton, K., Wark, G., Couch, R., Racine, T., & Krebs, D.L. (2002). Interpersonal moral conflicts between couples: Effects of type of dilemma, role, and partner's judgments on level of moral reasoning and probability of resolution. *Journal of Adult Development, 9*, 307–316.

Kundu, P., & Cummins, D.D. (2013). Morality and conformity: The Asch paradigm applied to moral decisions. *Social Influence, 8*, 268–279.

Mikulincer, M., & Shaver, P.R. (2007). *Attachment in adulthood: Structure, dynamics, and change.* New York: Guilford Press.

Murray, S.L., Holmes, J.G., & Collins, N.L. (2006). Optimizing assurance: The risk regulation system in relationships. *Psychological Bulletin, 132*, 641–666.

Oriña, M.M., Wood, W., & Simpson, J.A. (2002). Strategies of influence in close relationships. *Journal of Experimental Social Psychology, 38*, 459–472.

Paxton, J., & Greene, J. (2010). Moral reasoning: Hints and allegations. *Topics in Cognitive Science, 2*, 511–527.

Piaget, J. (1932). *Le jugement moral chez l'enfant*. Paris: F. Alcan.

Rai, T.S., & Fiske, A.P. (2011). Moral psychology is relationship regulation: Moral motives for unity, hierarchy, equality, and proportionality. *Psychological Review, 118*, 57–75.

Reis, H.T., & Shaver, P. (1988). Intimacy as an interpersonal process. In S. Duck (Ed.), *Handbook of personal relationships: Theory, research and interventions* (pp. 367–389). New York: John Wiley & Sons.

Rollins, B.C., & Bahr, S.J. (1976). A theory of power relationships in marriage. *Journal of Marriage and the Family, 38*(4), 619–626.

Rucker, D.D., Galinsky, A.D., & Dubois, D. (2012). Power and consumer behavior: How power shapes who and what consumers value. *Journal of Consumer Psychology, 22*, 352–368.

Shaver, P.R., & Mikulincer, M. (2012). An attachment perspective on morality: Strengthening authentic forms of moral decision making. In M. Mikulincer & P.R. Shaver (Eds.), *The social psychology of morality: Exploring the causes of good and evil* (pp. 257–274). Washington, DC: American Psychological Association.

Simpson, J.A., Farrell, A.K., Oriña, M.M., & Rothman, A.J. (2015). Power and social influence in relationships. In M. Mikulincer, P.R. Shaver, J.A. Simpson, & J.F. Dovidio (Eds.), *APA handbook of personality and social psychology: Vol. 3. Interpersonal relations* (pp. 393–420). Washington, DC: American Psychological Association.

Thibaut, J.W., & Kelley, H.H. (1959). *The social psychology of groups*. New York: Wiley.

Walster, E., Berscheid, E., & Walster, G.W. (1973). New directions in equity research. *Journal of Personality and Social Psychology, 25*, 151–176.

# 8

# WHEN PERSPECTIVE-TAKERS TURN UNETHICAL

*Adam D. Galinsky and Alice J. Lee*

Perspective-taking—the process of actively considering others' psychological experiences—has long been recognized as an invaluable tool for navigating one's social world, acting as the glue that binds and holds individuals together. Voluminous research consistently suggests that perspective-taking leads to prosocial and moral outcomes (Batson, 1994; Batson & Moran, 1999; Cialdini, Brown, Lewis, Luce, & Neuberg, 1997; Coke, Batson, & McDavis, 1978; Eisenberg & Miller, 1987; see also Crockett; Graziano & Schroeder; and Simpson, Farrell, & Marshall, this volume). People that take the perspective of others, compared to those that do not, are more likely to help others in need (Batson et al., 1991; Batson, 1994; Coke et al., 1978; Dovidio, Allen, & Schroeder, 1990), less likely to express stereotypes (Galinsky & Moskowitz, 2000), have less egocentric biases (Savitsky, Van Boven, Epley, & Wight, 2005; Wade-Benzoni, Tenbrunsel, & Bazerman, 1996), engage in less intergroup prejudice (Batson, Early, & Salvarani, 1997; Dovidio et al., 2004; Galinsky & Ku, 2004; Todd, Bodenhausen, Richeson, & Galinsky, 2011), and make more objective judgments of fairness (Epley, Caruso, & Bazerman, 2006). Perspective-taking has also been shown to expand the pie of resources and create economic value for the self *and* others (Galinsky, Maddux, Gilin, & White, 2008). The absence of perspective-taking, in contrast, has been linked to aggressive behavior that exacerbates interpersonal conflicts and leads to detrimental consequences in social interactions (Richardson, Hammock, Smith, Gardner, & Signo, 1994).

Despite this, wealth of research that documents the interpersonal benefits of perspective-taking, we propose that perspective-taking may not always build a royal road to morality. In fact, perspective-taking, which acts as the glue that holds individuals together in a cooperative context, can turn into gasoline that inflames an already fiery conflict when applied to a competitive context. Through a review of relevant studies, we demonstrate that perspective-taking acts as a relational amplifier that intensifies existing cooperative or competitive tendencies and can turn people into immoral antagonists.

## Perspective-Taking as *Glue* That Binds People Together in *Cooperative/Neutral* Contexts

### Empathy

We first examine how perspective-taking induces interpersonal benefits in a cooperative interaction by reviewing a number of key studies within the scope of two related but distinct dimensions: *empathy* and *self-other overlap*. Much of the earlier research on perspective-taking has focused on empathy—the ability to connect emotionally with another individual when witnessing their suffering (Batson, 1991; Batson, Fultz, & Schoenrade, 1987; Davis, 1994; Galinsky et al., 2008). Several empirical studies demonstrate that when individuals take the perspective of a target by imagining how the target is affected by his or her circumstance, they are more likely to express empathic concerns toward the target and, in turn, feel stronger motives to help the person in need (Batson, Early, and Salvarani, 1997; Coke et al., 1978; see also Forgas, this volume). For example, in one study conducted by Batson, Early, and Salvarani (1997), participants listened to a (bogus) pilot radio interview with a young woman named Katie Banks who lost her parents in a car accident and is struggling to stay in school while taking care of her younger siblings. Participants were assigned to one of three perspective-taking conditions. One-third were instructed to imagine how Katie feels (*imagine-other condition*); one-third to imagine how they would feel if they were in Katie's situation (*imagine-self condition*); and one-third to listen to the tape in an objective and detached manner (*objective condition*). The results showed that participants in the perspective-taking conditions (*imagine-other* and *imagine-self*) overall expressed more empathy and a greater motivation to help others compared to those in the objective condition. It is also interesting to note that the participants who imagined how Katie felt (*imagine-other condition*) reported the nature of their distress as more empathic distress (e.g., *sympathetic, softhearted, compassionate, tender, moved*), whereas the participants who imagined how they would feel in Katie's situation reported the nature of their distress as a combination of both empathic and personal distress (e.g., *alarmed, grieved, troubled, distressed, upset, disturbed, worried, perturbed*). In other words, focusing on the need of others may induce relatively pure altruistic motivation, whereas focusing on your own imagined suffering may evoke egoistic motivation to alleviate your own distress (Cialdini et al., 1987; Piliavin, Dovidio, Gaertner, & Clark, 1981). Regardless of the emotional source of the motivation, however, it is evident that perspective-taking leads one to feel more empathy and distress, and in turn, a greater motivation to help the counterpart in need.

While this study is helpful in understanding how taking the perspective of another evokes empathic motives for others in need, it does not directly show how empathy-aroused altruism translates into greater interpersonal cooperation. Batson and Moran's (1999) prisoner's dilemma study fills this gap by demonstrating how perspective-taking leads to empathy-induced altruism and motivates stronger social coordination. In this study, undergraduates participated in a one-trial prisoner's dilemma, where empathy for the target was manipulated through perspective-taking. Participants in the high-empathy condition were instructed to read an ostensible note—which described the woman's upsetting breakup with her long-term boyfriend—from a distressed woman's perspective, whereas participants in the low-empathy condition were instructed to remain objective, and participants in the control condition received no note at all. As a result, those who empathized with the distressful circumstances of the woman were more likely to cooperate with her in a subsequent prisoner's dilemma game due to empathy-induced altruistic motivations compared to those who did not engage in perspective-taking. Similar to the empirical findings of Batson, Early, and Salvarani (1997), the results of Batson and Moran (1999) demonstrate how perspective-taking works as a relational amplifier on social behavior, producing prosocial benefits—even if egoistically motivated—by activating empathy-induced altruism in cooperative interpersonal relations.

## Self-Other Overlap

More recently, researchers have examined perspective-taking from a self-other overlap context (e.g., Davis, Conklin, Smith, & Luce, 1996; Maner et al., 2002). The self-other overlap (Davis et al., 1996), simply understood as the application of the self to the other, leads people to share common values, beliefs, and morals (Turner, 1987), and has been demonstrated to create synchrony and foster social bonds by reducing social biases (Galinsky, Ku, & Wang, 2005). Many studies have shown that after perspective-taking, there is a greater self-target overlap such that the representation of the target comes to resemble that of the perspective-taker, and the perspective-taker ascribes the target's traits to be more "self-like" (Davis et al., 1996). As such, perspective-taking leads to a more personalized approach to the target, which can effectively reduce the accessibility and expression of stereotypes when forming impressions of the target (Brewer, 1996).

In accordance with this reasoning, Galinsky and Moskowitz (2000) conducted a study that investigated the role of perspective-taking in debiasing social thought, in which they had undergraduate students write a narrative essay about a day in the life of an elderly man—a member of a salient stereotyped group—in a photograph (Macrae, Bodenhausen, Milne, & Jetten, 1994). The participants were assigned to three conditions: *perspective-taking, stereotype suppression,* and *control.* Participants in the *perspective-taking* condition were told to take the perspective of the individual in the photograph; participants in the *stereotype suppression* condition were instructed to suppress any stereotypic preconceptions that might bias their writing; and participants in the *control* condition were given no explicit instructions on writing their narrative essays. Prior to writing the narrative essays about a day in the life of the elderly man, participants were asked to rate themselves according to 90 heterogeneous traits (Smith & Henry, 1996) to measure their tendency to stereotype. When participants were asked to rate general characteristics of the elderly with the same 90 traits after completing the essay task, perspective-takers rated the elderly less stereotypically and expressed greater overlap between representations of the self and representations of the elderly than did participants in the other two conditions. Furthermore, the results demonstrated that the perspective-taker's self-descriptive traits ascribed to the target extended to the social group that the target represented as well.

It is important to note that empathy-induced altruism and self-other overlap—while often used interchangeably—are distinct paths to the intersecting destination of closer social bonds. One may feel empathy-induced altruism toward another by taking their perspective without necessarily finding an overlap between the self and the target; and one can share common beliefs with the target without feeling empathy toward them. At the same time, empathy can lead to reduced social biases. For example, Batson, Polycarpou et al. (1997) showed that empathy can lead to more positive attitudes toward a stigmatized group by taking the perspective of a member of the group. In two separate studies, participants listened to a brief (bogus) broadcast pilot-testing project involving an interview of a young woman with AIDS in one study, and an interview of a homeless man in another study. In both studies, the authors manipulated the level of empathy for the member of the stigmatized group (*high vs. low*) and the member's responsibility for their adversity (*responsible vs. not responsible*).

Empathy was manipulated by either instructing participants to imagine how the victim feels in his or her situation (*high empathy*) or instructing participants to take an objective perspective toward the situation (*low empathy*). The member's responsibility was manipulated through the content of the interview that the participants listened to. The results showed that taking the perspective of a member of a stigmatized group led to more positive feelings toward the victim, regardless of whether the victim was responsible for the plight. Furthermore, these empathically evoked positive feelings toward the stigmatized individual led to more positive attitudes toward the stigmatized group as a whole.

As supported by these studies, it is evident how perspective-taking can lead to stronger social bonds—through empathy-induced altruistic motives and a heightened sense of self-other overlap—in a neutral or cooperative context. Perspective-taking elicits prosocial motivation by arousing empathy toward others and debiasing social thoughts, which can go a long way in assuaging interpersonal conflicts and promoting stronger social bonds (see also Graziano & Schroeder; Miller & Monin; and Simpson et al., this volume). However, the consequence of perspective-taking in a competitive, as opposed to a cooperative, context is not as apparent from the examples presented earlier. From sports games to politics and business rivalries, competition is ubiquitous in our daily lives. In the next section, we examine how, in a competitive context, perspective-taking can turn into gasoline that inflames an already heated competitive tendency.

## Perspective-Taking as *Gasoline* That Tears People *Apart* in Competitive Contexts

As illustrated in the previous section, taking the perspective of another by considering their thoughts and concerns can lead to a variety of positive outcomes in social interactions. It is important to note, however, that the relational context underlying the studies reviewed thus far are of individuals and groups that work together in a neutral or cooperative manner with converging interests and goals. In fact, contrary to the widespread belief that perspective-taking leads to prosocial behavior and stronger social bonds, recent studies suggest that in a competitive context, perspective-taking can lead to antisocial behavior and exacerbate social conflicts (Babcock & Loewenstein, 1997; Bazerman & Neale, 1982; Epley et al., 2006; Messick, 1995; Okimoto & Wenzel, 2011). In this section, we review a number of studies that demonstrate how perspective-taking can amplify social conflicts in a competitive context—a situation with opposing interests and beliefs among group members—by acting as gasoline that ignites already fiery competition.

By definition, perspective-taking guides people to imagine the thoughts, beliefs, and concerns of another from the other person's point of view. When such imagination highlights the other's self-centered motive rather than a cooperative one, perspective-taking may lead people to take defensive measures on their counterparts' potential actions against them, by acting even more selfishly in response (Epley et al., 2006). More specifically, in a competitive context—similar to the game-theoretical lens of backward induction—taking the perspective of a counterpart may lead an individual to focus on the counterpart's potential self-centered motive, and in anticipation, prompt the individual to act egoistically to gain a competitive advantage (Von Neumann & Morgenstern, 2004). This is especially so in resource dilemmas where the objective is to allocate a fixed amount of resource across the involved constituents in a "fair" manner (see also Bastian & Crimston, this volume). Resource dilemmas surround our everyday lives—from simple household examples (e.g., allocating chores among family members) to more complex business initiatives (e.g., distributing corporate funds across multiple teams)—and is thus essential to understand. When the underlying context of the resource dilemma is competitive, failure to understand the opposing side's perspective can lead to an egocentric evaluation of fairness and ignite interpersonal conflict (Babcock & Loewenstein, 1997; Bazerman & Neale, 1982; Messick, 1995). Not only do people believe they deserve a larger share of available resources than others believe is fair (Babcock & Loewenstein, 1997; Leary & Forsyth, 1987; Ross & Sicoly, 1979), they believe that others are in fact unfair and self-interested in an absolute sense (Kramer, 1994), which is likely to exaggerate the impact of self-interest on others' attitudes and thoughts (Miller, 1999; Miller & Ratner, 1998).

Perspective-taking can highlight such cynical attributions that may have been ignored if people were focusing on the self. In other words, when individuals expect others to behave egoistically—as in a competitive context with conflicting interests—individuals are motivated to behave even more selfishly in return from fear of exploitation (Kelley & Stahelski, 1970; Messé & Sivacek, 1979). Such "reactive egoism" could heighten, rather than diminish, conflict and dispute in social interactions, producing the opposite result that a cooperative context would predict from perspective-taking (Kruger & Gilovich, 1999). Epley et al. (2006) demonstrated through a number of studies that even though individuals may recognize what is objectively fair from taking the perspective of others and decrease self-centered biases in judgment, such perspective-taking may ironically increase egoistic behavior in a competitive context if perspective-takers expect their counterparts to behave in an unfair and selfish manner.

Epley et al. (2006) illustrated this in the laboratory through a negotiation study over a fixed pool of chocolate chip cookies. Half of the participants in this study were instructed to take the perspective of their other group members, whereas the other half were not instructed to do so. Furthermore, half of the groups were set up to compete against each other (i.e., the instructor announced that the single best cookie baker within the group would be eligible for a monetary award), whereas the other half were arranged to cooperate with one another (i.e., the instructor announced that the group that bakes the best cookie would win the monetary award as a group). Participants were only given a small amount of premium chocolate chips for the entire group, hence, creating a potentially competitive environment to attain the limited resource to use in their baking. The effect of perspective-taking on judgment versus behavior was measured by the amount of chocolate chips each participant reported they considered fair for themselves (or each of their group members) to take versus how much they actually ended up taking.

In the competitive situation, participants in the perspective-taking condition reported that it was fair for them to take fewer chocolate chips than the self-focused participants reported, but those in the perspective-taking condition ended up taking more chocolate chips in actuality than did the self-focused participants. On the other hand, perspective-taking in the cooperative context did not lead to such discrepancy in fairness judgment versus egocentric behavior. Notably, while taking the perspective of another decreased egocentric biases in both cooperative and competitive contexts, this judgment translated into an actual decrease in egoistic behavior only in the cooperative context. Additional analyses revealed that the increase in egocentric behavior in the competitive context was a result of participants believing that their counterparts would behave selfishly and competitively, leading participants to behave even more selfishly in a reactive and defensive manner.

Not only can perspective-taking lead to egocentric behaviors in a competitive environment, it can also lead to strong retributive responses to offenders. The self-other overlap from perspective-taking that debiases social thoughts and leads to prosocial behavior in a cooperative context can, in turn, make others' normative violations more threatening to one's social self-concept when applied to a competitive context (Okimoto & Wenzel, 2010). This is especially so when one's group membership is closely tied to one's self-identity, in which case consensus violations become personal and lead to particularly strong retributive responses as a way to alleviate threats to the self-relevant identity (Kerr, Hymes, Anderson, & Weathers, 1995).

When such threats arise, the transgressor—even if technically considered an in-group member—is viewed as a competitor as his or her interest is no longer aligned with the rest of the group. In line with this argument, a study conducted by Okimoto & Wenzel (2011) examined the effects of perspective-taking on revenge. More specifically, participants took part in an online study where they engaged in a joint decision-making situation, completing a number of shared tasks with an online partner (computer controlled, in actuality). Perspective-taking was manipulated by instructing half of the participants to imagine themselves from their partner's perspective and not providing such instructions to the other half. Ambiguity was also manipulated by framing the counterpart's decision as a random allocation (*ambiguous condition*) or a deliberate decision where the counterpart actively decided not to use the random assignment function (*clear condition*).

By giving participants the opportunity to assign their partner to an unfavorable task both in repulsion and duration, the authors found that participants were more likely to exact revenge when they took the perspective of the offender and when the violation was clearly intentional. It is important to note that such retributive responses were motivated by the desire for an individual to mitigate the self-relevant identity threat caused by the transgression. This finding is consistent with previous studies that point to self-other overlap (Davis et al., 1996) as a key effect of perspective-taking. However, while most studies point to the prosocial benefits of heightened self-other overlap from taking the perspective of others (Davis et al., 1996; Galinsky et al., 2005; Maner et al., 2002), this study shows that in a competitive situation where the underlying interests of people are misaligned, perspective-taking can actually lead to negative social outcomes that tear groups further apart by amplifying ethical violations as more detrimental and a direct threat to one's self-identity.

When a social identity is directly threatened—either by a transgressor within the in-group or a harmful out-group member—perspective-taking can elicit antagonism toward the counterpart among members most concerned about securing a positive social identity (Mallett, Huntsinger, Sinclair, & Swim, 2008; Zebel, Doosje, & Spears, 2009; see also Brandt, Wetherell, & Crawford, this volume). Whereas Okimoto and Wenzel (2011) highlighted how taking the perspective of a transgressive in-group member led to retributive reactions, Tarrant, Calitri, and Weston (2012) demonstrated how such negative consequences of perspective-taking can be extended to out-group members when the individual has a high degree of identification with the in-group. In particular, Tarrant et al. (2012) showed across two studies how taking the perspective of an out-group member led individuals with strong emotional and cognitive ties to the in-group (*high identifiers*) to express more negative attitude toward out-groups.

Participants were first measured on their level of identification with their group membership (e.g., university, nationality) across two separate studies. Perspective-taking was then manipulated by instructing half of the participants to imagine the typical day in the life of an out-group member while the other half in the control group were not given such instructions. As a result, perspective-takers who were highly identified with the in-group attributed more negative traits to describe the out-group, whereas those in the control group did not. These results are in line with the aforementioned studies that demonstrate how perspective-taking can lead to negative intergroup outcomes when people have divergent interests and beliefs that places them in competition with each other. Interestingly, in-group favoritism, which is considered a beneficial outcome of perspective-taking in a cooperative context, can have detrimental effects on interpersonal perceptions among competitive members by augmenting the members' needs to protect their salient social identity. This phenomena suggests that perspective-taking may trigger a downward spiral in competitive relationships—causing high in-group identifiers adopting the perspective of an out-group member to develop stronger in-group favoritism, which in turn evokes an even higher in-group identification and an even stronger distaste toward the out-group, that ultimately causes greater intergroup conflicts and so on.

Perspective-taking also has an effect on unethical behavior when applied to a competitive context. Recent studies have pointed to group identification and peer influence as key drivers to dishonest and illegal behavior (Gino, Ayal, & Ariely, 2009; Gino & Pierce, 2010). For example, Pierce, Kilduff, Galinsky, and Sivanathan (2013) examined how the nature of perspective-taking changes with the relational context—cooperative or competitive—to predict unethical behavior. In one study, participants of an online study purportedly engaged in a public goods game with another participant (a computer in actuality). In a public goods game, participants receive an allocation of points and can achieve the greatest joint benefit if both individuals contribute all of their points to the pool, whereas the greatest individual benefit is achieved if a participant contributes nothing to the pool while his or her counterpart contributes everything.

The relational context was manipulated by framing the counterpart's response to a question regarding the type of work they enjoy as either competitive (e.g., "I like work that challenges me and that is competitive") or cooperative (e.g., "I like working in teams or groups"). Perspective-taking was manipulated by asking participants to write about their own thoughts and strategy (*baseline condition*) versus what they think their counterpart is thinking and what they think their strategy is (*perspective-taking condition*). Finally, participants' (un)ethicality was measured by comparing the number of points the participants proclaimed to allocate in their messages versus the number of points they actually allocated in their final decision. Pierce et al. (2013) found that taking the perspective of a competitive counterpart resulted in participants engaging in greater deception, as a way to protect themselves from the potentially malicious actions of their competitors. This is consistent with the idea that perspective-taking leads to antisocial rather than prosocial behavior in a competitive context, as if adding gasoline to fire: it inflames already aroused competitive and self-protective impulses, exacerbating social conflicts and tearing individuals further apart.

## Conclusion

The research findings we have reviewed in this chapter demonstrate that perspective-taking acts as a relational amplifier that intensifies existing cooperative or competitive tendencies. Experimental research has consistently demonstrated that in neutral or cooperative contexts, perspective-taking acts as the glue that adheres individuals together by debiasing social thought and inducing prosocial behavior. On the other hand, emerging evidence suggests that perspective-taking is akin to pouring gasoline in a competitive context, by fueling individuals to focus on the selfish and unfair intentions of their counterpart, leading to reactive egoism and antisocial behavior that ignites an already fiery conflict.

We believe that understanding the divergent effects of perspective-taking in cooperative and competitive environments has important ramifications for our everyday lives. In particular, indiscriminate adoption of another's perspective carries the risk of severely damaging intergroup relations. For instance, it has become almost ubiquitous for corporations to implement diversity training as part of a formal initiative toward stronger employee relations. As suggested by Tarrant et al. (2012), however, one should be wary of how highly each member identifies with his or her social in-group, as mindless implementation of out-group perspective-taking may threaten members' social identity and lead to devastating consequences in social interactions. Thus, one needs to fully understand the divergent effects of perspective-taking on different relational contexts before haphazardly taking the perspective of another in blind expectation that it will lead to greater social bonds.

The crucial question remains, then, how one can reap the benefits of perspective-taking while circumventing the negative consequences in intergroup relations. While the answer is not straightforward, we propose a few practical solutions based on the aforementioned findings we have discussed. One suggestion is to draw attention to the common interests and values among otherwise competitive group members. The reoccurring reason behind individuals' cynical attributions to their counterparts—which in turn lead to self-protective egoistic reactions—is that individuals expect their counterparts to act in a selfish and competitive manner due to their conflicting interests. If one is able to highlight the shared—rather than the opposing—interests between group members, there is greater likelihood that the otherwise competitive individuals will be able to bridge their differences and reduce conflict. Epley et al. (2006) directly tested this in a study by simply altering the description of a group exercise (e.g., "*cooperative* alliance game" vs. "strategic *competition* game") to make cooperation a salient goal, while holding the competitive structure and incentive system of the game constant. This simple manipulation of the description led to behavioral changes consistent with the expected reactions discussed in the aforementioned studies from perspective-taking in cooperative and competitive contexts.

Another potential solution to harness the benefits of perspective-taking without incurring the harmful costs is to maintain both psychological and physical distance from competitors, rather than forcibly taking the perspective of one another. In other words, it may be better to keep the gasoline away from an already blazing fire to prevent the risk of igniting an even greater fire and exacerbating existing social conflict. This may seem counterintuitive and contrary to the contact hypothesis (Allport, 1954), but simply avoiding further contact with a competitor may sometimes be the most practical solution to prevent further aggravation. These are just a few of many possible solutions, but we are hopeful that our review of work on the disparate effects of perspective-taking in different relational contexts will pave the way for future explorations and offer some guidance to optimal perspective-taking in social interactions.

## References

Allport, G.W. (1954). *The nature of prejudice*. Reading, MA: Addison-Wesley.

Babcock, L., & Loewenstein, G. (1997). Explaining bargaining impasse: The role of self-serving biases. *Journal of Economic Perspectives, 11*, 109–126.

Batson, C.D. (1991). *The altruism question: Toward a social-psychological answer*. Hillsdale, NJ: Erlbaum.

Batson, C.D. (1994). Prosocial motivation: Why do we help others? In A. Tesser (Ed.), *Advanced social psychology* (pp. 333–381). Boston: McGraw-Hill.

Batson, C.D., Batson, J.G., Slingsby, J.K., Harrell, K.L., Peekna, H.M., & Todd, R.M. (1991). Empathic joy and the empathy-altruism hypothesis. *Journal of Personality and Social Psychology, 61*, 413–426.

Batson, C.D., Early, S., & Salvarani, G. (1997). Perspective taking: Imagining how another feels versus imagining how you would feel. *Personality and Social Psychology Bulletin, 23,* 751–758.

Batson, C.D., Fultz, J., & Schoenrade, P.A. (1987). Distress and empathy: Two qualitatively distinct vicarious emotions with different motivational consequences. *Journal of Personality, 55*(1), 19–39.

Batson, C.D., & Moran, T. (1999). Empathy-induced altruism in a prisoner's dilemma. *European Journal of Social Psychology, 29,* 909–924.

Batson, C.D., Polycarpou, M.P., Harmon-Jones, E., Imhoff, H.J., Mitchener, E.C., Bednar, L.L., . . . Highberger, L. (1997). Empathy and attitudes: Can feeling for a member of a stigmatized group improve feelings toward the group? *Journal of Personality and Social Psychology, 72,* 105–118.

Bazerman, M.H., & Neale, M.A. (1982). Improving negotiation effectiveness under final offer arbitration: The role of selection and training. *Journal of Applied Psychology, 67,* 543–548.

Brewer, M.B. (1996). When stereotypes lead to stereotyping: The use of stereotype in person perception. In C.N. Macrae, C. Stangor, & M. Hewstone (Eds.), *Stereotypes and stereotyping* (pp. 254–275). New York: Guilford Press.

Cialdini, R.B., Brown, S.L., Lewis, B.P., Luce, C., & Neuberg, S.L. (1997). Reinterpreting the empathy-altruism relationship: When one into one equals oneness. *Journal of Personality and Social Psychology, 73,* 481–494.

Cialdini, R.B., Schaller, M., Houlihan, D., Arps, K., Fultz, J., & Beaman, A.L. (1987). Empathy-based helping: Is it selflessly or selfishly motivated. *Journal of Personality and Social Psychology, 52*(4), 749–758.

Coke, J.S., Batson, C.D., & McDavis, K. (1978). Empathic mediation of helping: A two-stage model. *Journal of Personality and Social Psychology, 36,* 752–766.

Davis, M.H. (1994). *Empathy: A social psychological approach.* Madison, WI: Brown & Benchmark.

Davis, M.H., Conklin, L., Smith, A., & Luce, C. (1996). The effect of perspective taking on the cognitive representation of persons: A merging of self and other. *Journal of Personality and Social Psychology, 70,* 713–726.

Dovidio, J.F., Allen, J.L., & Schroeder, D.A. (1990). Specificity of empathy-induced helping: Evidence for altruistic motivation. *Journal of Personality and Social Psychology, 59,* 249–260.

Dovidio, J.F., ten Vergert, M., Stewart, T.L., Gaertner, S.L., Johnson, J.D., Esses, V.M., . . . Pearson, A.R. (2004). Perspective and prejudice: Antecedents and mediating mechanisms. *Personality and Social Psychology Bulletin, 30,* 1537–1549.

Eisenberg, N., & Miller, P.A. (1987). The relation of empathy to prosocial and related behaviors. *Psychological Bulletin, 101,* 91–119.

Epley, N., Caruso, E., & Bazerman, M.H. (2006). When perspective taking increases taking: Reactive egoism in social interaction. *Journal of Personality and Social Psychology, 91,* 872–889.

Galinsky, A.D., & Ku, G. (2004). The effects of perspective-taking on prejudice: The moderating role of self-evaluation. *Personality and Social Psychology Bulletin, 30,* 594–604.

Galinsky, A.D., Ku, G., & Wang, C.S. (2005). Perspective-taking and self-other overlap: Fostering social bonds and facilitating social coordination. *Group Processes & Intergroup Relations, 8,* 109–124.

Galinsky, A.D., Maddux, W.W., Gilin, D., & White, J.B. (2008). Why it pays to get inside the head of your opponent: The differential effects of perspective taking and empathy in negotiations. *Psychological Science, 19,* 378–384.

Galinsky, A.D., & Moskowitz, G.B. (2000). Perspective-taking: Decreasing stereotype expression, stereotype accessibility, and in-group favoritism. *Journal of Personality and Social Psychology, 78,* 708–724.

Gino, F., Ayal, S., & Ariely, D. (2009). Contagion and differentiation in unethical behavior: The effect of one bad apple on the barrel. *Psychological Science, 20,* 393–398.

Gino, F., & Pierce, L. (2010). Robin Hood under the hood: Wealth-based discrimination in illicit customer help. *Organization Science, 21,* 1176–1194.

Kelley, H.H., & Stahelski, A.J. (1970). Social interaction basis of cooperators' and competitors' beliefs about others. *Journal of Personality and Social Psychology, 16,* 66–91.

Kerr, N.L., Hymes, R.W., Anderson, A.B., & Weathers, J.E. (1995). Defendant–juror similarity and mock juror judgments. *Law & Human Behavior, 19,* 545–567.

Kramer, R.M. (1994). The sinister attribution error: Paranoid cognition and collective distrust in organizations. *Motivation and Emotion, 18,* 199–230.

Kruger, J., & Gilovich, T. (1999). "Naive cynicism" in everyday theories of responsibility assessment: On biased assumptions of bias. *Journal of Personality and Social Psychology, 76,* 743–753.

Leary, M.R., & Forsyth, D.R. (1987). Attributions of responsibility for collective endeavors. In C. Hendrick (Ed.), *Review of personality and social psychology: Group processes* (Vol. 8, pp. 167–188). Newbury Park, CA: Sage.

Macrae, C.N., Bodenhausen, G.V., Milne, A.B., & Jetten, J. (1994). Out of mind but back in sight: Stereotypes on the rebound. *Journal of Personality and Social Psychology, 67,* 808–817.

Mallett, R., Huntsinger, J.R., Sinclair, S., & Swim, J. (2008). Seeing through their eyes: When majority group members take collective action on behalf of an outgroup. *Group Processes & Intergroup Relations, 11,* 451–470.

Maner, J.K., Luce, C.L., Neuberg, S.L., Cialdini, R.B., Brown, S., & Sagarin, B.J. (2002). The effects of perspective taking on helping: Still no evidence for altruism. *Personality and Social Psychology Bulletin, 28,* 1601–1610.

Messé, L.A., & Sivacek, J.M. (1979). Predictions of others' responses in a mixed-motive game: Self-justification or false consensus? *Journal of Personality and Social Psychology, 37,* 602–607.

Messick, D.M. (1995). Equality, fairness, and social conflict. *Social Justice Research, 8,* 153–173.

Miller, D.T. (1999). The norm of self-interest. *American Psychologist, 54,* 1053–1060.

Miller, D.T., & Ratner, R.K. (1998). The disparity between the actual and assumed power of self-interest. *Journal of Personality and Social Psychology, 74,* 53–62.

Okimoto, T.G., & Wenzel, M. (2010). The symbolic identity implications of inter and intragroup transgressions. *European Journal of Social Psychology, 40,* 552–562.

Okimoto, T.G., & Wenzel, M. (2011). The other side of perspective taking. *Social Psychological and Personality Science, 2,* 373–378.

Pierce, J.R., Kilduff, G.J., Galinsky, A.D., Sivanathan, N. (2013). From glue to gasoline: How competition turns perspective takers unethical. *Psychological Science.*

Piliavin, J.A., Dovidio, J.F., Gaertner, S.L., & Clark, R.D., III. (1981). *Emergency intervention.* New York: Academic Press.

Richardson, D.R., Hammock, G.S., Smith, S.M., Gardner, W., & Signo, M. (1994). Empathy as a cognitive inhibitor of interpersonal aggression. *Aggressive Behavior, 20,* 275–289.

Ross, M., & Sicoly, F. (1979). Egocentric biases in availability and attribution. *Journal of Personality and Social Psychology, 37,* 322–336.

Savitsky, K., Van Boven, L., Epley, N., & Wight, W.M. (2005). The unpacking effect in allocations of responsibility for group tasks. *Journal of Experimental Social Psychology, 41,* 447–457.

Smith, E.R., & Henry, S. (1996). An in-group becomes part of the self: Response time evidence. *Personality & Social Psychology Bulletin, 22,* 635–642.

Tarrant, M., Calitri, R., & Weston, D. (2012). Social identification structures the effects of perspective taking. *Psychological Science, 23,* 973–978.

Todd, A.R., Bodenhausen, G.V., Richeson, J.A., & Galinsky, A.D. (2011). Perspective taking combats automatic expressions of racial bias. *Journal of Personality and Social Psychology, 100*(6), 1027.

Turner, J.C. (1987). The analysis of social influence. In J.C. Turner, M.A. Hogg, P.J. Oakes, S.D. Reicher, & M.S. Wetherell (Eds.), *Rediscovering the social group: A self-categorization theory* (pp. 68–88). Oxford: Blackwell.

Von Neumann, J., & Morgenstern, O. (2004). *Theory of games and economic behavior* (Commemorative ed.). Princeton, NJ: Princeton University Press.

Wade-Benzoni, K.A., Tenbrunsel, A.E., & Bazerman, M.H. (1996). Egocentric interpretations of fairness in asymmetric, environmental social dilemmas: Explaining harvesting behavior and the role of communication. *Organizational Behavior and Human Decision Processes, 67,* 111–126.

Zebel, S., Doosje, B., & Spears, R. (2009). How perspective-taking helps and hinders group-based guilt as a function of group identification. *Group Processes & Intergroup Relations, 12,* 61–78.

# 9

# CONFESSING TO AN IMMORAL ACT

## Consequences to Moral Beliefs and Inferences About Moral Dispositions

*Joel Cooper*

*What are the consequences of confessing to an immoral act? In this chapter, we will consider the dilemma of people who confess to immoral acts that they did not commit. In law enforcement, an all too common occurrence is for police to convince suspects to confess to a crime that they actually did not commit. Instances of physically coerced confessions notwithstanding, our focus is on the uncoerced confession in which the accused is cajoled to admit to a criminal action. People may be accused of moral transgressions in any number of situations such as cheating in school or committing fraud in the workplace. In this chapter, we will present evidence that situational events can lead innocent people to make false confessions. We will then present a view of the psychological consequences of false confessions. We will focus on people's belief that they actually committed the moral transgression, and we will consider the downstream consequences to their self-attributions of dispositional morality.*

On July 8, 1997, police in Norfolk, Virginia, approached US Navy sailor Daniel Williams and brought him to the police station for questioning regarding the murder of his neighbor, Michelle Moore-Bosko. After several hours of interrogation, Williams confessed to murdering Moore-Bosko. That confession was the primary evidence leading to a conviction for capital rape and murder. In his confession, Williams explained how he bludgeoned his neighbor with a shoe. When it came to light that the victim had not been bludgeoned but had been strangled, Williams signed a new confession that he had stabbed and strangled Moore-Bosko. The jurors' judgment of Williams' guilt was not affected by the change in the reported method of killing Moore-Bosko or by the fact that Williams recanted both confessions, claiming that the police had coerced him.

We know now that Daniel Williams neither raped nor killed his neighbor. At trial, he said the same to the 12 men and women who served as jurors. Why would jurors disbelieve his sworn verbal statement on the witness stand, preferring to make their judgments based on a recanted confession? In some ways, the jurors' decision was an easy one. We do not believe that people would confess to crimes they did not commit, especially given the extremity of the consequences that follow from a confession. Sadly, the data tell us otherwise. In the criminal justice system, cases such as Daniel Williams's and several others (Pratkanis & Aronson, 2001) make for poignant reading. Analyses of convictions that were ultimately overturned by subsequent evidence reveal that approximately 15% were based on false confessions (Bedau & Radelet, 1987; Garrett, 2008; Gudjonsson & Sigurdsson, 1994).

## False Confessions Outside the Courtroom

It is not only accused perpetrators of crimes who are pressured to confess to actions they did not commit. In the ordinary business of life, people occasionally admit to transgressions that are untrue. Sometimes, the confession is made to protect someone else as a gesture of prosocial morality (see also Graziano & Schroeder, this volume). A child in school may admit to breaking her teacher's vase in order to protect her best friend whom she believed really broke it. A parent may take the blame for a child's not doing his homework on a particular night in order to mitigate any punishment for the child. On other occasions, people may confess to a behavior because they succumb to social or moral pressure. A teenager in a pickup basketball game agrees that he stepped on the out-of-bounds line because several other players make the accusation. Although he believes his feet were entirely in bounds, he gives up the ball (i.e., confesses to stepping on the line). His confession is a result of social influence and his desire to allow the game to continue. Another reason for false confession is that the anticipated consequence of not confessing is greater than the consequence of confessing. A child who falsely confesses to his teacher that he broke the rules by speaking during a quiet period may anticipate fewer adverse consequences than truthfully revealing that it was the class bully who transgressed. In this chapter, we take the position that false confessions have consequences for how people view themselves. Because falsely confessing involves intrinsically moral decisions, such confessions may alter people's views of their own sense of morality as well as subsequent moral behavior (see Miller & Monin; and Simpson, Farrell, & Marshall, this volume).

## Attributions of Moral Dispositions to Others

The notion of how people make attributions about other people's personal characteristics has long been the focus of social psychological theorizing (Heider,

1958; Jones & Davis, 1965; Kelley, 1973). Our effectively navigating the social world is increased to the extent that we understand other people's propensity to act consistently across situations (see also Galinsky & Lee, this volume). Jones and Davis (1965) referred to such understandings as "dispositions" and delineated many of the principles we use to infer people's dispositions from an observation of their behaviors. The principles of correspondent inferences apply to making dispositional inferences about people's attitudes, kindness, maliciousness, or any other trait relevant to a person's actions. If we wish to gauge a person's level of helpfulness, for example, we can assess any occasions in which we have observed the person act in a helpful manner. According to Jones and Davis, we engage in a systematic process that allows us to make a reasonable guess about a person's intention to act in a helpful manner and use the intention to infer a disposition.

Consider a college student who is thought to have cheated on an examination. The unfair advantage that the student received can be dealt with in any number of ways, but we would not be surprised to see such a student suspended from school. The student's behavior suggests a level of morality inconsistent with what is expected from college students. The attribution of immorality as personal disposition suggests that the student cannot be trusted in subsequent situations in which moral behavior is expected. The attribution of a disposition allows us to predict the likelihood of future behavior that requires ethics and morality, which in turn prompts the separation of this student from his school.

How do we know if the student in this example actually engaged in the immoral behavior of which he stands accused? If we did not actually observe the behavior, we may rely on a second level of behavior—namely, the student's verbal statement about whether he did or did not cheat. If the student were to confess to cheating, we would have little doubt that the immoral behavior occurred. The attribution of immorality would not be difficult to make.

It is important to understand why we would be confident that the student who confessed to cheating is ethically challenged. Although various theories of attribution converge on similar sets of principles, our analysis can be guided by correspondent inference theory (Jones & Davis, 1965; Jones et al., 1972). Attributions of dispositions occur as a function of people's behavior, provided that we believe the behavior is informative. The two important variables in correspondence inference theory are the number of noncommon effects of a person's chosen behavior weighted by their social desirability. That is, does the behavior of confessing produce unique effects (compared to not confessing), and are those effects something that most people would enjoy having? Confessing to an immoral act has severe consequences and those consequences are markedly undesirable. It is straightforward to draw the correspondent inference and assume that a person who confesses to cheating is a cheater (i.e., has an immoral character disposition).

Behaviors that are coerced are not informative for the purpose of making a dispositional attribution. The attribution analysis that results in correspondent inferences cannot proceed when behavior is coerced because the actor did not intend to create the behavior or its effects. Yet, decades of research have shown that observers succumb to the correspondence bias (Gilbert & Jones, 1986) or the fundamental attribution error (Ross, 1977). Despite violating the logical rules of attribution, people have a tendency to make dispositional inferences on the basis of behavior, even when the behavior was coerced. In the classic research on correspondence bias, Jones and Harris (1967) informed participants that another university student had written an essay in favor of Cuban President Fidel Castro. Depending on experimental condition, some participants were told that the student had chosen to write in support of Castro whereas others were told that the student had been assigned the position. Although participants attributed highest pro-Castro attitudes to the student who chose to write on that side, they also attributed pro-Castro attitudes to those were assigned the task. The student's behavior in the latter condition should not have provided even a clue about his attitude toward Castro. Nonetheless, people engaged in the correspondence bias and made attitude attributions based on the coerced behavior.

## Jurors and the Correspondence Bias

According to Kassin and Wrightsman (1980, 1985), the most damning evidence given in court is a confession. Since most cases that are presented to juries involve not-guilty pleas, the confessions in question have typically been given to police prior to trial. Defendants often claim that their confessions were coerced or given under duress. Such explanations are rarely successful (Leo, 2008; Leo & Ofshe, 1998). Sauer and Wilkens (1999) found that the overwhelming majority of potential jurors reported that they believed that suspects would "almost never confess" to crimes they did not do. Leo (2008) quotes a Los Angeles Police Department psychologist who asserted "no amount of badgering would prompt the average person to admit to doing something that awful—or to admit to any crime" (p. 197).

The fact is that defendants *do* succumb to pressure to confess to immoral and illegal actions that they did not commit. For the past 80 years, US courts have forbidden the introduction of confessions that were coerced by physical means. In *Brown v. Mississippi* (1936), the Supreme Court reversed a guilty verdict on the grounds that the confession was extracted via brute force and that such tactics are a violation of defendants' rights to due process. As standards evolved over the decades, confessions became admissible to the extent that a judge, and sometimes a jury, finds that the confession was given willingly, knowingly, and in the absence of physical or psychological coercion.

One issue that the adversarial legal system must face is that police often question suspects with an array of psychological techniques designed to elicit confessions. A variety of procedural manuals detail the psychological and environmental pressures that can help produce confessions from suspects. Inbau, Reid, Buckley, and Jayne (2001) outline a nine-step procedure that is widely used by police to elicit confessions. These steps include convincing a suspect that firm evidence already exists to convict them of the crime and then working with the suspect to generate moral excuses to justify the crime. According to Kassin and McNally (1991), police interrogation techniques can be categorized into two main approaches: minimization and maximization. The former technique, minimization, relies on the interrogator's creating a sense of camaraderie with the suspect. The interrogator expresses sympathy and understanding, offers face-saving excuses, puts the blame on external factors, and downplays the severity of the offense. The latter technique, maximization, utilizes intimidation to scare the suspect, and exaggerates false incriminating evidence and the magnitude of the consequences that will occur in the absence of a confession. Because people do not believe an individual would confess to something he or she did not actually do (Sauer & Wilkens, 1999), the impact of a confession on jurors' attributions of guilt is maximal. They underestimate the social psychological factors at play during the interrogation, basing their ultimate judgment on the effect of consequence of the confession instead.

## The Effect of False Confessions on the Confessor

What is sometimes lost in discussions of false confessions is the effect of confessions on the perpetrator. In terms of the social psychology of attributions, does making a confession have an impact on people's own judgment of whether they actually engaged in the activity to which they confessed? Some celebrated legal cases suggest that the answer is sometimes yes. Eighteen-year-old Peter Reilly returned home one night to find his mother had been murdered. After Reilly called the police to report the incident, the police interrogated him. They claimed (falsely) that Reilly had failed his lie-detector test. Analysis of the transcripts of his confession (Barthel, 1976) showed Reilly progressing from denial to confusion to self-doubt. "Well, it looks like I really did it," he told police. Two years after his conviction, conclusive evidence was uncovered that exonerated him. He was not near his home on the night of the murder.

Recall the case against Daniel Williams who confessed to the murder of his neighbor. Although Williams was convicted on the basis of his confession, he continued to maintain that his confession was false and that he was innocent of the crime. A different story can be told for codefendant Joseph Dick, who was accused of being Williams's accomplice. Dick also confessed. However, he internalized his confession, coming to believe that he had actually been with Williams when they raped and murdered Ms. Moore-Bosko. He repeated his confession in court and testified against Daniel Williams. The Norfolk defendants were released from prison when DNA evidence showed that neither Williams nor Dick had anything to do with the crimes.

## False Confessions in a Social and Moral Context

Kassin and Kiechel (1996) addressed the underlying issue that renders confessions exceptionally powerful in courts. Would anyone actually confess to a transgression that he or she did not commit? To provide some experimental evidence to this debate, Kassin and Kiechel asked whether people who find themselves accused of transgressions could be systematically persuaded to make false confessions. They suggested that two elements in the interpersonal context of police interrogations seem to be present when false confessions are obtained. One is the creation of doubt about the events that took place, and the second is the creation of a belief that the accusers have proof of the suspect's guilt.

In a clever experimental laboratory procedure, Kassin and Kiechel (1996) had undergraduates participate in groups of two in what they thought was a reaction time task. One member of the pair was actually a confederate of the experimenter. On each trial of the reaction time task, the confederate read a list of words and the participant was to type them into a computer. The experimenter explained that it was imperative that the participant not touch the ALT key that was adjacent to the space bar because that would cause the computer to crash and the data to be lost. After a minute's activity, the computer seemed to crash. The experimenter hurried in to examine the computer and accused the participant of having pressed the forbidden key. Initially, all participants denied the allegation. In the high vulnerability condition, the participants were rendered less certain of what they had or had not done because the typing task was conducted at a frenetic pace. In the low vulnerability condition, it was conducted at a leisurely pace, allowing participants to be very certain of what they had typed. The second variable of interest was whether the participant believed there was incriminating evidence. This was manipulated in the form of testimony given by the confederate. In the false witness condition, the confederate admitted that she had seen the participant hit the ALT key that terminated the program. In the no-witness condition, the same confederate said she had not seen what happened.

To elicit compliance with the accusation, the experimenter told the participant to sign a statement that he or she hit the ALT key. They were not asked if they believed their confession, but only to make one as the experimenter demanded. The results showed that when there was no alleged witness and the pace of the typing had been slow, 65% of the participants refused to sign. On the other hand, when the pace was quick and thus the transgression less certain, 65% agreed to sign. That percentage rose to 100% when the uncertainty was combined with the witness's testimony. What happened next in Kassin and Kiechel's study assessed the degree to which people actually believed that they had transgressed. Another student confederate, posing as the next participant, approached the participant and asked what the commotion was about. The participants' responses were recorded and assessed for whether they stated unequivocally that they had hit the ALT key.

Although no one in the certain/no-witness condition admitted to having committed the forbidden behavior, 65% of participants who were in the fast-paced condition with an accusing witness freely stated that they had committed the behavior.

## Believing Your (False) Confession: An Empirical Study on Attributions of Morality

Under what conditions do people come to believe that their false confessions are true? From Kassin and Kiechel's (1996) work, we believe that people can be influenced to make false confessions and that people sometimes become convinced of the veracity of those confessions. In the current work, we examine the consequences of confessions for people's self-attributions of morality. If people confess, does it affect their attribution of their own dispositions? Are they likely to use the observation of their own behavior to draw inferences about the level of their own morality?

We speculate that people use their confessions as evidence of their dispositions but only to the extent that they feel they had a choice in making their confessions. This is consistent with analyses from cognitive dissonance theory (Festinger, 1957), self-perception theory (Bem, 1972), and attribution theory (Kelley, 1973). To the extent that people perceive their behavior to be freely chosen, that behavior is influential in determining their internal dispositions. Faced with knowledge that they described a transgression (i.e., confessed), people determine whether that description was coerced by the environment or whether it was given freely. If the latter, then it becomes information in determining their own dispositions.

We extended Kassin and Kiechel's research to an area of moral concern— namely, cheating. We established a situation in which students' performance on an exam could be improved if they cheated by taking extra time to complete the questions. We accused the students of having cheated on the exam and, using techniques drawn from existing police manuals (Inbau et al., 2001), induced them to confess to having cheated. We then assessed the degree to which the students believed that they had actually cheated. Finally, in a different context, we used an individual difference questionnaire to assess students' assessment of their own reality. We predicted that we could induce students to confess to cheating when, in fact, they had not done so. We also predicted that students would come to believe that their confessions were true to the extent that they felt they had a choice to confess. Finally, we predicted that if students confessed to cheating and believed (falsely) that they had committed the act, they would attribute to themselves a lower level of ethical and moral disposition.

In our empirical study, undergraduate students volunteered for a study investigating mental models to improve mathematical abilities. At the outset, participants were told that it was important to get an assessment of their current level of mathematics proficiency. To that end, they would take a difficult exam in mathematics and their scores would be published along with the scores of all other students taking the exam. The students were given 15 minutes to complete the test on the computer. The experimenter explained that they should work until they were finished but that they absolutely should not go beyond the time provided. The experimenter stated that he would leave the student alone with his or her work and would return in about 15 minutes. The student was told to use the clock that was prominently displayed on the computer as the official timer.

## The Alleged Transgression

The experimenter waited 17 minutes before returning to the room. When entering the room, he noted that he had intended to come back after 15 minutes so that he could monitor the student's adherence to the rules but, unfortunately, ran late. He asked participants whether they had used the extra time for anything related to the mathematics test. In a control condition, the student's denial that they had used extra time was taken at face value. Every student denied taking extra time, which was an honest and accurate portrait of what they had done.

## Accusing the Perpetrator

After inquiring about the student using extra time, the experimenter confronted the student with the notion that he or she must have used the time to work on the math test. He explained that the using extra time included such things as looking over your work, making changes, or just continuing to work after the timer reached zero. The experimenter adopted one of three interrogation techniques adopted from the police interrogation handbook.

## No Choice Confession

The experimenter in the no-choice condition told the students that, considering they had extra time available, it was required that they sign a statement saying that they had used the extra time on the math exam. The experimenter took responsibility for having allowed the extra time but explained that when such an event happens, he is required to get the student to sign a routine statement acknowledging use of extra time. Only then, he explained, can the study continue.

## Choosing to Confess: Minimization

Minimization is an interrogation approach in which the interrogator offers understanding of the alleged situation, offers face-saving excuses, and downplays the severity of the offense. To that end, the experimenter explained that it was not a major violation if the participant used extra time, evoking the notion that it was a common and justifiable occurrence, and that situations with this kind of temptation often lead to people violating the moral rules. He just needed the participant to acknowledge that he or she used extra time so that he could code the data differently for subsequent analysis. The experimenter stated, "Of course you do not have to sign the statement, but it would be very helpful if you do."

## Choosing to Confess: Maximization

In this condition, participants were told that cheating on a test, even in a laboratory, was a violation of the university's honor code. The penalties could be severe. Students were told that it would be much better to sign a statement confessing to using extra time because that would allow the data to be coded differently and still be used. On the other hand, failure to admit to using extra time—if they had actually used it—would result in severe consequences. Moreover, the experimenter revealed that he had hard evidence because the video camera on the computer had recorded the entire session. He indicated that he would check the video if the student did not admit to the transgression. The student was then given the choice about whether to sign the confession.

## Making the False Confession

The video camera on the computer had actually been used during the session. The videos revealed that no one, in any of the conditions, had actually violated the 15-minute limitation. No one in the control condition admitted to using extra time. However, the data in Figure 9.1 show the results for participants in the three experimental conditions. Nineteen of twenty participants in the no-choice conditions complied with the experimenter's instruction to sign a confession for a transgression that they did not commit. In the choice conditions, 72% of the participants agreed to confess, with the highest number coming in the maximization condition. The minimization and maximization conditions did not differ significantly from each other.

## Believing the False Confession

After participants either did or did not sign their false confessions, the experimenter indicated that he would have to terminate the study. He introduced the study's "principal investigator" who told participants that he needed to ask them questions. He first inquired about whether the participants had agreed to sign a statement about their having used extra time. He then administered a questionnaire that included the crucial item, "How much do you believe that you used

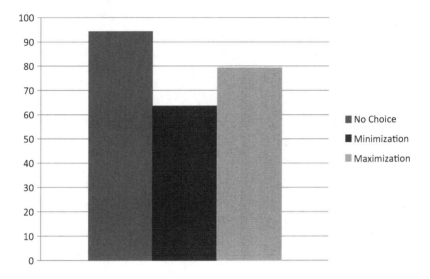

**FIGURE 9.1** Percentage of participants who signed a false confession.

extra time in completing the test?" The questionnaire also asked, "How much choice did you feel in confessing or not confessing?" All items were followed by 7-point scales.

Figure 9.2 presents the results of the degree to which students reported believing that they had actually used the extra time that they had confessed to. The results show that signing a confession had an impact on belief but, as expected, the effect varied by condition. The mean belief in the control condition in which people had been asked if they used the extra time but were not asked for a confession was 1.05. In the no-choice condition, the reported belief was minimally and nonsignificantly higher ($M = 1.15$). Students' beliefs in their own transgressions were significantly higher in the choice minimization ($M = 2.9$) and the choice maximization conditions ($M = 2.3$). The choice conditions were significantly different from the no-choice condition and marginally significantly different from each other ($p < .11$).

Not surprisingly, students' perceptions of the degree of choice they had to sign a confession were higher in the choice than in the no-choice condition. However, it is interesting that students perceived more choice in the minimization than the maximization condition. In other words, when threatened with severe consequences for failing to report a transgression (even though they had not transgressed), they saw their own freedom as more severely limited than when the inducements were minimal. In addition, the degree of belief that they had actually used extra time was correlated with the amount of decision freedom they thought they had ($r = .44$).

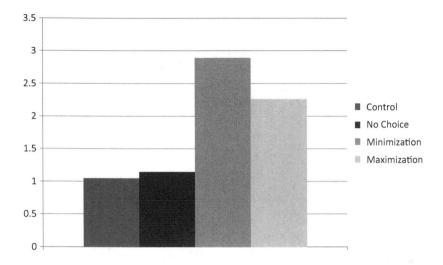

**FIGURE 9.2** Participants' mean beliefs in the substance of their confessions.

## *Impact of Confessions on Dispositions*

One day following the experimental procedure, student were contacted by e-mail and asked if they were willing to fill out some questions as part of an ongoing survey of personality instruments. No mention was made of any connection to the false confession study. If participants agreed (94% of the original participants agreed), they were asked to respond on the computer to a 10-item version of the Rosenberg Self-Esteem Scale. An 11th item was added to the scale that stated, "I feel I am an ethical person." The results showed that students who had signed a confession and believed that they had choice to sign the confession scored lower on the ethical person question ($M = 2.2$ vs. $M = 1.7, p < .02$) and lower on the Self-Esteem Scale overall ($M = 16.65$ vs. $M = 18.88, p < .05$).

## Implications of False Confessions: A Change in Moral Thinking

The new empirical work described in this chapter demonstrates that people can be induced to confess to immoral actions, even when their behavior was in fact moral, ethical, and legal. From the perspective of a third person, confessions of immoral, unethical behavior will almost certainly be grist for the attribution mill, allowing social perceivers to conclude that the confessor did indeed act in an immoral way and that immorality can be ascribed as a personal disposition.

The fact that false confessions have an impact on our own perception of ourselves is not as obvious. Nonetheless, various theories including cognitive dissonance (Cooper, 2007; Festinger, 1957) suggest that behavior does have a meaningful impact on attitudes and beliefs, provided that the behavior appears to have been freely chosen. The results of the current study support that notion. People who were accused of an action that they did not commit were nonetheless persuaded to confess to having cheated. If they believed that their confessions were made with personal free choice, they were more likely to believe their own confessions rather than trust their memories for what they had actually done. And those freely chosen confessions had consequences: people not only believed that they cheated, but also showed a lower sense of self-esteem and a lowered belief in their own sense of moral character.

The impact of false confessions on personal beliefs and subsequent moral inferences is systematic. First, a behavior must be elicited that confirms the transgression. The degree of coercion needs to be minimal. The justification for confessing must also be minimal. Recall that the maximization strategy in which the consequences of failing to confess were emphasized produced a confession but without as much internalization as the minimization strategy. Rather, the minimization strategy led people to believe that they had freely chosen to sign their confessions, which, in turn, led to belief change.

An interesting implication of false confessions is to consider their impact on subsequent behavior. Do they motivate people to compensate for their perceived immorality by engaging in moral, prosocial behavior, or do they motivate subsequent immoral behavior consistent with people's new self-image? In the current chapter, false confessions under the appropriate circumstances led people to make dispositional attributions about themselves that suggested a lack of morality. The intriguing question for future research is whether subsequent behaviors will be directed at finding opportunities for conveying that they are more morally worthy people, or whether they will act consistently with their newly formed view of their compromised morality. As Miller and Monin (this volume) point out, people often seek moral opportunities for conveying to themselves and others that they are morally worthy. This may be especially likely following morally costly behavior such as confessing to an immoral act.

On the other hand, in some of the foundational work on cognitive dissonance theory, Aronson and Carlsmith (1962) showed that people preferred to act consistently with their self-expectations, even at the expense of confirming negative traits. People who were led to expect that they had a low level of ability in a particular domain preferred to fail at a task rather than succeed. Aronson and Carlsmith suggested that confirming a self-expectancy is an important way of avoiding the negative state of dissonance. The extrapolation of that work to the current context suggests that people who falsely confess to immoral acts will not only lower their moral self-esteem but will also behave less morally in the future. If that is the case, then police and interrogators who obtain false confessions not only run the risk of falsely incarcerating the innocent, but may also be facilitating subsequent immoral behavior by those whom they have falsely accused.

# References

Aronson, E., & Carlsmith, J.M. (1962). Performance expectancy as a determinant of actual performance. *Journal of Abnormal and Social Psychology*, *65*, 178–182.

Barthel, J. (1976). *A death in Canaan*. New York: E.P. Dutton.

Bedau, H.A., & Radelet, M.L. (1987). Miscarriages of justice in potentially capital cases. *Stanford Law Review*, *40*, 21–179.

Bem, D.J. (1972). Self perception theory. In L. Berkowitz (Ed.), *Advances in experimental social psychology* (Vol. 6, pp. 1–62). New York: Academic Press.

Cooper, J. (2007). *Cognitive dissonance: Fifty years of a classic theory*. Los Angeles: Sage.

Festinger, L. (1957). *A theory of cognitive dissonance*. Stanford, CA: Stanford University Press.

Garrett, B.L. (2008). Judging innocence. *Columbia Law Review*, *108*, 55–142.

Gilbert, D.T., & Jones, E.E. (1986). Perceiver-induced constraints: Interpretations of self-generated reality. *Journal of Personality and Social Psychology*, *50*, 269–280.

Gudjonsson, G.H., & Sigurdsson, J.F. (1994). How frequently do false confessions occur? An empirical study among prison inmates. *Psychology, Crime and Law*, *1*, 21–26.

Heider, F. (1958). *The psychology of interpersonal relations*. New York: Wiley.

Inbau, F.E., Reid, J.E., Buckley, J.P., & Jayne, B.C. (2001). *Criminal interrogation and confessions* (4th ed.). Gaithersburg, MD: Aspen.

Jones, E.E., & Davis, K.E. (1965). From acts to dispositions: The attribution process in person perception. In L. Berkowitz (Ed.), *Advances in experimental social psychology* (Vol. 2, pp. 219–266). New York: Academic Press.

Jones, E.E., & Harris, V.A. (1967). The attribution of attitudes. *Journal of Experimental Social Psychology*, *3*, 1–24.

Jones, E.E., Kanouse, D.E., Kelley, H.H., Nisbett, S., Valins, S., & Weiner B. (1972). *Attribution: Perceiving the causes of behavior*. Morristown, NJ: General Learning Press.

Kassin, S.M., & Kiechel, K.L. (1996). The social psychology of false confessions: Compliance, internalization and confabulation. *Psychological Science*, *7*, 125–128.

Kassin, S.M., & McNally, K. (1991). Police interrogations and confessions: Communicating promises and threats by pragmatic implication. *Law and Human Behavior*, *15*, 233–251.

Kassin, S.M., & Wrightsman, L.S. (1980). Prior confessions and mock juror verdicts. *Journal of Applied Social Psychology*, *10*, 133–146.

Kassin, S.M., & Wrightsman, L.S. (1985). *The psychology of evidence and trial procedure*. Beverly Hills, CA: Sage.

Kelley, H.H. (1973). The process of causal attribution. *American Psychologist*, *28*, 107–128.

Leo, R.A. (2008). *Police interrogations and American justice*. Cambridge, MA: Harvard University Press.

Leo, R.A., & Ofshe, R.J. (1998). The consequences of false confessions: Deprivations of liberty and miscarriages of justice in the age of psychological interrogations. *Journal of Criminal Law and Criminology*, *88*, 429–496.

Pratkanis, A.R., & Aronson, E. (2001). *The Age of Propaganda*. New York: Freeman.

Ross, L. (1977). The intuitive psychologist and his shortcomings. Distortions in the attribution process. *Advances in Experimental Social Psychology*, *10*, 173–220.

Sauer, M., & Wilkens, J. (1999, May 16). Haunting questions: The Stephanie Crowe murder case. Part 6. *San Diego Union Tribune*.

# 10

# AFFECTIVE INFLUENCES ON MORAL DECISIONS

## Mood Effects on Selfishness Versus Fairness

*Joseph P. Forgas*

*Treating others fairly and equitably is a basic requirement for moral behaviour, yet in many everyday situations the impulse to be selfish and benefit ourselves at the expense of others remains a powerful motive. This chapter reports five experiments investigating the influence of positive and negative affect on moral decisions involving the allocation of resources to ourselves vs others, using strategic games such as the dictator game and the ultimatum game. In the dictator game, proposers have unconstrained power to be selfish, and the option of being fair to others is entirely voluntarily. In the ultimatum game, allocation decisions to self versus others require more sophisticated processing as they are subject to the veto power of recipients. All five experiments found that negative mood consistently increased, and positive mood reduced moral behaviour and concern with fairness. Allocators in a negative mood were consistently more fair and gave more resources to a partner than did those in a positive mood. These decisions also took longer to make, confirming mood-induced processing differences in moral decisions. The results are discussed in terms of recent affect-cognition theories, suggesting that positive affect recruits a more assimilative, internally focused processing style promoting greater selfishness, while negative affect induces more externally oriented, accommodative thinking and greater concern fairness and external moral norms. The implications of the findings for everyday interpersonal behaviors and interactions involving selfishness versus fairness are considered.*

Imagine that somebody gave you $100, with the simple request that you divide this sum between yourself and another person. How would you decide what to do? How much money would you keep for yourself? Although splitting the money 50–50 would appear to be a simple and manifestly 'fair' decision, in fact most people do display some degree of selfishness and favouritism towards themselves in such situations. Interestingly, doing the right thing by others—treating others fairly and equitably—lies at the core of some of the most common and important moral dilemmas people face in everyday life, with important implications for social relationships. Striking the right ethical balance between self-interest and fairness can also have a significant influence on developing interpersonal trust and team effectiveness (Jarvenpaa, Knoll, & Leidner, 1998).

Dealing with such decisions is often perplexing, involving a subtle conflict between internal motivations—selfishness—and external social norms mandating fairness towards others (see also Forgas, Jussim, & Van Lange; Graziano & Schroeder; and Simpson, Farrell, & Marshall, this volume). Could it be that feeling good and feeling bad might have a significant impact on the ethical decisions taken when allocating resources to ourselves and others? These experiments use the dictator game and the ultimatum game to investigate affective influences on how moral dilemmas involving selfishness versus fairness are resolved.

Surprisingly, the possibility that affective states may influence moral decisions has received little attention to date. Yet affect has long been recognized as one of the primary dimensions influencing social cognition and interpersonal behavior (Fiedler, 2001; Forgas, 2002; Forgas & Eich, 2012; Zajonc, 1980). Weak, low-intensity moods in particular have been found to exert a subtle yet powerful influence on thinking, judgments and social behaviors (Bless, 2000; Clore & Storbeck, 2006; Forgas, 2002, 2007). Moods are low-intensity, diffuse and relatively enduring affective states without a salient antecedent cause and therefore little conscious cognitive content. In contrast, emotions are more intense, short-lived and usually have a definite cause and conscious cognitive content (Forgas, 1995, 2002). It is the influence of moods rather than distinct emotions that will be of interest here, as moods typically produce more uniform, enduring and reliable cognitive and behavioral consequences than do more context-specific emotions (Forgas, 2002, 2006; Forgas & Eich, 2012). Before turning to the empirical evidence, some of the most relevant philosophical approaches to morality that have a direct bearing on how people deal with moral conflicts involving selfishness versus fairness will be considered.

## The Ethical Imperative of Fairness

The ethical conflict between selfishness versus fairness has been a major issue for religious and moral philosophers since time immemorial (see also Galinsky & Lee; Graziano & Schroeder; and Miller & Monin, this volume). The maxim of treating others as you would like to be treated yourself is a basic principle of several major religions. Since the Enlightenment, however, rationalist thinkers such as Adam Smith argued that *rational* self-interest—that is, selfishness—may often be socially beneficial and may legitimately guide many of our social and economic transactions if properly channelled.

In terms of the rational, *utilitarian philosophy* of Jeremy Bentham and John Stuart Mill, we ought to make decisions that will produce the greatest benefit and the least harm, resulting in the greatest good for the greatest number of people. This principle assumes that we should treat our own benefits and costs in the same rational, dispassionate manner as we assess the benefits and costs of others—in practice, not an easy task to accomplish.

The alternative *fairness or justice approach* is based on the work of Aristotle, who argued that fairness requires that we treat equals equally and avoid favoritism and discrimination. Again, living up to this norm is not always easy when decisions involve distributing benefits to ourselves versus others without favouritism to ourselves. Fairness to others as a social norm is also mandated by moral theories that emphasize the common interests of people within defined groups—treating them equitably is to everyone's advantage, and thus constitutes a powerful demand. This view is echoed in more recent evolutionary theories that suggest that humans and higher primates evolved a sophisticated sense of justice and fairness as an adaptive strategy to constrain selfishness and promote social cohesion (Forgas, Haselton, & von Hippel, 2007; see also von Hippel, Ronay, & Maddux, this volume). Thus, based on purely rational, philosophical consideration, being fair to others (and in our example, distributing resources equally) is clearly the desirable and preferred outcome to the ethical problem described earlier. Yet, in practice the fairness norm is rarely followed, but complete selfishness is also rare, suggesting that moral decisions of this kind involve far more than rational consideration (Güth, Schmittberger, & Schwarze, 1982).

This chapter will contribute to our understanding of how such ethical decisions are performed by describing a series of laboratory experiments exploring how everyday affective states and moods may influence the degree of selfishness and fairness people display when they are asked to divide scarce resources between themselves and another person in the *dictator game* and the *ultimatum game*.

## Selfishness Versus Fairness in Strategic Interactions

Interpersonal conflicts involving the contrary demands of selfishness (benefiting yourself) versus fairness (obeying moral norms and doing the right thing by others) represent a basic and recurring ethical problem in relating to others, and are the source of many historical and interpersonal conflicts. How can we study such moral decisions in a reliable and valid empirical manner? In this series of experiments we explored mood effects on selfishness and fairness in controlled strategic interpersonal situations, using interactive games such as the dictator game and the ultimatum game. In these interactions, benefiting the self or benefiting another represent clearly defined and easily operationalized alternative strategies, measured by comparing the allocation decisions made by people in positive and negative affective states.

## The Dictator Game and the Ultimatum Game

Economic games offer a reliable and valid method to study interpersonal strategies involving ethical conflicts, such as fairness, selfishness, trust and cooperation. In the dictator game, the allocator has the power to allocate a scarce resource (raffle tickets, a sum of money, etc.) between himself and another person in any way he sees fit, with no input by the receiver. In the ultimatum game, proposers face a more complex task. They can allocate a scarce resource between themselves and a responder who in turn has a veto power to accept or reject the offer; if rejected, neither side gets anything.

These games represent a highly realistic and controlled context in which to study the way people resolve the conflicting moral requirements of being selfish, or being fair when dealing with others. In a sense, the ethical dilemmas presented in these games model the realism and conflicts of many everyday social interactions. Such decisions are often characterized by an uncommon degree of realism and intimacy producing real personal involvement (Joinson, 2001; Tidwell & Walther, 2002; Walther, 1992). At a phenomenological level, computer-based communication can be just as real as face-to-face encounters (Walther, 1992).

In terms of classical economic theories, allocation decisions by rational actors should be designed to maximize benefits to the self as far as possible. In zero-sum situations such as the dictator game and the ultimatum game, earnings can only be maximized by keeping as much of the resource as possible. Contrary to this 'selfish' motive, moral philosophers emphasize the importance of fairness to others as a competing decision strategy (see earlier). Actual research suggests an intriguing pattern: instead of clear-cut selfishness or egalitarian fairness, decision makers frequently prefer a decision somewhere between these competing alternatives (Güth et al., 1982). Allocators often give over 30% to others instead of simply maximizing their own benefits. Interestingly, in ultimatum games where responders can veto unfair offers, they often do so and prefer to end up with nothing rather than feel unfairly treated (Bolton, Katok, & Zwick, 1998; Camerer & Thaler, 1995; Forsythe, Horowitz, Savin, & Sefton, 1994; Nowak, Page, & Sigmund, 2000).

In other words, ethical decisions involving selfishness versus fairness are influenced by a combination of motives, including the powerful ethical norm of fairness to others (Güth et al., 1982). Both in the dictator and ultimatum games selfishness must be balanced by attention to implicit fairness norms, confirming that ethical concern with fairness is a universal human characteristic, consistent with evolutionary evidence indicating that fairness norms serve important adaptive functions (Bolton et al., 1998; Camerer & Thaler, 1995; Forgas & East, 2008).

Thus, decision makers must necessarily weigh the conflicting *internal* demands of self-interest against the *external* norms requiring fairness to others (Haselhuhn & Mellers, 2005; Pillutla & Murnighan, 1995). It is precisely these kinds of elaborate, constructive social decisions that require judges to go beyond the available information that seem to be most commonly influenced by affective states, according to accumulating recent evidence (Fiedler, 2001; Forgas, 2002). For example, Andrade and Ariely (2009) found that angry individuals are more likely to reject unfair offers. In another study, Harlé and Sanfey (2007) report that unfair offers were more often rejected by people experiencing negative affect. Concern with fairness, once established, remains influential in subsequent strategic decisions. It seems that when making difficult moral judgments, people are influenced by the subtle interplay of the conflicting *internal* demands of self-interest and the *external* norm of fairness (Haselhuhn & Mellers, 2005; Pillutla & Murnighan, 1995). The present studies investigate the possibility that temporary mood states can play an important role in influencing how such internal and external demands are evaluated in moral decisions, consistent with recent affect-cognition research, to be reviewed next.

## Affective Influences on Ethical Decisions

Considerable recent research suggests that affective states have a dual effect on social decisions, by influencing both (1) the valence and content of the information considered (*informational effects*) and (2) the processing strategies people adopt (*processing effects*).

### Informational Effects

Affect may influence moral decisions either *directly* as a source of information (Clore & Storbeck, 2006; Schwarz, 1990), or *indirectly* by priming affect-congruent information in memory (Bower, 1981; Forgas & Bower, 1987). Both of these effects are likely to give rise to an affect-congruent bias in decisions: happy persons tend to access more positive information and behave in a more optimistic, confident and assertive manner (Forgas, 1999, 2002). Negative mood, in turn, by promoting the recall and use of more negative information, should produce more careful, cautious, pessimistic and socially constrained responses (Forgas, 1998, 2002; Schwarz, 1990).

Numerous experiments support this prediction. People in a positive mood tend to make more confident and less polite requests (Forgas, 1999), are more confident when negotiating (Forgas, 1998) and generally are more likely to impose their internal ideas on the social world (Bless & Fiedler, 2006). Happy mood may also function as a motivational resource (Trope, Ferguson, & Ragunanthan, 2001), allowing happy persons to better deal with more threatening information. Thus, positive affect should result in more self-serving and selfish allocations by *proposers*, but a greater tendency to reject unfair offers by *responders* in the ultimatum and the dictator games.

## Processing Effects

Affect can also influence *processing tendencies*, that is, *how* people process social information (Bless & Fiedler, 2006). Early work suggested that positive affect promotes a more superficial and lazy information-processing style, while negative affect improves attention and processing vigilance. More recent theories by Bless and Fiedler (2006) suggest that negative affect may function as an evolutionary alarm signal calling for more *accommodative*, externally focused processing. In contrast, positive affect tends to facilitate more internally focused, *assimilative* thinking (Clore & Storbeck, 2006; Schwarz, 1990). *Accommodation* and *assimilation* denote these two fundamental adaptive functions, where negative affect promotes a more externally focused processing style, as the individual seeks to *accommodate* to the demands of the external environment. In contrast, positive affect triggers a more *assimilative* processing style, focusing on internal inputs to the decision-making process.

Consistent with this processing dichotomy, negative affect can improve performance on tasks that require careful stimulus processing and attention to external norms and expectations (Forgas, 2007; Gasper & Clore, 2002; Walther & Grigoriadis, 2004). Positive affect, in contrast, improves performance on tasks that require assimilative processing—that is, reliance on internal, preexisting knowledge. For example, people experiencing negative affect tend to pay greater attention to new, external information, and as a result are better at detecting deception (Forgas & East, 2008), have better eyewitness memories (Forgas, Goldenberg, & Unkelbach, 2009), are less likely to rely on stereotypes (Bless et al., 1996; Unkelbach, Forgas, & Denson, 2008) and are less susceptible to judgmental errors (Forgas, 1998).

## The Present Studies

Extrapolating from this evidence, positive and negative affect may also have a significant influence on moral decisions involving selfishness versus fairness. Both informational and processing models predict that *proposers* should show greater selfishness when in a positive mood, and greater fairness when in a negative mood in both the dictator and the ultimatum games (Experiments 1, 2, 3; Forgas & Tan, 2013a, 2013b; Tan & Forgas, 2010). Informational theories imply that positive mood should produce more confident, assertive and selfish decisions, and negative mood should lead to more cautious and less selfish choices (Forgas & Eich, 2012). Processing models predict that positive affect should increase assimilative processing and attention to *internal* selfish impulses, while negative affect should trigger more accommodative and externally oriented processing and greater concern with fairness (Forgas, 2002; Tan & Forgas, 2010).

Can we distinguish between the effects of informational and processing theories? Although for proposers both theories predict greater selfishness in positive mood, and greater fairness in negative mood, in the case of *responders* (Experiment 5), informational and processing theories make divergent predictions. Informational theories suggest that positive mood should produce greater confidence and assertiveness, and thus the rejection of unfair offers. In contrast, processing theories such as the assimilative/accommodative model predict that *responders* in a negative mood should also pay greater attention to *external* norms of fairness and thus reject unfair offers more (Andrade & Ariely, 2009; Harlé & Sanfey, 2007). If positive mood *responders* reject unfair offers more, this supports informational theories. If unfair offers are more likely to be rejected by those in a negative mood, this would support processing explanations (Bless & Fiedler, 2006). These predictions will be evaluated in Experiment 5.

In summary, we hypothesized that (1) positive mood should increase and negative mood decrease selfishness by allocators in both the dictator game and the ultimatum game, and (2) receivers in the ultimatum game should show greater concern with fairness, and consequently should reject unfair offers more when they are in a negative rather than in a positive mood. This second prediction is consistent with processing theories such as the assimilation/accommodation model, but could not be explained by informational theories of mood effects.

## Can Negative Mood Improve Fairness?

The first study (Tan & Forgas, 2010, Exp. 1) explored mood effects on moral decisions by allocators in the dictator game, where they have unfettered freedom to impose their will—in other words, the dictator game represents an almost 'pure' measure of selfishness. The status of the receiver (in-group vs. out-group member) was also manipulated here. The experiment comprised of a 2 × 2 between-subjects design, with mood (happy, sad) and relationship (in-group, out-group other) as the independent variables. It was expected positive mood should increase and negative mood reduce selfishness overall, and these mood effects should be smaller when the decision concerns a partner who is an in-group member, where the norms of fairness may constrain mood effects (Forgas & Fiedler, 1996).

As part of the mood induction, student volunteers ($N = 45$) first received manipulated positive and negative feedback about their performance on a bogus test of cognitive abilities. Next, they played the dictator game on a computer link-up and made allocations either to an in-group member or an out-group member. The game was introduced as requiring the allocator to distribute 10 raffle tickets between themselves and another person, with a $20 voucher as the ultimate prize, so that every raffle ticket gained would increase one's chances of winning the prize. All participants were told that they had been 'randomly' assigned to be allocators. In the in-group condition, they were also told that they will be allocating tickets to a fellow student in their own faculty (the in-group manipulation) or a student in another faculty (out-group).

An analysis of variance (ANOVA) of self-rated mood confirmed that the mood induction was effective: those in the negative mood condition felt significantly worse than those in the positive condition ($M$ = 5.44, $SD$ = 1.60 vs. $M$ = 3.06, $SD$ = 1.09; $F(1,43)$ = 45.74; $p$ = .01). Next, a 2 (mood) × 2 (in-group/out-group partner) ANOVA showed a significant mood main effect on allocations, $F(1,44)$ = 5.02; $p$ < .05, but no other effects, $p$ > .05 (Figure 10.1). Happy players kept more raffle tickets to themselves than did sad students ($M$ = 5.61 vs. 4.68). There was also a nonsignificant trend for greater selfishness towards a stranger in positive mood ($M$ = 5.17 vs. 6.09) than in negative mood ($M$ = 4.69 vs. 4.67) (Figure 10.1). The results of this first experiment confirm that affect had a significant influence on ethical decisions involving fairness vs. selfishness, such that negative mood promoted greater fairness. The next experiment was designed to confirm and extend these findings.

## How Robust Is the Mood Effect on Selfishness Versus Fairness?

In this study (Tan & Forgas, 2010, Exp. 2) a different mood induction (affect-inducing films) was used, and rather than using a single allocation task, a series of eight allocations was used to different partners, with the names and photos of partners also displayed for each task to increase the realism of the task. Participants ($N$ = 72) first evaluated 'films for use in a later study' (in fact, the mood induction) before participating in an 'unrelated' second task, a computer-mediated interaction involving the allocation of 10 points to gain movie passes between themselves and a partner in a dictator game in each of eight encounters. The mood induction films contained excerpts from a popular British comedy series (*Fawlty Towers*) and excerpts from a sad movie dealing with family misfortune (*Angela's Ashes*) (Forgas, 2002, 2007).

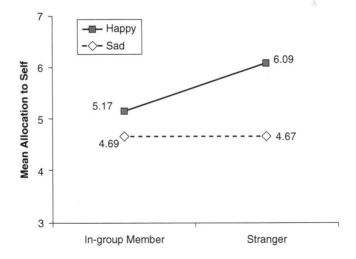

**FIGURE 10.1** The effects of mood (good, bad) and relationship (in-group member vs. stranger) on the selfishness of allocations in a dictator game.

The mood induction was again successful, as self-ratings showed that those in the happy condition were significantly happier than those in the sad condition, $F(1,70) = 274.21; p = .01$ ($M = 1.89; SD = 1.04$ vs. $-1.33; SD = 0.49$). Next, an ANOVA of allocation decisions again revealed a significant mood main effect. Overall, happy individuals were again more selfish and kept more points to themselves ($M = 6.68$ out of 10; $SD = 1.47$) than did sad individuals ($M = 5.82$; $SD = 1.63; F(1,70) = 5.45; p < .05$), supporting the main hypothesis. A further $2 \times 8$ mixed ANOVA showed a significant interaction between mood and the eight trials, $F(7,64) = 3.31; p < .01$, as well as a significant trial by mood linear trend, $F(1,70) = 8.17; p < .01$. As the trials progressed, happy individuals actually became *more* selfish, and sad individuals became more *fair* (Figure 10.2).

Thus, this study again confirmed that mood had a significant influence on selfishness and fairness, and these effects were repeated across eight trials, using a different mood induction procedure and a more realistic decision context. As in Experiment 1, positive affect increased selfishness, and negative mood reduced selfishness, consistent with both the informational and processing theories of mood effects on cognition.

## The Influence of Fairness Norms

In both Experiments 1 and 2, positive mood reduced and negative mood increased fairness. It is noteworthy that even when having complete power in a dictator game, there is nevertheless a marked tendency towards some degree of fairness. What

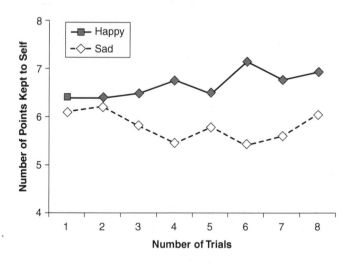

**FIGURE 10.2** The effects of mood on selfishness vs. fairness: happy persons kept more rewards to themselves, and this effect is more pronounced in later trials.

would happen if we explicitly manipulate the fairness norm? In Experiment 3 (Tan & Forgas, 2010, Exp. 3), the fairness norm was explicitly manipulated by giving allocators selective information about the alleged fair or unfair behaviours of *previous* players, so as to reinforce or undermine the social norm of fairness. It was expected that mood effects on ethical decisions should be strongest when the prior behaviour by others undermines the external social norm of fairness.

The procedure was similar to Experiments 1 and 2. Participants ($N = 64$) first viewed affect inducing films before playing the dictator game with a randomly assigned partner. The mood induction videos included excerpts from *Monty Python's Life of Brian* (positive mood), and scenes from the movie *My Life* (negative mood). Before the game, participants were also exposed to information about *fair* or *unfair* offers of "past proposers" to emphasize or de-emphasize the fairness norm. The experiment employed a $2 \times 2$ between subject design with mood (positive and negative) and prior allocations (fair vs. unfair) as the independent variables, and selfishness (the number of points kept) as the dependent variable.

The mood induction was again successful: happy participants rated their mood as significantly better than did the negative group ($M = 1.91$, $SD = 1.08$ vs. $M = -1.24$, $SD = 0.86$; $F(1,60) = 215.56, p = .001$). Neither the fairness manipulation ($F(1,60) = 3.19, p > .05$) nor a mood by fairness interaction influenced self-rated mood ($F(1,606) = 1.18, p > .20$).

Allocations were next analyzed using a $2 \times 2$ ANOVA. There was a significant interaction between mood and fairness norm, $F(1,60) = 4.35; p < .037$ (Figure 10.3). When prior allocators were unfair, there was a significant difference between happy and sad people, $F(1,33) = 3.79; p < .05$: happy allocators were significantly more selfish ($M = 7.56; SD = 2.47$) than the sad group ($M = 5.59; SD = 3.44$). In contrast, when fairness by prior allocators was emphasized there was *no difference* in allocations between happy and sad participants, $F(1,27) = 1.18; p < .287$ ($M = 6.56; SD = 1.78; M = 7.38; SD = 2.29$).

These results show that prior emphasis on the ethical fairness norms indeed reduced mood effects on allocations. In contrast, when selfish behaviour by prior allocators was emphasized, undermining the fairness norm, there was less external pressure and greater latitude for mood-induced differences to emerge. This pattern suggests that mood effects on selfishness are greatest when fairness norms are weak, allowing greater scope for mood-induced differences in processing style to influence outcomes.

These three experiments looked at mood effects on ethical decisions in the dictator game, characterized by unrestricted freedom by the allocators to do as they wish. What happens when this 'dictatorial' choice is constrained, because an allocation can be rejected by the other party, in which case neither side receives anything? By its very nature, the ultimatum game forces allocators to give more careful consideration to the expectations of the recipient, who can veto any proposition. The next two experiments explored affective influences on ethical decisions by allocators and recipients in the ultimatum game.

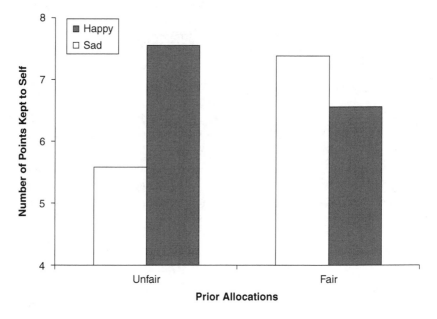

**FIGURE 10.3** The effects of mood and emphasizing or de-emphasizing the norm of fairness on allocations in the dictator game: Mood effects are stronger when the fairness norm is de-emphasized (prior allocators are unfair) rather than emphasized (prior allocators are fair).

## Mood Effects on Fairness in the Ultimatum Game

This study (Forgas & Tan, 2013b, Exp. 1) sought to replicate the kind of mood effects on fairness demonstrated in Experiments 1–3 in the more complex decisional environment of the ultimatum game, where proposers must also consider the willingness of responders to accept or reject their offers. The second main aim of this experiment was to collect direct evidence about the processing strategies involved in producing these effects, by directly measuring the time taken to reach their decisions by happy and sad participants. It was expected that the more accommodative and externally oriented processing recruited in a negative mood should result in increased processing latencies compared to assimilative processing and reliance on internal information in a positive mood.

On arrival, participants were informed that they will be participating in two unrelated experiments, a film evaluation task (in fact, the mood induction) and an interaction task (the ultimatum game). Both tasks were presented consecutively on a computer using the DirectRT program. First, positive and negative moods were induced by watching a short film. Participants viewed brief 10-minute positive (excerpts from the *Fawlty Towers* comedy series) or negative (excerpts from *Angela's Ashes*) edited video clips, and were instructed to view the films as if they were watching TV at home.

Next, all participants ($N$ = 81) were 'randomly' assigned to be *proposers*, and played the ultimatum game dividing 10 points between themselves and a responder, each worth one ticket in a draw to win free movie passes. Thus, mood (positive and negative) was the independent variable, and *fairness level* (number of points kept) and *response latencies* (in seconds) were the dependent variables. To make the task more realistic, bogus photos of responders were displayed and participants believed that their own photo taken at the start of the session was visible to responders.

An ANOVA confirmed that the mood induction was successful, $F(1,79)$ = 146.61; $p$ = .001, showing that participants in the positive condition were in a significantly better mood than those in the negative condition ($M$ = 1.62 vs. −1.12). An analysis of the fairness of allocations also showed a significant mood main effect, $F(1,79)$ = 4.58; $p$ < .05. As hypothesized, those in a negative mood were more fair and allocated significantly more points ($M$ = 5.90; $SD$ = 0.94) to others than did happy individuals ($M$ = 5.33; $SD$ = 1.44). An ANOVA of response latencies also revealed a significant mood effect, $F(1,79)$ = 9.19; $p$ = .003. As expected, sad individuals took longer to make allocation decisions ($M$ = 10.40 s) than did happy individuals ($M$ = 9.62 s), consistent with their predicted more accommodative and attentive processing style.

This experiment is the first to demonstrate that mood-induced differences in selfishness and fairness can be directly linked to different processing strategies and processing latencies. Those in a negative mood were significantly more fair and also performed the allocation task more slowly than did participants in a positive mood (Bless & Fiedler, 2006; Forgas, 2002; Schwarz, 1990). Only processing theories such as the assimilative/accommodative processing theory imply differences in processing style and processing latency, as found here. By focusing attention externally, negative mood increased processing latencies and resulted in more fair and equitable decisions. The next experiment will look at mood effects on the behavior of *responders* rather than proposers in the ultimatum game.

## Mood Effects on Willingness to Accept Unfair Decisions in the Ultimatum Game

Experiment 5 was designed to show that mood can also influence the degree of fairness recipients are willing to *accept* in the ultimatum game (Forgas & Tan, 2013b, Exp. 2). If negative mood indeed promotes more accommodative and norm-aware processing, responders in a negative mood should be more concerned with fairness norms and thus be more likely to reject unfair offers. In contrast, according to *informational models*, positive affect should increase confidence and assertiveness and the tendency to reject unfair offers. Thus, analyzing mood effects on the behaviour of respondents will allow a direct evaluation of the differential predictions of informational and processing theories of mood effects.

The same procedure was employed as in Experiment 4, but this time all participants ($N = 90$) were 'randomly' allocated to be *responders* rather than allocators. The same mood induction procedure was employed. Each participant received four offers of different levels of fairness (2, 3 or 4 out of 10 points) in four consecutive allocation trials by two male and two female proposers in a random order, and indicated their decision to accept or reject each offer. The experiment employed a 2 × 4 mixed design, with *mood* (positive, negative) and *fairness offer type* (2, 2, 3 or 4 points) as the independent variables and *acceptance rate* as the dependent variable. The mood induction was again highly effective, as those in the positive mood condition rated their mood as significantly better than did those in the negative mood condition, $F(1,88) = 176.31; p = .001$ ($M = 4.88$ vs. 2.69). An ANOVA of responders acceptance or rejection of allocations found a significant mood main effect on acceptance, $F(1,88) = 4.55; p < .05$. Overall, 57% of those in negative mood rejected unfair offers compared to only 45% in the positive condition (see Figure 10.4). This mood effect was most marked in reactions to the less fair, 2- and 3-point offers, but disappeared for the most fair 4-point offers, accepted by 98% of respondents.

Acceptance for unfair offers of 2 points was low, but acceptance gradually increased as offers became more fair (26%, 48% and 98% for the 2-, 3- and 4-point offers, respectively). No significant mood by offer size interaction effect was found, $F(3,88) = 1.41, p > .20$. This result confirms that rejections were consistently higher in negative than in positive mood, a finding that clearly supports processing theories that predict that negative mood should increase and positive mood reduce attention to external fairness norms. This pattern is not readily explained by informational models that imply greater confidence and assertiveness, and higher rejection rates by those in a positive mood.

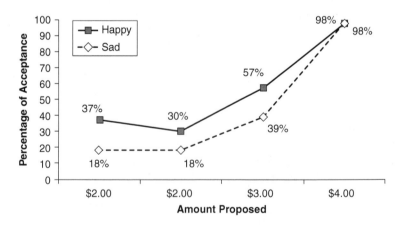

**FIGURE 10.4** The effects of mood (good, bad) and offer fairness on the acceptance of offers by responders in the ultimatum game.

## General Discussion

Deciding between selfishness and fairness, how much to keep and how much to give to others, is one of the more common ethical dilemmas we encounter in everyday life (see also Graziano & Schroeder, this volume). These experiments are the first to show that mild positive and negative moods can have a significant and consistent influence on such moral decisions. The dictator game and the ultimatum game offer particularly suitable methods for exploring such effects, as they represent well-defined and realistic decision contexts. All five experiments consistently showed that fairness was greater when people experienced *negative* rather than *positive* moods.

Positive affect in contrast increased selfishness and reduced fairness both in the dictator game (Experiments 1–3), and in the ultimatum game (Experiments 4 and 5). We also found that decisions in a negative mood took longer to perform than in a positive mood, providing direct evidence that mood-induced differences in processing style may be responsible for these effects (Experiment 2). The final experiment, Experiment 5, provides selective support for processing rather than informational theories of mood effects on moral decisions. These results have some interesting theoretical and practical implications for understanding mood effects on how people resolve ethical dilemmas.

## *Theoretical Implications*

The dictator game used in Experiments 1, 2 and 3 represents a simple, almost pure framework in which to behave selfishly. Interestingly, even when allocators faced no constraint on how selfish they wanted to be, they still displayed some degree of fairness and allocated some resources to their partners. Across all conditions examined, negative mood significantly increased, and negative mood reduced fairness, consistent with those in a negative mood paying more attention to external norms mandating fairness. These results are consistent with theories predicting mood-induced differences in processing strategies (Bless & Fiedler, 2006). Those in a negative mood, thinking more accommodatively, were more willing to follow the external ethical norm of fairness, while those in a good mood, thinking more assimilatively, were more willing to follow their internal selfish dispositions.

Focusing more on external information when in a negative mood is also in line with recent findings showing that negative mood improves eyewitness memory, reduces stereotyping, increases politeness, and reduces judgmental errors (Forgas, 1998, 1999; Forgas et al., 2009; Unkelbach et al., 2008). These findings converge towards indicating that affect has an important signalling function when performing complex decisions (Clore & Storbeck, 2006; Forgas et al., 2007; Schwarz, 1990), with negative affect calling for more externally focused, accommodative thinking, and positive affect promoting a more assimilative, internally focused strategy (Bless, 2000; Bless & Fiedler, 2006; Fiedler, 2001). Greater concern with fairness when in a negative mood in all five experiments here is consistent with this prediction.

An analysis of mood effects on the behaviour of recipients (Experiment 5) showed that their concern with fairness was also greater in negative than in positive mood, supporting processing theories. This pattern is also consistent with other research showing that happy persons are generally more likely to follow their internal inclinations (in this case, selfishness) (De Vries, Holland, & Witteman, 2008; Unkelbach et al., 2008), consistent with affect having an important adaptive signalling function directing attention to internal versus external information (Clore & Storbeck, 2006; Schwarz, 1990). Processing accounts are also supported by recent findings showing that negative mood improves attention to the external world (Foerster, 2010; Forgas, 1998, 1999; Forgas et al., 2009; Unkelbach et al., 2008; Walther & Grigoriadis, 2004).

We should note that the encounters we studied did not involve real face-to-face communication, although the partners' photos were displayed, and participants did believe that they are interacting with a real person. As similar effects have now been obtained in a wide range of laboratory as well as real-life situations, we believe that face-to-face communication should show similar mood effects.

## Practical Implications

Many scenarios in our private as well as our working lives involve some conflict between acting selfishly and acting fairly (see also Galinsky & Lee; and Simpson et al., this volume). Social cognitive processes, such as the ones examined here, can play an important role in such ethical conflicts. Despite some evidence for mood effects on social decisions (Forgas & Eich, 2012), the effects of moods on selfishness in ethical conflicts have received little empirical attention in the past. The kind of mood effects on selfishness demonstrated here may have important implications for real-life behaviours in romantic relationships, organizational decisions, and many other everyday situations where decisions by one person have incontestable consequences for others.

Interestingly, our results further challenge the common assumption in much of applied, organizational, clinical and health psychology that positive affect has universally desirable social and interpersonal consequences. Together with other recent experimental studies, our findings confirm that negative affect often produces adaptive and more socially sensitive and ethical outcomes. For example, negative moods can improve the detection of deception (Forgas & East, 2008), improve impression formation (Forgas, 1998), benefit eyewitness accuracy (Forgas, Vargas, & Laham, 2005) and result in more effective interpersonal communication strategies (Forgas, 2007). The present experiments confirm this pattern by demonstrating that mild negative moods also increase fairness and sensitivity to the needs of others.

## Limitations and Future Prospects

We focused on selfishness versus fairness here, one of the most important and ubiquitous ethical conflicts people face in interpersonal situations. Other kinds of interpersonal decisions may well recruit different processing approaches, and may produce different results, as also found in the voluminous literature on altruism and helping (Batson, 1991; Carlson & Miller, 1987; Dovidio, Piliavin, Schroeder, & Penner, 2006). Having the power to impose one's preferences (as in the dictator game), or making the first move to propose a sharing of resources (as in the ultimatum game) represents a complex, yet highly controlled setting with considerable face validity in which to investigate mood effects on interpersonal strategies.

Behavior in economic games can also be influenced by framing and context effects, such as playing with a real versus a hypothetical person (Fantino, Gaitan, Kennelly, & Stolarz-Fantino, 2007), whether partners are able or not to propose a counteroffer (Stephen & Pham, 2007) and the personal relevance of the task (Forgas & Fiedler, 1996). Investigating such issues deserves further attention. Even though the decisions studied here did not involve face-to-face contact, affect is likely to have similar consequences on ethical decisions in a face-to-face situation (Joinson, 2001; Joinson, McKenna, & Postmes, 2007; Wallace, 1999).

As we have seen, mood effects on selfishness are highly dependent on the processing strategies adopted by allocators (Fiedler, 2001; Forgas, 1995, 2002; Sedikides, 1995), which in turn are often influenced by a variety of contextual and situational factors. For example, when normative information was provided about the fair behavior of others, reinforcing the norm of fairness, the size of mood effects decreased (Experiment 3), suggesting that external, normative pressures can reduce the extent to which people are willing to engage in open, generative and constructive processing, thus impairing mood effects as also found in other research (Forgas & Eich, 2012).

As the results were conceptually consistent across the five experiments, and are also in line with findings obtained in conceptually similar studies (Andrade & Ariely, 2009; Harlé & Sanfey, 2007; Tan & Forgas, 2010), we can be reasonably confident that they are reliable. However, further research may also look at the consequences of more intense and specific emotions on moral decisions such as anger, disgust, pride or embarrassment (Lerner & Keltner, 2001; Srivastava, Espinoza, & Fedorikhin, 2009).

## Conclusions

In conclusion, interpersonal decisions involving a moral conflict between selfishness and fairness represent a common everyday task that seems open to affective influences. There is an urgent need to investigate how affective states impact the way people deal with everyday moral conflicts. These experiments extend research on affect and social cognition (Bower, 1981; Fiedler, 2001; Fiedler & Bless, 2000; Forgas, 1995, 2002) to the new domain of moral conflicts, and show that negative mood can increase and positive mood reduce attention to external fairness norms in such encounters. Our results are broadly consistent with recent affect cognition theorizing in experimental social psychology (Bless & Fiedler, 2006), and extend this work to the area of solving ethical dilemmas. We hope that these studies will stimulate further empirical interest in this interesting and relevant field.

# References

Andrade, E.B., & Ariely, D. (2009). The enduring impact of transient emotions on decision making. *Organizational Behavior and Human Decision Processes, 109*, 1–8.

Batson, C.D. (1991). *The altruism question: Toward a social-psychological answer.* Hillsdale, NJ: Erlbaum.

Bless, H. (2000). The interplay of affect and cognition: The mediating role of general knowledge structures. In J.P. Forgas (Ed.), *Feeling and thinking: The role of affect in social cognition* (pp. 131–152). New York: Cambridge University Press.

Bless, H., Clore, G.L., Schwarz, N., Golisano, V., Rabe, C., & Wolk, M. (1996). Mood and the use of scripts: Does happy mood really lead to mindlessness? *Journal of Personality and Social Psychology, 71*, 665–679.

Bless, H., & Fiedler, K. (2006). Mood and the regulation of information processing and behavior. In J.P. Forgas (Ed.), *Affect in social thinking and behavior* (pp. 65–84). New York: Psychology Press.

Bolton, G.E., Katok, E., & Zwick, R. (1998). Dictator game giving: Rules of fairness versus acts of kindness. *International Journal of Game Theory, 27*(2), 269.

Bower, G.H. (1981). Mood and memory. *American Psychologist, 36*, 129–148.

Camerer, C., & Thaler, R.H. (1995). Anomalies: Ultimatums, dictators and manners. *Journal of Economic Perspectives, 9*(2), 209–219.

Carlson, M., & Miller, N. (1987). Explanation of the relation between negative mood and helping. *Psychological Bulletin, 102*, 91–108.

Clore, G.L., & Storbeck, J. (2006). Affect as information about liking, efficacy and importance. In J.P. Forgas (Ed.), *Affect in social thinking and behavior* (pp. 123–143). New York: Psychology Press.

De Vries, M., Holland, R.W., & Witteman, C.L.M. (2008). In the winning mood: Affect in the Iowa gambling task. *Judgment and Decision Making, 3*, 42–50.

Dovidio, J.F., Piliavin, J.A., Schroeder, D.A., & Penner, L.A. (2006). *The social psychology of prosocial behavior.* Mahwah, NJ: Erlbaum.

Fantino, E., Gaitan, S., Kennelly, A., & Stolarz-Fantino, S. (2007). How reinforcer type affects choice in economic games. *Behavioural Processes, 75*, 107–114.

Fiedler, K. (2001). Affective influences on social information processing. In J.P. Forgas (Ed.), *Handbook of affect and social cognition* (pp. 163–185). Mahwah, NJ: Lawrence Erlbaum Associates.

Fiedler, K., & Bless, H. (2000). The formation of beliefs in the interface of affective and cognitive processes. In N. Frijda, A. Manstead, & S. Bem (Eds.), *The influence of emotions on beliefs* (pp. 144–170). New York: Cambridge University Press.

Foerster, J. (2010). A systems account of global versus local processing. *Psychological Inquiry*, *21*, 175–197.

Forgas, J.P. (1995). Mood and judgment: The Affect Infusion Model (AIM). *Psychological Bulletin*, *117*(1), 39–66.

Forgas, J.P. (1998). Happy and mistaken? Mood effects on the fundamental attribution error. *Journal of Personality and Social Psychology*, *75*, 318–331.

Forgas, J.P. (1999). Feeling and speaking: Mood effects on verbal communication strategies. *Personality and Social Psychology Bulletin*, *25*(7), 850–863.

Forgas, J.P. (2002). Feeling and doing: Affective influences on interpersonal behavior. *Psychological Inquiry*, *13*(1), 1–28.

Forgas, J.P. (Ed.). (2006). *Affect in social thinking and social behaviour*. New York: Psychology Press.

Forgas, J.P. (2007). When sad is better than happy: Mood effects on the effectiveness of persuasive messages. *Journal of Experimental Social Psychology*, *43*, 513–128.

Forgas, J.P., & Bower, G.H. (1987). Mood effects on person perception judgements. *Journal of Personality and Social Psychology*, *53*, 53–60.

Forgas, J.P., & East, R. (2008). On being happy and gullible: Mood effects on scepticism and the detection of deception. *Journal of Experimental Social Psychology*, *44*, 1362–1367.

Forgas, J.P., & Eich, E.E. (2012). Affective influences on cognition: Mood congruence, mood dependence, and mood effects on processing strategies. In A.F. Healy & R.W. Proctor (Eds.), *Handbook of Psychology: Vol. 4. Experimental psychology* (I.B. Weiner, Editor-in-Chief) (pp. 61–82). New York: Wiley.

Forgas, J.P., & Fiedler, K. (1996). Us and them: Mood effects on intergroup discrimination. *Journal of Personality and Social Psychology*, *70*, 28–40.

Forgas, J.P., Goldenberg, L., & Unkelbach, C. (2009). Can bad weather improve your memory? A field study of mood effects on memory in a real-life setting. *Journal of Experimental Social Psychology*, *54*, 254–257.

Forgas, J.P., Haselton, M., & von Hippel, W. (Eds.). (2007). *Evolution and the social mind*. New York: Psychology Press.

Forgas, J.P., & Tan, H.B. (2013a). To give or to keep? Affective influences on selfishness and fairness in computer-mediated interactions in the dictator game and the ultimatum game. *Computers and Human Behavior*, *29*, 64–74.

Forgas, J.P., & Tan, H.B. (2013b). Mood effects on selfishness versus fairness: Affective influences on social decisions in the ultimatum game. *Social Cognition*, *31*, 504–517.

Forgas, J.P., Vargas, P., & Laham, S. (2005). Mood effects on eyewitness memory: Affective influences on susceptibility to misinformation. *Journal of Experimental Social Psychology*, *41*, 574–588.

Forsythe, R., Horowitz, J.L., Savin, N.E., & Sefton, M. (1994). Fairness in simple bargaining experiments. *Games and Economic Behavior*, *6*(3), 347–369.

Gasper, K., & Clore, G.L. (2002). Attending to the big picture: Mood and global versus local processing of visual information. *Psychological Science*, *13*(1), 34.

Güth, W., Schmittberger, R., & Schwarze, B. (1982). An experimental analysis of ultimatum bargaining. *Journal of Economic Behavior & Organization*, *3*(4), 367–388.

Harlé, K.M., & Sanfey, A. (2007). Incidental sadness biases social economic decisions in the ultimatum game. *Emotion*, *7*, 876–881.

Haselhuhn, M.P., & Mellers, B.A. (2005). Emotions and cooperation in economic games. *Cognitive Brain Research*, *23*, 24–33.

Jarvenpaa, A.L., Knoll, K., & Leidner, D. E. (1998). Is there anybody out there? Antecedents of trust in global virtual teams. *Journal of Management Information Systems, 14*, 22–34.

Joinson, A.N. (2001). Self-disclosure in computer-mediated communication: The role of self-awareness and visual anonymity. *European Journal of Social Psychology, 31*, 177–192.

Joinson, A., McKenna, K.Y.A., & Postmes, T. (Eds.). (2007). *Oxford handbook of internet psychology*. Oxford: Oxford University Press.

Lerner, J. S & Keltner, D. (2001). Fear, anger, and risk. *Journal of Personality & Social Psychology, 81*, 146–159.

Nowak, M.A., Page, K.M., & Sigmund, K. (2000). Fairness versus reason in the ultimatum game. *Science, 289*, 1773–1775.

Pillutla, M.M., & Murnighan, J.K. (1995). Being fair or appearing fair: Strategic behavior in ultimatum bargaining. *Academy of Management Journal, 38*, 1408–1426.

Schwarz, N. (1990). Feelings as information: Informational and motivational functions of affective states. In E.T. Higgins & R. Sorrentino (Eds.), *Handbook of motivation and cognition: Foundations of social behavior* (Vol. 2, pp. 527–561). New York: Guilford Press.

Sedikides, C. (1995). Central and peripheral self-conceptions are differentially influenced by mood: Test of the differential sensitivity hypothesis. *Journal of Personality and Social Psychology, 69*, 759–777.

Srivastava, J., Espinoza, F., & Fedorikhin, A. (2009). Coupling and decoupling of unfairness and anger in ultimatum bargaining. *Journal of Behavioral Decision Making, 22*, 475–489.

Stephen, A.T., & Pham, M.T. (2007). On feelings as a heuristic for making offers in ultimatum negotiations. *Psychological Science, 19*(10), 1051–1058.

Tan, H.B., & Forgas, J.P. (2010). When happiness makes us selfish, but sadness makes us fair: Affective influences on interpersonal strategies in the dictator game. *Journal of Experimental Social Psychology, 46*(3), 571–576.

Tidwell, L.C., & Walther, J.B. (2002). Computer-mediated communication effects on disclosure, impressions, and interpersonal evaluations. *Human Communications Research, 28*, 317–348.

Trope, Y., Ferguson, M., & Ragunanthan, R. (2001). Mood as a resource in processing self-relevant information. In J.P. Forgas (Ed.), *Handbook of affect and social cognition* (pp. 213–234). Mahwah, NJ: Lawrence Erlbaum Associates.

Unkelbach, C., Forgas, J.P., & Denson, T.F. (2008). The turban effect: The influence of Muslim headgear and induced affect on aggressive responses in the shooter bias paradigm. *Journal of Experimental Social Psychology, 44*, 1409–1413

Wallace, P. (Ed.). (1999). *The psychology of the internet*. Cambridge: Cambridge University Press.

Walther, J.B. (1992). Interpersonal effects of computer-mediated interaction: a relational perspective. *Communications Research, 19*, 52–90.

Walther, E., & Grigoriadis, S. (2004). Why sad people like shoes better: The influence of mood on the evaluative conditioning of consumer attitudes. *Psychology and Marketing, 21*, 755–773.

Zajonc, R.B. (1980). Feeling and thinking: Preferences need no inferences. *American Psychologist, 35*, 151–175.

# PART III

# Ironic and Paradoxical Effects of Morality

# 11

# CAN HIGH MORAL PURPOSES UNDERMINE SCIENTIFIC INTEGRITY?

*Lee Jussim, Jarret T. Crawford, Sean T. Stevens,*
*Stephanie M. Anglin, and Jose L. Duarte*

*In this chapter, we review basic processes by which moral purposes can sometimes motivate immoral behavior, and then suggest how moral agendas can sometimes lead social psychology astray through an array of questionable interpretive practices (QIPs). These practices can be used to advance a moral agenda by permitting researchers to interpret the data as supporting that agenda even when it does not. The QIPs reviewed here include: blind spots (overlooking or ignoring data inconsistent with one's moral agenda), selective preference (accepting research supporting one's agenda at face value, but subjecting opposing research of comparable or greater quality to withering criticism), and phantom facts (making declarations or drawing implications without evidence). Four major areas of social psychological research—sex differences, stereotype threat, attitudes toward climate science, and the ideology-prejudice relationship—are reviewed and shown to be characterized by unjustified conclusions plausibly reflecting high moral purposes. The chapter concludes with a discussion of how to reduce QIPs in research that has moral undertones.*

Social psychological research and historical events have repeatedly shown that moral righteousness can and has led to immoral behavior in many contexts outside of science. This chapter suggests that social psychological research itself, when driven by high moral concerns, can and often does produce distorted and invalid claims. First we discuss historical and social psychological evidence that high moral purposes can lead to immoral behavior. Next we briefly review recently identified statistical and methodological threats to the validity of social psychological research. We then introduce a set of heretofore unrecognized threats involving distortions to the *claims* made on the basis of scientific research—what we term questionable interpretive practices (QIPs). When researchers have high moral purposes, they may be enticed into using QIPs to advance their moral goals at the expense of making scientifically true claims. This chapter reviews the psychological processes by which this can happen, applies them to scientists' own behavior, shows how such processes have likely led to distortions in several areas of social psychological research, and identifies ways to limit such distortions.

## The Moral Irony of High Moral Purposes: Can High Moral Purposes "Justify" Immoral Behavior?

The answer from history is a clear "yes." History is littered with harm committed in the name of high moral purposes. Destruction or subjugation of indigenous peoples in the Americas, Australia, and Asia was believed to constitute the "advancement" of civilization. The Spanish Inquisition was conducted by the Catholic Church in the name of God. The abuses of McCarthyism were conducted to fight communist tyranny. Terrorism, suicide bombings, and the mass murder of civilians are typically conducted by those who deeply believe their cause is righteous (Baumeister, 2012). Certainly, not all who act with moral justifications commit atrocities. Nonetheless, the historical evidence indicates that believing one's cause is righteous can and has been used to justify discrimination, oppression, and violence.

Recent social psychological research on the nature of morality and the psychology of ideology is consistent with these historical observations, and may help explain how moral justifications can and have been used to perpetrate moral transgressions (see, e.g., Graham & Haidt, 2012; Skitka & Morgan, 2014). Consider the notion of "moral licensing": people who have committed a good deed feel license to behave immorally afterward (e.g., Conway & Peetz, 2012). Morality includes codes of conduct that guides people's actions (Forgas, Jussim, & Van Lange, this volume). The purpose of such codes is to produce "good" behavior, but good can be so subjective that one person's good behavior is another's bad behavior (e.g., protecting the sanctity of marriage by forbidding gay couples to marry). Sacredness refers to "the human tendency to invest people, places, times, and ideas with importance far beyond the utility they possess" (Graham & Haidt, 2012, p. 14). Holding something sacred can provide justification for immoral behavior.

For instance, Graham and Haidt (2012) presented a qualitative interpretation of *The Turner Diaries*, a fictional work that is considered a "bible of the racist right" by the Southern Poverty Law Center (Jackson, 2004). It depicts the overthrow of the US government by an Aryan movement to restore White supremacy, which later leads to a race war. This analysis revealed that loyalty to and self-sacrifice for the Aryan rebellion, as well as the purity of the White race, were treated as moral ideals. Graham and Haidt (2012) also analyzed press releases from the Weather Underground, a militant left-wing group that engaged in terrorist attacks against the US government. They concluded that the Weather Underground sacralized non-White populations, the poor, and the oppressed as victims of evil White capitalist America, which required extermination. This narrative drew primarily on the moral concerns associated with the provision of care and the prevention of harm. Thus, the laudable moral ideals of providing care for and preventing harm to the disadvantaged was used to justify actions that harmed others (e.g., bombing police stations and other government-affiliated buildings).

Political ideology is often anchored in moral intuitions that can help "bind" people into moral communities possessing shared values, worldviews (Graham & Haidt, 2012; Haidt, 2012) and moral social identities (Parker & Janoff-Bulman, 2013). Moral convictions, which reflect a strong and absolute belief that something is right or wrong without the need for proof or evidence, have a dark side (see Skitka, 2010; Skitka & Morgan, 2014). When people strongly identify with such groups, they are routinely intolerant of those with different values and worldviews (e.g., Chambers, Schlenker, & Collisson, 2013; Crawford & Pilanski, 2014; Wetherell, Brandt, & Reyna, 2013; for reviews, see Brandt, Wetherell, & Crawford, this volume; Brandt, Reyna, Chambers, Crawford, & Wetherell, 2014). For instance, self-identified American liberals and conservatives display equal willingness to deprive each other of constitutionally protected rights (Crawford, 2014; Crawford & Pilanski, 2014).

The fact that laypeople can and at times do use moral imperatives to justify immoral acts raises the possibility that they may also, at least sometimes, obstruct scientists' focus on "getting it right." How might this manifest? One possibility is that researchers may sometimes allow their moral purposes to influence how they conduct and interpret their research. The most extreme possibilities are that high moral purposes may distort or even invalidate their research. To understand how, it is necessary to understand (1) what we mean by scientific integrity and (2) common threats to scientific integrity.

## Can High Moral Purposes Undermine the Integrity of Social Psychology?

### What Is Scientific Integrity?

"Scientific integrity" refers to two related but separate ideas: (1) the personal honesty of individual scientists in the conduct and reporting of their research; and (2) developing robust bodies of conclusions that are valid and unimpaired by errors and biases. Even when researchers suffer no lack of personal integrity, conventional practices common in their field may produce findings that are misleading or invalid. Nonetheless, "getting it right" is the sine qua non of science (Funder et al., 2013). Science can tolerate individual mistakes and flawed theories, but only if it has reliable mechanisms for efficient correction. This is perhaps most obvious in engineering (where, for example, a poorly designed product may not work or, in some cases, be dangerous) and medical interventions (some of which make people less rather than more healthy). However, even within psychology, large amounts of time, effort, and resources can and have been wasted chasing phenomena that only appeared to be real (e.g., fewer options increases satisfaction with one's choice; thinking about Florida leads people to walk slowly) through a combination of p-hacking and publication biases (e.g., Lakens, 2015; Simonsohn, Nelson, & Simmons, 2014).

## Known Threats to the Integrity of Social Psychology

### Statistical and Methodological Threats

Questionable research practices, failures to replicate, faulty statistical practices, lack of transparency, publication biases, and political biases all potentially threaten scientific integrity (Begley & Ellis, 2012; Cummings, 2013; Ioannidis, 2005; Jussim, Crawford, Stevens, & Anglin, in press; Simmons, Nelson, & Simonsohn, 2011). Individuals and organizations have begun addressing scientific integrity failures through reforms primarily targeting transparency, statistics, and methods.

Nonetheless, there is a set of practices unrelated to methods or statistics that has not received much attention in ongoing scientific integrity discussions, but which can similarly threaten the validity of scientific conclusions: questionable interpretive practices. Because these practices involve subjective decisions about which there may often be no clearly right or wrong methodological or statistical guidelines, they are easily triggered by morally righteous motivations. The rest of this chapter addresses how these subjective judgments can threaten scientific integrity.

### Confirmation Bias Among Laypeople

People's motivations can influence their reasoning. Motivated reasoning refers to biased information processing that is driven by goals unrelated to accurate belief formation (Kahan, 2011; Kunda, 1990). A specific type of motivated reasoning, confirmation bias, occurs when people seek out and evaluate information in ways that confirm their preexisting views while downplaying, ignoring, or discrediting information opposing their views (Nickerson, 1998; also referred to as "myside bias," see Stanovich, West, & Toplak, 2013). People intensely scrutinize counter-attitudinal evidence while easily accepting information supporting their views (e.g., Ditto & Lopez, 1992; Lord, Ross, & Lepper, 1979). Although these processes are affectively driven (e.g., Jacks & Devine, 2000; Munro & Ditto, 1997; Zuwerink & Devine, 1996), people generate convincing arguments to justify their automatic evaluations, producing an illusion of objectivity (Haidt, 2001; Nickerson, 1998).

## Confirmation Bias Among Social Scientists

Scientists are not immune to confirmation bias (Ioannidis, 2012; Lilienfeld, 2010). Reviewers' theoretical (Epstein, 2004; Mahoney, 1977) and ideological (Abramowitz, Gomes, & Abramowitz, 1975) views influence their evaluation of research reports. Values influence each phase of the research process, including how people interpret research findings (Duarte et al., 2015). Although scientists strive to be objective, confirmation biases have considerable potential to influence study design and the evaluation and interpretation of evidence.

## Questionable Interpretive Practices as an "Under the Radar" Threat to the Integrity of Social Psychological Science

Even if methods and statistics are impeccable, it is *still* possible to reach distorted conclusions through questionable interpretive practices (QIPs)—conceptual and narrative tools for reaching desired conclusions, even when data are inconsistent with those conclusions (Jussim et al., in press). QIPs are a mechanism by which researcher confirmation biases (e.g., Lilienfeld, 2010) can distort conclusions, even with untainted data.

Although there are many QIPs (Jussim et al., in press; see Brandt & Proulx, 2015, for a discussion of the related phenomenon of QTIPs, or questionable theoretical and interpretive practices), this chapter focuses on:

- *blind spots*: overlooking data and studies that conflict with one's preferred conclusions.
- *selective preference*: highlighting studies consistent with one's preferred conclusions and downplaying, criticizing, or dismissing equally high quality studies inconsistent with those conclusions.
- *phantom facts*: declaring something true, or making an implicit assumption that something is true, without providing empirical evidence.

We next review four areas of research in which a plausible case can be made that high moral purposes have led to scientific distortions.

## High Moral Purpose I: Combating "Isms"

Social psychology has a rich history of advocacy research designed to combat inaccurate stereotypes, unjustified prejudices, and many types of discrimination. These are undoubtedly high moral aims—and many social psychologists may take "making a difference" as a high moral purpose (Unger, 2011). Furthermore, many valuable social scientific insights have emerged from the long-standing efforts of social psychologists toward understanding these enduring social problems.

Conducting research to reduce oppression, however, is exactly the type of worthy moral purpose that risks compromising the scientific integrity of social psychology. Morally motivated scientists may suborn their subtle and complex theories to generate false or misleading claims that advance their agenda. This vulnerability was aptly captured by the recently proposed Paranoid Egalitarian Meliorism (PEM) model (Winegard, Winegard, & Geary, 2015):

> We do not mean paranoid pejoratively; rather we mean it as a form of error-management (Haselton & Nettle, 2006). In this view, paranoid refers to a heightened sensitivity to perceive injustices and/or threats to equality. Because of this, many social psychologists: (1) study topics that are related to perceived injustices (stereotyping, prejudice, hierarchies, immorality of the wealthy, obedience); (2) ignore topics that are perceived to threaten egalitarianism (heritability, stereotype accuracy, possible benefits of conformity/hierarchy); and (3) become hostile/biased against research suggesting that some outcome differences among individuals and/or groups are at least partially caused by differences in personal traits rather than by discrimination or social oppression (e.g., that sex differences in STEM field representation are partially caused by cognitive differences and the different occupational preferences of men and women). At its most extreme, PEM can lead to the creation of "victim groups" who become quarantined from objective scientific analysis. Protection of such perceived victim groups becomes a sacred value (Tetlock, 2003), and those who are perceived as violating this sacred value are assailed. Biased reviews, funding, and hiring decisions are justified because they are means to protecting a sacred cause.

Although the term "paranoid" may be too strong, the phenomena they described strongly implicate high moral purposes as threats to scientific integrity. Indeed, it is even possible that some scientists view research that exposes and combats the evils of oppression, discrimination, and injustice as a "moral opportunity" (Miller & Monin, this volume) to advance the impression that they are good, decent egalitarians. The following examples strongly suggest that the PEM can give some insight into how social psychologists sometimes get their science wrong and, therefore, inform current and future perspectives about how to get it right.

### The Science and Politics of Minimizing Gender Differences

The systematic study of gender similarities and differences became a prominent area of research in psychology in the 1970s, coinciding with the modern feminist movement in the US. Many psychologists studied sex differences from a feminist perspective, seeking to demonstrate that gender differences are small to nonexistent in order to promote gender equality and advance women's status in society (Eagly, 1995). Although the goal of improving women's access to equal opportunity was undeniably moral, the evidence for trivial or nonexistent gender differences was decidedly mixed. This constituted a classic case of a series of QIPs, whereby research that contested claims of gender equivalence was consistently overlooked, dismissed, or downplayed.

Starting with Maccoby and Jacklin's (1974) classic review downplaying the size and importance of many gender differences, many feminist and social psychological scholars, with the manifest and worthy agenda of breaking down barriers to women, followed suit. In "The Science and Politics of Comparing Women and Men," an early classic article showing how worthy moral goals (in this case, gender equality) can obstruct scientific progress, Eagly (1995, p. 149) described this state of affairs as follows:

> To the extent that the "gender-neutral" strategy of making no distinctions between women and men leads to gender equality (see Bem, 1993), scientific research showing that women are not different from men should help ensure women equal access to a variety of roles from which they were excluded. In contrast, evidence of differences might be seen as disqualifying women in relation to certain roles and opportunities and as justifying unequal treatment under the law.

As a result, research showing substantial gender differences was intensely scrutinized and challenged. As Eagly (1995, p. 149) continues:

> Feminist writing of the 1970s generally portrayed research purportedly demonstrating sex differences as largely prescientific and obviously faulty, or, if the research was more modern, as riddled with artifacts, methodological deficiencies, and unexplained inconsistencies in findings (e.g., Sherif, 1979).

One possibility is that these criticisms were scientifically well justified and that subsequent research would eliminate the artifacts and deficiencies and then demonstrate the validity of perspectives downplaying gender differences. However, another possibility is that this reflects the QIP of *selective preference*: perhaps these scholars engaged in confirmation biases, aggressively seeking flaws in research they disliked (demonstrating gender differences) and not applying the same critical standards to research they liked (demonstrating little or no gender differences). As noted earlier, people (including scientists; Abramowitz et al., 1975; Ceci, Peters, & Plotkin, 1985) often work harder to discredit disliked than liked findings. However, in a manner entirely consistent with Haidt's (2001) intuitionist model of morality, they deploy their logical reasoning skills to make it appear as if their reasoning explains their evaluation, when in fact it was their evaluation that triggered their reasoning. This raises the possibility that decades of declaring research demonstrating gender differences as trivial and fatally flawed reflected the motivated biases and QIPs of the researchers, not the quality of the research itself.

So, which was it? By the late 1990s, the empirical answer was vividly clear. The size of gender differences varies a great deal across different characteristics. Some are trivially small. But many are at least moderate, and some are quite large. Several meta-analyses show at least moderate gender differences for characteristics such as restlessness, math test scores, helping, leadership, a slew of nonverbal skills and characteristics, and many cognitive/academic characteristics among children (e.g., Briton & Hall, 1995; Halpern, Straight, & Stephenson, 2011; Swim, 1994). To be sure, men and women have many characteristics on which they, in fact, do not greatly differ (Hyde, 2005); however, even Hyde acknowledges that differences are quite large in certain physical skills, sexuality, and aggression (and see Eagly, 2013, for an analysis that suggests Hyde understates the size and power of gender differences).

Unfortunately, the outdated consensus on the ostensibly trivial size of sex differences continued to appear in textbooks and reviews, independent of the growing evidence to the contrary, and sometimes could be found even post-Eagly's (1995) exposé of these dysfunctions in the scientific literature (see Eagly, 2013, for a review). As Eagly (1995, 2013) has pointed out, achieving equal opportunities for women is an undeniably moral goal. However, the clear record of so many scientists allowing their benevolent moral intentions to distort their scientific conclusions constitutes one of the clearest records of good morals going bad in ways that obstructed the advancement of valid scientific conclusions.

## But for Stereotype Threat, White and African-American Standardized Test Scores Would (Not) Be Equal

Alongside fighting sexism, fighting racism has long been one of many social psychologists' high moral purposes. The fight for civil rights and equality of opportunity is undoubtedly a high moral good. The question addressed by the present chapter, however, is whether this high moral purpose has sometimes led to distorted scientific conclusions. There are many reasons to believe that it has, and here we focus on one (see Jussim, 2012, and Jussim et al., in press, for others): the erroneous and misleading interpretations of stereotype threat research.

The difference between White and African-American academic achievement is one of the great social problems plaguing the US. One manifestation of this problem is the very large gap in standardized achievement test scores, averaging about a full standard deviation, or the equivalent of 100 SAT points on each test (e.g., Neisser et al., 1996). A simple situational tweak that could eliminate these very large differences would have dramatic implications. It would dispel biological explanations, suggest that race differences have social causes, and reduce obstacles to racial equality.

Psychologists once claimed that they had found just such a magic bullet: stereotype threat. In a classic early study, Steele and Aronson (1995) examined the performance of African-American and White students under various conditions designed to lead African-Americans to become concerned about confirming stereotypes of African-American inferiority (the stereotype threat conditions) or designed to eliminate such threats. The results, which are reproduced here in Figure 11.1, appeared to be striking. Under threat, there seemed to appear the typical, dramatic race differences in performance. But under no threat conditions, there seemed to be no race difference.

The Figure 11.1 caption statement is technically incorrect (they are covariate adjusted means, not "mean test performance" scores, thereby rendering the figure deeply misleading). The nearly equal covariate adjusted means in the nondiagnostic condition *do not mean* that Blacks and Whites had equal scores. Instead, they mean that the *preexisting differences* (of about 40 points) were maintained in the nondiagnostic condition. Stereotype threat increased achievement test differences; removing it did not eliminate the mean differences between African-Americans and Whites.

It is clear that stereotype threat researchers once routinely presented their findings in this manner (see Sackett, Hardison, & Cullen, 2004, for a review). Referring to Steele and Aronson (1995), Aronson et al. (1999, p. 30) claimed that African-American students performed "about as well as Whites when the same test was presented as a nonevaluative problem solving task." Wolfe and Spencer

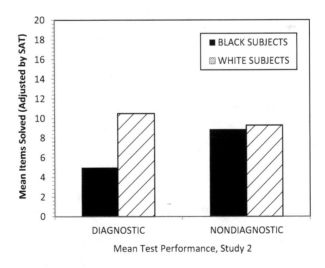

**FIGURE 11.1**  Based on Figure 2 from Steele, C. M., & Aronson, J. (1995). Stereotype threat and the intellectual test performance of African Americans. *Journal of Personality and Social Psychology, 69*, 797–811, page 802.

(1996, p. 180) declared that "one simple adjustment to the situation (changing the description of the test) eliminated the performance differences between Whites and African-Americans."

As the American Psychological Association (2006, n.p.) puts it on its web page:

> In the no stereotype-threat condition, in which the exact same test was described as a lab task that did not indicate ability, Blacks' performance rose to match that of equally skilled Whites. Additional experiments that minimized the stereotype threat endemic to standardized tests also resulted in equal performance.

And then later on the same page: "At the very least, the findings undercut the tendency to lay the blame on unsupported genetic and cultural factors, such as whether African Americans 'value' education or girls can't do math" (American Psychological Association, 2006, n.p.).

This latter sentence demonstrates the moral purpose driving some of the promotion of stereotype threat research. The problem, however, is not the moral posturing. It is the unjustified *scientific* claim. The original stereotype threat research *never* showed that removing threat eliminates race differences in standardized test scores. This is a *phantom fact*. How can that possibly be, given the results displayed in Figure 11.1?

## The Confusing (Misre)presentation

The widespread misinterpretation probably derived from two sources: a confusing presentation of the original result, and the failure to correct this misleading presentation by subsequent stereotype threat researchers. Although Steele and Aronson's (1995) text clearly states that they performed an *analysis of covariance* (ANCOVA) and reported *adjusted means*, their Figure 2 presents the *covariate adjusted means* labeled only as "Mean test performance Study 2" (p. 802; see Figure 11.1). The figure shows that the (adjusted) mean performance of the African-American students was equal to the (adjusted) mean performance of the White students.

Misinterpreting this study is easy absent a close reading of the text and a sophisticated understanding of adjusted means in ANCOVA. Because the adjusted means for African-American and White students were nearly identical in the no threat (nondiagnostic test) condition, it is easy to come away with the false impression that removing stereotype threat eliminated racial differences. Equal adjusted means in ANCOVA occur because preexisting differences are unaffected by the manipulation, not because the means are equal. The equal adjusted means indicate that preexisting differences (52 SAT points, in their sample) were *maintained* (not eliminated) when not under stereotype threat.

## Misleading Presentations 2.0

This situation changed, slightly, after Sackett et al. (2004) pointed all this out. In a reply that primarily defended the validity of stereotype threat research, Steele and Aronson (2004) acknowledged that "in fact, without this [covariate] adjustment, they would be shown to perform still worse than Whites" (p. 48). They claimed that ANCOVA was conducted in order to reduce error variance. This is a valid use of ANCOVA, and one could view this exchange as a nice example of science (eventually) self-correcting. Why it took so long, and did not occur until after Sackett et al.'s (2004) critique, remains unclear.

One possibility is that the high moral purpose of combating racism impelled stereotype threat researchers to promote the idea that there were no "real" race differences in academic test score performance. Indeed, if the priority is to "get the science right," one might expect stereotype threat researchers to describe Steele and Aronson's (1995) results simply and accurately subsequent to Sackett et al.'s (2004) critique. This can be done in 13 words: "Stereotype threat *increased* the achievement gap; removing threat left the prior gap intact."

Alternatively, however, modern stereotype threat researchers might go to considerable lengths to retain the original claim of racial equivalence under non-threatening conditions in their earnest pursuit of egalitarianism. Perhaps this explains why modern stereotype threat researchers *still* promote a technically true but misleading claim. For example, Schmader, Johns, and Forbes (2008, p. 336) claimed that Steele and Aronson (1995) showed that:

> African American college students performed worse than their White peers on standardized test questions when this task was described to them as being diagnostic of their verbal ability but that their performance was equivalent to that of their White peers when the same questions were simply framed as an exercise in problem solving (and after accounting for prior SAT scores).

Similarly, Walton, Spencer, and Erman (2013, p. 5) wrote:

> In a classic series of studies, Black students performed worse than White students on a GRE test described as evaluative of verbal ability, an arena in which Blacks are negatively stereotyped. But when the same test was described as nonevaluative—rendering the stereotype irrelevant—Blacks performed as well as Whites (controlling for SAT scores; Steele & Aronson, 1995).

These latter statements take 50–60 words, whereas the true result of the study can be summarized in 13. These latter statements must be convoluted in order to (1) be technically true and (2) maintain the claim that "remove stereotype threat, and African-American/White standardized test score differences disappear." To be true, the declaration that African-American and White scores are "equivalent" in nonthreatening conditions needs to be walked back by adding the parenthetical regarding controlling for prior SAT scores. The actual result—preexisting differences were maintained under nonthreatening conditions—is never explicitly stated in these articles.

After Sackett et al.'s (2004) exposé, stereotype threat researchers have a special responsibility to insure that their statements are accurate and not likely to be misinterpreted. The persistence of misleading statements strongly suggests that insuring that readers understand that removing stereotype threat did not significantly reduce the achievement gap in Steele and Aronson's (1995) research has taken a backseat to the high moral purpose of combating racism. Instead, despite Sackett et al.'s (2004) best attempt to bury the *phantom fact* that "remove threat, and the gap disappeared," the undead claim (with the newer addition of the parenthetical but easily missed and misunderstood caveat, "controlling for prior scores," which makes it deeply misleading rather than false) continues to appear in some of psychology's most influential outlets.

## High Moral Purpose II: Deploying Science to Crush Our Political Opponents

People with strong ideological views are often intolerant of those who hold different views (Brandt et al., 2014; Brandt et al., this volume). People view opposing partisans as more extreme than they really are, as immoral, as holding illogical beliefs, and as not deserving the same rights and protections as other people (e.g., Chambers, Baron, & Inman, 2006; Chambers & Melnyk, 2006; Crawford, 2014; Crawford & Pilanski, 2014; Graham, Nosek, & Haidt, 2012).

What does this have to do with high moral purposes undermining scientific integrity? There is no reason to think social psychologists are personally immune from these attitudes, or that the scientific method offers immunity from the biases such attitudes often produce (Duarte et al., 2015; Jussim et al., 2015, in press). If scientists believe that it is their moral obligation to marginalize their ignorant and immoral ideological opponents, they put themselves at risk for purveying invalid scientific claims. Because strongly held ideological beliefs subjectively feel like objective truths (Morgan, Skitka, & Lytle, 2014), it is possible that such scientists are unaware of the biased nature of their science; squashing their ideological opponents may be subjectively experienced as a core component of advancing science.

When there is abundant objective evidence that some widely held belief is false, scientists are justified for challenging such beliefs. However, we are not confident that scientists with high moral purposes can always distinguish between, on one hand, overwhelming objective evidence and, on the other, promoting their own personal moral and political agendas, even in the absence of overwhelming objective evidence. Next, we next present two examples of how attempts to vilify one's ideological opponents has distorted science.

## The Curious Case of Condemning Climate Skeptics as Conspiracy Theorists

Global warming may be one of the greatest social and scientific problems of our era. The potential disruption produced by melting polar ice, rising seas, expanding deserts, and increased extreme weather outbreaks is vast, and the evidence is overwhelming that humans have either created or exacerbated the pace with which warming has occurred (United Nations, 2014). Nonetheless, it is very difficult to get people, organizations, and especially governments to do anything to address the problem.

Further compounding the problem are active efforts to thwart major policy changes by challenging the scientific basis for evidence of human-caused global warming. Thus, to some, fighting the "deniers" of global warming may have taken on a high moral purpose.

Into this mix stepped Lewandowsky et al. (2013) with a paper titled, "NASA Faked the Moon Landing—Therefore (Climate) Science Is a Hoax"—which strongly implies that people who doubt global warming believe bizarre conspiracy theories. As Lewandowsky et al. (2013, p. 622) put it, "conspiratorial thinking contributes to the rejection of science."

One possibility is that this was true—that a disproportionately high number of people who disbelieve climate science also believe in something as silly as the faking of the moon landing. Another, however, was that this was essentially trumped up in order to cast those who are most skeptical of the climate science as fools. Fortunately, and to their credit, Lewandowsky et al. (2013) publicly posted their data, so we can evaluate these two alternative explanations for the claim in the title.

Their evidence for these conclusions was drawn from 1,145 readers of environmentalist blogs who completed a web survey asking about their belief in conspiracies and acceptance of scientific conclusions (HIV causes AIDS, burning fossil fuels increases atmospheric temperatures, etc.). Lewandowsky et al. (2013) subjected responses to latent variable modeling and did indeed find that "conspiracist ideation" negatively predicted (−.21, standardized regression coefficient) acceptance of climate science. So, where is the problem?

The implication that climate skeptics believe in the faking of the moon landing is another phantom fact. Out of over 1,145 respondents, there was a grand total of 10 who believed the moon landing was faked. Among the 134 of participants who "rejected climate science," only *three* people (2%) endorsed the moon-landing hoax. The link asserted in the title of the paper did not exist in the sample. Correlations primarily resulted from covariance in levels of agreement among reasonable positions (i.e., people varied in how much they *disbelieved* hoaxes and in how strongly they *accepted* science). It would be fair to characterize their results as indicating "the more strongly people disbelieved hoaxes, the more strongly they believed in climate science"—people varied in *how strongly* they rejected hoaxes and accepted science, but almost no one believed the moon hoax.

Understanding when people are and are not persuaded by science is an interesting and important area of research. But this curious case highlights the threat to scientific integrity that can stem from high moral missions. The notion that skeptics believed something so silly as the faking of the moon landing is yet another myth essentially concocted by the researchers. No matter how worthy the efforts to advance policy changes to combat human sources of global warming, the goal of "getting it right" is jeopardized when scientists claim their data shows their ideological opponents hold silly beliefs when they, in fact, do not. As such, this constitutes another example of high moral purposes undermining scientific integrity.

## The Unjustified Claim That Prejudice Is a Province of the Right

Several theoretical perspectives disproportionately blame conservatives for prejudice, discrimination, and political intolerance (e.g., Jost, Glaser, Kruglanski, & Sulloway, 2003; Lindner & Nosek, 2009; Sibley & Duckitt, 2008). We next consider two nonmutually exclusive possible explanations for this pattern: (1) conservatives really do hold more prejudices and are more intolerant than are those on the left; and (2) this pattern reflects the biases and moral agendas of the researchers studying the relationship between ideology and prejudice.

Conservatives are indeed prejudiced against many groups, including racial and ethnic minorities, women, and homosexuals (e.g., Altemeyer, 1996; Jost et al., 2003). However, is prejudice restricted to oppressed or disadvantaged target groups? One might reasonably consider prejudice against corporate executives or wealthy White men to be irrelevant to advancing egalitarian *political and moral* goals, but does that render such prejudice impossible, uninteresting, nonexistent, or psychologically inconsequential? The answer can be yes only if one limits the scientific purpose of social psychology to the political/moral action agenda of advancing the status of disadvantaged groups.

If prejudice simply refers to negative attitudes toward groups and is not restricted to oppressed demographic groups, it becomes clear that *any* group can be the target of prejudice. Considering only prejudices against the subset of demographic groups who are disadvantaged does not fully answer the question, "Is prejudice the particular province of the right?"

There is another problem with limiting prejudice to the study of such demographic groups. These are the groups that are of highest concern to people on the left, and in fact, most such groups are themselves left-wing or left-aligned groups (e.g., African-Americans; gay men and lesbians; see Brandt et al., 2014, for a discussion). Restricting prejudice to such groups constituted a large *blind spot* in the "psychology of prejudice" induced by the overwhelmingly left-wing worldviews of social psychologists (see Duarte et al., 2015, for a review), which until recently rarely addressed prejudice against right-wing or right-aligned groups.

If conservatives are *generally* more prejudiced than liberals, then they should also show more prejudice against right-wing groups. This, however, has not happened. Research supporting the *ideological conflict hypothesis* (ICH; see Brandt et al., 2014, for a review) shows that conservatives are prejudiced against left-aligned groups (e.g., atheists, welfare recipients) to about the same degree as liberals are prejudiced against right-aligned groups (e.g., evangelical Christians, businesspeople). Such findings have replicated across convenience and nationally representative samples, with a variety of social target groups, and various operationalizations of intergroup antipathy, including prejudice (Chambers et al., 2013; Crawford, 2014; Wetherell et al., 2013), political intolerance (Crawford, 2014; Crawford & Pilanski, 2014), and outright discrimination (i.e., dictator game; Crawford et al., 2014). Thus, despite extant efforts to explain prejudice as a symptom of conservatism, this recent ICH research shows that antipathy toward ideologically dissimilar others characterizes the left and right in approximately equal measure.

Reducing intergroup antipathy such as prejudice and discrimination is a justified moral concern. However, adopting this moral concern has made some social and political psychologists blind to contradictory evidence, and has narrowed the very definitions of prejudice and related constructs in ways that, intentionally or not, unjustifiably advance the notion that conservatives are morally inferior to liberals. The subsequent conclusions typify, perhaps unintentionally, Lilienfeld's (2015) conclusion that conservatism is often characterized as deficient and in need of explanation, relative to "normal" liberalism. These decisions demonstrate yet again how a particular moral agenda—combating the demographic prejudices of conservatives—has distorted scientific practice and constituted an obstacle to advancing our understanding of prejudice.

## Recommendations for Limiting the Distorting Effects of High Moral Missions

In this chapter, we have identified how moral purposes can lead to QIPs that undermine the validity of social psychology. Although it may be difficult, we believe that social psychologists, in their roles as authors, reviewers, and editors, can engage in practices that avoid, reduce, and defuse QIPs. A few such practices are discussed here (see Duarte et al., 2015 and Jussim, Crawford, Anglin, & Stevens, 2015, and Jussim, Crawford, Stevens, & Anglin, in press, for additional recommendations).

## Acknowledging Competing Perspectives

Clark and Hatfield (1989) provide a useful template for how to interpret results in a balanced manner that might otherwise have been exploited to advance a particular moral agenda. Instead of relying on a pet theory to interpret their results (showing huge differences between men and women in willingness to accept an offer from a stranger to have casual sex), they offered several potential explanations (some of which were ideologically contradictory) rather than excluding disfavored over favored options. Such an approach is not only more scientifically honest, but helps advance scholarship by providing authors multiple alternative testable hypotheses for future research.

## Adversarial Collaboration and Popperian Falsification

We echo the Popperian imperative that scientific practices are often at their best when researchers, in their own work and in reviewing that of others, attempt to falsify rather than confirm their pet hypotheses. This approach can help researchers identify how their own biases can be scrutinized, which can reduce morally motivated blind spots and selective preferences.

One way to maximize falsification attempts is through adversarial collaborations (Kahneman, 2003; Van Lange, 2013). There are challenges to such an approach, and projects may break down over disagreements prior to data collection. Nonetheless, if researchers can get past their personal (including moral) commitments to particular outcomes, there are both personal and scientific advantages to such collaborations. Personally, such collaborations are likely to advance the careers of all involved by yielding highly publishable findings. Scientifically, adversaries will likely be highly motivated to disconfirm one another's theories, thereby stacking the scientific deck in favor of Popperian falsification. Consequently, such collaborations are likely to (and have already) constructively advance(d) the field by resolving scientific controversies (Crawford, Collins, & Brandt, 2015; Silberzahn, Simonsohn, & Uhlmann, 2014).

## Meta-Analytic Thinking

A single study cannot resolve a question of human thought or behavior. By focusing on single studies, we have considerable freedom to allow our moral concerns to bias just what evidence we see as informative. It is very easy to cherry-pick studies and results in narrative reviews in such a manner as to create the impression that there is widespread support for our preferred claims, even when there is not (as indicated by the research one has, in classic *blind-spot* manner, intentionally or unintentionally overlooked). Instead, whether or not we conduct actual meta-analyses, we should get into the habit of compiling, citing, including, and considering broad swaths of evidence (whether individually or collectively; see Tsuji, Bergmann, & Cristia, 2014) pertinent to our research question, regardless of whether it supports or contests our pet hypotheses. Efforts to create checklists that can encourage a balanced and meta-analytic approach (see Washburn, Morgan, & Skitka, 2015, for such an example) can reduce morally motivated biases at multiple stages of the research process.

## Ways Forward

We generally oppose adding onerous bureaucratic requirements to the already difficult research process (see also Fiedler, this volume). However, one method social psychologists can use to limit their potential for motivated reasoning and confirmation biases is to ask themselves a few pointed questions. In that spirit, we conclude our chapter with this *Personal Use Checklist*, which we envision as something for personal use, not to be required by journals or other organizations. Furthermore, just because this version of the checklist works for us does not mean it will necessarily work for others. We encourage researchers to adapt this as they see appropriate, or develop their own. This is intended to assist well-meaning researchers to become more aware of their own potential for biases, in order to be more able to limit or eliminate them, *without mandates from authorities, editors, or organizations.*

The following *Personal Use Checklist* is for increasing confidence that our empirical research is relatively free of motivated biases:

1.  What do I want to happen and why?* An honest and explicit self-assessment is a good first step toward recognizing our own tendencies toward bias, and is, therefore, a first step to building in checks and balances in our research to reduce them.
2.  Do I have a long track record of research that does not systematically validate a particular political or social justice narrative or agenda? Note this is not about one's *intentions*. It is about one's *results*. If one's results consistently validate a particular set of beliefs, values, or ideology, one has failed this check, and this suggests attempts at falsification may be in order.
3.  Have I generated theoretical arguments for *competing and alternative hypotheses* and designed studies to incorporate and test them?* Honest tests of alternatives can go a long way to reducing personal bias.
4.  Have I carefully edited my manuscript to eliminate the use of pejorative terms to refer to the psychological characteristics of types of people I dislike or disagree with?
5.  Have I read some of the literature highlighting the invidious ways our motivated biases, morals, and politics can creep into our scientific scholarship? Doing so can alert one to ways in which our politics and values might distort

our science. After having done so, have I made a good faith attempt to eliminate such biases from my scholarship?

6.   Have I sought feedback from colleagues with very different theoretical and political views than mine or with track records of scholarship that often contests my preferred narratives?

Starred (*) items are from the checklist first developed by Washburn, Morgan, and Skitka (2015).

It may not always be possible for researchers to meet all six of these checks. However, as a starting heuristic, meeting five of the six probably justifies confidence that the research has kept bias mostly in check. What to do if one cannot meet at least five of the six (or, alternatively, one fails too many of one's own such questions)? Although that, too, is a matter of judgment, one possibility will be to *start over*. The first check may appear to be an open-ended question that one can neither pass nor fail. However, if one has strong preferences for how a study "should" come out, then one's ego may be invested in the outcome and one has failed this check. Checks 2 and 3 are easy enough to conduct, though *implementing* Check 3 after one has realized one has not met it may require new research. Check 4 is no more difficult than eliminating sexist language from manuscripts. Check 5 requires a little reading and probably can do double duty as a required assignment in advanced undergraduate and graduate courses on methodology, social cognition (confirmation bias among scientists!), and scientific practices. The hardest part about Check 6 is finding enough people so that the ones from whom one seeks feedback are not overburdened.

## Conclusion

In this chapter, we have reviewed evidence that people sometimes engage in immoral actions when they are motivated by high moral principles. One possible manifestation of this sort of moral irony is that when researchers are motivated by high moral principles, such as combating global warming or advancing egalitarianism, such motivations may lead to practices that threaten scientific integrity. This can occur because scientists are subject to the same sorts of motivated reasoning and tendencies toward confirmation bias as are laypeople. When they are highly motivated by moral, political, or social action agendas, therefore, they may be at heightened risk of engaging in questionable interpretive practices—discursive techniques for reaching desired conclusions even when the data do not support those conclusions. In this chapter, we have reviewed how blind spots (overlooking data and studies that conflict with one's preferred conclusions), selective preference (highlighting studies consistent with one's preferred conclusions and downplaying, criticizing, or dismissing equally high-quality studies inconsistent with those conclusions), and phantom facts (declaring something true, or making an implicit assumption that something is true, without providing empirical evidence) have led to underestimating the size of gender differences, claims that removing stereotype threat eliminated racial differences in standardized test scores when it did not do so, and claims that climate skeptics believe bizarre conspiracy theories that, in fact, they do not believe.

Such researcher biases are undoubtedly well intentioned (or, at least, we are sympathetic to the moral values of egalitarianism and to the importance of combating global warming). However well intentioned they are, such biases are also generally subtle and invidious, and, as such, many researchers may be unaware of the potentially unintentional ways in which they can lead to unjustified conclusions. Thus we ended our chapter by reviewing specific steps researchers can take to limit their vulnerability to such biases. Our hope is that by making such processes salient, researchers will be more willing and able to prevent them, and thereby lead to a more credible and valid psychological science.

# References

Abramowitz, S.I., Gomes, B., & Abramowitz, C.V. (1975). Publish or perish: Referee bias in manuscript review. *Journal of Applied Social Psychology, 5*, 187–200.

Altemeyer, R.A. (1996). *The authoritarian specter.* Cambridge, MA: Harvard University Press.

American Psychological Association. (2006). Stereotype threat widens achievement gap. Retrieved December 28, 2014, from http://www.apa.org/research/action/stereotype.aspx

Aronson, J., Lustina, M.J., Good, C., Keough, K., Steele, C.M., & Brown, J. (1999). When white men can't do math: Necessary and sufficient factors in stereotype threat. *Journal of Experimental Social Psychology, 35*, 29–46.

Baumeister, R.F. (2012). Human evil: The myth of pure evil and the true causes of violence. In M. Mikulincer & P.R. Shaver (Eds.), *The social psychology of morality: Exploring causes of good and evil* (pp. 367–380). Washington, DC: American Psychological Association.

Begley, C.G., & Ellis, L.M. (2012). Drug development: Raise standards for preclinical cancer research. *Nature, 483*, 531–533.

Brandt, M.J., & Proulx, T. (2015). QTIPS: Questionable theoretical and interpretive practices in social psychology: Commentary on Duarte et al. *Behavioral and Brain Sciences, 38*, 19–20.

Brandt, M.J., Reyna, C., Chambers, J.R., Crawford, J.T., & Wetherell, G. (2014). The ideological-conflict hypothesis: Intolerance among both liberals and conservatives. *Current Directions in Psychological Science, 23*, 27–34.

Briton, N.J., & Hall, J.A. (1995). Beliefs about female and male nonverbal communication. *Sex Roles, 32*, 79–90.

Ceci, S.J., Peters, D., & Plotkin, J. (1985). Human subjects review, personal values, and the regulation of social science research. *American Psychologist, 40*, 994–1002.

Chambers, J.R., Baron, R.S., & Inman, M.L. (2006). Misperceptions in intergroup conflict: Disagreeing about what we disagree about. *Psychological Science, 17*, 38–45.

Chambers, J.R., & Melnyk, D. (2006). Why do I hate thee? Conflict misperceptions and intergroup mistrust. *Personality and Social Psychology Bulletin, 32*, 1295–1311.

Chambers, J.R., Schlenker, B.R., Collisson, B. (2013). Ideology and prejudice: The role of value conflicts. *Psychological Science*, *24*, 140–149.

Clark, R.D., & Hatfield, E. (1989). Gender differences in receptivity to sexual offers. *Journal of Psychology & Human Sexuality*, *2*, 39–55.

Conway, P., & Peetz, J. (2012). When does feeling moral actually make you a better person? Conceptual abstraction moderates whether past moral deeds motivate consistency or compensatory behavior. *Personality and Social Psychology Bulletin*, *38*, 907–919.

Crawford, J.T. (2014). Ideological symmetries and asymmetries in political intolerance and prejudice toward political activist groups. *Journal of Experimental Social Psychology*, *55*, 284–298.

Crawford, J.T., Brandt, M.J., Chambers, J.R., Inbar, Y., Motyl, M., & Wance, N.M. (2014). *A multi-dimensional approach to political prejudice: Social and economic ideologies differentially predict prejudice across the political spectrum*. Manuscript in preparation.

Crawford, J.T., Collins, T.P., & Brandt, M.J. (2015). *Ideological symmetry in people's avoidance of dissonance-arousing situations: A failure to closely or conceptually replicate Nam, Jost and Van Bavel (2013)*. Manuscript in preparation.

Crawford, J.T., & Pilanski, J.M. (2014). Political intolerance, right *and* left. *Political Psychology*, *35*, 841–851.

Cummings, G. (2013). The new statistics why and how. *Psychological Science*, *25*, 7–29.

Ditto, P.H., & Lopez, D.F. (1992). Motivated skepticism: Use of differential decision criteria for preferred and nonpreferred conclusions. *Journal of Personality and Social Psychology*, *63*, 569–584.

Duarte, J.L., Crawford, J.T., Stern, C., Haidt, J., Jussim, L., & Tetlock, P. (2015). Political diversity will improve social psychological science. *Behavioral and Brain Sciences*, *38*, 1–13.

Eagly, A. (1995). The science and politics of comparing women and men. *American Psychologist*, *50*, 145–158.

Eagly, A.H. (2013). The science and politics of comparing men and women: A reconsideration. In M.K. Ryan & N.R. Branscombe (Eds.), *Sage handbook of gender and psychology* (pp. 11–28). London: Sage.

Epstein, W.M. (2004). Informational response bias and the quality of the editorial processes among American social work journals. *Research on Social Work Practice*, *14*, 450–458.

Funder, D.C., Levine, J.M., Mackie, D.M., Morf, C.C., Vazire, S., & West, S.G. (2013). Improving the dependability of research in personality and social psychology: Recommendations for research and educational practice. *Personality and Social Psychology Review*, *18*, 3–12.

Graham, J., & Haidt, J. (2012). Sacred values and evil adversaries: A moral foundations approach. In M. Mikulincer, & P.R. Shaver (Eds.), *The social psychology of morality: Exploring the causes of good and evil* (pp. 11–31). Washington, DC: American Psychological Association.

Graham, J., Nosek, B.A., & Haidt, J. (2012). The moral stereotypes of liberals and conservatives: Exaggeration of differences across the political spectrum. *PLOS ONE*, *7*, e50092.

Haidt, J. (2001). The emotional dog and its rational tail: A social intuitionist approach to moral judgment. *Psychological Review*, *108*, 814–834.

Haidt, J. (2012). *The righteous mind: Why good people are divided by religion and politics*. New York: Pantheon Books.

Halpern, D.F., Straight, C.A., & Stephenson, C.L. (2011). Beliefs about cognitive gender differences: Accurate for direction, underestimated for size. *Sex Roles*, *64*, 336–347.

Haselton, M.G., & Nettle, D. (2006). The paranoid optimist: An integrative evolutionary model of cognitive biases. *Personality and Social Psychology Review, 10,* 47–66.

Hyde, J.S. (2005). The gender similarities hypothesis. *American Psychologist, 60,* 581–592.

Ioannidis, J.P.A. (2005). Why most published research findings are false. *PLOS Medicine, 2,* e124.

Ioannidis, J.P.A. (2012). Why science is not necessarily self-correcting. *Perspectives on Psychological Science, 7,* 645–654.

Jacks, J.Z., & Devine, P.G. (2000). Attitude importance, forewarning of message content, and resistance to persuasion. *Basic and Applied Social Psychology, 22,* 19–29.

Jackson, C. (2004). *The Turner Diaries,* other racist novels, inspire extremist violence. *Intelligence Report,* Southern Poverty Law Center. Retrieved December 30, 2014, from https://www.splcenter.org/fighting-hate/intelligence-report/2004/turner-diaries-other-racist-novels-inspire-extremist-violence

Jost, J.T., Glaser, J., Kruglanski, A.W., & Sulloway, F.J. (2003). Political conservatism as motivated social cognition. *Psychological Bulletin, 129,* 339–375.

Jussim, L. (2012). *Social perception and social reality: Why accuracy dominates bias and self-fulfilling prophecy.* New York: Oxford University Press.

Jussim, L., Crawford, J.T., Anglin, S.M., & Stevens, S.T. (2015). Ideological bias in social psychological research. In J. Forgas, K. Fiedler, & W. Crano (Eds.), *Sydney Symposium on Social Psychology and Politics* (pp. 91–109). New York: Taylor & Francis.

Jussim, L. Crawford, J.T., Stevens, S.T., & Anglin, S.M. (in press). Political distortions in the social psychology of intergroup relations. To appear in P. Valdesolo & J. Graham (Eds.), *Bridging ideological divides: Claremont Symposium on Applied Social Psychology.* Wiley-Blackwell.

Kahan, D.M. (2011). Neutral principles, motivated cognition, and some problems for constitutional law. *Harvard Law Review, 125,* 1–77.

Kahneman, D. (2003). Experiences of collaborative research. *American Psychologist, 58,* 723–730.

Kunda, Z. (1990). The case for motivated reasoning. *Psychological Bulletin, 108,* 480–498.

Lakens, D. (2015). *Professors are not elderly: Evaluating the evidential value of two social priming effects through p-curve analysis.* Unpublished manuscript.

Lewandowsky, S., Oberauer, K., & Gignac, G.E. (2013). NASA faked the moon landing—therefore, (climate) science is a hoax: An anatomy of the motivated rejection of science. *Psychological Science, 24,* 622–633.

Lilienfeld, S.O. (2010). Can psychology become a science? *Personality and Individual Differences, 49,* 281–288.

Lilienfeld, S.O. (2015). Lack of political diversity and the framing of findings in personality and clinical psychology: Commentary on Duarte et al. *Behavioral and Brain Sciences, 38,* 31–32.

Lindner, N.M., & Nosek, B.A. (2009). Alienable speech: Ideological variations in the application of free-speech principles. *Political Psychology, 30,* 67–92.

Lord, C.G., Ross, L., & Lepper, M. (1979). Biased assimilation and attitude polarization: The effects of prior theories on subsequently considered evidence. *Journal of Personality and Social Psychology, 37,* 2098–2109.

Maccoby, E.E., & Jacklin, C.N. (1974). *The psychology of sex differences.* Stanford, CA: Stanford University Press.

Mahoney, M.J. (1977). Publication prejudices: An experimental study of confirmatory bias in the peer review system. *Cognitive Therapy and Research, 1,* 161–175.

Morgan, G.S., Skitka, L.J., & Lytle, B.L. (2014). *Objectively and universally true: Psychological foundations of moral conviction*. Paper presented at the annual meeting of the Society for Personality and Social Psychology, Austin, TX.

Munro, G.D., & Ditto, P.H. (1997). Biased assimilation, attitude polarization, and affect in reactions to stereotype-relevant scientific information. *Personality and Social Psychology Bulletin, 23*, 636–653.

Neisser, U., Boodoo, G., Bouchard, T.J., Jr., Boykin, A.W., Brody, N., Ceci, S.J., . . . Urbina, S. (1996). Intelligence: Knowns and unknowns. *American Psychologist, 51*, 77–101.

Nickerson, R.S. (1998). Confirmation bias: A ubiquitous phenomenon in many guises. *Review of General Psychology, 2*, 175–220.

Parker, M.T., & Janoff-Bulman, R. (2013). Lessons from morality-based social identity: The power of outgroup "hate," not just ingroup "love." *Social Justice Research, 26*, 81–96.

Sackett, P.R., Hardison, C.M., & Cullen, M.J. (2004). On interpreting stereotype threat as accounting for African American–White differences on cognitive tests. *American Psychologist, 59*, 7–13.

Schmader, T., Johns, M., & Forbes, C. (2008). An integrated process model of stereotype threat effects on performance. *Psychological Review, 115*, 336–356.

Sibley, C.G., & Duckitt, J. (2008). Personality and prejudice: A meta-analysis and theoretical review. *Personality and Social Psychology Review, 12*, 248–279.

Silberzahn, R., Simonsohn, U., & Uhlmann, E.L. (2014). Matched-names analysis reveals no evidence of name-meaning effects: A collaborative commentary on Silberzahn and Uhlmann (2013). *Psychological Science, 25*(7), 1504–1505.

Simmons, J.P., Nelson, L.D., & Simonsohn, U. (2011). False-positive psychology. *Psychological Science, 22*, 1359–1366.

Simonsohn, U., Nelson, L.D., & Simmons, J.P. (2014). P-curve and effect size: Correcting for publication bias using only significant results. *Perspectives on Psychological Science, 9*, 666–681.

Skitka, L.J. (2010). The psychology of moral conviction. *Personality and Social Psychology Compass, 4*, 267–281.

Skitka, L.J., & Morgan, G.S. (2014). The social and political implications of moral convictions. *Advances in Political Psychology, 35*, 95–110.

Stanovich, K.E., West, R.F., & Toplak, M.E. (2013). Myside bias, rational thinking, and intelligence. *Current Directions in Psychological Science, 22*, 259–264.

Steele, C.M., & Aronson, J. (1995). Stereotype threat and the intellectual test performance of African Americans. *Journal of Personality and Social Psychology, 69*, 797–811.

Steele, C.M., & Aronson, J.A. (2004). Stereotype threat does not live by Steele & Aronson (1995) alone. *American Psychologist, 59*, 47–48.

Swim, J.K. (1994). Perceived versus meta-analytic effect sizes: An assessment of the accuracy of gender stereotypes. *Journal of Personality and Social Psychology, 66*, 21–36.

Tetlock, P.E. (2003). Thinking the unthinkable: Sacred values and taboo cognitions. *Trends in Cognitive Sciences, 7*, 320–324.

Tsuji, S., Bergmann, C., & Cristia, A. (2014). Community-augmented meta-analyses toward cumulative data assessment. *Perspectives on Psychological Science, 9*, 661–665.

Unger, R. (2011). SPSSI leaders: Collective biography and the dilemma of value-laden action and value-neutral research. *Journal of Social Issues, 67*, 73–91.

United Nations. (2014). Climate change impacting entire planet, raising risk of hunger, floods, conflict. Retrieved December 28, 2014, from http://www.un.org/apps/news/story.asp?NewsID=47471

Van Lange, P.A.M. (2013). What we should expect from theories in social psychology: truth, abstraction, progress, and applicability as standards (TAPAS). *Personality and Social Psychology Review, 17,* 40–55.

Walton, G.M., Spencer, S.J., & Erman, S. (2013). Affirmative meritocracy. *Social Issues and Policy Review, 7,* 1–35.

Washburn, A.N., Morgan, G.S., & Skitka, L.J. (2015). A checklist to facilitate objective hypothesis testing: Commentary on Duarte et al. *Behavioral and Brain Sciences, 38,* 42–43.

Wetherell, G., Brandt, M.J., & Reyna, C. (2013). Discrimination across the ideological divide: The role of perceptions of value violations and abstract values in discrimination by liberals and conservatives. *Social Psychology and Personality Science, 4,* 658–667.

Winegard, B., Winegard, B., & Geary, D.C. (2015). Too paranoid to see progress: Social psychology is probably liberal, but it doesn't believe in progress: Commentary on Duarte et al. *Behavioral and Brain Sciences, 38,* 43.

Wolfe, C., & Spencer, S. (1996). Stereotypes and prejudice. *American Behavioral Scientist, 40,* 176–185.

Zuwerink, J.R., & Devine, P.G. (1996). Attitude importance and resistance to persuasion: It's not just the thought that counts. *Journal of Personality and Social Psychology, 70,* 931–944.

# 12

# CONCEPT CREEP

## Psychology's Expanding Notions of Harm and Their Moral Basis

*Nick Haslam*

*In recent years many of psychology's concepts have quietly undergone semantic shifts. I argue that these shifts reveal a consistent trend: many concepts that refer to the negative aspects of human experience and behavior have expanded their meanings. These concepts increasingly extend outward to capture qualitatively new phenomena ("horizontal expansion") and downward to capture quantitatively less extreme phenomena ("vertical expansion"). I illustrate these forms of semantic creep by reviewing changes in the concepts of abuse, bullying, trauma, mental disorder, and prejudice over recent decades. In each case, the concept's boundary has stretched and its meaning has dilated. I argue that this pattern of "concept creep" reflects a dominant moral agenda within social, developmental, and clinical psychology, involving an escalating sensitivity to harm. The mixed implications of this spreading definition of harm and being harmed are discussed.*

Concepts in the social and behavioral sciences will not sit still. Their meanings shift in response to new research findings, new theories, new forms of measurement, and changing intellectual fashions. The fields in which they operate traffic in what the philosopher Ian Hacking (1991) calls *human kinds*: "kinds of people, their behaviour, their condition, kinds of action, kinds of temperament or tendency, kinds of emotion, and kinds of experience" (pp. 351–352). Unlike *natural kinds*—objectively existing categories that carve nature at its immobile joints— human kinds are fundamentally fluid.

Human kinds matter because their fluidity can have real social effects. Rather than merely mirroring changes in society, alterations in how we conceptualize human kinds can influence social reality. Hacking (1995) referred to these social consequences of social concepts as *looping effects*. Our understandings of human kinds forms the basis for social judgments and policies, and the ways in which we define and label people and their experiences shapes how they understand themselves. Hacking's historical analyses of child abuse, autism, and multiple personality disorder show how these evolving concepts, which emanated from the social and behavioral sciences, came to mold the behavior and identity of people who recognized themselves in these ideas.

Hacking's work shows that we should not be surprised to find that psychology's concepts are moving targets, and that their movements influence how people make sense of themselves and others. In this chapter I argue that many psychological concepts have moved in a consistent direction in recent decades. These movements represent alterations in the range of phenomena to which concepts apply, or their semantic extension. I propose that these alterations take two forms. The first, *vertical expansion*, occurs when a concept's meaning becomes less stringently defined, so that it encompasses quantitatively milder variants of the phenomenon to which it originally referred. For example, the concept of obesity would have undergone vertical expansion if the critical body mass index threshold was lowered, thereby increasing the number of people defined as obese. The second form, which I call *horizontal expansion*, occurs when a concept extends to a qualitatively new class of phenomena, including application to a new semantic context. For example, the concept of *refugee* has expanded to include people displaced by environmental catastrophe, whereas it originally referred only to those displaced by conflict.

My main contention in this chapter is that some of psychology's key concepts have changed in a systematic way, involving particular kinds of concept moving in a particular direction. Baldly stated, it is the field's negative concepts—those referring to undesirable, harmful, or pathological forms of experience and behavior—whose meanings have changed, and those changes have involved a systematic semantic expansion, both horizontal and vertical. The concepts in question continue to encompass their original meanings—their semantic core remains unchanged—but they now refer to a substantially wider and deeper range of phenomena.

This pattern of semantic inflation is not widely appreciated by psychologists. Changes in particular concepts have been noted in a piecemeal fashion but the general tendency has been missed, along with any discussion of its causes and consequences. In the following pages I illustrate my concept creep hypothesis by reviewing changes in five concepts drawn from developmental, clinical, and social psychology: abuse, bullying, trauma, mental disorder, and prejudice. My approach throughout is to describe the semantic evolution of the concepts neutrally rather than to evaluate the merits of the changes. I then speculate on what has driven this dilation in the meaning of these concepts and what its implications might be, drawing on moral psychology.

## Case Study 1: Abuse

The concept of abuse has become more salient in recent decades through our growing awareness of the prevalence and damaging psychological effects of maltreatment. In addition to gaining currency, the concept has also gained semantic territory. Hacking (1991) presented a historical analysis of shifting meanings of abuse from the 19th century to the 1970s, but my focus here is on spreading shifts that have taken place since the end of that period.

Early psychological investigations of abuse recognized two forms, physical and sexual, the exposure to which increases vulnerability to psychopathology and other forms of ill-being. Physical abuse involved the intentional infliction of bodily harm, whereas sexual abuse involved inappropriate sexual contact. In the past three decades, three changes to the conceptualization of abuse have expanded it horizontally so that it encompasses qualitatively new phenomena. First, *emotional abuse* (Thompson & Kaplan, 1996)—sometimes labeled *psychological abuse*—was introduced as a new abuse subtype that need not involve bodily contact, but includes verbal aggression and other behavior that is domineering, threatening, rejecting, degrading, possessive, inconsistent, or emotionally unresponsive. Second, this form of abuse was commonly studied within the context of adult domestic relationships, whereas abuse had been traditionally referred to the behavior of adults toward children. Third, the concept of abuse came to incorporate neglect, the lack of provision of adequate care and concern. In the early literature on child maltreatment, neglect and abuse were considered separately, but increasingly neglect has been understood as a form of abuse. Cicchetti and Barnett's (1991) taxonomy of child abuse, for example, considers physical neglect as one of its subtypes. Similarly, Goldsmith and Freyd (2005) consider emotional neglect, or "emotional unavailability," to be a form of emotional abuse.

Emotional abuse expands the concept of abuse into the realm of nonphysical harm, and neglect-as-abuse expands it into acts of omission: the failure to commit desirable acts of care. The broadened understanding of abuse that results also vertically expands the concept, so that abuse comes to incorporate less severe phenomena than it did previously. Emotional abuse encompasses forms of interpersonal maltreatment that are more diffuse and ambiguous than those that fall within the realms of physical and sexual abuse. Deciding whether a particular interaction represents humiliation or teasing, possessiveness or protectiveness, and aggressiveness or assertiveness is inevitably subjective and dependent on perspective. What counts as emotional abuse from the standpoint of a self-identified victim might seem innocuous from the standpoint of the supposed perpetrator, or even from an independent observer's standpoint, but it is typically the victim's perception that is privileged in contemporary psychological assessments of whether emotional abuse or neglect have taken place. A similar vertical expansion of the concept of abuse can result from the incorporation of neglect. Criteria for judging omissions are less concrete that those for judging commissions, resulting in an indistinct boundary between neglect and its absence. This indistinctness allows the concept of neglect to become overinclusive, identifying behavior as negligent that is substantially milder or more subtle than other forms of abuse.

This abbreviated examination of the abuse concept reveals that it has undergone significant horizontal and vertical creep. As Frank Furedi (2006) pungently observed, there has been a "continuous expansion of the range of human experiences which can be labelled as abusive," such that "neglect and unintended insult become equated with physical violence and incorporated into an all-purpose generic category" (p. 86).

## Case Study 2: Bullying

Whereas abuse originally referred to damaging behavior directed toward children by adults, bullying originally referred to a form of damaging behavior whose victims and perpetrators were both children. Dan Olweus, who originated the concept in the 1970s, proposed three defining elements. Bullying involves aggressive or otherwise negative actions that are directed toward a child by one or more other people, where that behavior is (1) intentional, (2) repetitive, and (3) carried out in the context of a power imbalance (i.e., the victim has less power—whether in number, size, strength, age, status, or authority—than the bully). Bullying, which prototypically involves physical or verbal harassment or indirect relational behaviors such as rumor-spreading and isolation, is therefore conceptually distinct from peer aggression, where the aggression may not be repeated and the parties may have equal power.

The concept of bullying has undergone several forms of horizontal expansion since Olweus's original formulation. It has spread to include new forms of technologically mediated behavior collectively referred to as *cyberbullying*, which involves not only a new medium but also some distinctive behaviors that have no direct equivalent in traditional bullying. It has also expanded to refer to behavior occurring in adult workplaces rather than schoolyards (e.g., Salin, 2003), becoming a focus of study in occupational and organizational psychology just as much as in developmental and educational psychology.

Although there are clear resemblances or analogies between the sorts of behavior that qualify as bullying in school and work settings, applying the concept in the workplace amounts to an expansion of the concept into new semantic territory, both with regard to setting and to the age of participants. A third form of horizontal creep of the bullying concept involves types of behavior rather than medium or setting. Increasingly definitions of bullying include acts of omission and behaviors that manipulate relationships with people other than the victim of bullying, such as excluding, shunning, and ignoring, whereas early definitions emphasized direct physical and verbal attacks. As Mishna (2012) notes, "it is only fairly recently that indirect and social exclusionary forms of peer victimization were labelled as bullying" (p. 41). The same expansion can be seen in the workplace bullying literature, which now defines giving a coworker the silent treatment as bullying (Fox & Stallworth, 2005).

The concept of bullying has also crept vertically to include milder, less extreme phenomena through the progressive relaxation of each of Olweus's three criteria. First, the repetitiveness criterion has been relaxed by allowing the posting of a single offensive image or message to qualify as cyberbullying and by revisions of bullying assessment tools that loosen the requirement. The most widely used instrument (the Olweus Bullying Questionnaire), for example, originally specified that "when we talk about bullying, these things happen repeatedly," but a later revision stated that "these things *may* happen repeatedly" or "are *usually* repeated" (emphasis added).

A second kind of vertical expansion has occurred through the relaxation of the power imbalance criterion. The originally recognized forms of power differential (bullies' greater age, size, or number relative to victims) have been supplemented by new kinds of difference (differential peer-group status, popularity, and even self-confidence; Olweus, 2013), which expand the number of ways in which a power imbalance can be said to exist. Similarly, in the cyberbullying context, where the bully may be anonymous and the power differential relative to the victim is uncertain, bullying scholarship now considers differences in "technological know-how between perpetrator and victim, relative anonymity, social status, number of friends, or marginalized group position" (Smith, del Barrio, & Tokunaga, 2012, p. 36) to constitute power imbalances. Another relaxation of the power imbalance can be found in the workplace bullying literature, where interactions between same-rank coworkers can be counted as bullying, and where there is the added complexity that power imbalances within organizations are often legitimate and intrinsic to the relationship between coworkers.

A third form of vertical creep can be seen in the relaxation of the intentionality criterion. As Salin (2003) observes, in the context of workplace bullying, "intent is typically not part of the definition, but instead the subjective perception of the victim is stressed" (pp. 1215–1216). Thus bullying can be said to occur even if the behavior is inadvertent. This opening of the definition of bullying to the subjectivity of victims arguably represents a fourth form of vertical creep. Olweus (2013), for example, proposes that "the ultimate 'power of definition' must reside with the targeted student" (p. 757) as to when a power imbalance occurs. Similarly, Mishna (2012) argues that victims' judgments of whether they have been bullied should take precedence over those of perpetrators and adult observers, such as parents and teachers. Thus, if a child perceives social exclusion to have been deliberate, repeated, and hurtful, or "jokes" to have been said with malice rather than jest, then bullying has occurred. Giving power of definition to victims is likely to vertically expand the concept because many of the behaviors that may be taken to constitute bullying are ambiguous and intrinsically perspectival: one listing of potential workplace bullying includes occasions when a person "limited your ability to express an opinion," "gave excessively harsh criticism of your performance," "made unreasonable work demands," and "applied rules and punishments inconsistently" (Fox & Stallworth, 2005). People who see themselves as victims of these acts are likely to have a lower threshold for identifying them than neutral observers.

Like abuse, the concept of bullying has spread far beyond its original meaning. It has crept horizontally into online behavior, into adult workplaces, and into forms of social exclusion that target victims with hurtful omissions rather than actions. It has also expanded vertically to include behavior that is less extreme than prototypical bullying by loosening requirements that the behavior repeated, intentional, or occurring in the context of a traditionally conceived power imbalance, and by privileging the victim's perspective in defining the phenomenon. As Cascardi, Brown, Iannarone, and Cardona (2014) have argued, this definitional inflation has significant practical consequences. It erodes distinctions between bullying, harassment, and peer aggression, which require different therapeutic and legal remedies; it has potentially troubling implications for free speech rights; and it can impose excessive regulatory burdens on institutions, potentially requiring schools "to report and investigate every aggressive transgression, from playground teasing and roughhousing to aggravated assault" (p. 255).

## Case Study 3: Trauma

Trauma, from the Greek for "wound," originally referred to a morbid condition of the body produced by a physical insult. Its cause was an external event and its effect was an organic disturbance. This meaning was operative in mid-20th century psychiatry, the first edition of the *Diagnostic and Statistical Manual of Mental Disorders* (DSM-I; APA, 1952) describing a class of "brain disorders" caused by gross force, electricity, infection, poison, or congenital factors. Trauma now refers to a much broader set of phenomena, although the earlier meaning persists, as in "traumatic brain injury." DSM-III (APA, 1980) was a turning point, recognizing "posttraumatic stress disorder" (PTSD) as a mental disorder for the first time. Contrary to the DSM-I understanding of trauma, PSTD symptoms were understood to spring not from an organic injury to the brain but from a psychological injury to the mind. This broadening of the meaning of trauma is a classic case of horizontal creep.

Trauma can now refer to psychological effects of troubling experiences as well as to the experiences or events themselves, but I will focus on the latter meaning. Defining what counts as a traumatic event has been an enduring source of controversy (Long & Elhai, 2009) because "there is a continuum of stressor severity and there are no crisp boundaries demarcating ordinary stressors from traumatic stressors" (Weathers & Keane, 2007, p. 108). The working definition of *traumatic event* is embodied in Criterion A of the DSM's diagnostic rules for PTSD. In DSM-III (APA, 1980), this criterion required that a traumatic event "would evoke significant symptoms of distress in almost everyone" and be "outside the range of usual human experience": rape, assault, military combat, natural disasters, car accidents, and torture were listed as events that would typically meet the criterion, and bereavement, chronic illness, business losses, or marital conflict as events that would not. DSM-III-R (APA, 1987) expanded the definition of trauma to include indirect experiences, such as witnessing serious injury or death in another person, threats posed to one's kin or friends rather than oneself, or merely learning about an event that had afflicted them. DSM-IV (APA, 1994) further stretched this elastic concept by listing developmentally inappropriate sexual experiences as potential traumatic events—a break with the earlier understanding that traumas must involve threats of serious injury or death—and by increasing the emphasis on the person's subjective response to the event over its objective properties.

These revisions of Criterion A significantly enlarge the definition of trauma and have been labelled "conceptual bracket creep" by one critic (McNally, 2004). By encompassing less extreme stressors they substantially increase the range of experiences that count as traumas and the number of people who count as traumatized. Breslau and Kessler (2001) found that only 14 of 19 experiences that would qualify as potentially traumatic by DSM-IV's Criterion A1 would have met Criterion A in DSM-III-R, resulting in a 22% increase in the number of traumatic events to which their sample had been exposed.

The inclusion of indirect and noncatastrophic events within a widened definition of trauma exemplifies vertical expansion. The changes enlarge the range of events seen as possible triggers of PTSD by lowering the threshold of severity. In recent years, trauma scholars have proposed that childbirth, sexual harassment, infidelity, and abandonment by a spouse exceed that threshold. Some recent definitions of trauma go even further. According to the US government's Substance Abuse and Mental Health Services Administration (SAMHSA):

> Individual trauma results from an event, series of events, or set of circumstances that is experienced by an individual as physically or emotionally harmful or threatening and that has lasting adverse effects on the individual's functioning and physical, social, emotional, or spiritual well-being.
>
> (SAMHSA, 2012, p. 2)

By this definition a traumatic event need not be a discrete event, involve serious threats to life or limb, fall outside normal experience, be likely to create marked distress in almost everyone, or even produce marked distress in the traumatized person, who must merely experience it as harmful.

## Case Study 4: Mental Disorder

It is well known that mental disorders have proliferated over successive editions of the DSM, from around 100 in DSM-I (APA, 1952) to well over 300 in

DSM-IV-TR (APA, 2000). The rapidly growing population of mental disorders has led critics to accuse DSM of disease-mongering, but it need not entail an expansion of the concept of mental disorder itself. Later editions may merely subdivide the same psychopathological territory into smaller plots. However, systematic comparison of DSM's editions reveals that later iterations have expanded into new territory.

The full history of this expanding frontier has not been written, but a few examples should suffice. DSM-I (APA, 1952) contained seven groupings of mental disorders: acute and chronic brain disorders, mental deficiency, psychotic disorders, psychophysiologic disorders, psychoneurotic disorders, personality disorders (which included addiction), and transient situational personality disorders. DSM-II (APA, 1968) expanded the range of psychiatric conditions in three ways. First, it introduced a new "special symptoms" grouping that included problems with sleep and eating, domains that were not covered in DSM-I. Second, it extended the range of conditions afflicting young people beyond DSM-I's "mental deficiency" category, recognizing a new grouping of behavior disorders of childhood and adolescence. Third, it added sexual deviations to DSM-I's list of personality disorders.

DSM-III (APA, 1980) split up and reorganized several of DSM-II's disorder groupings, but it also crept horizontally by recognizing several new kinds of disorders. New classes of factitious, impulse-control, and dissociative disorders were instituted, none of their conditions corresponding to those described in previous DSM editions. DSM-III also added new disorders within existing groupings: disorders involving cognitive difficulties were added to the class of disorders first diagnosed in childhood and adolescence; sexual disorders were expanded to include gender identity disorder (a condition of gender, not sexuality); anxiety disorders incorporated social fears and extreme shyness for the first time; and substance-related disorders expanded to include problematic usage ("substance abuse") that fell short of addiction.

DSM-IV (APA, 1994) and DSM-5 (APA, 2013) have introduced further horizontal creep, which will not be reviewed here. The key point is that although a core of organic brain disorders and psychotic and neurotic conditions have persisted through every edition of DSM, an assortment of new conditions and domains of psychopathology has spread outward from it. Phenomena that might previously have been understood as moral failings (e.g., substance abuse, impulse control, and eating problems), personal weaknesses (e.g., sexual dysfunctions, shyness), medical problems (e.g., sleep disturbances), or ordinary vicissitudes of childhood now find shelter under the umbrella concept of mental disorder.

The expanding register of mental disorders indicates horizontal creep, but the concept of mental disorder has also undergone vertical creep. Recent editions of DSM commonly loosen the criteria for determining where normality ends and mental disorder begins, allowing milder, less disabling psychological phenomena to qualify as disordered. Sometimes this relaxation of criteria takes the form of recognizing new "spectrum" conditions, as with cyclothymia, binge eating disorder, and Asperger's syndrome, which represent less severe variants of bipolar disorder, bulimia nervosa, and autism, respectively. Sometimes the relaxation occurs in the definition of existing conditions. Horwitz and Wakefield (2007, 2012), for example, present historical evidence that DSM criteria for depression conflate contextually justified sadness with pathological melancholy, and adaptive fear with phobia, resulting in systematic overdiagnosis and overmedication.

Much of the recent controversy surrounding DSM-5 (APA, 2013) hinges on vertical creep of this sort, the target of a campaign by Allen Frances, the architect of DSM-IV, to "save normality" from the new edition (Frances, 2013). His critique targets the relaxation of diagnostic rules, such as the removal of the bereavement exclusion (allowing recently bereaved people to receive a depression diagnosis) (Wakefield, Schmitz, First, & Horwitz, 2007), the loosening of criteria for diagnosing attention deficit hyperactivity disorder (ADHD) among adults, and the invention of a new "somatic symptom disorder" for people with worries about physical symptoms that fall well short of earlier definitions of hypochondriasis.

Conceptual creep exists not only within formal psychiatric classifications such as DSM, but also in the clinical psychology literature. The concept of addiction, for example, does not occur within DSM, but has crept horizontally to incorporate new "behavioral" or "process" addictions, characterized not by a physiological dependence on an ingested substance but by a psychological dependence on a compulsive activity. Addictions to sex, gambling, pornography, shopping, online gaming, food, chocolate, exercise, social media, TV, work, and tanning have been proposed, among others (Potenza, 2006). The concept of addiction has also underdone a vertical expansion, best illustrated by the concept of "soft" addictions (Wright, 2006). Persistent activities that have some self-defeating aspects, these behavior patterns lack the sense of powerlessness, dependency, and compulsion that is typical of standard addictions and the harm they cause is relatively innocuous.

Once again, we see evidence that a concept's meaning has stretched elastically to include an increasingly broad variety of phenomena. In the past half century, the concept of mental disorder has expanded sideways into new forms of psychopathology and downward into milder forms. The proportion of humanity warranting a mental disorder diagnosis has correspondingly swelled.

## Case Study 5: Prejudice

Abuse, bullying, trauma, and mental disorder fall within the domains of developmental and clinical psychology. By examining concept creep in the domain of prejudice we move into the realm of social psychology. Since the publication of Gordon Allport's (1954) *The Nature of Prejudice*, this has been one of the field's most well-researched topics. As Dixon, Levine, Reicher, and Durrheim (2012) document, Allport understood prejudice to involve intergroup antipathy: the prejudiced person holds hostile attitudes toward members of an outgroup. This understanding has broadened substantially in the last three decades.

First, new conceptualizations of modern and symbolic prejudice incorporated attitudes that were not directly hostile to outgroups. McConahay (1986) drew a distinction between old-fashioned racism, exemplified by explicit Allportian bigotry, and a subtler and more prevalent modern racism. Modern racists, like symbolic racists (Sears, Henry, & Kosterman, 2000), do not endorse blatant hostility toward traditional targets of prejudice but instead deny the continuing existence of racism and oppose affirmative action. These attitudes were taken to indicate prejudice because they were associated with discriminatory behavior and understood to reveal tacit negative evaluations, suppressed because they were socially undesirable.

Second, the concept of aversive prejudice (Dovidio & Gaertner, 2004) was coined to account for aversions to other-race people, often unconscious, held by liberal-minded people who deny personal prejudice. These aversions were understood to reflect fear, unease, or discomfort rather than hostile antipathy. The related concept of implicit prejudice (Dovidio, Kawakami, & Gaertner, 2002) captured people who unconsciously associate outgroups with negative concepts, as demonstrated by tasks such as the Implicit Association Test. The idea of modern or symbolic prejudice allows that prejudiced people may not directly admit to holding hostile attitudes to outgroups, although they are aware of doing so, but the concepts of implicit and aversive prejudice imply that prejudiced people may not be aware of holding negative intergroup attitudes, and these attitudes may be grounded in sentiments other than hostility.

A third expansion of the concept of prejudice comes from research on sexism. Modern, symbolic, aversive, and implicit prejudices are less blatant and hostile than the old-fashioned variant that dominated early prejudice research, but they retain the view that prejudice involves negative group evaluations. The concept of benevolent sexism (Glick & Fiske, 1996), which refers to the view that women are too delicate and morally superior to inhabit the hurly-burly public world of men, relaxes this requirement, counting group evaluations that are at least superficially positive as prejudiced.

A final expansion of the concept of prejudice can be seen in the concept of microaggression (Sue et al., 2007), which refers to subtle demonstrations of prejudice such as slights and oversights that are ambiguous and that the supposed perpetrator denies. As with concepts of implicit and aversive prejudice, the theory of microaggressions proposes that prejudice may be unconscious and prejudiced acts may be driven by anxiety rather than hostility, as with the faltering speech of White therapists discussing racial issues with minority clients (Sue et al., 2007). However, the concept of microaggression goes further in expanding the concept of prejudice by suggesting that it exists at least partly in the eyes of the target, whose perspective is privileged in determining whether a microaggression has taken place. The target's subjective perception of prejudice decides whether it exists.

These recent understandings of prejudice reflect a vertical creep of the concept to encompass milder and subtler phenomena than those captured by Allport's view of prejudice-as-antipathy. Prejudice is no longer exclusively blatant, but can be subtle, inferred, and disguised in political principle. It is not necessarily available to awareness, but can be unconscious. It may not be hostile or even derogatory, but can be anxiously avoidant or patronizingly positive. It may not even be inherent in the acts or attitudes of a prejudiced person, existing instead in another person's perception.

Horizontal creep can also be seen in the psychology of prejudice. Early social psychologists who studied prejudice primarily examined varieties of racism, including anti-Semitism, whereas researchers now also study prejudices based on sexual orientation, gender identity, religion, physical appearance and stature, marital status, and even species. (Some of these newer prejudices—homophobia, transphobia, Islamophobia—also illustrate the horizontal creep of the concept of phobia from irrational fear to attitudinal aversion.) The concept of prejudice today is thus vastly wider and more inclusive than it was in 1954.

## Overview of the Case Studies

These conceptual case studies reveal a consistent pattern of semantic inflation that involves a few basic similarities. First, most of the concepts have stretched to include milder, subtler, or less extreme phenomena than those to which they referred in previous decades. This stretching is evident in definitions of abuse that can count angry arguments as instances of emotional abuse, definitions of bullying that include once-off office tyranny, definitions of trauma that include vicarious experiences, relaxed diagnostic criteria for mental disorders such as depression, and the recognition of nonconscious forms of prejudice.

Second, some of the concepts that initially referred to the commission of undesirable acts have stretched to include acts of omission and avoidance. This pattern is illustrated by the inclusion of neglect within the concept of abuse, the growing recognition of exclusionary forms of bullying, and the concept of aversive prejudice.

Finally, several concepts have acquired a more subjective aspect. Emotional abuse may be claimed if one party feels abused, bullying if a person perceives that their work has been criticized too harshly, trauma if a victim experiences significant distress even if the triggering event would not otherwise quality as traumatic, and prejudice if its target perceives it despite the sincere protestations of the supposed perpetrator. In short, creep has occurred across many diverse concepts, commonly involving an increased sensitivity to negative experience and behavior, an increased focus on harmful forms of inaction, and an increased acceptance of subjective criteria for deciding when the concepts apply.

## Explaining Concept Creep

If we are to make sense of concept creep, we must explain what drives it. A satisfactory explanation should answer three key questions. First, why does creep specifically affect negative concepts? All five concepts refer to undesirable experiences or events and evidence that these concepts have enlarged is rife, but it is difficult indeed to find comparable examples of inflatable positive concepts. Second, why do these concepts expand rather than contract? If human kinds are intrinsically fluid, as Hacking maintained, why have their meanings spread rather than receded? Any adequate account of concept creep must explain why negative concepts creep outward rather than back into the shadows. Third, why does the expansion take both vertical and horizontal forms? A good explanation of creep should encompass its two varieties, the quantitative and the qualitative.

Before examining how well some possible explanations answer these questions, it might be queried whether concept creep is indeed unique to negative concepts. Arguably some positive concepts have also expanded. For example, the concept of intelligence has seen some horizontal expansion with the introduction of emotional, kinesthetic, and other supposed intelligences. Similarly, it could be claimed that the concept of self-esteem has expanded from its original core meaning through the concept of collective self-esteem, although in this case it could be counterargued that this idea merely refers to a group-level source of self-worth rather than a shift in what self-worth itself is taken to be. At this point, in the absence of a thorough historical review of a wider assortment of concepts, it is not possible to rule out the possibility that concept creep also affects positive concepts such as these. Nevertheless, my simple assertion is that creep is readily observed for a variety of negative concepts and that positive examples are less salient.

In addition to answering the three questions just posed, a good explanation of concept creep should also be parsimonious, accounting for why the pattern occurs across disparate concepts rather than explaining each concept's changes in its own terms. For example, although the expansion of mental disorder could be attributed to medicalization (Frances, 2013), the expansion of abuse and trauma to an emerging culture of fear or victimhood (Dineen, 1999; Furedi, 2006), and the expansion of prejudice to "political correctness," the fact that similar semantic enlargements replicate across the concepts argues for a more generalized explanation.

One superficially appealing but entirely deficient explanation for creep is that human kind concepts are always in flux because they are dependent on social practices and conventions and because everything social falls on a seamless continuum. This may all be true—for example, there is strong evidence that most mental disorders are not discrete categories (Haslam, Holland, & Kuppens, 2012)—but it fails to answer our three questions. The malleability and continuity of social concepts is consistent with conceptual change taking vertical and horizontal forms, but it does not explain why concepts should move outward, not inward, or why negative concepts should be especially prone to expansion. Nor does this explanation offer any specific account of what the general pattern of change represents.

A second possible explanation invokes processes internal to academic scholarship. Concepts that attract extensive scholarly attention may tend to expand their meanings as theorists and researchers attempt to find new ways to formulate and apply them. Successful concepts, by this account, like memes, expand their semantic territories just as successful species expand their environmental niches. The five concepts presented in this chapter are each highly successful in this sense. This explanation can in principle explain why expansion rather than contraction occurs and why expansion should take vertical and horizontal forms. However, it cannot explain why this expansion should be specific to negative concepts, as there is no shortage of successful positive psychological concepts that should show the same pattern but do not. In addition, the "Darwinian concepts" explanation offers no parsimonious general account of why the disparate negative concepts enlarge aside from their academic popularity.

A third explanation implicates psychology as a cultural force. Writers have pointed to the growing "psychologization" of experience in postwar society (De Vos, 2010). The discipline has grown steeply in public influence and visibility, and as Horwitz and Wakefield (2007) observe, "all professions strive to broaden the realm of phenomena subject to their control" (p. 213). The psychologization account can explain why psychological concepts would expand their meanings and why expansion could take horizontal and vertical forms. However, again it cannot explain why expansion should be relatively specific to psychology's negative concepts or account for what the negative concepts have in common that accounts parsimoniously for that expansion.

A fourth explanation invokes social and technological change outside of psychology. Some expansion of psychology's concepts may simply reflect new social or technical realities. Bullying cannot extend to cyberbullying without the advent of the Internet and mobile devices, and prejudice would not extend to new outgroups if social and cultural change did not bring them into existence or make them salient. By this account psychological concepts accrue new meanings as side effects of large-scale societal changes. This form of explanation can explain why concepts expand rather than contract, but it is otherwise unpersuasive. It can explain horizontal expansion to new kinds of phenomena much more readily than vertical expansion to milder variants, and it cannot explain why expansion should be limited to negative concepts. It also offers only piecemeal accounts of why specific concepts undergo alterations rather than a general account that can encompass parallel changes in the concepts of abuse and prejudice, bullying and mental disorder.

Much more promising is a fifth explanation that invokes a broad cultural shift rather than general societal change or factors intrinsic to psychology or academic scholarship. In *The Better Angels of Our Nature*, Steve Pinker (2011) documents the relentless decline in violence over several timescales. In the recent decades that are the focus of my analysis, Pinker identifies the "rights revolutions" as the driver of this reduction. Movements for the rights of women and minorities have led a "civilizing offensive" that targeted previously accepted forms of aggression, "propelled by an escalating sensitivity to new forms of harm" (Pinker, 2011, p. 460). Pinker's analysis, resting on this increasing sensitivity to harm, can explain why concept creep should involve expansion rather than contraction and why it should apply asymmetrically to negative (i.e., harm-related) concepts. Its claim that the relevant changes involve enhanced sensitivity to "new forms of harm" and to "the slightest trace of a mindset that might lead to it" (Pinker, 2011, p. 469) indicates that it can explain both horizontal and vertical creep.

The only limitation of Pinker's analysis as an account of concept creep is that it specifically addresses violence rather than the more general pattern of expanding negative concepts that I have proposed. The idea that the rights revolutions were based on "a rising abhorrence to violence" (Pinker, 2011, p. 469) may help to explain the expansion of concepts directly related to violence, such as abuse and bullying, but would have to be significantly stretched to explain the enlargement of concepts, such as prejudice and trauma, that need not implicate violence. However a violence-based analysis cannot account for the expansion of completely unrelated concepts such as mental disorder.

I would argue that concept creep is best explained by a modified version of Pinker's account, involving a gradual sensitization to harm in general rather than to violence in particular. The five concepts examined earlier each represent ways of harming (abuse, bullying, prejudice) or being harmed (trauma, mental disorder), and their vertical and horizontal expansions are manifestations within the discourse of academic psychology of this increased sensitivity to harm. This harm-based account offers a unifying account of why psychology's concepts have stretched to encompass potentially damaging acts, ideas, and events that their earlier versions of these concepts would had overlooked. From this standpoint, expanded concepts of bullying and abuse define a wider variety of forms of maltreatment as unacceptable, and expanded concepts of prejudice define a wider variety of attitudes as inappropriate. In addition, expanded concepts of trauma and mental disorder define a wider variety of people as needful of protection and care.

## The Moral Basis of Concept Creep

If psychology's concept creep reflects an increased sensitivity to harm, harming, and being harmed, what does that pattern say about the field? This question can be approached from the standpoint of moral psychology, whose concepts clarify several fundamental aspects of the phenomenon.

Most basically, concept creep can be understood as an expansion of the "moral circle" (Laham, 2009; Singer, 1981), the domain of entities taken to be deserving of moral treatment and concern. Just as the moral circle has tended to expand over the course of human history, expanding concepts of abuse, bullying, trauma and the like extend the range of people that the discipline of psychology identifies as deserving of professional concern. Horizontal creep stretches the boundary of concern to include people experiencing new kinds of difficulty, such as the victim of cyberbullying, the insomniac, or the emotionally abused spouse, and ratifies them as suitable targets for protective or therapeutic intervention. Vertical creep has the same effect by stretching conceptual boundaries to include people whose difficulties were not previously adjudged severe enough to warrant intervention: the office-worker intimidated by a colleague, the vicariously traumatized, the binge eater. This understanding of concept creep as a form of circle expansion aligns with Pinker's (2011) analysis of the widening sensitivity to harm that characterized the rights revolutions, each of which has been a movement with an agenda of moral expansion. It also recognizes that the psychological concepts that are subject to creep do not identify phenomena or kinds of person merely as objects of academic study, but also as objects of professional concern.

Moral psychology also clarifies the basis of this concern. According to Moral Foundations Theory (Graham et al., 2011), moral reasoning can be based on five distinct kinds of moral consideration: harm/care, fairness/reciprocity, ingroup/loyalty, authority/respect, and purity/sanctity. My contention is that psychology's concept creep is driven by a rising moral sensitivity to harm, the common element in the five case studies I presented, implying that one moral foundation—harm and its linked value of care—is paramount in it. The concept creep phenomenon broadens moral concern by defining new sorts of behavior and events as harming and new classes of people as harmed, and it identifies these people as needful of professional care and protection. The harm/care foundation is significant because it is strongly associated with political liberalism (Graham, Haidt, & Nosek, 2009), as well as with empathy, compassion, and being female (Graham et al., 2011). Arguably concept creep reflects the way in which soft (developmental, social, and clinical) psychology has aligned with a liberal social agenda of enhanced sensitivity to harm and care for the harmed. For example, expansion of the concept of bullying can be seen as serving a progressive agenda of protecting the vulnerable, including people at lower rungs of the workplace hierarchy, from the powerful. Similarly, the expansion of the concept of abuse to include emotional variants, which are commonly invoked in the context of close relationships, aligns with a feminist agenda of protecting women from all forms of domestic violence.

To this point the moral implications of concept creep would appear to be overwhelmingly positive. It expands the moral circle, defines previously tolerated forms of abusive, domineering, and discriminatory behavior as problematic, and extends professional care to people who experience adversity and suffering that would once have been ignored. However, a third concept from moral psychology suggests that concept creep may have a downside. Research on "moral typecasting" (Gray & Wegner, 2009) shows that people who are ascribed moral patiency (the capacity to be acted on in moral or immoral ways, which depends on the perceived capacity to be sensitive to harm and to suffer) tend not to be ascribed moral agency (the capacity to engage in moral or immoral action). In the context of immoral actions, people tend to be morally typecast either as victims who suffer harm but lack responsibility and the capacity to act intentionally, or as perpetrators who are blameworthy but lack the capacity to suffer.

Concept creep represents an increased sensitivity to forms of harm and being harmed. It therefore amounts to an expansion of moral patiency, representing more and more people as hurt and vulnerable. According to moral typecasting theory, this expansion is likely to reduce the perceived agency of these people, in effect defining them as helpless, acted-upon victims. The expanding reach of harm brought on by concept creep also risks creating a growing class of typecast moral villains: abusers, bigots, bullies, and traumatizers who are seen as deserving of blame but are denied their own moral patiency. If the moral typecasting account is correct, concept creep may therefore extend moral concern to the vulnerable while also cultivating a sense of victimhood and polarized images of innocent sufferers and guilty evildoers. This kind of morally saturated polarization can be observed in the growing intolerance of ideological outgroups documented by Brandt, Wetherell, and Crawford (this volume). A similar dynamic may underpin some case of scientific malpractice, where a concern for protecting groups seen as vulnerable from real or symbolic harm can motivate failures of scientific integrity (Jussim, Crawford, Stevens, Anglin, & Duarte, this volume).

The theory of moral typecasting suggests that concept creep may have mixed blessings. It may have other unwanted effects as well. First, by extending the meaning of harm-related concepts to cover milder variants through vertical expansion it may dilute and even trivialize those meanings. If everyday sadness becomes "depression" and everyday stressors become "traumas," then those ideas lose their semantic punch. This concern is magnified by the likelihood that academic psychology's definitions will be further diluted and vulgarized by laypeople. Second, and conversely, remedies that are geared to narrower definitions of harm-related concepts may become inappropriate when they are extended to the less severe phenomena captured by broader definitions. Medication that may be appropriate for more severe variants of a condition may be inappropriate for its milder variants, and legal interventions that are suitable for severe bullying or abuse may be unduly harsh and counterproductive when applied to less extreme forms. Finally, concept creep can generate terminological confusion as previously distinct ideas come to overlap. The expansion of trauma to include relatively mild maltreatments, of bullying to encompass single incidents, and of abuse to include events causing emotional harm creates redundancy among their meanings. One person using an ethnic slur toward another can now count as abuse, bullying, trauma, and prejudice by some definitions. This redundancy breeds conceptual confusion and parallel literatures.

## Conclusions

This is not the place to attempt a balanced appraisal of the pros and cons of concept creep. What matters is that it exists and that it has significant social implications. Creep represents a previously unacknowledged tendency for concepts associated with harm to undergo semantic inflation, so that more and more experiences and actions are viewed as harming and more and more people as harmed. My contention is that concept creep represents a real trend within psychology that aligns with changes in the culture at large. It is also likely to have real effects on that culture as psychological concepts filter into everyday life and discourse. A moral psychology framework can help us understand what concept creep means, what propels it, and what its consequences—sure to be ambivalent—might be.

## References

Allport, G. (1954). *The nature of prejudice*. New York: Addison-Wesley.

American Psychiatric Association (1952). *Diagnostic and Statistical Manual of Mental Disorders* (1st ed.) [DSM-I]. Washington, DC: Author.

American Psychiatric Association (1968). *Diagnostic and Statistical Manual of Mental Disorders* (2nd ed.) [DSM-II]. Washington, DC: Author.

American Psychiatric Association (1980). *Diagnostic and Statistical Manual of Mental Disorders* (3rd ed.) [DSM-III]. Washington, DC: Author.

American Psychiatric Association (1987). *Diagnostic and Statistical Manual of Mental Disorders* (3rd ed., revised) [DSM-III-R]. Washington, DC: Author.

American Psychiatric Association (1994). *Diagnostic and Statistical Manual of Mental Disorders* (4th ed.) [DSM-IV]. Washington, DC: Author.

American Psychiatric Association (2000). *Diagnostic and Statistical Manual of Mental Disorders* (4th ed., text revision) [DSM-IV-TR]. Washington, DC: Author.

American Psychiatric Association (2013). *Diagnostic and Statistical Manual of Mental Disorders* (5th ed.) [DSM-5]. Washington, DC: Author.

Breslau, N., & Kessler, R.C. (2001). The stressor criterion in DSM-IV posttraumatic stress disorder: An empirical investigation. *Biological Psychiatry, 50*, 699–704.

Cascardi, M., Brown, C., Iannarone, M., & Cardona, N. (2014). The problem of overly broad definitions of bullying: Implications for the schoolhouse, the statehouse and the ivory tower. *Journal of School Violence, 13*, 253–276.

Cicchetti, D., & Barnett, D. (1991). Toward the development of a scientific nosology of child maltreatment. In D. Cicchetti & W.M. Grove (Eds.), *Thinking clearly about psychology: Essays in honor of Paul E. Meehl: Vol. 2. Personality and psychopathology* (pp. 346–377). Minneapolis: University of Minnesota Press.

De Vos, J. (2010). From Milgram to Zimbardo: The double birth of postwar psychology/psychologization. *History of the Human Sciences, 23*, 156–175.

Dineen, T. (1999). *Manufacturing victims: What the psychology industry is doing to people*. London: Constable.

Dixon, J., Levine, M., Reicher, S., & Durrheim, K. (2012). Beyond prejudice: Are negative evaluations the problem and is getting us to like each other more the solution? *Behavioral and Brain Sciences, 35*, 411–425.

Dovidio, J.F., & Gaertner, S.L. (2004). Aversive racism. *Advances in Experimental Social Psychology, 36,* 1–52.

Dovidio, J., Kawakami, K., & Gaertner, S.L. (2002). Implicit and explicit prejudice and interracial interaction. *Journal of Personality and Social Psychology, 82,* 62–68.

Fox, S., & Stallworth, L.E. (2005). Racial/ethnic bullying: Exploring links between bullying and racism in the US workplace. *Journal of Vocational Behavior, 66,* 438–456.

Frances, A. (2013). *Saving normal: An insider's revolt against out-of-control psychiatric diagnosis, DSM-5, big Pharma, and the medicalization of ordinary life.* New York: William Morrow.

Furedi, F. (2006). *Culture of fear revisited: Risk-taking and the morality of low expectation* (4th ed.). London: Continuum.

Glick, P., & Fiske, S.T. (1996). The Ambivalent Sexism Inventory: Differentiating hostile and benevolent sexism. *Journal of Personality and Social Psychology, 70,* 491–512.

Goldsmith, R.E., & Freyd, J.J. (2005). Awareness for emotional abuse. *Journal of Emotional Abuse, 5,* 95–123.

Graham, J., Haidt, J., & Nosek, B.A. (2009). Liberals and conservatives rely on different sets of moral foundations. *Journal of Personality and Social Psychology, 96,* 1029–1046.

Graham, J., Nosek, B.A., Haidt, J., Iyer, R., Koleva, S., & Ditto, P.H. (2011). Mapping the moral domain. *Journal of Personality and Social Psychology, 101,* 366–385.

Gray, K., & Wegner, D.M. (2009). Moral typecasting: Divergent perceptions of moral agents and moral patients. *Journal of Personality and Social Psychology, 96,* 505–520.

Hacking, I. (1991). The making and molding of child abuse. *Critical Inquiry, 17,* 253–288.

Hacking, I. (1995). The looping effect of human kinds. In D. Sperber, D. Premack, & A.J. Premack (Eds.), *Causal cognition: A multi-disciplinary debate* (pp. 351–383). New York: Oxford University Press.

Haslam, N., Holland, E., & Kuppens, P. (2012). Categories versus dimensions in personality and psychopathology: A quantitative review of taxometric research. *Psychological Medicine, 42,* 903–920.

Horwitz, A.V., & Wakefield, J.C. (2007). *The loss of sadness: How psychiatry transformed normal sorrow into depressive disorder.* New York: Oxford University Press.

Horwitz, A.V., & Wakefield, J.C. (2012). *All we have to fear: Psychiatry's transformation of natural anxieties into mental disorders.* New York: Oxford University Press.

Laham, S.M. (2009). Expanding the moral circle: inclusion and exclusion mindsets and the circle of moral regard. *Journal of Experimental Social Psychology, 45,* 250–253.

Long, M.E., & Elhai, J.D. (2009). Posttraumatic stress disorder's traumatic stressor criterion: History, controversy, clinical and legal implications. *Psychological Injury and Law, 2,* 167–178.

McConahay, J.B. (1986). Modern racism, ambivalence, and the modern racism scale. In J.F. Dovidio & S.L. Gaertner (Eds.), *Prejudice, discrimination, and racism* (pp. 91–125). Orlando, FL: Academic Press.

McNally, R.J. (2004). Conceptual problems with the DSM-IV criteria for posttraumatic stress disorder. In G.M. Rosen (Ed.), *Posttraumatic stress disorder: Issues and controversies* (pp. 1–14). New York: Wiley.

Mishna, F. (2012). *Bullying: A guide to research, intervention, and prevention.* New York: Oxford University Press.

Olweus, D. (2013). School bullying: Development and some important challenges. *Annual Review of Clinical Psychology, 9,* 751–780.

Pinker, S. (2011). *The better angels of our nature: A history of violence and humanity.* London: Penguin.

Potenza, M.N. (2006). Should addictive disorders include non-substance-related conditions? *Addiction, 101,* 142–151.

Salin, D. (2003). Ways of explaining workplace bullying: A review of enabling motivating and precipitating structures and processes in the work environment. *Human Relations, 56,* 1213–1232.

Sears, D.O., Henry, P.J., & Kosterman, R. (2000). Egalitarian values and contemporary racial politics. In D.O. Sears, J. Sidanius, & L. Bobo (Eds.), *Racialized politics: The debate about racism in America* (pp. 75–117). Chicago: University of Chicago Press.

Singer, P. (1981). *The expanding circle.* Oxford: Clarendon Press.

Smith, P.K., del Barrio, C., & Tokunaga, R. (2012). Definitions of bullying and cyberbullying: How useful are the terms? In S. Bauman, D. Cross, & J. Walker (Eds.), *Principles of cyberbullying research: Definitions, measures, and methods* (pp. 29–40). Philadelphia, PA: Routledge.

Substance Abuse and Mental Health Services Administration. (2012). *SAMHSA's working definition of trauma and guidance for trauma-informed approach.* Rockville, MD: Substance Abuse and Mental Health Services Administration.

Sue, D.W., Capodilupo, C.M., Torino, G.C., Bucceri, J.M., Holder, A.M., Nadal, K.L., & Esquilin, M. (2007). Racial microaggressions in everyday life: Implications for clinical practice. *American Psychologist, 62,* 271–286.

Thompson, A.E., & Kaplan, C.A. (1996). Childhood emotional abuse. *British Journal of Psychiatry, 168,* 143–148.

Wakefield, J.C., Schmitz, M.F., First, M.B., & Horwitz, A.V. (2007). Extending the bereavement exclusion for major depression to other losses: Evidence from the National Comorbidity Survey. *Archives of General Psychiatry, 64,* 433–440.

Weathers, F.W., & Keane, T.M. (2007). The criterion A problem revisited: Controversies and challenges in defining and measuring psychological trauma. *Journal of Traumatic Stress, 20,* 107–121.

Wright, J. (2006). *The soft addiction solution: Break free of the seemingly harmless habits that keep you from the life you want.* London: J.P. Tarcher/Penguin.

# 13

# ETHICAL NORMS AND MORAL VALUES AMONG SCIENTISTS

## Applying Conceptions of Morality to Scientific Rules and Practices

*Klaus Fiedler*

*The purpose of this chapter is to apply theoretical approaches to the social psychology of morality to the moral evaluation of scientists' own behavior. It will be seen that the current discourse on questionable research practices, usability of science, and fraud, mainly fueled by whistle-blowers who are themselves members of the scientific community, does not live up to higher levels of moral judgment according to Piaget and Kohlberg. This discourse can also not be explained within the modern intuitionist approach to morality. It can, however, be understood in terms of the current Zeitgeist of compliance with unreflected norms, related to the social psychology of conformity and obedience. Transgressions of arbitrary norms (e.g., of sober significance testing) are given more weight than violations of more fundamental norms (e.g., theoretical reasoning; cost-benefit assessment). The age-old principle of reciprocity is largely neglected when powerful players in the game (editors', reviewers', or whistle-blowers' motives or conflicts of interest) are not treated according to the same rules as weaker players (authors, students, applicants). A recent critique by Fiedler and Schwarz (2015) of John et al.'s (2012) evidence on questionable research practices is used for illustration. The final discussion is concerned with practical and theoretical implications of the moral values among scientists.*

## Introduction

According to the *Stanford Encyclopedia of Philosophy*,[1] the term morality can be defined either descriptively "to refer to some codes of conduct put forward by a society" or normatively "to refer to a code of conduct that, given specified conditions, would be put forward by all rational persons." Traditionally, the seminal research by Piaget (1932/1965), Kohlberg (1963), and Kelley (1971) on the psychology of morality was apparently driven by the latter, normative perspective, presupposing that morality constitutes an integral aspect of rationality. Jean Piaget's (1932/1965) monograph conveys the message that the development of moral judgment in the child is closely linked to the maturation of intelligence. He was obviously influenced by Kant's (1788/1999) belief in the a priori existence of both cognitive and moral categories, the ontogenetic acquisition of which Piaget believed to follow a regular sequence of developmental stages. This assumption can also be encountered in Lawrence Kohlberg's (1963) writings. From a slightly different, attributional perspective, Harold Kelley (1971) proposed:

> *The moral evaluation process is, in part, based on the processes of reality evaluation and achievement evaluation.* By this, I mean that judgments of right and wrong, good or bad (moral evaluations), derive their properties in part from the same processes as are involved in judgments of correct or incorrect (reality evaluations) and as are involved in judgments of personal success or failure (achievement evaluations). (p. 293)

In contrast to these rationalist approaches, which lead to the assumption of universal principles of moral judgment, a growing body of recent research is apparently motivated by a descriptive approach referring to moral intuition (Haidt, 2001; Saltzstein & Kasachkoff, 2004), to heuristics, ideological narratives (Haidt, Graham, & Joseph, 2009), the blinding function of morality (Haidt, 2013), and the affective influence of sacred values (Graham & Haidt, 2012). Rather than implying universals, this intuitionist and affective approach assumes variation between cultures, groups and ideologies, pluralism in moral values (Berlin, 1998), and distinct relations between moral rules and (left vs. right) political orientations (Haidt & Graham, 2009; van Leeuwen & Park, 2009). Moral judgment is strongly qualified by cultural values, group conventions, religions, or political and epistemic authorities. As Haidt and Graham (2009) put it, the domain of morality cannot be restricted to harm and fairness, its classical issues. It must be broadened to include community (ingroup), authority, and sacredness (Durkheim, 1925/1973) as distinct sources of bias and irrationality. Haidt (2013) raises this new research trend to the level of a prescriptive advice: "I offer three principles that I think should characterize moral psychology in the twenty-first century: (1) Intuitions come first, strategic reasoning second, (2) There's more to morality than harm and fairness and (3) Morality binds and blinds" (p. 281).

## Ethical Norms and Moral Attribution Among Scientists

The present chapter is neither concerned with the moral dilemma (Crockett, this volume; Nichols & Mallon, 2006), the currently most prominent experimental paradigm, nor does it directly speak to harm, justice, ingroup, authority, and sacredness, the key concepts in the intuitionist approach to morality. It is rather concerned with ethical and moral evaluation of scientific practices—an issue that has recently become the focus of a widely attended, self-critical and sometimes self-deprecating debate. Although this topic may appear a bit self-centered and detached from more common areas of morality research (e.g., existential moral dilemmas), it has considerable consequences for the public image of science, for funding schemes, and for the future development of scientific methods and practices. Above all, this topic affords a reality test of whether the two prominent approaches can account for an up-to-date moral debate.

## Compliance as an End in and of Itself

It will soon be apparent that this current discourse on ethical violations, immoral transgressions, and questionable practices in science neither meets the criteria of mature stages of moral judgment according to Piaget, Kohlberg, or Kelley, of reciprocity, and mastery, nor can it be understood within the intuitionist framework. Rather, this debate appears to be mainly driven by a well-known heuristic that has been almost forgotten in the pertinent research, namely, the impact of conformity and compliance with existing rules conceived as a normative end in and of itself, independent of its rationality and utility and often detached from real authority, solidarity, or sacred value. Regardless of the lessons provided in Hannah Arendt's (1963) *Eichmann in Jerusalem: A Report on the Banality of Evil* and in Asch's (1956) or in Milgram's (1963) memorable demonstrations of conformity, the mere compliance with given rules, instructions, or conventions continues to dominate the discourse on good practices in science. Pertinent evidence for this claim will be provided in the next section.

It may indeed be no exaggeration to say that compliance has hardly ever enjoyed the same popularity as in these days, given virtually unlimited access to personal data and technologies for the monitoring and storage of everyday compliance. Almost every large or midsize company has its own compliance department to monitor and control ethical behavior, well below the threshold of legal transgression. Conformity with shortsighted norms is given more attention than compatibility with higher-order legal principles and human rights. Good or bad intentions are hardly considered when sanctioning noncompliant people (like Edward Snowden). What is politically correct and conformist not only determines what is feasible in politics, but even in science (using citation indices as a conformist diagnostic criterion) and in interpersonal behavior. Even the social status of young children depends on their compliance with brand names, popular idols, jargon, and behavioral routines. Asch (1956) already found that experimental participants who provide nonconformist responses become disliked and devalued. And modern experiments on group decision making continue to demonstrate that dissenters who dare to utter unshared information are disliked (cf. Wittenbaum, Hubbell, & Zuckerman, 1999). All these observations testify to the leading role played by compliance for the present zeitgeist of morality, both within science and in society as a whole.

## Moral Reasoning Among Scientists

Note that uncritical compliance with haphazard standards and instructions, even in the absence of strong authorities or forces of ingroup solidarity, cannot be rational or due to sacred values and evolutionary or cultural foundations or morality. An interesting and thought-provoking question is, therefore, why rational scientists—especially those who did take their lessons from Asch, Arendt, and Milgram—should exhibit mere compliance rather than living up to a mature and rational level of moral judgment. Are the ethical norms and moral values that characterize scientists' behavior not obliged to broadminded social ideals and interests, without regard for the presence of interest holders, and without regard to the individual's own interest (cf. Kelley, 1971, p. 294)? Should the moral evaluations and attributions of scientists be determined by the same shallow rules of compliance that have been shown to characterize social behavior at modest levels of reflection? And, should scientists be only concerned with failure on moral tests as distinguished from success on moral opportunities (Miller & Monin, this volume)?

In the remainder of this chapter, I first provide a sketch of the recent debate on violations of ethical and moral norms and rules of good scientific practices. I will then argue that this debate is neither characterized by Kelley's (1971) notion that judgments of reality (correct vs. incorrect) and achievement (success vs. failure) underlie moral evaluation, nor does it reflect the affective impact of actual harm, injustice, ingroup interests, real authority, and violations of any sacred norms. It rather seems to reflect the zeitgeist of a compliance type of "good-boy" morality (Kohlberg, 1963) that does not appear to be sensitive to higher levels of attribution (see Table 13.1) or even intuitive judgments of honesty, fairness, and hypocrisy.

## Major Topics of the Current Debate on Ethical and Moral Conduct in Science

What are the major topics or types of morally questionable behaviors that have been the focus of so many recent articles?

## Plain Fraud

First of all, there have been a few cases of actual fraud, in which behavioral scientists finally admitted to have committed intentional and systematic data fabrication. These are severe transgressions that not only give unfair advantages to fraudsters, who surreptitiously profit from major publications in high-reputation journals. These cases also serve to undermine the public image and the trust in scientific work. Everybody will agree that the scientific community has a vital interest in diagnosing, understanding, and sanctioning data fabrication.

**TABLE 13.1** Heider's (1958) levels of attribution of responsibility, using formulations borrowed from Shaw & Sulzer (1964).

| Level | Attributions at this level are characterized by the following moral rules: | Roughly corresponding to Piaget's (1932/1965): |
| --- | --- | --- |
| Level I: Global association | Person is responsible for any effect associated with the person. Mere presence might be enough. | Syncretistic, pseudocausal reasoning |
| Level II: Extended commission | Person is responsible for any effect of his or her actions, even when effects were unintended and could not be foreseen. | Objective responsibility |
| Level III: Careless commission | Person is responsible for any foreseeable effect of his or her actions, even when unintended. | |
| Level IV: Purposive commission | Person is responsible for any foreseeable and intentional effect of his or her actions. | Subjective responsibility |
| Level V: Justified commission | Even when action effects are intentional, person is only partially responsible if most other persons would have felt and acted the same. | |

## Plagiarism and Violations of Authorship Rights

The same holds for obvious cases of plagiarism, which have become a popular issue in Germany due to the revelation that prominent politicians' dissertations had been stolen. However, despite the negative mass media influence of these prominent affairs on the image of academic institutions, plagiarism does not appear to play much of a role in current psychology. On the contrary, the scientific community appears to be quite insensitive to plagiarism and disinterested in protecting authorship as a valuable good. We never care much about whether every individual in a long list of authors really made a substantial contribution, or whether the senior author in the last position contributed more than equipment and resources. We do not even care about a useful criterion for authorship. The recent claim for unlimited access to data and research tools reflects wide compliance with the transparency claim but little sensitivity for protecting authorship in the creative science process, obviously because there is no majority or proponent of authorship or intellectual origin.

## Harmful Consequences of Applied Research

There is also a conspicuous lack of interest in ethical problems associated with applied psychology, comparable to the ethical debates about genetically modified crops, therapeutic use of stem cells, or animals killed in biology and the life sciences. Although applied psychology is much more likely to cause manifest harm, costs, and personal injustice than fundamental research (due to inappropriate diagnosis, treatment, or faulty methodology), there is nothing comparable in applied psychology, outside the lab, to the ongoing ethics debate revolving around practices within the lab. Lawyers, journalists, and peer researchers do not care much about payment for ineffective or inappropriate psychotherapy, the failure of older therapists to participate in further vocational training, malpractice and methodological mistakes of expert witnesses leading to wrong legal decisions (see Cooper, this volume), discrimination and bias in personnel selection, vested interested and subtle forms of corruption, unwarranted use of questionable survey data, or irresponsible publications of scientifically dubious findings or unwarranted interpretations—an issue to be taken up shortly.

## Attribution of Fraud

If my perception is correct, severe forms of fraud, plagiarism, or corruption do not appear to play strong roles in psychological research, and the ethical debate largely excludes those applied areas, where they are most likely because much is at stake. Still, even when fraud exists in psychological research, one might ask whether an attributional analysis using Kelley's (1971) criteria would justify an association of fraud with psychology. Using Heider's (1958) levels of attribution scale—borrowed from Shaw and Sulzer (1964) and summarized in Table 13.1—it would be interesting to see whether the attribution of fraud in science exceeds even the most primitive level of global associations (of fraud with psychology).

On the one hand, granting a rate of nonzero deception in all domains of life, a logical truism is that deliberate sampling of negative cases will always discover a few existence proofs of fraud. If so, the very existence of a highly selective nonzero sample does not tell us anything about the prevalence of fraud. On the other hand, only a small minority of documented fraud cases came from within psychology; the prevalence of fraud is much higher in the life sciences (Stroebe, Postmes, & Spears, 2012). An even more telling comparison could be based on a systematic assessment of fraud in all areas of cultural life, such as politics, banking, business, journalism, legal affairs, sports, or close relationships. From such a broader perspective, science may turn out to represent an idyllic place of relatively high rates of mutual trust and honesty.

Whether this is true or not, any reasonable moral judgment ought to try going beyond the most primitive level of global association, also known as the fundamental attribution error (Tetlock, 1985), and instead try to take external circumstances and constraints into account. Crucial to attaining a more mature level of attribution is the mastery of the tradeoff between intentionality and effect strength (Piaget, 1932/1965). While young children believe that a large (expensive) window broken by a clumsy football kick is more severe than a small window broken by an intentional kick, the moral judgments of older children give more weight to intention than to the effect. More generally, an advanced stage of morality is evident in shifting weight from the (visible) effect to the (latent) cause.

## Questionable Research Practices

The failure to reach such an advanced level of moral reasoning is apparent in the malicious discussion of so-called questionable research practices that, unlike severe deception, appear to be quite common in behavioral science. Thus, the greatest part of the discourse revolves around such behaviors as not reporting all obtained findings in a published paper, selectively reporting studies that yielded significant findings supporting hypotheses ("studies that worked"), or claiming to have predicted unexpected results. A frequently cited paper by John, Loewenstein, and Prelec (2012) came to conclude, based on a survey among active scientists, that such "questionable practices may constitute the prevailing research norm" (p. 524) and that their prevalence "raises questions about the credibility of research findings and threatens research integrity" (p. 531). These conclusions are so far-reaching and threatening for the scientific community that a more informed assessment of the underlying evidence is in place.

First of all, it is unfortunate and unjustified that the discussion of these questionable research practices is often immediately linked to the recent cases of deliberate fraud, which are not comparable in terms of severity and underlying motives. There is no reason to assume that questionable practices of the aforementioned kind cause fraud. If somebody is hard-boiled enough to engage in plain cheating, he or she does not have to exhibit these subtle biases in self-presentation and selective reporting. Placing questionable practices and fraud in close context only serves to further enhance the global association of psychology with a diffuse meaning of immoral behavior.

More importantly, a closer analysis of questionable research practices reveals that most of them may be attributed to external circumstances and attributes of the scientific system rather than internal dispositions of the individual researcher. Selectively reporting studies that have worked may simply reflect the truism that editors and reviewers do not allow for the publication of results that did not work. The very fact that authors do not continue to try it again and again simply means that they are anticipating the publication bias that exists as a system constraint.[2] Interpreting these cases as "researcher practices" may thus be a misnomer, an ordinary example of the fundamental attribution error—that is, to mistake external conditions for personal dispositions. Similarly, not reporting all the results that were obtained in a study and in the subsequent data analysis (often including simulations and subanalyses motivated by diverse ideas emergent in a dialectic process) may be neither unusual nor motivated by bad intentions. People who endorse not reporting all they have done may be just honest, sincere, and maybe even a bit proud of how carefully and richly they analyze their studies.

In a slightly different vein, raising the impression that all unexpected results were predictable from the beginning may reflect a normal (unintended) hindsight illusion (Fischhoff, 1975). In the light of the evidence obtained in a study, theoretically minded researchers may spontaneously engage in reconstructive attempts to give theoretical meaning to those results, and this may indeed create the hindsight illusion that "I knew it all along." Or, hindsight interpretations may simply reflect the impact of reviewers or editors who force authors to articulate an account of all reported findings. In any case, the behavior may not originate in the researcher's intention to raise too positive an impression of his or her work. The actual motive may indeed be prosocial (helping readers to understand the research), compliant (adhering to an implicitly learned writing norm), or self-deceptive (not remembering the original prediction).[3] Note also that the epistemological status of a hypothesis, whether and when it was adopted by the researcher, is unlikely to have any substantial effect on the data analysis (which is typically determined by the design), on the assessment of internal and external validity, on the chances of the study to be included in reviews and meta-analyses, or on any other theoretical and practical consequence of the study. If so, "admitting" that one has not fully anticipated a hypothesis is rather just a humble act of compliance, like an arbitrary item in a lie detection test or a lying subscale of a personality inventory.

### Minor Deceptions

To be sure, the survey by John et al. (2012) also included some other, less equivocal practices that come closer to dishonest behaviors with unwanted consequences for the scientific process, such as rounding off $p$-values or claiming that results are unaffected by demographic variables when this was actually not tested. Let us assume that such behaviors actually represent minor cases of dishonesty or white lies, apparently aimed at getting a paper past editors or reviewers who may not publish a study because of an unexpected gender effect or because a significance test resulted in $p = .052$ rather than $p = .049$. Some support for such an interpretation was already found by Van Lange, Taris, and Vonk (1997). Even when one (like the present author) does not want to excuse plain lying even on minor details, a fair assessment of morality cannot fully exclude the role of external causes. Is such hypocritical, petty-minded behavior not to a notable degree reflective of features in the scientific system, which evokes hypocrisy (in adaptive players) and therefore calls for external attributions?

## Compliance as a Consequence of Single-Sided Morality

The current discussion of questionable research practices is not only superficial and unsophisticated from an attributional point of view; it is also narrow-minded in terms of the behaviors under focus. The greatest part of the published debate is concerned with practices that undermine the assumptions of statistical hypothesis testing, increasing the danger of $\alpha$-errors in particular (Simmons, Nelson, & Simonsohn, 2011). Stopping data collection after obtaining the desired results or excluding outliers after looking at the impact of doing so are unwanted behaviors because they violate the assumption of random sampling and stochastic independence in hypothesis testing. As a consequence, the nominal $\alpha$ in significance testing is no longer the actual error probability that an effect observed in a sample will be obtained under the null hypothesis. Not complying with these rules enforced by inference statistics is considered a sin that undermines valid and replicable science. All other facets of methodology related to theorizing, logic of science, terminological precision, research design, and modeling are largely ignored and virtually never considered morally relevant.

### *Compliance With the Demon of Statistical-Significance Testing*

To illustrate this hypocrisy, consider the recent research on the enhanced memory for faces associated with the cheater detection motive, a topic of great interest in evolutionary psychology. For instance, in a study by Buchner, Bell, Mehl, and Musch (2009), participants were presented with a series of faces along with text passages that either referred to cheater detection ("Cheater K.S. is a second-hand car dealer. Regularly, he sells restored crash cars as supposedly accident-free and conceals serious defects from the customers") or not ("Cooperator N.G. is a mechanic. He is always eager to provide spare parts as cheap as possible for his clients and to fulfill his jobs efficiently"). Significance tests clearly confirm that in a subsequent recognition test, memory for faces associated with cheating is clearly superior to memory for faces associated with cooperation or neutral themes. This well-replicated finding is consistent with the notion that cheater detection and social exchange motives are evolutionarily significant and cognitive abilities as old as the time of hunter-gatherers (Cosmides & Tooby, 2004).

Could the late exclusion of a few outliers (who have apparently not understood the instructions) or a questionable stopping rule (ceasing to sample participants when the available evidence already demonstrates the expected results) greatly reduce the scientific value of this kind of research? An informed answer clearly depends on an analysis of the alternative condition, namely, the same research in the absence of those statistical malpractices. Can strict adherence to the rules of significance testing be presupposed to result in unbiased and valid inferences about the cheater-detection hypothesis?

Some closer inspection reveals that under most study conditions the strong assumptions of significance testing are unlikely to be met anyway. In a recognition test involving dozens of faces, it is hardly justified to assume that memory measures for different faces are stochastically independent, that discriminability and response bias are stable over the entire test time, that all assumptions about scaling and measurement resolution are met, or that the sample of participants can be considered truly random.[4] So, it would only be honest to admit that the nominal $\alpha$ is virtually never the true $\alpha$ and, even more directly, a significance test is never more than a crude heuristic to judge the viability of a hypothesis, not a sound basis for inferring the validity of the hypothesis. Again, honesty and morality require rational reasoning: A significant finding only means that $p$(obtained effect | $H_0$) is very low (< $\alpha$). There is no rationale for making inferences about $p(H_0$ | obtained effect) or $p(H_1$ | obtained effect). Let me quickly add that this logical restriction is also not overcome when significance testing relies on Bayesian (rather than Fisherian) tools. The strong dependence of Bayesian statistics on prior odds, $p(H_1)$ / $p(H_0)$, highlights the fact that the posterior odds (i.e., that $H_1$ rather than $H_0$ is true) depend crucially on other factors than the statistical properties of the obtained effect in a sample.

Provided some more modest consensus can be reached about the omnipotence of statistics, the question is why the morality debates centers on prescriptions derived from statistics. The most reasonable answer that comes to mind—namely, that precision is a major asset in science—is unwarranted when no precise inference about $p(H_1$ | obtained effect) is possible anyway. On the contrary, strict adherence to statistical rules of the game might foster an illusion of confidence in the validity of findings that ought to be regarded as rather local in value. Alternatively, one might contend that discipline and commitment to rules of the game are fundamental assets, symbolic symptoms of trustworthiness or of a general disposition to be honest and committed to the scientific community. In my opinion, though, a more convincing answer would have to point out that blind compliance with unreflected rules is at work. Any other account could hardly explain why so many other sources of invalidity, bad research design, measurement and sampling error, and sloppy interpretation are not also treated as dangerous for scientific precision and integrity and as morally relevant.

## Conspicuous Insensitivity to Nonstatistical Dangers

A more open-minded valuation of dangers that might undermine the trust in and reliance on science has to realize, first of all, that randomized sampling of participants represents but one of a variety of sampling filters (Fiedler, 2011). Inferences about the validity of the cheater-detection hypothesis not only depend on the size and the allegedly pure randomness of the sample of participants. They also depend on the sampling of stimuli (faces used), treatments (text passages referring to cheating or other behaviors), levels manipulated on independent variables (in a typical fixed-effects design), indices used to measure the dependent variable, different wordings of instructions, task settings (including time delays, attentional constraints, list length, etc.), or psychologically relevant boundary conditions of recognition performance (e.g., mood, regulatory focus, etc.). The principle of representative sampling (Brunswik, 1955; Dhami, Hertwig, & Hoffrage, 2004) calls for study designs that treat all these aspects as random factors rather than fixed-effect factors restricted to two or very few arbitrarily selected study conditions (cf. Wells & Windschitl, 1999). However, while perfect compliance with the norm of random sampling of participants is considered crucial for good practices in science, the failure to render a study representative of all these other respects is not part of the arbitrary behavioral code. Not checking on the degree to which face memory is peculiar to the specific text passages presented with the faces, to the strength of the cheating appeals, to demand effects inherent in specific instructions, or to boundary conditions like incidental versus intentional memory settings would not be considered questionable a practice.

A provocative paper by Vul, Harris, Winkielman, and Pashler (2009) that focused on inflated correlations ("voodoo correlations") in neuroscience is telling about the serious validity problem that results from selective sampling of measurement points ("voxels"). The authors had pointed out that correlations as high as $r = .70$ or more between brain measures and behavioral measures of traits or performance might be due to the fact that such correlations are often based on a highly selective subset of those voxels (out of 150,000 or so) that bear the strongest relation to the behavioral criterion. If so, this might not only undermine the validity of neuroscience but actually border on invalidity of a morally significant kind. However, neuroscientists were quick to deny that 150,000 degrees of freedom are reduced like that. They rather pointed out that the selection of voxels in state-of-the-art neuro-research is based on regions of interest (ROIs), or brain areas that have been shown previously, or in pilot studies, to be relevant to the explanation of behavioral correlates. In other words, to exculpate a researcher from any accusation, the reframing of a voxel selection stage as a pilot study is sufficient. If researchers use early participants (framed as a pilot study) to select voxels defining an ROI empirically, this is deemed to be logically (and morally) different from a selection framed as the initial stage of a single main study. The example highlights the weakness of the underlying moral code that is used to classify behaviors as questionable or not, and it highlights again the need to anchor moral valuation in a refined attributional analysis, beyond global associations and moral intuition.

## Failure to Engage in Deep and Responsible Theorizing

The need to engage in moral reasoning proper is most evident when it comes to careless (and often self-serving or self-deceptive) theorizing. Consider again the cheater-detection example. If the failure to stop sampling according to a predetermined rule and the post hoc exclusion of invalid participants constitute morally questionable practices, then how serious is a premature theoretical explanation of a finding for which there is no logical foundation? Indeed, Bell and Buchner (2012) first succeeded in gathering strong evidence for the hypothesis *If cheater, then enhanced memory* across several replication experiments, using large samples and apparently clean sampling methods. However, reminiscent of Peter Wason's (1960) lesson on conditional reasoning—that *If p, then q* does not imply that only *p* affects *q*—they then ran another experiment to see whether cheater detection is really the crucial causal factor. Granting that the text passages used to induce cheater detection could also serve to induce cheater-independent negative meaning, they also associated faces with other negative meanings and, not too surprisingly, they obtained a similar increase in memory performance.

I anticipate that hardly anybody will blame researchers who fail to take logical rules into account, even though Peter Wason's lesson is as popular as the rules of significance testing. However, I ask myself why careless logical reasoning is less relevant for good conduct than complying with statistical norms. The only plausible answer that comes to my mind, related to distinction of compliance and conversion (Moscovici & Personnaz, 1991), is that statistical norms are a matter of compliance whereas logical reasoning calls for critical, emancipated reasoning, lying outside the realm of common interpretations of good scientific practices.

Deeper reflection and analysis show that careless theoretical reasoning—which is of course not haphazard but typically favoring researchers' beloved hypotheses—is a widespread phenomenon (Fiedler, Kutzner, & Krueger, 2012). Wason (1960) had shown that when trying to identify the rule underlying a sequence like 2, 4, 8, people quickly come up with overly specified rules (such as $2^N$) and restrict their hypothesis test to checking the predictions of the selected rule, finding out that, say, 16, 32, and 64 also provide positive examples of the rule. Using such non-Popperian strategies, they never find out that the correct rule might not be $2^N$ but some less specific rule that includes $2^N$ as a special case. For instance, they fail to find out that the actual rule might be superlinearly increasing integers, or increasing integers, or any series of integers, or any real numbers, any numbers, or any set of symbols (whether numbers or not).

By analogy, researchers—even when their work is published in the best journals—interpret that impact of exposure to a funeral or a mortality-related essay topic on conservative behavior as an impact of mortality salience (Greenberg, Solomon, & Pyszczynski, 1997). They hardly test whether the manipulation affects some superordinate construct that includes mortality as a special case. Rather than mortality, it might reflect the priming of existential values (implying similar effects for birth as for mortality), or self-referent affect, or simply priming of incompleteness (implying similar effects for mortality-unrelated incompleteness; Wicklund & Braun, 1987). In a similar vein, the manipulation of exposure frequency is presupposed to causally induce fluency, rather than other, more general aspects of density in memory. Or, returning to Bell and Buchner (2012), one need not take it for granted that vignettes manipulate cheater detection, rather than other negative meaning or other nonnegative affective meaning.

The naïve belief in the validity of one preferred theoretical account, and the failure to check for a whole variety of alternative causal models of the same findings, is particularly evident in the epidemic use of mediation analysis (Fiedler, Schott, & Meiser, 2011), which is generally considered a gold standard of good practice and strong science worthy of imitation. Closer inspection shows that the vast majority of all published research that uses mediation analysis only ran a statistical test that focused on one favorite mediator. It rarely happens that researchers engage in comparative tests of several mediator candidates, and researchers virtually never test for alternative causal models but mediation (cf. Danner, Hagemann, & Fiedler, 2015). Thus, rather than mediating the influence of X on Y according to a causal mediation model $X \rightarrow Z \rightarrow Y$, the third variable Z might be a covariate of Y in a common-cause model $X \rightarrow X, Z$, or all three variables might just be drawn at random from a set of homogeneously correlated measures of the same syndrome. Simulation results make it crystal clear that statistical tests of Z as a mediator cannot discriminate between these different causal models (Fiedler et al., 2011). Statistical tests will also be often significant when the actual causal model is different from mediation. However, whereas careless mistakes in conducting and reporting a statistical mediation test would be a candidate for questionable practice, leading to the downgrading or even disqualification of scientists who commit the mistake, the widely shared practice of drawing premature and often wrong inferences from highly selective, single-eyed mediation tests is hardly recognized as problematic. Eventually, misleading, hypothesis-confirming, and self-serving mediation analyses would be considered better than not running a mediation test. After all, the latter involves compliance with a majority habit, and less emancipation is required to diagnose a formal statistical mistake than to reason critically about alternative causal models.

More generally, the new interest in quantitative model fitting is quite in line with a compliance-oriented valuation system. By conducting mathematical model tests, researchers subscribe symbolically to precision and strictness as laudable norms of scientific research. In contrast, critical questions about whether metric data qualities assumed in quantitative models are met, whether model fit entails capitalizing on chance, and the insight that a fitting model need not underlie the data to be explained (Roberts & Pashler, 2000) would run against the easily executed compliance rule. Such critical counterarguments are therefore not appreciated as manifestations of good scientific practices and of researchers' honesty and responsibility.

## Reciprocity, Equality, and Generally Binding Moral Rules

So far, I have argued that the behavioral scientists' ethical norms and behavioral codes do not live up to higher levels of attribution that would allow them to go beyond the fundamental attribution bias (i.e., blaming the researcher rather than the system) and beyond compliance with superficial rules. The aim of the present section is to demonstrate that even more primitive moral rules of fairness, such as the age-old reciprocity principle or the equal-rights-and-equal-duty rule, are not visible in the current debate. Rather, there appears to be an asymmetric allocation of roles in the science game, with some people being "prosecutors" or monitors of ethical standards and other taking the role of "defendants" or targets of evaluation. Good practices are expected of and controlled in authors who want their manuscripts to be published in journals, but good practices are hardly ever assessed in reviewers and editors, the major determinants in the publication system. Similarly, good practices and minimal standards are obligatory for grant-proposal writers, for Ph.D. students, and for original researchers, but hardly for reviewers of grant proposals, doctoral advisors, or scholars who blame others in published articles of questionable practices. It appears that those agents who take the offensive role of referees, evaluators, and censors need not be afraid that they will themselves be evaluated according to the same rules of good conduct that they evaluate in the targets or patients of the unidirectional compliance game.

Thus, John et al.'s (2012) widely cited survey study entailed a grave and generalized accusation that questionable research practices of the type discussed earlier have become a prevailing research norm so that the credibility of research findings and integrity are questioned. However, granting that John et al. are driven by a moral (compliance) norm, there is little interest in the question of whether their survey itself lives up to standards of good science. We already discussed that no deliberate attempt was made to avoid, or to diagnose, misunderstandings of questionable practices. Moreover, other rules of good survey research related to the logic of conversation were not attended to. For instance, the only way for a respondent to appear innocent would have been to respond "no" to all items, which cannot be expected in a survey.

However, the most serious shortcoming is that John et al. assessed the proportion of people who ever committed a behavior (e.g., ever stopped sampling once the desired results were obtained) at least once in their life, and the resulting proportions were then treated like evidence on the prevalence of these behaviors. This is, of course, a category mistake, because researchers conduct many hypothesis tests in their lives, and the prevalence of the behavior is some multiplicative function of the proportion of scientists with a nonzero rate times the average repetition rate across all studies (cf. Fiedler & Schwarz, 2015). Nobody would come to doubt that the prevalence of lying is magnitudes lower than the proportion of people who ever told a lie. So why should we believe that the proportion of scientists who ever committed a behavior equals the behavior's prevalence? What gives us the right to believe that any sound inference from the survey to the behavioral prevalence is possible at all?

Indeed, our own experience with a critical test of the John et al. (2012) data (leading to strongly divergent results) is that editors and reviewers do not appreciate any attempt to blame prosecutors. Without strong arguments against the validity of our critique (Fiedler & Schwarz, 2015), they continue to believe that John et al. were driven by a laudable motive, and reviewers feel intuitively that their pessimistic prevalence estimates are probably closer to the truth than the more optimistic estimates obtained in a survey with different measures for prevalence and nonzero proportions. They also don't mind that their own behavior prevents a potentially very informative paper from seeing the light of publication, although they seem to agree that not reporting unwanted findings is a bad practice. Crucial to understanding the contradiction is of course the fact that the John et al. article fits neatly into what is considered politically correct and therefore likely to become a compliance norm.

In a similar vein, Simonsohn, Nelson, and Simmons (2014) refer to $p$-hacking as an explanation of the conspicuously high rate of $\alpha$ values slightly lower than .05 in significance tests of published articles. The action verb "$p$-hacking" entails an internal attribution to researchers' intentional, deliberate actions, although an obvious external attribution would be to understand the peak at slightly below $\alpha = .05$ as a reflection of a filter in the publication system. Even though I sensitized them to the surplus meaning of the verb and its implications, they decided to continue using the term $p$-hacking. Obviously, if one is on the appropriate side of a compliance game, one need not refrain from questionable depreciation of peer researchers.

A slightly different but related example concerns the unfortunate publication of Bem's (2011) parapsychological paper on precognition—which also contributed a lot to the current zeitgeist of questioning scientific standards. Obviously, the decision to publish this paper was driven by compliance with the norm to treat all submissions according to the same (mainly statistical) rules and not to be prejudiced against research in parapsychology (Judd & Gawronski, 2011). Afterward, the published critique of Bem's work was largely restricted to issues of appropriate significance testing—another compliance domain. Other serious problems with the logic of science and the validity of Bem's research, which I pointed out repeatedly as a reviewer from the beginning, were hardly ever noted and only published in a low-publicity journal (cf. Fiedler & Krueger, 2013). In leading empirical journals, there is little room and little interest in publishing enlightening debates if they do not refer to statistical significance testing. This neglect of critical debates—serving an emancipation rather than a compliance function—is noteworthy because a few exceptional cases of published theory debates have been extremely successful and inspiring (e.g., the debate on the issue of genuine altruism; Batson, 1997; Neuberg et al., 1997).

From all perspectives, as an editor, a reviewer, and as an author who submits his own papers to leading journals, I have witnessed reviewers deliberately arguing against the publication of research that works against their own interests or previous results. If this occurs—and it does occur regularly when reviewers are really expert in a field—my impression is not that reviewers have much to lose in ethical reputation if they engage in clearly one-sided critique and obvious attempts to turn down a paper. They possess an evaluator role. Similarly, it is relatively easy for reviewers to allude to the alleged fact that some evidence is not new, without indicating a reference, or simply to express that they do not like what researchers have done. My impression is that strong editors who act as arbiters rather than simply counting and following reviewer votes are the exception rather than the rule. Although the impact of reviewers and especially of editors on publication decisions is much stronger than the impact of the authors' practices, the former are unlikely to become the target of moral valuation. The implicit norm is apparently that editors publish an article if they want to publish it and that reviewers are doing valuable honorable work that does not deserve to be judged morally. The only role that is weak enough to be assigned a patient part in the compliance game is the author, who has to provide signed declarations of good conduct and worry about being responsible for published data and interpretations. There is little need for the more powerful roles in the game to develop guilty feelings, although their impact on the publication output is strongest and most direct.

## Conclusions: Can Social Psychology Account for Morality in Science?

Thus, it seems obvious that the reality of a recent moral debate among, in, and around the scientific community can be neither explained in terms of the old rationalist approaches to morality nor in terms of modern intuitionist approaches. On the one hand, the manner in which questionable practices are defined and in which scientists are held responsible for any effects of their actions, regardless of intention and foreseeability and regardless of how many people engage in similar behavior, would be at best classified as Level II in Heider's scale (cf. Table 13.1). The underlying moral principles are far away from Levels V or IV, which ought to be reached according to Piaget (1932/1965) and Heider (1958) by moral maturation alone. In fact, I do believe that many scientists would defend the rigid Level II rules as an asset, a precondition for objectivity in good science. But note that Piaget's (1932/1965) use of the term "objective responsibility" for Level II was meant to denote unsophisticated moral judgments that are insensitive to motives and intentions, rather than objectivity in checking violations of compliance rules. Apparently, the current zeitgeist is more interested in establishing the latter meaning of objectivity than in overcoming the former meaning.

On the other hand, scientists' moral judgments are not only insensitive to higher levels of attribution, lying outside the domain of rationalist theories in the traditions of Piaget and Kant. They also lie outside the domain of the modern intuitionist approach, with focuses on affective heuristics and sacred values, which do not appear to motivate the current debate. With respect to the key concepts harm, justice, ingroup, authority, and sacredness (Haidt, 2013), it has to be noted that in this debate that (1) no cost-benefit analysis is conducted to assess harm; (2) no fairness rules of justice are applied to everybody; (3) no ingroup-serving bias prevents whistleblowers from blaming their own ingroup members; (4) no natural authority is apparent behind the debate; and (5) there is hardly anything sacred in the most widely respected statistical norms.

My motivation here is not to criticize my peers or my scientific community for a moral attribution style that others have considered immature. Rather, it is to point out that the most prominent psychological approaches to morality may not be applicable to real-world manifestations of moral evaluation. I hasten to add that focusing on morality in other parts of real life—such as the conduct of politicians or journalists, democratic rights and duties, commercial business rules, or faithfulness in close relationships—would probably lead to the same conclusion: neither rational rules (cost-benefit analysis, reciprocity, consideration of norm distributions) nor phylogenetically inherited moral heuristics capture the essence of moral judgment under realistic conditions (see also the critique by Saltzstein & Kasachkoff, 2004).

The one approach that in my view comes closest to understanding the motives, monitoring mechanisms, and moral judgment rules in contemporary science can be found in the seminal writings of Hannah Arendt (1963), Solomon Asch (1956), Stanley Milgram (1963), and Moscovici (1980) on uncritical and strict reliance on compliance rules, contrasted against rational and intellectually advanced rules of argumentation and mature attribution. New evidence by Bocchiaro, Zimbardo, and Van Lange (2012) suggests a major reason why people adopt compliant behaviors so readily. When asked to comply with an unethical request, a vast majority of people "cooperates" but grossly underestimates the high rate of people who comply.

I believe that content validity for broadly assessed morality issues in real life should not be neglected in social psychological research. I am not taking for granted that the analysis I have outlined in the present chapter is the only viable perspective. Proponents of intuitionist research may have other reality domains in mind, which I have overlooked, and maybe some scientists involved in the pursuit of good scientific practices can convince me that the underlying moral rules are more sophisticated than I could see. For such counterarguments to be really convincing, though, they would have to come up with real evidence that goes beyond experiments in which moral dilemmas are described in vignettes that enforce sacred values and emotional instincts that are rarely invoked in everyday reality.

To the extent, however, that moral judgment and action in real life is indeed driven by compliance with (often arbitrary but objectively applicable) norms of conduct, this has not only implications for a refined theory of moral judgment, but it also has obvious practical implications. Scientists and practitioners—in politics, law, economy, education, and therapy—have to reflect on whether morality is of practical value and, if so, to analyze the relation between moral means and moral ends. Are there good reasons to assume that objectively applicable compliance will foster the attainment of such moral ends as validity in science (Jussim, Crawford, Stevens, Anglin, & Duarte, this volume), reducing inequality in the global world (von Hippel, Ronay, & Maddux, this volume), affirming human rights and personal dignity, and fairness in sports and courtrooms? Or might a comprehensive analysis—which has to be both moral and scientific—reveal that it is functional and worthwhile in the long run to strive for higher levels of moral attribution, beyond mere compliance and sacred values?

## Notes

1 http://plato.stanford.edu/entries/morality-definition/#toc
2 While this could be considered a case of collective immorality, it is just another symptom of compliance.
3 Note in passing, however, that what appears like a benevolent form of compliance at the individual level may be not at all benevolent at the collective level.
4 To be sure, these limitations of statistics do not justify other violations of methodological rules. The purpose here is only to point out the uncritical compliance with statistical norms.

## References

Arendt, H. (1963). *Eichmann in Jerusalem: A report on the banality of evil*. London: Faber & Faber.
Asch, S.E. (1956). Studies of independence and conformity: I. A minority of one against a unanimous majority. *Psychological Monographs: General and Applied, 70*(9), 1–70.
Batson, C.D. (1997). Self–other merging and the empathy–altruism hypothesis: Reply to Neuberg et al. (1997). *Journal of Personality and Social Psychology, 73*(3), 517–522.
Bell, R., & Buchner, A. (2012). How adaptive is memory for cheaters? *Current Directions in Psychological Science, 21*(6), 403–408.
Bem, D. (2011). Feeling the future: Experimental evidence for anomalous retroactive influences on cognition and affect. *Journal of Personality and Social Psychology, 100*, 407–425.
Berlin, I. (1998, 14 May). My intellectual path. *New York Review of Books*.
Bocchiaro, P., Zimbardo, P.G., & Van Lange, P.A.M. (2012). To defy or not to defy: An experimental study of the dynamics of disobedience and whistle-blowing. *Social Influence, 7*(1), 35–50.
Brunswik, E. (1955). Representative design and probabilistic theory in a functional psychology. *Psychological Review, 62*(3), 193–217.
Buchner, A., Bell, R., Mehl, B., & Musch, J. (2009). No enhanced recognition memory, but better source memory for faces of cheaters. *Evolution and Human Behavior, 30*(3), 212–224.

Cosmides, L., & Tooby, J. (2004). Social exchange: The evolutionary design of a neuro-cognitive system. In M.S. Gazzaniga (Ed.), *The cognitive neurosciences* (3rd ed., pp. 1295–1308). Cambridge, MA: MIT Press.

Danner, D., Hagemann, D., & Fiedler, K. (2015). Mediation analysis with structural equation models: Combining theory, design, and statistics. *European Journal of Social Psychology, 45*(4), 460–481.

Dhami, M.K., Hertwig, R., & Hoffrage, U. (2004). The role of representative design in an ecological approach to cognition. *Psychological Bulletin, 130*(6), 959–988.

Durkheim, E. (1973). *Moral education* (E. Wilson & H. Schnurer, Trans.). New York: Free Press. (Original work published 1925)

Fiedler, K. (2011). Voodoo correlations are everywhere—not only in neuroscience. *Perspectives on Psychological Science, 6*(2), 163–171.

Fiedler, K., & Krueger, J.I. (2013). Afterthoughts on precognition: No cogent evidence for anomalous influences of consequent events on preceding cognition. *Theory & Psychology, 23*(3), 323–333.

Fiedler, K., Kutzner, F., & Krueger, J.I. (2012). The long way from α-error control to validity proper: Problems with a short-sighted false-positive debate. *Perspectives on Psychological Science, 7*(6), 661–669.

Fiedler, K., Schott, M., & Meiser, T. (2011). What mediation analysis can (not) do. *Journal of Experimental Social Psychology, 47*(6), 1231–1236.

Fiedler, K., & Schwarz, N. (2016). Questionable research practices revisited. *Social Psychological and Personality Science, 7*, 45–52.

Fischhoff, B. (1975). Hindsight is not equal to foresight: The effect of outcome knowledge on judgment under uncertainty. *Journal of Experimental Psychology: Human Perception and Performance, 1*(3), 288–299.

Graham, J., & Haidt, J. (2012). Sacred values and evil adversaries: A moral foundations approach. In M. Mikulincer & P.R. Shaver (Eds.), *The social psychology of morality: Exploring the causes of good and evil* (pp. 11–31). Washington, DC: American Psychological Association.

Greenberg, J., Solomon, S., & Pyszczynski, T. (1997). Terror management theory of self-esteem and cultural worldviews: Empirical assessments and conceptual refinements. In M.P. Zanna (Ed.), *Advances in experimental social psychology* (Vol. 29, pp. 61–139). San Diego, CA: Academic Press.

Haidt, J. (2001). The emotional dog and its rational tail: A social intuitionist approach to moral judgment. *Psychological Review, 108*, 814–834.

Haidt, J. (2013). Moral psychology for the twenty-first century. *Journal of Moral Education, 42*(3), 281–297.

Haidt, J., & Graham, J. (2009). Planet of the Durkheimians, where community, authority, and sacredness are foundations of morality. In J.T. Jost, A.C. Kay, & H. Thorisdottir (Eds.), *Social and psychological bases of ideology and system justification* (pp. 371–401). New York: Oxford University Press.

Haidt, J., Graham, J., & Joseph, C. (2009). Above and below left–right: Ideological narratives and moral foundations. *Psychological Inquiry, 20*(2–3), 110–119.

Heider, F. (1958). *The psychology of interpersonal relations.* Oxford: Wiley.

John, L.K., Loewenstein, G., & Prelec, D. (2012). Measuring the prevalence of questionable research practices with incentives for truth telling. *Psychological Science, 23*, 524–532.

Judd, C.M., & Gawronski, B. (2011). Editorial comment. *Journal of Personality and Social Psychology, 100*(3), 406.

Kant, I. (1999). Critique of practical reason. In M. Gregor (Ed. & Trans.), *The Cambridge edition of the works of Immanuel Kant: practical philosophy* (pp. 137–276). Cambridge: Cambridge University Press. (Original work published 1788)

Kelley, H.H. (1971). Moral evaluation. *American Psychologist, 26*(3), 293–300.

Kohlberg, L. (1963). The development of children's orientations toward a moral order: I. Sequence in the development of moral thought. *Vita Humana, 6*(1–2), 11–33.

Milgram, S. (1963). Behavioral study of obedience. *Journal of Abnormal and Social Psychology, 67*(4), 371–378.

Moscovici, S. (1980). Toward a theory of conversion behavior. *Advances in Experimental Social Psychology, 13*, 209–239.

Moscovici, S., & Personnaz, B. (1991). Studies in social influence: VI. Is Lenin orange or red? Imagery and social influence. *European Journal of Social Psychology, 21*(2), 101–118.

Neuberg, S.L., Cialdini, R.B., Brown, S.L., Luce, C., Sagarin, B.J., & Lewis, B.P. (1997). Does empathy lead to anything more than superficial helping? Comment on Batson et al. (1997). *Journal of Personality and Social Psychology, 73*(3), 510–516.

Nichols, S., & Mallon, R. (2006). Moral dilemmas and moral rules. *Cognition, 100*, 530–542.

Piaget, J. (1965). *The moral judgment of the child.* New York: Free Press. (Original work published 1932)

Roberts, S., & Pashler, H. (2000). How persuasive is a good fit? A comment on theory testing. *Psychological Review, 107*, 358–367.

Saltzstein, H.D., & Kasachkoff, T. (2004). Haidt's Moral Intuitionist Theory: A psychological and philosophical critique. *Review of General Psychology, 8*(4), 273–282.

Shaw, M.E., & Sulzer, J.L. (1964). An empirical test of Heider's levels in attribution of responsibility. *Journal of Abnormal and Social Psychology, 69*(1), 39–46.

Simmons, J.P., Nelson, L.D., & Simonsohn, U. (2011). False-positive psychology: Undisclosed flexibility in data collection and analysis allows presenting anything as significant. *Psychological Science, 22*(11), 1359–1366.

Simonsohn, U., Nelson, L.D., & Simmons, J.P. (2014). P-curve: A key to the file-drawer. *Journal of Experimental Psychology: General, 143*(2), 534–547.

Stroebe, W., Postmes, T., & Spears, R. (2012). Scientific misconduct and the myth of self-correction in science. *Perspectives on Psychological Science, 7*, 670–688.

Tetlock, P.E. (1985). Accountability: A social check on the fundamental attribution error. *Social Psychology Quarterly, 48*(3), 227–236.

Van Lange, P.A.M., Taris, T.W., & Vonk, R. (1997). Dilemmas of academic practice: Perceptions of superiority among social psychologists. *European Journal of Social Psychology, 27*(6), 675–685.

Van Leeuwen, F., & Park, J.H. (2009). Perceptions of social dangers, moral foundations, and political orientation. *Personality and Individual Differences, 47*(3), 169–173.

Vul, E., Harris, C., Winkielman, P., & Pashler, H. (2009). Puzzlingly high correlations in fMRI studies of emotion, personality, and social cognition. *Perspectives on Psychological Science, 4*, 274–290.

Wason, P.C. (1960). On the failure to eliminate hypotheses in a conceptual task. *Quarterly Journal of Experimental Psychology, 12*, 129–140.

Wells, G.L., & Windschitl, P.D. (1999). Stimulus sampling and social psychological experimentation. *Personality and Social Psychology Bulletin, 25*(9), 1115–1125.

Wicklund, R.A., & Braun, O.L. (1987). Incompetence and the concern with human categories. *Journal of Personality and Social Psychology, 53*(2), 373–382.

Wittenbaum, G.M., Hubbell, A.P., & Zuckerman, C. (1999). Mutual enhancement: Toward an understanding of the collective preference for shared information. *Journal of Personality and Social Psychology, 77*(5), 967–978.

# PART IV

# Morality and Collective Behavior

# 14

# MORALIZATION AND INTOLERANCE OF IDEOLOGICAL OUTGROUPS

*Mark J. Brandt, Geoffrey Wetherell, and Jarret T. Crawford*

*Moral conflicts are pervasive and potentially corrosive to democratic politics; however, little is known about where moral convictions come from. We review evidence for the role of emotions, beliefs, and the self-concept, in predicting moralization. To the extent that moral convictions are emotionally relevant, tightly intertwined with the self, and, in some cases, associated with harms and benefits may help to explain their potency in predicting political behaviors and perceptions. In support of this idea we review recent work suggesting that both political liberals and conservatives are equally intolerant toward ideological outgroups and that this intolerance is often based on perceived moral and value differences. Neither liberals nor conservatives are uniquely (im)moral, but rather both seek to defend the meaning provided by their political beliefs that are connected to their fundamental moral beliefs. Possible solutions to reduce moral conflict and promote cooperation are discussed.*

Conflicts arise for many reasons. Some conflicts are over scarce resources, such as natural resources like fresh water or social resources like power. Other conflicts are over values, such as religious, moral, political, and even scientific values (see Fiedler, this volume). Conflicts over resources, in some ways, make sense (see also Bastian & Crimston, this volume). These are resources that people and societies need, and one frequent necessity for acquiring those resources is to engage in conflict with people and societies that have resources you do not. Conflicts over values are different. Many attitudes do not inherently cause conflict. I (MJB) prefer the band Jawbreaker. They are a particularly good representation of the punk/emo amalgamation that occurred during the late '80s and early '90s, but if you do not share the same view we can still have a reasonable interaction and perhaps even be friends. However, both personal experience and history teaches us that other kinds of attitudes, particularly those that are experienced as morally relevant, are more likely to lead to conflict. Most scholars would predict that differences in preferences for early '90s punk bands are less likely to ruin a relationship than differences in moral values or a moral issue (e.g., whether or not abortion is permissible). In this chapter, we first examine recent social psychological research on the moralization process by which people go from having a preference for an issue to a moral conviction. That is, we examine the question, "Where do moral convictions come from?" Then, we review research on conflicts over moral values and other ideological worldviews.

## Moral Conviction

Attitudes held with a sense of moral conviction are different from attitudes that are nonmoral preferences or conventions. Moral conviction is a person's subjective metacognitive belief that a particular attitude or value is connected to his or her fundamental sense of right or wrong (Skitka & Morgan, 2014). These attitudes are often perceived as objective and universal, and motivate behavior (Morgan, Skitka, & Lytle, 2014; Skitka, Bauman, & Sargis, 2005). One of the major findings of the moral conviction research program is that the extent to which a particular attitude is held with a sense of moral conviction differs from person to person. Some people consider abortion to be a moral issue, whereas others consider it a nonmoral preference (e.g., Ryan, 2014; Skitka et al., 2005). Similarly, some people consider their attitudes toward presidential candidates, same-sex marriage, gun control, Jawbreaker, and taxes as moral convictions, whereas other people consider these very same issues as unrelated to their moral values (e.g., Ryan, 2014; Skitka et al., 2005). Individuals can even construe rather boring issues, such as whether students should study, in moral terms (Van Bavel, Packer, Haas, & Cunningham, 2012). One clear but potentially controversial conclusion of this research is that there is no clear-cut set of moral or nonmoral issues, but rather different individuals construe different issues along a continuum from morally relevant to morally irrelevant (see also Haslam, this volume).

The moral conviction research program has made it quite clear that moral convictions differ from their nonmorally convicted counterparts. For example, moral convictions are easily accessible (Wisneski, Lytle, & Skitka, 2009), and people perceive moral convictions as independent of majority influence (Aramovich, Lytle, & Skitka, 2012) and independent of authority (Skitka, Bauman, & Lytle, 2009). For example, when the US Supreme Court—a branch of the government that is typically perceived as highly legitimate—ruled in favor of physician assisted suicide (PAS), only people who were both opposed to and morally convicted about PAS perceived less legitimacy of the court after, compared to before, the court's ruling (Skitka et al., 2009). This result suggests that people who view their opposition to PAS with a sense of moral conviction follow their convictions and ignore the suggestions of a typically legitimate authority, perhaps finding it easier to change their opinion of the court rather than their deeply held moral conviction. The effects reported in these studies often use large samples of adults, and the effects hold when controlling for a host of plausible demographic and attitudinal variables (including, critically, attitude strength) suggesting that the effects of moral conviction are both far-reaching and robust.

## Where Do Moral Convictions Come From?

A recent extension of the moral conviction research program tries to understand why some people consider an issue to be a moral issue, but other people do not view the very same issue with a sense of moral conviction. What makes an issue a nonmoral issue for some people, but a strong moral conviction for others? Why do some people see an issue as slightly moral, whereas others see the same issue as *the* prototype of a moral issue? That is, what causes moralization? In this section we review evidence for three possibilities, but there may be many more.

### *Emotions and Beliefs*

The most well-known examinations of moralization were conducted by Paul Rozin and colleagues to understand the moralization of vegetarianism and smoking (Rozin, Markwith, & Stoess, 1997; Rozin & Singh, 1999). The primary reason these papers are cited in the contemporary literature is because they find that feelings of disgust are robust correlates of moralization (cf. Petrescu & Parkinson, 2014). This has inspired the relatively few additional studies that test moralization. For example, work by Wheatley and Haidt (2005) finds that manipulations of disgust lead people to see a morally neutral behavior (e.g., a student council representative selected topics for the upcoming meetings that would stimulate discussion) as morally wrong (for a review of the slim empirical literature relevant to this moralization claim see Avramova & Inbar, 2013). The idea that emotions lead to moralization is consistent with the gist of Haidt's (2001) influential social intuitionist model of moral judgment, which predicts that judgments of right or wrong are based on people's intuitive, gut-level, and emotional reactions to the issue. It is also consistent with cross-sectional studies finding a correlation between issue-based anger and other negative emotions and moral conviction (Mullen & Skitka, 2006; Skitka & Wisneski, 2011).

There is also reason to believe that less emotional and more cognitive considerations, like people's beliefs about the harms and benefits of a particular issue, may also play a role. A less well-known finding from Rozin and colleagues' work is that people's perception that eating meat or smoking is harmful was also associated with moralization (Rozin et al., 1997; Rozin & Singh, 1999). Other recent work has found that even moral judgments of scenarios that have removed all obvious instances of harm are thought to contain some degree of harm by participants (Gray, Schein, & Ward, 2014), and that anthropomorphizing a social cause (and thus highlighting the potential for harm) increases donations to that cause (Ahn, Kim, & Aggarwal, 2014; see also Haslam, this volume). This suggests that moralization may occur via the strong emotions people attach to particular issues and/or via beliefs that an issue, attitude, or behavior has particularly harmful or beneficial outcomes.

Making firm conclusions about these interesting ideas is hampered because prior work on moralization has primarily used cross-sectional surveys that cannot capture changes in moralization (e.g., Rozin et al., 1997). Some work has used experimental manipulations of emotions (Wheatley & Haidt, 2005); however, these studies are rare, often small, and test moralization of unimportant issues (because they are more likely to be seen as morally irrelevant) and with limited types of emotions (i.e., disgust). It is more common for studies to manipulate emotions (or some other concept, like cleanliness; Horberg, Oveis, Keltner, & Cohen, 2009; Zhong, Strejcek, & Sivanathan, 2010) and examine their effects on the moral wrongness of particular actions that are (likely) already moralized (e.g., a man having [safe] sex with a dead chicken).

To build on previous work addressing moralization, a longitudinal design is preferable. With this design it is possible to observe how emotions or beliefs about harms and benefits at one point in time predict moral conviction at a later time point while controlling for moral conviction at the previous time point. A recent study of the 2012 US presidential election tested the routes of both the emotion and beliefs about harms and benefits to the moralization of people's preferences for president (Barack Obama or Mitt Romney) in a longitudinal design (Brandt, Wisneski, & Skitka, 2015). In this case, the path estimates for the emotions and harms and benefits represent the ability of these variables to predict changes in moral conviction (i.e., moralization) over time. Participants completed two waves of the survey prior to the election, including one in the week prior to the election.

In the longitudinal study, measures of emotions often relevant for morality and politics were used (Rozin, Lowery, Imada, & Haidt, 1999; Valentino, Brader, Groenendyk, Gregorowicz, & Hutchings, 2011). Hostility (consisting of items like anger, disgust, hostility, etc.) toward participants' nonpreferred candidate and enthusiasm (consisting of items like happy, joyful, excited, etc.) for participants' preferred candidate were included, so that the possible moralizing effects of both positive and negative emotions could be examined.[1] Participants also reported the possible consequences of their preferred and nonpreferred candidate winning the election and then rated the degree of harms and benefits of these consequences to capture their beliefs about harms and benefits (cf. Eagly, Mladinic, & Otto, 1994). Both the emotions and beliefs measures were used to predict standard measures of moral conviction (Skitka & Morgan, 2014). This study uncovered several interesting findings:

1.  We found that enthusiasm predicted increased moral conviction of people's preferred candidate and hostility predicted increased moral conviction of people's nonpreferred candidate. That is, emotions particularly relevant to the target of moral conviction (i.e., the candidates) predicted greater moralization.
2.  Moral conviction predicted increased hostility, joviality, and perceived harms and benefits. That is, the relationship between emotions and moral conviction are bidirectional, whereas moral conviction appears to be a cause but not a consequence of perceived harms and benefits.
3.  We also examined how the emotional and harms/benefits based antecedents of moral conviction might differ between liberals, conservatives, and moderates. Liberals, conservatives, and moderates showed similar patterns of results across most of the measures. The key difference was the measures of harms and benefits. For partisans, harms and benefits were both related to moralization, whereas for moderates both measures were associated with reduced moralization, or demoralization.

Combined, these three findings help move research on moralization forward and highlight possible questions for future studies. For example, the emotion-related findings replicate the spirit of Rozin's original research and Haidt's social intuitionist model, but also go further and suggest that irrelevant emotions may not be sufficient to increase moralization (see also Landy & Goodwin, 2015). That is, only the emotions that were most relevant to the target of moral conviction were associated with greater moral conviction over time (e.g., enthusiasm for the preferred candidate *did not* predict moral conviction of the nonpreferred candidate). The results for harms and benefits also suggest some support for Haidt's (2001) social intuitionist model because beliefs about harms and benefits were more clearly an outcome (and not a cause) of moral conviction. At the same time, there was some evidence that harms and benefits could have different effects on moralization depending on participants' stake in the election as either an ideologue or more of a moderate.

The precise mechanism between moral convictions and beliefs about harms and benefits, however, could be further teased apart. Are these beliefs about harms and benefits post hoc rationalizations of the moral convictions participants felt, or do they arise because morally convicted participants are more likely to attend to positive and negative information about the issue (see also Gawronski, Conway, Armstrong, Friesdorf, & Hütter, this volume)? Another interesting question revolves around the nonsignificant differences between liberals and conservatives. Although liberals and conservatives may differ in the *content* of the issues they believe to be morally relevant (Graham, Haidt, & Nosek, 2009; Hofmann,

Wisneski, Brandt, & Skitka, 2014), the *processes* underlying moral conviction appear to be very similar. Perhaps liberals and conservatives are more psychological similar, in terms of process, than typically assumed (for a review of additional evidence on this point see also Frimer, this volume; Skitka & Washburn, in press).

Investigations of moralization have typically focused on emotions and cognitions because these are the same type of constructs adopted by the original moral psychologists (e.g., David Hume, Adam Smith). However, it is not clear that these emotions and cognitions are enough to create moralization on their own. People are very emotional about sports teams and they have perceptions of harms and benefits for a number of relatively mundane activities. Yet, these things are not necessarily felt with the vigor of a moral conviction. To help fill this gap, we have also examined other routes to moralization, such as via connections with the self-concept.

## Self-Concept

Core conceptions of the self are guiding principles in people's lives, and impact important outcomes such as psychological well-being (Diener, Oishi, & Lucas, 2003; Higgins, 1987) and relationship satisfaction (Vinokur, Price, & Caplan, 1996). Psychologists have often suggested a link between the self-concept and morality. For example, psychologists note that human life is driven by the search for things of value (Flanagan, 1991) and that identity is an orientation based on things that a person sees as admirable, worthwhile, or of value (Taylor, 1989). One end goal of moral development is to infuse one's sense of self with one's morals (Blasi, 1995), and to experience personal and moral goals as one and the same, leading the self to be defined by moral values (Colby & Damon, 1993). In short, people integrate conceptions of the self and morality (see also Frimer & Walker, 2009; Hart, 2005; Lapsley & Narvaez, 2004).

The idea that morality is integrated with the self suggests that moralization may be especially likely to occur for attitudes that are connected with the self (see also Pyszczynski, this volume). In early work on moral conviction, Skitka (2002) wrote that moral convictions are "self-expressive stands on a specific issue" that "result from heavily internalized norms . . . and personal commitment to terminal values" (p. 589); however, these ideas were never directly tested. Other early work on moralization speculated that people moralize attitudes (e.g., about smoking) as they become aware that they have consequences relevant to the self (e.g., potential harm; Rozin, 1999). However, these examinations lack empirical tests of the extent to which the self-relevance of attitudes relate to moral conviction, and the possible causal directions underlying these relationships. For example, it could be the case that as people experience an attitude as self-relevant, they will feel more morally convicted about it. It could also be the case that as people become morally convicted about an attitude, they become more likely to see it as relevant to the self-concept.

To provide empirical tests of the idea that moral convictions are experienced as self-relevant, and that the self-relevance of attitudes drives moral conviction, researchers (Wetherell, Brandt, & Reyna, 2014) examined the extent to which facets of attitude strength relevant to the self—importance and centrality—are related to the extent to which people are morally convicted about attitudes. Some past evidence found that, for a respondent-nominated set of attitudes, the importance and centrality of an attitude was correlated with moral convictions about the attitude (Skitka et al., 2005). However, these effects did not always replicate. This most recent investigation analyzed over 40 different attitudes using a multilevel approach. In this approach, participants rate many different attitudes on moral conviction, importance, and centrality as well as several additional facets of attitude strength, such as certainty, extremity, and religious conviction. This analytic strategy is an important addition, as previous research (Skitka et al., 2005) examined a smaller number of purely between-subjects correlations between attitude strength and moral conviction, limiting the certainty that correlations are not driven by specific attitudes under study. Within participants, importance and centrality were the strongest predictors of moral conviction across attitudes compared to attitude extremity, certainty, and even religious conviction. Across studies, the effect sizes of importance and centrality were approximately two to three times stronger of a predictor than the next strongest predictor. These initial studies suggest that within people attitudes experienced as core to the self are more likely to be imbued with a sense of moral conviction.

Although compelling, these results are cross-sectional, and thus do not provide evidence of a causal path between the self-concept and moral beliefs. To provide a test of the possible routes from the self-concept to moral conviction, additional longitudinal analyses of the relationship between moral conviction and importance and centrality over time were conducted (Wetherell et al., 2014). The time points in each study were one to two months apart. Participants' moral conviction about nuclear power, government bailouts, gun control, abortion rights, and immigration were measured. Across two studies, importance predicted moral conviction over time, but moral conviction did not predict importance over time. Interestingly, when examining centrality, the reverse path was present: moral conviction predicted centrality over time, but centrality did not predict moral conviction over time.

These studies provide initial evidence that the self-concept is related to moral convictions within individuals. They also build upon previous theory (Colby & Damon, 1993; Rozin, 1999), suggesting that self-relevant beliefs become intertwined with moral beliefs over time. These results suggest a potential reciprocal relationship between the self-concept and morality. When people see an attitude as important, they may focus on it over time and imbue it with greater central-ity and moral relevance, and as attitudes become more morally relevant, they may become increasingly central to the self. These results both mirror and build upon previous philosophical perspectives and psychological studies, suggesting that people search for things of value in life and incorporate them into the self-concept. To the extent that people experience something as important, they may see it as of greater moral value, and incorporate it into the self-concept to a greater extent.

## Summary

Emotions, connections with the self-concept, and in some cases harms and ben-efits may be possible routes to moral conviction. These routes may be distinct pathways, but they may also represent three different ways that moral convictions can be embedded into a person's identity. The more that a particular attitude is embedded, the more people imbue the attitude with a sense of moral conviction. Whether these routes are distinct, partially overlapping, or different manifestations of the same psychological process await future research.

## Moral Convictions and Dissimilar Others

Understanding the root of moral convictions is not just a theoretical exercise. It is important because conflicts often arise with morally dissimilar others, and these conflicts contribute to not only the angst of the populace but also humanitarian disasters (see also Frimer, this volume). Historical examples abound: the Ameri-can "culture wars," the expansion of ISIS, the Cold War, war protestors, and so on. As in real life, in the lab researchers have found that people feel high levels of self-involvement (Kouzakova, Ellemers, Harinck, & Scheepers, 2012), see less common ground with their opponents (Kouzakova et al., 2012), and experience a cardiovascular threat response (Kouzakova, Harinck, Ellemers, & Scheepers, 2014) in conflicts over moral issues compared to conflicts over resources. This may be the reason moral conflicts become so heated so quickly, why people are willing to discriminate and deny political rights to those they disagree with on moral issues (Skitka et al., 2005), why moral conviction predicts greater perceived disagree-ment with ideological opponents (Crawford, Wire, & Chambers, 2014), and why some researchers claim that perceived value and moral conflicts are the biggest and most consistent predictors of prejudice (Henry & Reyna, 2007). People even have a difficult time determining the procedures that might be used to resolve a moral disagreement (Skitka et al., 2005), and tend to marry people with similar political and moral views over and above demographic and personality similarities (Alford, Hatemi, Hibbing, Martin, & Eaves, 2011).

## Ideological-Conflict Perspective

One important question is, why do moral and value conflicts appear to be so potent? Our work points to one possible answer. Moral beliefs (and other belief systems) provide people with a sense of meaning (Greenberg, Simon, Pyszczynski, Solomon, & Chatel, 1992; Kosloff, Greenberg, & Solomon, 2010; Proulx & Major, 2013; see also Pyszczynski, this volume). That is, it gives people a sense of how the world should and does work (Denzau & North, 1994; Proulx & Inzlicht, 2012). These expectations help people efficiently navigate their social, political, and moral world. Although meaning is the current popular term, other terms from the history of social, cognitive, and developmental psychology could also work (Abelson, 1979; Proulx & Inzlicht, 2012). For example, the answer to the question at the start of the paragraph could read: Moral beliefs (and other belief systems) provide people with a [schema / mental representation / paradigm / working model].

There is ample evidence for this idea spanning decades: political scientists can measure political belief systems with the same tools that cognitive scientists use to measure mental representations (Conover & Feldman, 1984; Hamill, Lodge, & Blake, 1985; Lodge & Hamill, 1986); computers can be programmed with a rudimentary political belief system just as they can be programmed with a rudimentary mental representations (Abelson & Carroll, 1965; Carbonell, 1978); political schemas facilitate schema-consistent memories similar to the effects with nonpolitical schemas (Lodge & Hamill, 1986); and threats to meaning in one domain increase adherence to salient moral, political, or religious beliefs (e.g., Bassett, Van Tongeren, Green, Sonntag, & Kilpatrick, 2015; Castano et al., 2011; Farias, Newheiser, Kahane, & de Toledo, 2013; Greenberg et al., 1992; Kosloff et al., 2010; Randles, Inzlicht, Proulx, Tullett, & Heine, 2015). Treating a belief system—including a moral belief system—as a complicated type of mental representation is not necessarily new (for one extensive model see Axelrod, 1973), but this characterization of belief systems allows us to make predictions about how people will respond to people with different belief systems.

People do not like it when their sense of meaning is violated. People have a schema for how the world should work, and when the world does not conform to this expectation they experience anxiety and work to alleviate the anxiety (Jonas et al., 2014; Proulx et al., 2012; Randles et al., 2015). The precise resolution to meaning violation (or schema violation, or mental representation violation, etc.) likely depends on the context, but we know that one way people affirm their sense of meaning is by being intolerant of people with different moral worldviews. For example, a variety of meaning-related threats increases the affirmation of an unrelated moral schema (i.e., the amount of bond set for a prostitute; Proulx & Heine, 2008; Proulx, Heine, & Vohs, 2010). Other work has shown that affirming people's sense of meaning reduces the amount of prejudice they express (Fein & Spencer, 1997).

In our work we have built on these ideas to propose the ideological-conflict hypothesis (Brandt, Reyna, Chambers, Crawford, & Wetherell, 2014). Most generally, and consistent with a variety of work on worldview conflicts (e.g., Tetlock, 1998; Tetlock, Kristel, Elson, Green, & Lerner, 2000) and attraction-similarity principles (Byrne, 1971; van Osch & Breugelmans, 2012) as far back as at least Heider's (1958) balance theory, the hypothesis predicts that people will be intolerant of those who hold on to different worldviews. This hypothesis is most interesting when used to make predictions about when liberals and conservatives will show intolerance. Past work has suggested that conservatives should be particularly intolerant because they are more concerned about their ingroups (Graham, Haidt, & Nosek, 2009), are less open to experience (Sibley, Osborne, & Duckitt, 2012), or have higher needs for structure and closure (Jost, Glaser, Kruglanski, & Sulloway, 2003) which make them more adverse to people with opposing worldviews. The ideological conflict hypothesis, however, predicts that both liberals and conservatives will be intolerant of people with opposing worldviews. The idea is that because both liberal and conservative ideologies are belief systems that provide people with meaning, both liberals and conservatives should, in turn, express intolerance toward those who violate their sense of meaning.

The ideological-conflict hypothesis has been tested directly by several different labs. Across a range of target groups and student, community, and representative samples, liberals tend to be intolerant of people they perceive to be conservative (e.g., evangelical Christians, rich people) and conservatives tend to be intolerant of people they perceive to be liberal (e.g., gays and lesbians, atheists; Chambers, Schlenker, & Collisson, 2013; Crawford, Modri, & Motyl, 2013; Crawford & Pilanski, 2014; Wetherell, Brandt, & Reyna, 2013). In one recent study (Waytz, Young, & Ginges, 2014), Democrats assumed that Republicans were motivated by outgroup hate while fellow Democrats were motivated by ingroup love. Similarly, Republicans assumed that Democrats were motivated by outgroup hate while fellow Republicans were motivated by ingroup love. Both liberals and conservatives even prefer ideologically similar authorities (Frimer, Gaucher, & Schaefer, 2014; see also Frimer, this volume). The aforementioned findings all suggest that liberals and conservatives alike will express intolerance of people with differing worldviews and support those with similar worldviews.

Related experimental work has examined the extent to which the correlation between political beliefs and prejudice might be due to the perceived political ideology of the targets used in the studies. For example, manipulating the perceived ideology of African Americans to be either liberal or conservative is enough to eliminate any association between conservative political ideology and intolerant views of African Americans (Chambers et al., 2013; Iyengar & Westwood, 2015), a finding typical in political science and social psychology (e.g.,

Cunningham, Nezlek, & Banaji, 2004; Federico & Sidanius, 2002). This suggests that conservatism's association with racism may be driven (at least in part) by presumed ideological differences with African Americans. Similarly, manipulating the perceived ideology of gay men or atheists to be conservative also eliminates the association between conservative political ideology and intolerant views of these groups (Brandt & Spälti, 2014).

We suggest that ideological conflict is caused by the underlying meaning that ideologies provide. Consistent with this, when people's sense of meaning is threatened, both liberals and conservatives compensate by affirming their political beliefs (Castano et al., 2011; Greenberg et al., 1992; Kosloff et al., 2010; Proulx & Major, 2013; Randles et al., 2015). In an unpublished study (Brandt & Hagens, 2013), a community sample from the Netherlands completed measures of political ideology. After this, they wrote about one of two self-threats (a type of meaning threat; Park & Maner, 2009) or a trip to the grocery store (a control condition). After either of the self-threat conditions, participants on both the political left and the political right expressed a larger ideological intergroup bias compared to participants in the control condition (see Figure 14.1). Combined with previous work using meaning threats such as mortality salience, reverse-colored playing cards, or the induced-compliance task (e.g., Kosloff et al., 2010; Proulx & Major, 2013; Randles et al., 2015), this study suggests that political ideologies on the left and the right provide people with meaning.

Another way to examine how the meaning ideologies provide is responsible for ideological conflict is to test mediators of the association between political ideology and intolerance. In our initial studies we found that a generalized sense of threat (Crawford & Pilanski, 2014) or perceived value (moral) violations (Wetherell et al., 2013) were consistent mediators of the association. This suggests that perceptions that a group is threatening or morally dissimilar are important drivers of the ideological-conflict effect. In more recent work, Crawford (2014) examined the roles of several different types of threat in predicting prejudice against and political intolerance of ideological dissimilar groups. Across four samples, results showed that symbolic threat—that is, threat to people's important values and beliefs—was the most robust predictor of prejudice against ideologically dissimilar groups. Importantly, this effect was observed toward both left-wing and right-wing groups and implies similar psychological processes in intolerance across the political spectrum.

Interestingly, however, different types of threats underlay political intolerance (i.e., denial of constitutional rights), and further, the type of threat depended on the ideological orientation of the group itself. Specifically, consistent with evidence suggesting that people on the right are most concerned about the consequences of social disorder and upheaval (Stenner, 2005), safety threat predicted political intolerance of left-wing groups. However, political intolerance of right-wing groups was predicted by the perception that the group itself threatened

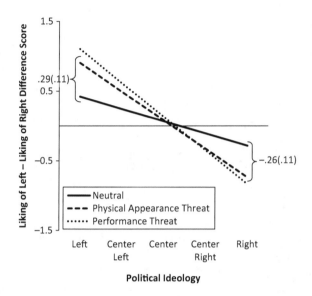

**FIGURE 14.1** Self-threat increases ideological intergroup bias among the political-left and the political-right.

*Note:* Coefficients are unstandardized betas and standard errors in parentheses. Coefficients were both significantly different from zero, $p = .02$. The political ideology scale ranges from extreme-left to extreme-right; however, no participants indicated they were extreme-left and only one participant indicated they were extreme-right, and so the predicted values of these data-points are not displayed. The two threat conditions did not differ from one another. $N = 182$.

the rights of other people (a form of "intolerance of intolerance" by liberal participants). Together, these results imply that pure dislike of ideologically dissimilar targets is tied to perceived violations of the types of values and beliefs that provide meaning to groups. However, attitudes that extend beyond mere dislike to outright suppression (i.e., political intolerance) may require more tangible types of threats (i.e., safety, rights violations).

## Solutions to Ideological Conflict?

People may think that if the "other side" of political conflict would just take their perspective, there would not be any conflict. This intuition, however, would likely exacerbate the problem as taking the perspective of an adversary can add flames to the fire (see Galinsky & Lee; and Simpson, Farrell, & Marshall, this volume; but see Tuller, Bryan, Heyman, & Christenfeld, 2015, for evidence that perspective taking *can reduce* political conflict). However, taking the idea that meaning threats underlie political conflict seriously suggests several possibilities for alleviating the conflict. For example, in other domains research has demonstrated that self-affirmations (i.e., affirming participants' sense of meaning) reduce stereotyping and prejudice of outgroups (e.g., Fein & Spencer, 1997). In the political domain, similar effects have been found, such that people with both liberal and conservative views of the issues are more willing to compromise in negotiations over politically and morally charged issues (Cohen et al., 2007; see also Binning, Sherman, Cohen, & Heitland, 2010). Other work has highlighted that, prior to negotiations, expressing respect for the other side and affirming their status is useful for promoting more conciliatory behavior (Bendersky, 2014). Both of these intervention strategies take advantage of the tendency for people to incorporate important moral and political issues into their self-concept (Wetherell et al., 2014) to find a way to promote political cooperation. The success of these interventions in promoting cooperation for both liberals and conservatives is in contrast to what might be expected by perspectives that highlight the different psychological processes potentially underlying conservatism (e.g., Jost et al., 2003). If these differential processes are the problem, then the solutions should also be different; however, this does not appear to be the case.

## Conclusion

Over the course of this chapter we have taken you from the underpinnings of moral convictions to the conflict between political rivals. Through this journey we've highlighted several underpinnings of moral convictions that may explain why moral convictions are particularly difficult to change and become the source of conflict. Social psychologists are not exempt from such pitfalls of their moral convictions (see Fiedler; and Jussim, Crawford, Stevens, Anglin, & Duarte, this volume). These studies are just the first step in understanding the moralization process beyond sterile lab studies and cross-sectional surveys. We encourage more intensive studies into the underpinnings and dynamics of moral convictions because understanding the roots of these beliefs will help us understand how people with moral differences might be able to get along. This is currently a problem for different political and moral backgrounds, with only a few studies suggesting possible solutions. Helping to solve and ameliorate the negative effects of moral conflict is a practically and theoretically important domain that will benefit from the insights of social psychologists.

## Note

1 Validated subscales of the affective reactions of the PANAS inventory were used as measures in this study (Watson & Clark, 1994). Fear was also included and did not find any consistent results.

# References

Abelson, R.P. (1979). Differences between belief and knowledge systems. *Cognitive Science, 3*, 355–366.

Abelson, R.P., & Carroll, J.D. (1965). Computer simulation of individual belief systems. *American Behavioral Scientist, 8*, 24–30.

Ahn, H.-K., Kim, H.J., & Aggarwal, P. (2014). Helping fellow beings: Anthropomorphized social causes and the role of anticipatory guilt. *Psychological Science, 25*, 224–229.

Alford, J.R., Hatemi, P.K., Hibbing, J.R., Martin, N.G., & Eaves, L.J. (2011). The politics of mate choice. *Journal of Politics, 73*, 362–379.

Aramovich, N.P., Lytle, B.L., & Skitka, L.J. (2012). Opposing torture: Moral conviction and resistance to majority influence. *Social Influence, 7*, 21–34.

Avramova, Y.R., & Inbar, Y. (2013). Emotion and moral judgment. *Wiley Interdisciplinary Reviews: Cognitive Science, 4*, 169–178.

Axelrod, R. (1973). Schema theory: An information processing model of perception and cognition. *American Political Science Review, 67*, 1248–1266.

Bassett, J.F., Van Tongeren, D.R., Green, J.D., Sonntag, M.E., & Kilpatrick, H. (2015). The interactive effects of mortality salience and political orientation on moral judgments. *British Journal of Social Psychology, 54*, 306–323.

Bendersky, C. (2014). Resolving ideological conflicts by affirming opponents' status: The tea party, Obamacare and the 2013 government shutdown. *Journal of Experimental Social Psychology, 53*, 163–168.

Binning, K.R., Sherman, D.K., Cohen, G.L., & Heitland, K. (2010). Seeing the other side: Reducing political partisanship via self-affirmation in the 2008 presidential election. *Analyses of Social Issues and Public Policy, 10*, 276–292.

Blasi, A. (1995). Moral understanding and the moral personality: The process of moral integration. In W.M. Kurtines & J.L. Gewirtz (Eds.), *Moral development: An introduction* (pp. 229–253). Boston: Allyn & Bacon.

Brandt, M.J., & Hagens, R. (2013). *Political ideology and prejudice in response to self-threats: Coping, negativity bias, or meaning maintenance?* Unpublished manuscript.

Brandt, M.J., Reyna, C., Chambers, J.R., Crawford, J.T., & Wetherell, G. (2014). The ideological-conflict hypothesis: Intolerance among both liberals and conservatives. *Current Directions in Psychological Science, 23*, 27–34.

Brandt, M.J., & Spälti, A.K. (2014). *Shared political ideology overrides differences in race, religion, and sexual orientation across seven measures of intolerance.* Unpublished manuscript.

Brandt, M.J., Wisneski, D., & Skitka, L. (2015). Moralization and the 2012 presidential election. *Journal of Social and Political Psychology, 3*, 211–237.

Byrne, D. (1971). *The attraction paradigm.* New York: Academic Press.

Carbonell, J.G. (1978). POLITICS: Automated ideological reasoning. *Cognitive Science, 2*, 27–51.

Castano, E., Leidner, B., Bonacossa, A., Nikkah, J., Perrulli, R., Spencer, B., & Humphrey, N. (2011). Ideology, fear of death, and death anxiety. *Political Psychology, 32*, 601–621.

Chambers, J.R., Schlenker, B.R., & Collisson, B. (2013). Ideology and prejudice: The role of value conflicts. *Psychological Science, 24*, 140–149.

Cohen, G.L., Sherman, D.K., Bastardi, A., Hsu, L., McGoey, M., & Ross, L. (2007). Bridging the partisan divide: Self-affirmation reduces ideological closed-mindedness and inflexibility in negotiation. *Journal of Personality and Social Psychology, 93*, 415–430.

Colby, A., & Damon, W. (1993). The uniting of self and morality in the development of extraordinary moral commitment. In G.G. Noam, T.E. Wren, G. Nunner-Winkler, & W. Edelstein (Eds.), *The moral self* (pp. 149–174). Cambridge, MA: MIT Press.

Conover, P.J., & Feldman, S. (1984). How people organize the political world: A schematic model. *American Journal of Political Science, 28*, 95–126.

Crawford, J.T. (2014). Ideological symmetries and asymmetries in political intolerance and prejudice toward political activist groups. *Journal of Experimental Social Psychology, 55*, 284–298.

Crawford, J.T., Modri, S.A., & Motyl, M. (2013). Bleeding-heart liberals and hard-hearted conservatives: Subtle political dehumanization through differential attributions of human nature and human uniqueness traits. *Journal of Social and Political Psychology, 1*(1), 86–104.

Crawford, J.T., & Pilanski, J.M. (2014). Political intolerance, right *and* left. *Political Psychology, 35*(6), 841–851.

Crawford, J.T., Wire, S., & Chambers, J.R. (2014). *Moral conviction predicts perceived disagreement with ideological opponents.* Unpublished manuscript.

Cunningham, W.A., Nezlek, J.B., & Banaji, M.R. (2004). Implicit and explicit ethnocentrism: Revisiting the ideologies of prejudice. *Personality and Social Psychology Bulletin, 30*, 1332–1346.

Denzau, A.T., & North, D.C. (1994). Shared mental models: ideologies and institutions. *Kyklos, 47*, 3–31.

Diener, E., Oishi, S., & Lucas, R.E. (2003). Personality, culture, and subjective well-being: Emotional and cognitive evaluations of life. *Annual Review of Psychology, 54*, 403–425.

Eagly, A.H., Mladinic, A., & Otto, S. (1994). Cognitive and affective bases of attitudes toward social groups and social policies. *Journal of Experimental Social Psychology, 30*, 113–137.

Farias, M., Newheiser, A.K., Kahane, G., & de Toledo, Z. (2013). Scientific faith: belief in science increases in the face of stress and existential anxiety. *Journal of Experimental Social Psychology, 49*, 1210–1213.

Federico, C.M., & Sidanius, J. (2002). Racism, ideology, and affirmative action revisited: The antecedents and consequences of "principled objections" to affirmative action. *Journal of Personality and Social Psychology, 82*, 488.

Fein, S., & Spencer, S.J. (1997). Prejudice as self-image maintenance: Affirming the self through derogating others. *Journal of Personality and Social Psychology, 73*, 31–44.

Flanagan, O. (1991). *Varieties of moral personality: Ethics and psychological realism.* Cambridge, MA: Harvard University Press.

Frimer, J.A., Gaucher, D.G., & Schaefer, N.K. (2014). Political conservatives' affinity for obedience to authority is loyal, not blind. *Personality and Social Psychology Bulletin, 40*, 1205–1214.

Frimer, J.A., & Walker, L.J. (2009). Reconciling the self and morality: An empirical model of moral centrality development. *Developmental Psychology, 45*, 1669–1681.

Graham, J., Haidt, J., & Nosek, B.A. (2009). Liberals and conservatives rely on different sets of moral foundations. *Journal of Personality and Social Psychology, 96*, 1029–1046.

Gray, K., Schein, C., & Ward, A.F. (2014). The myth of harmless wrongs in moral cognition: Automatic dyadic completion from sin to suffering. *Journal of Experimental Psychology: General, 143*, 1600–1615.

Greenberg, J., Simon, L., Pyszczynski, T., Solomon, S., & Chatel, D. (1992). Terror management and tolerance: Does mortality salience always intensify negative reactions to others who threaten one's worldview? *Journal of Personality and Social Psychology*, *63*, 212–220.

Haidt, J. (2001). The emotional dog and its rational tail: A social intuitionist approach to moral judgment. *Psychological Review*, *108*, 814–834.

Hamill, R., Lodge, M., & Blake, F. (1985). The breadth, depth, and utility of class, partisan, and ideological schemata. *American Journal of Political Science*, *29*, 850–870.

Hart, D. (2005). The development of moral identity. In G. Carlo & C.P. Edwards (Eds.), *Nebraska symposium on motivation: Vol. 51. Moral motivation through the lifespan* (pp. 165–196). Lincoln: University of Nebraska Press.

Heider, F. (1958). *The psychology of interpersonal relations*. New York: John Wiley & Sons.

Henry, P.J., & Reyna, C. (2007). Value judgments: The impact of perceived value violations on American political attitudes. *Political Psychology*, *28*, 273–298.

Higgins, E.T. (1987). Self-discrepancy: A theory relating self and affect. *Psychological Review*, *94*, 319–340.

Hofmann, W., Wisneski, D.C., Brandt, M.J., & Skitka, L.J. (2014). Morality in everyday life. *Science*, *345*, 1340–1343.

Horberg, E.J., Oveis, C., Keltner, D., & Cohen, A.B. (2009). Disgust and the moralization of purity. *Journal of Personality and Social Psychology*, *97*, 963–976.

Iyengar, S., & Westwood, S.J. (2015). Fear and loathing across party lines: New evidence on group polarization. *American Journal of Political Science*, *59*, 690–707.

Jonas, E., McGregor, I., Klackl, J., Agroskin, D., Fritsche, I., Holbrook, C., . . . Quirin, M. (2014). Threat and defense: From anxiety to approach. *Advances in Experimental Social Psychology*, *49*, 219–286.

Jost, J.T., Glaser, J., Kruglanski, A.W., & Sulloway, F.J. (2003). Political conservatism as motivated social cognition. *Psychological Bulletin*, *129*, 339–375.

Kosloff, S., Greenberg, J., & Solomon, S. (2010). The effects of mortality salience on political preferences: The roles of charisma and political orientation. *Journal of Experimental Social Psychology*, *46*, 139–145.

Kouzakova, M., Ellemers, N., Harinck, F., & Scheepers, D. (2012). The implications of value conflict: How disagreement on values affects self-involvement and perceived common ground. *Personality and Social Psychology Bulletin*, *38*, 798–807.

Kouzakova, M., Harinck, F., Ellemers, N., & Scheepers, D. (2014). At the heart of a conflict: Cardiovascular and self-regulation responses to value versus resource conflicts. *Social Psychological and Personality Science*, *5*, 35–42.

Landy, J.F., & Goodwin, G.P. (2015). Does incidental disgust amplify moral judgment? A meta-analytic review of experimental evidence. *Perspectives on Psychological Science*, *10*, 518–536.

Lapsley, D.K., & Narvaez, D. (2004). A social-cognitive approach to the moral personality. In D.K. Lapsley & D. Narvaez (Eds.), *Moral development, self and identity* (pp. 189–212). Mahwah, NJ: Lawrence Erlbaum Associates.

Lodge, M., & Hamill, R. (1986). A partisan schema for political information processing. *American Political Science Review*, *80*, 505–520.

Morgan, G.S., Skitka, L.J., & Lytle, B.L. (2014). *Objectively and universally true: Psychological foundations of moral conviction*. Paper presented at the annual meeting of the Society for Personality and Social Psychology, Austin, TX.

Mullen, E., & Skitka, L.J. (2006). Exploring the psychological underpinnings of the moral mandate effect: Motivated reasoning, group differentiation, or anger? *Journal of Personality and Social Psychology*, *90*, 629–643.

Park, L.E., & Maner, J.K. (2009). Does self-threat promote social connection? The role of self-esteem and contingencies of self-worth. *Journal of Personality and Social Psychology, 96*, 203–217.

Petrescu, D.C., & Parkinson, B. (2014). Incidental disgust increases adherence to left-wing economic attitudes. *Social Justice Research, 27*, 464–486.

Proulx, T., & Heine, S.J. (2008). The case of the transmogrifying experimenter: Affirmation of a moral schema following implicit change detection. *Psychological Science, 19*, 1294–1300.

Proulx, T., Heine, S.J., & Vohs, K.D. (2010). When is the unfamiliar the uncanny? Meaning affirmation after exposure to absurdist literature, humor, and art. *Personality and Social Psychology Bulletin, 36*, 817–829.

Proulx, T., & Inzlicht, M. (2012). The five "A"s of meaning maintenance: Finding meaning in the theories of sense-making. *Psychological Inquiry, 23*, 317–335.

Proulx, T., & Major, B. (2013). A raw deal: Heightened liberalism following exposure to anomalous playing cards. *Journal of Social Issues, 69*, 455–472.

Randles, D., Inzlicht, M., Proulx, T., Tullett, A., & Heine, S.J. (2015). Is dissonance reduction a special case of fluid compensation? Evidence that dissonant cognitions cause compensatory affirmation and abstraction. *Journal of Personality and Social Psychology, 108*, 697–710.

Rozin, P. (1999). The process of moralization. *Psychological Science, 10*, 218–221.

Rozin, P., Lowery, L., Imada, S., & Haidt, J. (1999). The CAD triad hypothesis: A mapping between three moral emotions (contempt, anger, disgust) and three moral codes (community, autonomy, divinity). *Journal of Personality and Social Psychology, 76*, 574–586.

Rozin, P., Markwith, M., & Stoess, C. (1997). Moralization and becoming a vegetarian: The transformation of preferences into values and the recruitment of disgust. *Psychological Science, 8*, 67–73.

Rozin, P., & Singh, L. (1999). The moralization of cigarette smoking in the United States. *Journal of Consumer Psychology, 8*, 321–337.

Ryan, T.J. (2014). Reconsidering moral issues in politics. *Journal of Politics, 76*(02), 380–397.

Sibley, C.G., Osborne, D., & Duckitt, J. (2012). Personality and political orientation: Meta-analysis and test of a threat-constraint model. *Journal of Research in Personality, 46*, 664–677.

Skitka, L.J. (2002). Do the means always justify the ends, or do the ends sometimes justify the means? A value protection model of justice reasoning. *Personality and Social Psychology Bulletin, 28*(5), 588–597.

Skitka, L.J., Bauman, C.W., & Lytle, B.L. (2009). The limits of legitimacy: Moral and religious convictions as constraints on deference to authority. *Journal of Personality and Social Psychology, 97*, 567–578.

Skitka, L.J., Bauman, C.W., & Sargis, E.G. (2005). Moral conviction: Another contributor to attitude strength or something more? *Journal of Personality and Social Psychology, 88*, 895–917.

Skitka, L.J., & Morgan, G.S. (2014). The social and political implications of moral conviction. In H. Lavine (Ed.), *Advances in political psychology, 35*, 95–110.

Skitka, L.J., & Washburn, A. (in press). Are conservatives from Mars and liberals from Venus? Maybe not so much. In P. Valdesolo & J. Graham (Eds.), *Bridging ideological divides.*

Skitka, L.J., & Wisneski, D.C. (2011). Moral conviction and emotion. *Emotion Review, 3*, 328–330.

Stenner, K. (2005). *The authoritarian dynamic.* Cambridge: Cambridge University Press.

Taylor, C. (1989). *Sources of the self: The making of the modern identity.* Cambridge, MA: Harvard University Press.

Tetlock, P.E. (1998). Close-call counterfactuals and belief-system defenses: I was not almost wrong but I was almost right. *Journal of Personality and Social Psychology, 75,* 639–652.

Tetlock, P.E., Kristel, O.V., Elson, S.B., Green, M.C., & Lerner, J.S. (2000). The psychology of the unthinkable: taboo trade-offs, forbidden base rates, and heretical counterfactuals. *Journal of Personality and Social Psychology, 78,* 853–870.

Tuller, H.M., Bryan, C.J., Heyman, G.D., & Christenfeld, N.J. (2015). Seeing the other side: Perspective taking and the moderation of extremity. *Journal of Experimental Social Psychology, 59,* 18–23.

Valentino, N.A., Brader, T., Groenendyk, E.W., Gregorowicz, K., & Hutchings, V.L. (2011). Election night's alright for fighting: The role of emotions in political participation. *Journal of Politics, 73,* 156–170.

Van Bavel, J.J., Packer, D.J., Haas, I.J., & Cunningham, W.A. (2012). The importance of moral construal: moral versus non-moral construal elicits faster, more extreme, universal evaluations of the same actions. *PLOS ONE, 7,* e48693.

van Osch, Y.M., & Breugelmans, S.M. (2012). Perceived intergroup difference as an organizing principle of intercultural attitudes and acculturation attitudes. *Journal of Cross-Cultural Psychology, 43,* 801–821.

Vinokur, A.D., Price, R.H., & Caplan, R.D. (1996). Hard times and hurtful partners: how financial strain affects depression and relationship satisfaction of unemployed persons and their spouses. *Journal of Personality and Social Psychology, 71,* 166–179.

Watson, D., & Clark, L.A. (1994). *Manual for the positive and negative affect schedule—Expanded form.* Iowa City: University of Iowa. Retrieved from http://www2.psychology.uiowa.edu/faculty/watson/PANAS-X.pdf

Waytz, A., Young, L.L., & Ginges, J. (2014). Motive attribution asymmetry for love vs. hate drives intractable conflict. *Proceedings of the National Academy of Sciences, 111,* 15687–15692.

Wetherell, G.A., Brandt, M.J., & Reyna, C. (2013). Discrimination across the ideological divide: The role of value violations and abstract values in discrimination by liberals and conservatives. *Social Psychological and Personality Science, 4,* 658–667.

Wetherell, G.A., Brandt, M.J., & Reyna, C. (2014). *Moralization and the self.* Unpublished manuscript

Wheatley, T., & Haidt, J. (2005). Hypnotic disgust makes moral judgments more severe. *Psychological Science, 16,* 780–784.

Wisneski, D.C., Lytle, B.L., & Skitka, L.J. (2009). Gut reactions: Moral conviction, religiosity, and trust in authority. *Psychological Science, 20,* 1059–1063.

Zhong, C.B., Strejcek, B., & Sivanathan, N. (2010). A clean self can render harsh moral judgment. *Journal of Experimental Social Psychology, 46,* 859–862.

# 15

# SIN, MORALITY, AND OPPONENT MOTIVES FOR PROSOCIAL BEHAVIOR

## William G. Graziano and David A. Schroeder

*The literature linking morality and prosocial behavior is difficult to coordinate due to its sheer size. Furthermore, the variables differ in scope from the molecular to the sociocultural level. A multilevel approach is one way to integrate these variables into coherent scientific explanations. The multilevel approach was used to link macro-level forces to the evolution of moral and prosocial norms. Specifically, we applied it to the relations among concepts of sin, debt, reparations and prosocial acts. Next, we discussed a micro-level opponent process mechanism that links variables at different levels to the expression and acquisition of prosocial behavior.*

We plan to discuss sin, social norms, and morality. We will discuss the impact of these concepts on overt acts of prosocial behavior. For long sweeps of human history, these variables were tightly connected. Perhaps they still are (e.g., Muller, 1997). We will draw on literatures that are off the beaten path for most social, personality, and cognitive psychologists. Before attacking such weighty topics, however, let us consider some overarching issues.

Is prosocial behavior simply a social construction of relatively recent vintage or something buried far deeper in psychological processes (e.g., Laurin, Kay, & Fitzsimons, 2012; Pagels, 1996)? A restrained scholarly answer would suggest a need for qualifications; the label used to describe a complex phenomenon implies a demarcation and narrowing of the boundaries. First, the "behavior" aspect limits the domain to overt, observable actions. Narrowing the boundary further, the "prosocial" aspect refers to a subset of actions that bring desirable outcomes to the other people. It is a broad umbrella that would include under it helping, cooperating, caregiving, volunteering, and sharing, to name but a few of the most obvious cases. Outside this boundary are behaviors that are negative, destructive, antisocial, or even neutral in terms of their effects on others (see Vachon, Lynam, & Johnson, 2014). The prosocial behavior label by itself does not require costs to the actor, feelings of tender concern, or consistency in the actor's actions, nor does it require a selfless intent to bring benefits exclusively or even preponderantly to the recipient. In this scheme, a special subcase of prosocial behavior labeled altruism occurs when consideration of the actor's intent (to benefit the recipient) is included (e.g., Batson, 1991, 2011).

To start us down our path, we offer some explicit assumptions. First, as a behavioral phenomenon, prosocial behavior has an ancient lineage, almost certainly appearing early in the biological and social evolution of our species (e.g., de Waal, 2008, 2014; Eastwick, 2009; Tomasello, 2014). Prosocial and cooperative behavior in other primates and their links to other forms of social behavior suggests biological substrates evolving over millions of years. Also supporting the argument for a long history is information from written records in Aramaic, Greek, and Hebrew dating back more than 3,000 years (e.g., Anderson, 2009; Brunschweig & Lloyd, 2000). The second assumption qualifies the first: the interpretation of prosocial behavior varies across time, theory, and research literatures. This is especially true if prosocial behavior is conceptualized as an aspect of (1) moral reasoning, (2) a correlate of redemption from sin, or (3) the result of empathic concern. Like most other social behaviors, the nature of prosocial behavior may appear simple on the surface, but it is an end product of a sequence of antecedent predispositions and events, combined with the circumstances of the immediate situations, that contributes to the final expression of overt action.

One of the most important unresolved issues in prosocial research is the status of an actor's intent. Inferences about the actor's intent play some role in the interpretation of prosocial action by others but may also serve a role in the way the actor expresses overt action. Assessing intent in ourselves and in others seems to be a basic human activity (Haidt, 2012; Haidt & Graham, 2007; Lieberman, 2014; Malle, 2011). When trying to understand why one person might help or benefit another, intent is a covert variable. It can only be inferred, not directly observed, either in the self or in others.

Intent seems important intuitively, but arguments have been made for ignoring intent, suggesting that it is as a kind of human conceit (e.g., Camus, 1958; Sartre, 1960). In other cases, it might be prudent to overlook intent for functional reasons, concentrating instead on the positive outcomes of prosocial behavior (e.g., Dorff, 2005). There is an even bigger reason to ignore intent, however, and it is rooted in the history of psychology. From the 1890s to 1960s, as part of its commitment to creating a scientific psychology, many psychologists promoted behaviorism (e.g., Watson, 1924), both as a conceptualization and as a methodology. Other approaches were treated as prescientific and obsolete. In the behaviorist's heyday, psychology was defined as the science of *behavior*, with explicit proximate environmental stimuli seen as causes and behaviors as effects (e.g., Watson, 1913).

Behaviorism claimed pride of place as a scientific approach because behavior is directly observable whereas internal thoughts and feelings (including intentions) can only be inferred. Following Enlightenment philosophers such as Locke (1690/2009), behaviorists treated prosocial behavior as a manifestation of morality, which was largely learned from experiences with the social environment. During the behaviorist era, unobservable variables like intent moved off center of the explanatory stage.

Despite its near-hegemonic successes early in its reign, behaviorism was later challenged by other approaches within psychology. Notable among these approaches was the gradual adoption of an information-processing metaphor for psychology (e.g., Neisser, 1967; Reed, 2007). Increased attention was given to internal psychological processes of cognition and emotion. It became increasingly clear that an exclusive focus on behavior would not yield the comprehensive scientific account of psychological processes that was desired (Baumeister, Masicampo, & Vohs, 2011; Carlston & Graziano, 2010; Finkel, 2014; Prot et al., 2014). Swept along in this cognitive revolution was prosocial behavior. Now intent could be summoned for an encore.

Even after the shift toward information-processing explanations, no major theorist denied that prosocial performance was influenced by rewards and incentives. Nor did they deny that many, if not most, forms of prosocial behavior were learned either as a result of direct, personal reinforcement (e.g., Skinner, 1953) or as a consequence of observing the rewards or punishments experienced by others (e.g., Bandura, 1977; see Galinsky & Lee, this volume). With the wisdom of hindsight, it is possible to observe a sea change that renewed interest in internal cognitive and emotional states associated with prosocial behavior. Many theorists were still careful not to claim that thoughts actually caused prosocial behavior (e.g., Jordan & Wesselmann, 2015; Weinstein & Ryan, 2010), but cognitive activities like intent became "interesting covariates" of behavior. The philosopher of science, Wesley Salmon (2006), might describe this kind of association as a "damn strange coincidence." Intention and thinking may not have moved quickly to the center of the stage, but they came back into the explanatory theater.

## Can Prosocial Behavior Be Explained Scientifically?

According to Allport (1985), if any one individual deserves credit for being the founder of the field of social psychology as a science, his nominee would be Auguste Comte. (Comte was also the person credited with coining the term "altruism.") In keeping with his French Revolution zeitgeist, Comte was also credited with framing a skeptical, even antagonistic, relation between religion and the abstract sciences in a series of three volumes written in 1830–1842 and 1851–1854. Comte believed that the abstract sciences (e.g., mathematics, astronomy, chemistry, physics, and biology) emerged in a definite, invariant order as they passed through three stages of development. The first stage was the *theological* stage, in which phenomena are explained in terms of supernatural intervention. The second stage explained events in *metaphysical* terms. The final stage involved the *positivist* stage of development. For example, the infections of bubonic plague, syphilis, or AIDS could be explained as God's wrath for sin (theological); as a result of life being nasty, brutish, and short (metaphysical); or as natural phenomena, the results of infections from biological pathogens (positivist). The abstract sciences could emerge from sole reliance on theological explanations only in a definite order, with mathematics first, followed by astronomy, physics, chemistry, and biology.

Allport (1985) believed that Comte ran into difficulties when he dealt with sciences of living things and, more particularly, in dealing with sentient life; many of these problematic phenomena lie within the domains we would now call psychology and sociology. Comte believed that these matters would be the last kinds of individual, mentalistic phenomena to escape from theology toward more objective, positive explanations. As a result, clear scientific explanations have been obscured for these domains. For our purposes, a theological explanation for prosocial behavior includes compliance with or violation of moral rules, which are given by God or God's designated representatives. Sometimes the theological explanation is disguised, that is, explanations for prosocial behavior that were primarily moral evaluations, along a bad-to-good continuum. Most religions teach that prosocial behavior is laudatory: to share, to give alms to the poor, and to follow communal rules (e.g., Anderson, 2013; Berkson, 2010; Dorff, 2005). Some behavior that is clearly not prosocial is blameworthy: to be greedy, to injure the disadvantaged, and to break rules. In this framing, persons who have not behaved in prosocial ways are guilty of sin and must bear a burden for their transgressions. If the nature of the sin is serious, then public sanctions are justified. (See Miller & Monin, this volume, regarding moral tests vs. moral opportunities.)

Comte's skeptical approach seems to have been influential among historians and philosophers (Barzun, 2001; de Botton, 2012; Freeman, 2002). Perhaps its most powerful effect, however, may have been in framing the very definition of phenomena that could and could not be explained scientifically. It seems to have fed into the historical development of the "demarcation problem" (Pigliucci & Boudry, 2013; Popper, 1957). This problem involves how to separate scientific phenomena and their associated explanations from those that are myths, prescientific, religious, or pseudoscientific.

Salmon (2006) observed an interesting pattern in the evolution of modern thinking about valid scientific explanation. In the so-called received view that dominated the philosophy of science of the sort created by the Vienna Circle or the Berlin Circle (e.g., Feigl, 1970; Hempel & Oppenheim, 1948; Humphreys, 2006), the logical positivists saw part of their mission "to expunge from science any contamination of super-empirical factors" (Salmon, 2006, p. 4), such as supernatural beings, teleology, entelechies, deference to religious texts, and vital forces.

These philosophers focused on physics, and this allowed them to sidestep the kinds of problems that troubled Comte with regard to social behavior (e.g., Feigl, 1970; Meehl, 1978).

Many of the variables linked to morality and prosocial behavior have uncanny surface similarities to elements the logical positivists hoped to expunge, namely purposes, goals, teleology, religion, and even vital forces. Salmon (2006) notes that there are two sorts of facts: evidentiary facts and explanatory facts (Carnap, 1962). Salmon illustrates this distinction using Velikovsky's (1950) attempt to explain various Old Testament miracles, singling out Joshua causing the earth to cease to rotate during the Siege of Gibeon (Josh. 10:13–14, New King James Version). In Joshua's case, however, suspension of the earth's rotation, even if time-limited, would be in violation of the well-established Newtonian physical law of the conservation of angular momentum. As an evidentiary fact, therefore, this biblical event is unlikely to have occurred and, thus, it requires no scientific explanatory account. These problems arise with theological stage explanations. Overall, the prior probability of the miraculous event is vanishingly small in light of the nomothetic reliability of Newtonian mechanics (Meehl, 1978).

Applying this to prosocial behavior, the logical positivists would probably question the legitimacy of a claim that preferential prosocial action to kin over non-kin had the purpose of putting an individual's genes into the next generation. Similarly, they would question the legitimacy of the question, "Does a person's intent to benefit another person cause prosocial behavior?" But what is at issue with this question is not evidentiary but explanatory. That is, evidentiary fact in this case would be that ratings of self-reported intent to benefit another person, which may be reliably correlated with observed helping behavior. Explanatory facts would require nonobserved inferences to theoretical processes such as purposes and goals. Purposes and intent are extra-empirical variables, so in Comte's terms their interrelations are metaphysical at best and theological at worst. One consequence of this approach is to give the impression that scientific explanations for prosocial behaviors involving sentient persons were beyond the pale of sound scientific explanation.

## Explaining Morality and Prosocial Behavior in Sentient Beings Historically

The logical positivists like Hempel and Popper were reacting to limitations in centuries of theological explanations (Israel, 2001; James, 1902; Menand, 2001, pp. 100–101; Pigliucci & Boudry, 2013). For at least 3,000 years, most explanations of prosocial behavior were tied to a providential God, morality, and ethics. They had clear religious and theological content.

Substantively, Canto-Sperber (2000) notes an especially important historical development that has implications for the contemporary view of prosocial behavior. It was the gradual emergence of a spiritual principle, psyche (the soul), during the 6th century B.C.E. This soul was no longer just the departure of breath from the body at death but the indicator of an independent being that persisted past death. Until that time, immortality was seen as the privilege of the gods, not as a characteristic of humans. This idea of a soul promotes the notion that the individual is the locus for intentional actions for which that person is ultimately accountable. After death, the individual could be punished or receive retribution. A picture begins to emerge here: in Jewish and Christian theological and philosophical accounts, individuals' intentions make people accountable for their actions. The existence of an individual soul implies that prosocial actions could be rewarded not only in the present world but in the world to come. Conversely, failure to engage in prosocial acts could be conceptualized as sin, which creates a burden and a need for restitution.

During the emergence of Christianity, Palestine was at the heart of a "new world" of Hellenism created by Alexander and his Macedonian followers (Le Boulluec, 2000). In Palestine, the numerically small but powerful elite wrote and spoke Greek, whereas ordinary people used Aramaic. Gradually a core of educated families gave their children a Greek education of high quality. Without this educated class, it would have been difficult to construct the Septuagint, the translation of the text of the Pentateuch from Hebrew into Greek. According to Bardet (2000), the translation of sacred texts from one language into another is contrary to most traditions in the Levant and Near East. Apparently the Jewish society, largely in the Diaspora, perceived a need for the Greek text because they were unable to read the Hebrew version. Bickermann (1988) observed that the translation fixed the text from a philological as well as a theological perspective, increasing the importance of the words at the expense of actual living practice. Here we see how both history and language affected the framing of Abrahamic and Judeo-Christian ideas about prosocial behavior.

At last we have found sin and its links to morality and prosocial behavior. Sociopolitical history and language shaped Abrahamic and Judeo-Christian ideas and norms about prosocial behavior. An important part of the answer lies more in the linguistic evolution of ancient Hebrew and Aramaic texts than in the Greek speculations on the good life. From a theological perspective, sin may be the primary cause of evil in the world, but efforts to repair its effects are the cause of prosocial behavior. Anderson (2009) reports careful linguistic analyses of religious texts that track the transformation of the concepts and language used to describe sin. One of the oldest descriptions appears in Leviticus (1000–580 B.C.E.). In it, the Day of Atonement (Lev. 16:21–22) is described in terms of the removal of the sins of all of Israel by a priest putting his hands on a goat that then assumed the weight of Israel's sins as it escaped into the desert. The desert was seen as beyond the reach of God, and the sins of the Israelites would thus disappear from God's view. Repentance for sin was not enough, as the physical thing that was sin rested on the head of every Israelite, and it had "to be carted into oblivion" (Anderson, 2009, p. 6). Almost half a millennium later however, in the Gospel according to Matthew, Jesus speaks of sin using a different metaphor, namely one of debt: "Forgive us our debts as we forgive our debtors." Scholars noted that this sin-as-debt metaphor was derived from contemporary Hebrew and Aramaic idioms of the time. If a person was not able to settle his debts, the creditor could have the debtor sold as a debt-slave, along with his wife, children, and all his property in payment of the debt.

Anderson (2009) observed that a major shift in thinking about sin—from weight to debt—was seen during the era of Persian rule (538–333 B.C.E.). This period was associated with the rising prestige and influence of the Aramaic language, the official language of the Persian Empire. When the Babylonians sacked the First Temple in Jerusalem (587 B.C.E.), the Israelites were sentenced to years of captivity in Babylon. Using descriptions suiting Comte's most basic theological level, the prophet Isaiah explained why the Temple was sacked: it was due to the great sinfulness of the people of Israel. During that exile, Jews in Babylon became bilingual in both Hebrew and Aramaic. In Aramaic, but not in Hebrew, sin was construed as "debt," and a person in debt had to raise currency to repay it.

Anderson (2009) described a critical and revolutionary change in thinking as a result of shifting from Hebrew to Aramaic language use. In the idiom of Rabbinic Hebrew, following the Jews' return from their Babylonian captivity, the semantic opposite of "debt" is "credit." Before the sacking of the Temple, however, the idiom of "bearing the weight of one's sins" did not have a natural opposite. For the first time, Jewish thinkers had means for describing and encouraging positive, virtuous behavior. Just as sin brought debt, virtue brought merit. Accordingly, humans could build credits for themselves through good works (i.e., prosocial behavior). These credits were duly noted by God and deposited as treasure in a heavenly bank. In this approach, human agency becomes a force for counteracting the ravages of sin. Daniel (Dan. 4:27) tells King Nebuchadnezzar, the Babylonian who destroyed the First Temple in Jerusalem, that he can redeem himself by giving away money to the poor.

According to Anderson, these changes in ideas represents one of the most important developments in early Judaism, namely that almsgiving became widely seen as the prime commandment (Dorff, 2005). The Rabbinic literature made further distinctions. Almsgiving to the poor was especially commendable. Deeds of loving kindness were superior to charity, because the former can be done to both the poor and the rich and apply to both the living and the dead. The Rabbinic literature values acts of loving-kindness for the objective good they do, regardless of the motive that prompted them (*Babylonian Talmud*, reported in Dorff, 2005). The early Christian church inherited this view of prosocial acts from the Jews. In Matthew (Matt. 25:34–40), Jesus himself is reported to have said that at the end of the world, the sheep will be separated from the goats based on their good works directed to the needy ("for I was hungry, and you gave me food, I was thirsty . . .").

As Anderson (2009) noted, these issues of sin, debt, and good works reemerged with special vigor during the Protestant Reformation. How can a penitent's almsgiving and prosocial acts cancel the debt of sin and restore that penitent to good graces? Can the benefits be transferred through the penitent to another person, thereby reducing the debt of a dead relative in purgatory? The sale of church-authorized indulgences in particular drew criticism from Martin Luther for its promise that money could repay the debts of sin. Such repayment was not only for the self but could be transferred to other persons (MacCulloch, 2003, pp. 12–13). Luther's challenge was that charity, almsgiving, and helping the poor were all admirable acts, but good works alone could not guarantee salvation. Perhaps good works and almsgiving genuinely motivated by an underlying faith were the keys (Anderson, 2013, pp. 8–9).

This has been an extended discussion. In terms of our focus here, the merit of good works and prosocial behavior presumably depended on its intent and underlying motivation. The theological issues are complex and nuanced (see Anderson, 2009, pp. 160–163), but from a psychological perspective, given these Reformation controversies, ambivalent reactions toward people in need of help may be common, then and now (e.g., Cohen & Rozin, 2001; Regnerus, Smith, & Sikkink, 1998). How does sin affect the help-giver's choices? For example, should mental illnesses like schizophrenia and depression be better regarded as diseases or as the wages of sin, for which the sufferer must atone before receiving help (e.g., Wesselmann & Graziano, 2010)? The Reformation Protestants no longer accepted the Mass as a sacrificial act that remitted sins. Once the sacramental aspects of almsgiving were removed, the donor had no need to meet the beneficiary in person, and alms to the indigent could be delivered by civic organizations (see also Dijker & Koomen, 2007). Do third-party contributions count in sin-debt reduction? Whatever else this might be, the Reformation set into motion a perspective on prosocial behavior and corresponding norms that was different from the Judeo-Christian heritage that preceded it (Israel, 2001; MacCulloch, 2003, "Outcomes," pp. 645–683).

## From Distal Norms to Psychological Processes

The norm-centered approach outlined previously tells us more about "when" than about "why." It tells us about the kinds of social norms that evolved (descriptive norms), but also about the explicit and implicit rules and behaviors required in a given situation (injunctive norms). Within the literature on prosocial behavior, some studies have raised questions about the explanatory power of norms for prosocial behaviors. Darley and Batson (1973), for example, manipulated norm salience by having seminarians give a sermon either about the Good Samaritan (prosocial norm) or about job opportunities for seminarians. Norm salience was pitted against a situational variable by manipulating whether the seminarians were in a hurry to give their talks. The norm salience effect was not significant, whereas the situational variable of being in a hurry was. Darley and Batson concluded that "this lack of effect for sermon topic raises certain difficulties for an explanation of helping behavior involving helping norms and their salience" (p. 107). To address these sorts of issues, some writers noted that distinctions need to be made among various kinds of norms. Besides the descriptive/injunctive distinction, Dovidio, Piliavin, Schroeder, and Penner (2006) noted two broad categories of prosocial norms, namely fairness norms (e.g., reciprocity, equity, justice) and social responsibility norms. What became clear was that more attention was needed on the psychological processes underlying specific injunctive norms that promoted or inhibited prosocial behavior. Phrased another way, norms are social-cognitive representations for expected behaviors when other situational cues are weak or ambiguous. Situational cues can overwhelm the implicit social influence of injunctive norms. By themselves, norms lay general foundations but must be augmented with information about psychological processes operating within individuals. One step toward linking these divergent issues and building a model of morality and prosocial behavior may be found in work by Dijker and Koomen (2007). Substantively, they focus on stigmatization and the biased treatment individuals can receive when they violate group norms. Dijker and Koomen note that the same person can show strong bias against one class of "deviants" (e.g., drug addicts), yet show almost loving concern for a different class of deviants (e.g., homeless children). Such variability in bias is not easily explained by a single personality variable, a single norm, or even a single process.

Dijker and Koomen proposed an innovative, integrative approach to stigmatization that included two evolved, preverbal systems of motivation. Each system reflects human evolutionary history. The older component is a Fight/Flight system that we carry as part of our paleo-reptilian heritage. Encounters with "unusual cases" ("deviance" in Dijker & Koomen) activates this system without conscious deliberation, priming a system that impels individuals to flee from danger or to fight if forced to do so. The second system is newer in evolutionary time and is part of the parental care system associated with kin selection (e.g., Hamilton, 1964; Trivers, 1972). Furthermore, the two motivational systems have the capacity to elicit characteristic emotions when exposed to certain specific environmental triggers. Because humans evolved in small groups of genetically related individuals, aggressive reactions to unusual cases had to be inhibited. Some of the unusual cases probably involved kin, for whom repair of deviance would be more beneficial than aggression or exclusion. The Care system has the capacity to suppress the Fight/Flight system.

It is possible to extend the theoretical system presented by Dijker and Koomen (2007) further toward morality and prosocial behavior. Let us assume that prosociality is the psychological manifestation of the Care system. If this is correct, then prosociality may not only relate to sympathetic care given to the weak and disadvantaged but may also operate to suppress the responses associated with the more primitive Fight/Flight system. Some prosocial phenomena may be fairly direct expressions of Care, and others may be a product of Care-based suppression of Fight/Flight (Graziano & Habashi, 2015). Furthermore, persons with prosocial predispositions (e.g., persons high in agreeableness) may feel an intent-like empathic concern directly for victims of misfortune (Graziano & Eisenberg, 1997; Graziano, Habashi, Sheese, & Tobin, 2007), but they may also suppress (perhaps effortfully) negative reactions to traditional targets of prejudice generated by their Fight/Flight system (Graziano, Bruce, Sheese, & Tobin, 2007).

Moving the system a bit beyond description, let us assume some connections between the Fight/Flight and Care systems of potential relevance to prosociality. If we assume that both Fight/Flight and Care systems are part of the human evolutionary legacy and present in almost all people (albeit at varying strengths), and that Fight/Flight occurs faster than Care upon exposure to an environmental oddity, then the two may operate as opponents to each other's preponderant responsive activation tendencies. If so, we can generate explanations for apparent paradoxes and anomalies. In helping contexts similar to those studied by Batson (1991, 2011), personal distress may inhibit prosocial acts because it is part of Fight/Flight, not Care; empathic concern, however, promotes helping because it is part of Care. Despite having opposite effects on helping, both personal distress and empathic concern are present in most people, explaining the positive correlation. Personal distress is the first, immediate response to a victim because it is connected to the faster Fight/Flight system. If there is an opportunity for easy escape from the victim when personal distress is high, then the victim will not receive help. If the potential helper cannot escape quickly, or if the observer must remain in proximity to the victim, then enough time may pass for the slower empathic concern system to become active. The result would be suppression of the Fight/Flight system by the Care system and increase the chances that the victim would receive help. This account would explain why outcomes of research on Ease/Difficulty of Escape are unstable. The key variable—the time interval between exposure to the victim and the window of opportunity for escape—is unmeasured.

Graziano and Habashi (2010) advanced this logic one step further. They proposed that the system we describe may be a case of the opponent process model of motivation presented by R.L. Solomon (Solomon, 1980; Solomon & Corbit, 1974). In a search of the published literature, Graziano and Habashi could find only two uses of the Solomon opponent process model for either helping or prejudice (Baumeister & Campbell, 1999; Piliavin, Callero, & Evans, 1982). In both cases, the focus of attention was primarily on Solomon's opponent explanation for cycles of addictive behavior. Their version of the opponent approach as applied to prosocial behavior is presented in Figure 15.1. In keeping with Solomon, the first process activated is labeled Process A. Its activation is virtually automatic, a kind of unconditioned response to the onset of an environmental stimulus. It remains active while the evocative stimulus is present and ends when the stimulus is removed. The second process activated is an opponent, labeled Process B. It is slower to come online but persists well after Process A ends. Because A and B are opponents, but A occurs first and more quickly in response to an environmental event for some brief part of the sequence, Process A operates initially in almost pure form (without an opponent). Concretely, if Process A is personal distress and Process B is empathic concern, then the first response to a victim should be unopposed personal distress. If escape is possible in this interval, the victim will not receive help. By the same logic, initial reactions to unusual cases (e.g., victims of misfortune) as well as to members of out-groups would be personal distress and avoidance. With time, however, Process B can be activated and oppose the processes of Process A, and the empathic concern may eventually dominate and lead to prosocial action. These opponent processes may be what Pryor, Reeder, Yeadon, and Hesson-Mclnnis (2004) index in their behavior correction research. Initial negative reactions are replaced by more positive ones.

The Solomon opponent process approach offers several additional insights about prosociality. Repeated exposure to the evocative (unconditioned) stimuli produces systematic changes in the relative strengths of Process A and Process B: Process A becomes weaker, and Process B becomes stronger. For Solomon, the prototype is drug addiction, in which repeated exposure to substances like cocaine create smaller and shorter states of euphoria and longer states of withdrawal. In

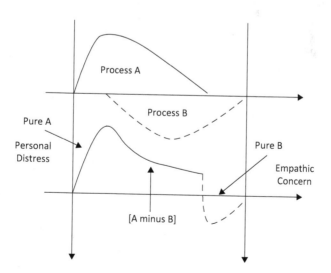

**FIGURE 15.1** Opponent process model of motivation.

*Note:* Adapted from Solomon, R.L., & Corbit, J.D. (1974). An opponent-process theory of motivation: I. Temporal dynamics of affect. *Psychological Review, 57,* 119–145.

our application, repeated exposure to victims of misfortune should lead to smaller and shorter periods of personal distress and, at least in theory, to longer states of empathic concern. This connection might explain why there are individual differences, and why they appear in the form that they do. In most of these cases, the kinds of individual differences in motivation for helping reported by Oliner and Oliner (1988/1992) and by others reflect the fact that the helpers had repeated exposure to various kinds of "unusual cases" of people earlier in their lives.

The Solomon approach also raises questions about the conceptual status of individual differences related to helping (e.g., agreeableness), the decomposition of molar social behavior into constituent components, and the role of time in the expression of complex social behavior. How long is the temporal extension of a prosocial "situation," and when does one situation end and a different one begin? Regarding the first of these questions, at some level each individual is born prepared for a life trajectory by a set of inherited tendencies and motivation systems. Evolution may have left us with two powerful motive systems in Fight/Flight and Care (Dijker & Koomen, 2007), but there are probably individual differences in the relative strength of these two motivations. Observers might detect and label these socially important behavioral differences as, say, neuroticism and agreeableness, respectively. At this point, we might be satisfied to build structural models or collect data showing intercorrelations among variables like Care, agreeableness, and some other dispositions like self-esteem. Such an approach would grossly underestimate the dynamic quality of the major dispositions and probably the range of influence of the individual difference under consideration. That being said, repeated exposure to certain kinds of environmental events alters the basic parameters of the inherited dispositions and motives.

Regarding the second question, the expression of complex social behavior like helping is almost certainly the outcome of several different but related systems. When these systems operate at the same time, one system may reduce the influence of another. In the opponent process model, the influence of Process A is much reduced once Process B is activated. From observing a single episode of helping or prejudice, a researcher might conclude that a single process is operative, but it is likely that the process is better studied only by observing the operation of the components over time.

The opponent process model linking multiple motives to interpersonal behaviors and to more general self-regulatory processes (Graziano & Tobin, 2013) is novel, so many issues are unresolved. Are personality dispositions related to prosociality (e.g., empathy, agreeableness) tied to the Care system only or to Fight/Flight as well? Are they tied to both personal distress and empathic concern, to both prejudice and the suppression of prejudice, or to just one of the elements in each pair? We believe that the opponent process approach allows us to anticipate phenomena that are not described elsewhere. Here we offer a few tentative ideas.

To the best of our knowledge no empirical research has addressed the issue of delayed helping (but see Penner, Dovidio, Piliavin, & Schroeder, 2005; Piliavin, Dovidio, Gaertner, & Clark, 1981). In general, a common assumption is that the influence of a manipulation of victim need, mood state, or empathic concern will dissipate for most or all people over time (for example, see the arousal: cost-reward model in Piliavin et al. [1981]). That is, rates of helping are affected by the interval between provision of information and the request for help and the opportunity to provide it. Note the analogue to the correction of prejudice outcomes reported by Pryor et al. (2004). If the opponent process system operates roughly as described here, then some forms of helping may be greater after a short delay than they are following an immediate request. The initial Fight/Flight reaction may come under the control of the opponent Care system, in effect disinhibiting helping with time. Undoubtedly, we would also see characteristic emotions, such as relief, at finally having an opportunity to provide assistance. Based on the previous rationale, we would also expect persons with more frequent exposure to victims to offer more help, sooner and with less influence of delay, than persons with fewer exposures to such victims. These experiences produced quasi-personality predispositions, emerging as a result of social learning. At this point, such conjectures are speculative.

## Concluding Thoughts

Understanding the social characteristics of moral decisions and behavior has been a major challenge to thinkers since the first written records of human activities were created. Social psychology can make contributions to our understanding of current moral judgments and behavior, and, in turn, conceptions of morality can inform social psychological theories and research. This chapter focused on prosocial behavior, a potentially rich source of information about the contextual connections among morality-related thoughts, feelings, and behavior. In this chapter, we described linguistic influences on the evolution of injunctive prosocial norms. We then worked backward from overt prosocial behavior toward its contextual influences and causes. The key idea is that prosocial behaviors are often influenced by injunctive norms, which stand at an intermediate meso-level position, between macro-level variables like language and patterns of infections at one end, and micro-level variables like physiological processes at the other end (Penner et al., 2005). We offered a multilevel approach with the goal of integrating processes at different levels of abstraction. The evolution of the concept of sin influenced corresponding changes in injunctive prosocial norms, and in acts presumed to redeem sinners from the stain and guilt of their normative transgressions. Building on work by Murray and Schaller (2014), Graziano and Schroeder (2015) proposed another historical force influencing prosocial norm evolution, namely cultural differences in reactions to pathogen prevalence and infections. Both language and pathogen prevalence represent macro-level contextual variables that contribute to the evolution of morality and injunctive prosocial norms. By themselves, norms provide an incomplete picture of prosocial behavior; links are needed to the micro level. Basing ideas on previous social psychology work on stigmatization (Dijker & Koomen, 2007), we proposed an opponent-process, social learning mechanism that could help to explain patterns of prosocial behavior, including differences in willingness to aid victims.

The ideas we proposed are synthetic, in that they are built as extensions on top of ideas found outside the literature of prosocial behavior. Rather than being outsiders, however, these ideas provide an opportunity for a fresh look at phenomena and processes in need of further explanation. How well they will fare in the long run is largely an empirical question.

## References

Allport, G.W. (1985). The historical background of social psychology. In G. Lindzey & E. Aronson (Eds.), *Handbook of social psychology: Vol. 1. Theory & method* (3rd ed., pp. 1–46). Reading, MA: Addison-Wesley.

Anderson, G.A. (2009). *Sin: A history*. New Haven, CT: Yale University Press.

Anderson, G.A. (2013). *Charity: The place of the poor in the biblical tradition*. New Haven, CT: Yale University Press.

Bandura, A. (1977). *Social learning theory*. Englewood Cliffs, NJ: Prentice Hall.

Bardet, S. (2000). Hellenism and Judaism. In J. Brunschweig & G.E.R. Lloyd (Eds.), *Greek thought: A guide to classical knowledge* (pp. 870–881). Cambridge, MA: Belknap of Harvard University Press.

Barzun, J. (2001). *From dawn to decadence: 500 years of Western cultural life from 1500 to the present*. New York: Harper Collins.

Batson, C.D. (1991). *The altruism question: Toward a social-psychological answer*. Hillsdale, NJ: Erlbaum.

Batson, C.D. (2011). *Altruism in humans*. New York: Oxford University Press.

Baumeister, R.F., & Campbell, W.K. (1999). The intrinsic appeal of evil: Sadism, sensational thrills, and threatened egotism. *Personality and Social Psychology Review, 3*, 210–221.

Baumeister, R.F., Masicampo, E.J., & Vohs, K.D. (2011). Do conscious thoughts cause behavior? *Annual Review of Psychology, 62*, 331–361.

Berkson, W. (2010). *Pirke avot: Timeless wisdom for modern life*. Philadelphia, PA: Jewish Publication Society.

Bickermann, E.J. (1988). *The Jews of the Greek age*. Cambridge, MA: Harvard.

Brunschweig, J., & Lloyd, G.E.R. (Eds.). (2000). *Greek thought: A guide to classical knowledge*. Cambridge, MA: Belknap of Harvard University Press.

Camus, A. (1958). The guest. (Justin O'Brien, trans.). *London Magazine, 5*(14), 14–25.

Canto-Sperber, M. (2000). Ethics. In J. Brunschweig & G.E.R. Lloyd (Eds.), *Greek thought: A guide to classical knowledge* (pp. 94–124). Cambridge, MA: Belknap of Harvard University Press.

Carlston, D., & Graziano, W.G. (2010). Individuals, behavior, and what lies between the two. In C.R. Agnew, D.E. Carlston, W.G. Graziano, & J.R. Kelly (Eds.), *Then a miracle occurs: Focusing on behavior in social psychological theory and research* (pp. 57–67). New York: Oxford University Press.

Carnap, R. (1962). *Logical foundations of probability* (2nd ed.). Chicago: University of Chicago Press.

Cohen, A.B., & Rozin, P. (2001). Religion and the morality of mentality. *Journal of Personality & Social Psychology, 81*, 697–710.

Darley, J.M., & Batson, C.D. (1973). "From Jerusalem to Jericho": A study of situational and dispositional variables in helping behavior. *Journal of Personality & Social Psychology, 27*, 100–108.

de Botton, A. (2012). *Religion for atheists: A non-believer's guide to the uses of religion.* New York: Vintage.

De Waal, F. (2014, April). *Prosocial behavior in primates.* Colloquium, Purdue University, West Lafayette, IN.

De Waal, F.B. (2008). Putting the altruism back in altruism: The evolution of empathy. *Annual Review of Psychology, 59*, 279–300.

Dijker, A., & Koomen, W. (2007). *Stigmatization, tolerance and repair: An integrative psychological analysis of responses to deviance.* Cambridge: Cambridge University Press.

Dorff, E.N. (2005). *The way into Tikkun Olam (repairing the world).* Woodstock, VT: Jewish Lights.

Dovidio, J.F., Piliavin, J.A., Schroeder, D.A., & Penner, L.A. (2006). *The social psychology of prosocial behavior.* Mahwah, NJ: Erlbaum.

Eastwick, P.W. (2009). Beyond the Pleistocene: Using phylogeny and constraint to inform the evolutionary psychology of human mating. *Psychological Bulletin, 135*, 794–821.

Feigl, H. (1970). The "orthodox" view of theories: Remarks in defense as well as critique. In M. Radner & S. Winokur (Eds.), *Analysis of theories and methods of physics and psychology: Minnesota studies in the philosophy of science* (Vol. 4, pp. 3–16). Minneapolis: University of Minnesota Press.

Finkel, E.J. (2014). The I3 model: Metatheory, theory and evidence. In J.M. Olson & M.P. Zanna (Eds.), *Advances in experimental social psychology* (Vol. 49, pp. 1–104). San Diego, CA: Academic Press.

Freeman, C. (2002). *The closing of the Western mind: The rise of faith and the fall of reason.* New York: Vintage.

Graziano, W.G., Bruce, J.W., Sheese, B.E., & Tobin, R.M. (2007). Attraction, personality, and Prejudice: Liking none of the people most of the time. *Journal of Personality and Social Psychology, 93*, 565–582.

Graziano, W.G., & Eisenberg, N. (1997). Agreeableness: A dimension of personality. In R. Hogan, J. Johnson, & S. Briggs (Eds.), *Handbook of personality psychology* (pp. 795–824). San Diego, CA: Academic Press.

Graziano, W.G., & Habashi, M.M. (2010). Motivational processes underlying both prejudice and helping. *Personality and Social Psychology Review, 14*, 313–331.

Graziano, W.G., & Habashi, M.M. (2015). Searching for the prosocial personality. In D. Schroder & W.G. Graziano (Eds.), *Oxford handbook of prosocial behavior* (pp. 231–255). New York: Oxford.

Graziano, W.G., Habashi, M.M., Sheese, B.E., & Tobin, R.M. (2007). Agreeableness, empathy, and helping: A person × situation perspective. *Journal of Personality and Social Psychology, 93*, 583–599.

Graziano, W.G., & Schroeder, D.A. (2015). Gaining the big picture: Prosocial behavior as an end product. In D.A. Schroeder & W.G. Graziano (Eds.), *Oxford handbook of prosocial behavior* (pp. 721–737). New York: Oxford.

Graziano, W.G., & Tobin, R.M. (2013). The cognitive and motivational foundations underlying agreeableness. In M.D. Robinson, E. Watkins, & E. Harmon-Jones (Eds.), *Handbook of Cognition and Emotion* (pp. 347–366). New York: Guilford.

Haidt, J. (2012). *The righteous mind: Why good people are divided by politics and religion.* New York: Pantheon.

Haidt, J., & Graham, J. (2007). When morality opposes justice: Conservatives have moral intuitions that liberals may not recognize. *Social Justice Research, 20,* 98–116.

Hamilton, W.D. (1964). The genetical evolution of social behaviour I and II. *Journal of Theoretical Biology, 7,* 1–32.

Hempel, C.G., & Oppenheim, P. (1948). Studies in the logic of explanation. *Philosophy of Science, 15,* 135–175.

Humphreys, P. (2006). Foreword. In W.C. Salmon (Ed.), *Four decades of scientific explanation* (pp. x–xi). Pittsburgh, PA: University of Pittsburgh.

Israel, J.I. (2001). *Radical enlightenment: Philosophy and the making of modernity 1650–1750.* Oxford: Oxford University Press.

James, W. (1902). *The varieties of religious experience.* New York: Modern.

Jordan, S. J., & Wesselmann, E.D. (2015). The contextually grounded nature of pro-social behavior: A multi-scale, embodied approach to morality. In D.A. Schroeder & W.G. Graziano (Eds.), *Oxford handbook of prosocial behavior* (pp. 153–165). New York: Oxford.

Laurin, K., Kay, A.C., & Fitzsimons, G.M. (2012). Divergent effects of activating thoughts of God on self-regulation. *Journal of Personality & Social Psychology, 102,* 4–21.

Le Boulluec, A. (2000). Hellenism and Christianity. In J. Brunschweig & G.E.R. Lloyd (Eds.), *Greek thought: A guide to classical knowledge* (pp. 858–869). Cambridge, MA: Belknap of Harvard University Press.

Lieberman, M.D. (2014). *Social: Why our brains are wired to connect.* New York: Crown.

Locke, J. (2009). *An essay concerning human understanding.* New York: Oxford University Press. With commentary by Pauline Phemister. (Original work published 1690)

MacCulloch, D. (2003). *The reformation: A history.* New York: Viking.

Malle, B.F. (2011). Time to give up the dogmas of attribution: An alternative theory of behavior explanation. In J.M. Olson & M.P. Zanna (Eds.), *Advances in experimental social psychology* (Vol. 44, pp. 297–352). Burlington, MA: Academic Press.

Meehl, P.E. (1978). Theoretical risks and tabular asterisks: Sir Karl, Sir Ronald and the slow progress of soft psychology. *Journal of Consulting & Clinical Psychology, 46,* 806–834.

Menand, L. (2001). *The metaphysical club: The story of ideas in America.* New York: Farrar Straus & Giroux.

Muller, J.Z. (Ed.). (1997). *Conservatism: An anthology of social and political thought from David Hume to the present.* Princeton, NJ: Princeton University Press.

Murray, D.R., & Schaller, M. (2014). Pathogen prevalence and geographic variation in traits and behavior. In P.J. Rentfrow (Ed.), *Geographical psychology: Exploring the interaction of environment & behavior* (pp. 51–70). Washington, DC: American Psychological Association.

Neisser, U. (1967). *Cognitive psychology.* New York: Appleton-Century Crofts.

Oliner, S.P., & Oliner, P.M. (1992). *The altruistic personality: Rescuers of Jews in Nazi Europe. What lead ordinary men and women to risk their lives on behalf of others?* New York: Simon & Schuster. (Original work published 1988)

Pagels, E. (1996). *The origins of Satan.* New York: Random House.

Penner, L.A., Dovidio, J.F., Piliavin, J.A., & Schroeder, D.A. (2005). Prosocial behavior: A multilevel perspective. *Annual Review of Psychology, 56,* 365–392.

Pigliucci, M., & Boudry, M. (Eds.). (2013). *Philosophy of pseudoscience: Reconsidering the demarcation problem.* Chicago: University of Chicago Press.

Piliavin, J.A., Callero, P.L., & Evans, D.E. (1982). Addiction to altruism? Opponent-process theory and habitual blood donation. *Journal of Personality and Social Psychology, 43,* 1200–1213.

Piliavin, J.A., Dovidio, J.F., Gaertner, S. L., & Clark, R.D., III (1981). *Emergency intervention.* New York: Academic Press.

Popper, K. (1957). Philosophy of science: A personal report. In C.A. Mace (Ed.), *British philosophy at mid-century* (pp. 155–191). London: Allen & Unwin.

Prot, S., Gentile, D.A., Anderson, C.A., Suzuki, K., Swing, E., Lim, K.M., . . . Lam, B.C.P. (2014). Long-term relations among prosocial-media use, empathy, and prosocial behavior. *Psychological Science, 25*(2), 358–368.

Pryor, J.B., Reeder, G.D., Yeadon, C., & Hesson-Mclnnis, M. (2004). A dual-process model of reactions to perceived stigma. *Journal of Personality and Social Psychology, 87,* 436–452.

Reed, S.K. (2007). *Cognition: Theory & applications* (7th ed.). Belmont, CA: Thomson.

Regnerus, M.D., Smith, C., & Sikkink, D. (1998). Who gives to the poor? The influence of religious tradition, and the political location on the personal generosity of Americans toward the poor. *Journal for the Scientific Study of Religion, 37,* 481–493.

Salmon, W.C. (2006). *Four decades of scientific explanation.* Pittsburgh, PA: University of Pittsburgh.

Sartre, J.-P. (1960). *Intimacy.* London: Panther.

Skinner, B.F. (1953). *Science and human behavior.* New York: Macmillan.

Solomon, R. (1980). The opponent-process theory of acquired motivation: The costs of pleasure and the benefits of pain. *American Psychologist, 35,* 691–712.

Solomon, R.L., & Corbit, J.D. (1974). An opponent-process theory of motivation: I. Temporal dynamics of affect. *Psychological Review, 57,* 119–145.

Tomasello, M. (2014). The ultra-social animal. *European Journal of Social Psychology, 44,* 187–194.

Trivers, R. (1972). Parental investment and sexual selection. In B. Campbell (Ed.), *Sexual selection and the descent of man: 1871–1971* (pp. 136–179). Chicago: Aldine.

Vachon, D., Lynam, D., & Johnson, J.A. (2014). The (non)relation between empathy and aggression: Surprising results from a meta-analysis. *Psychological Bulletin, 140,* 751–773.

Velikovsky, I. (1950). *Worlds in collision.* New York: Doubleday.

Watson, J.B. (1913). Psychology as the behaviorist views it. *Psychological Review, 20,* 158–177.

Watson, J.B. (1924). *Behaviorism.* New York: Norton.

Weinstein, N., & Ryan, R.M. (2010). When helping helps: Autonomous motivation for prosocial behavior and its influence on well-being for the helper and recipient. *Journal of Personality & Social Psychology, 98,* 222–244.

Wesselmann, E., & Graziano, W.G. (2010). Sinful or possessed? Religious beliefs and mental illness stigma. *Journal of Social and Clinical Psychology, 29,* 402–437.

# 16

# THE MORAL PSYCHOLOGY OF RESOURCE USE

*Brock Bastian and Daniel Crimston*

*Resource decision making is not based on human needs alone and regularly requires achieving a balance between the protection of animal rights, rare species, and entire ecosystems. This balance is under pressure from two current trends. First, human (over)population of the planet is growing exponentially, placing pressure on limited resources. Second, there is a growing human tendency to afford moral rights to nonhumans, and these nonhumans are sometimes the resources themselves. We will review research that examines this conflict. First, we will focus on how people's own morality may play a role in resource decision making, demonstrating that our increasing sensitivity to the needs and rights of nonhumans has clear costs for humans. Second, we will focus on how competing motivations (satisfaction of human needs vs. upholding moral principles) may shape and bend our moral worlds, changing our attitudes and perceptions in ways that ultimately allow us to satisfy those needs. By taking account of how the satisfaction of human needs interacts with moral reasoning about the rights of those more distant from us, we will aim to provide new insights into how research, policy, and practice may be best positioned to address the inevitable rise of resource conflicts.*

In December 2012, the Australian government approved a minerals mine in north-west Tasmania, an area that was also proposed for a World Heritage Site listing and a location known to house the endangered Tasmanian Devil (Ford, 2012). For those interested in protecting this native ecosystem the mine approval was seen as a tragic loss. Only a month prior to this announcement the government declared the establishment of a marine reserve on the coast of Australia covering 2.3 million square kilometres of ocean (Duffy, 2012). They also announced a $100 million fund to buy out affected fisheries. Opponents of this decision expressed grave concerns for the impact this would have on fishing communities and food stocks.

What these examples make clear is that decisions around resource use are not only based on human needs. Resource decision making is also beholden to the value placed on the protection of rare species and entire ecosystems. These examples also demonstrate that the needs of humans and nonhumans are often in conflict: marine parks interfere with the use of fish for food, and mining has damaging consequences for the natural environment. This same conflict can also be located in many more common cases, such as the production of meat. With a growing human population the need for cheap affordable meat is also on the rise. The mass production of affordable meat also comes into direct conflict with animal rights issues. Factory farming raises the specter of cruel and inhumane conditions in which animals are both raised and slaughtered for food. For this reason, many choose to eat meat that they believe has been produced outside of these environments. Of course, the additional cost associated with these alternative and more humane approaches is often prohibitive for those on low incomes, further highlighting the tension that exists between moral sensitivity and resource availability and affordability.

In this chapter we draw attention to an increasing pressure point in decision making around resource use and resource allocation. With a growing human population, the requirements for resources to meet basic human needs are also increasing. At the same time, humans globally are becoming more sensitive to the needs and rights of nonhumans (Pinker, 2011; Singer, 1981), leading to an increased desire to protect natural environments and other species from harm. In some cases these decisions are based on human needs, such as the importance of protecting the Amazon River basin due its role in producing about 20% of Earth's oxygen. However, just as often they are based on qualities that are considered of intrinsic value alone.

This is most clear in the case of animals, many of whom are believed to be sentient creatures that have the right to be protected from harm. In fact, increasingly animals are afforded other rights too, such as Sandra the Orangutan in an Argentine zoo who now has the legal right to freedom (ABC, 2014). Yet, these same concerns can be observed in the desire to protect other entities that are not themselves "sentient." Take for instance the criteria for World Heritage Site listings. In deciding which things to protect, the United Nations Educational, Scientific and Cultural Organization (UNESCO) focuses on qualities such as uniqueness or beauty—intrinsic qualities. Indeed, the decision to grant the Whanganui River in New Zealand the status of personhood is clearly motivated by consideration of its intrinsic value (Fairbrother, 2012). Just like a person, the Whanganui River now has the right to be protected from harm, meaning that it is unlikely to be available for the production of hydroelectricity or agricultural irrigation any time soon.

## Why a *Moral* Psychology of Resource Use?

At first blush it may seem a little strange to invoke the notion of morality when talking about resource use. Traditionally, moral considerations have been reserved for issues surrounding equity and fairness in the satisfaction of human needs. Take for instance the many "games" that have been developed to bring insights into resource dilemmas, or what is often referred to as "the tragedy of the commons" (Hardin, 1968). Almost exclusively these dilemmas are investigated from the point of view of human needs alone. Issues relating to how resource use may impact on nonhuman needs, or even the various ways in which resources may be valuable in their own right (intrinsic value) as opposed to their usefulness in satisfying human needs, are rarely if ever considered.

We believe there has been a critical oversight in approaches to understanding resource decision making. Almost exclusively scholars have sought to understand how people share resources with other humans. In this previous work, core moral concepts of harm, fairness, equity, and rights are invoked in describing the satisfaction of human needs. Critically, however, these same moral concerns are also relevant for thinking about the rights and needs of nonhumans (see Haslam, this volume). Moral concerns are clearly evident in the animal rights movements, and whilst animals provide an important source of labor as well as meat, leather, fur, or any number of animal-based products such as lanolin, keratin, elastin, or collagen, they also form psychologically meaningful bonds with humans (Amiot & Bastian, 2014). The extension of intrinsic moral value to entire species, ecosystems, and the biosphere also demonstrates that these entities are often firmly within our circle of moral consideration (Feinberg & Willer, 2013; Pinker, 2011; Singer, 1981; Stern & Dietz, 1994). Focusing our analysis on the morality of human need satisfaction alone cannot account for the rapid rise of these organizations and the ways in which they are impacting on resource decision making.

## What Makes a Resource Morally Relevant?

The first step in developing a moral psychology of resource use is to develop insights into why and when a resource may be viewed as possessing morally relevant qualities. Perhaps the most obvious way to account for why a nonhuman may be afforded moral status is the extent to which that entity is considered "human-like" (Bastian, Laham, Wilson, Haslam, & Koval, 2011). The importance of human-likeness has been well illustrated in a study by Plous (1993), which showed that animals that are perceived to be more similar to humans are also perceived as having a greater capacity for pain. Moreover, when watching human-like animals being mistreated, observers experience greater autonomic arousal (Plous, 1993) and are more likely to recommend harsher sentences for those who abuse them (Allen et al., 2002). Of course, human-like is also a vague term that incorporates a broad array of qualities, many of which may not be morally relevant themselves—for instance having fingernails is unlikely to be a prime mover of moral concern. One critical human-like quality is the capacity to think and feel—that is the extent to which an entity is considered to possess a "mind."

There is now an extensive body of work focusing on the role of mind in our perception of and orientation toward nonhumans. In developing a psychological theory of anthropomorphism (the tendency to attribute human-like qualities to nonhumans), Epley, Waytz, and Cacioppo (2007) argued that there are three reasons that humans are likely to view nonhumans as possessing a mind. The first is related to the general tendency of humans to rely on their own experiences when inductively reasoning about the experiences of others. The second relates to the usefulness of mental state attribution in making sense of the actions of others. For instance Waytz, Gray, Epley, and Wegner (2010) found that when motivated to predict the actions of nonhuman agents, people are more likely to attribute mental qualities to them. Finally, they argue that loneliness or a lack of social connection to others increases the tendency to attribute mind to nonhumans—especially those qualities that are important for creating and maintaining social relations (Epley, Akalis, Waytz, & Cacioppo, 2008). The work of Epley and colleagues provides important insights into why pets are often anthropomorphized in cultures low in social capital.

Attributing mind to others, including nonhumans, is a critical social cognitive skill that is motivated by a number of factors and serves a number of functions. Most importantly for our analysis, it also has significant moral implications (Gray, Young, & Waytz, 2012; Waytz et al., 2010). Yet, not all things that are considered morally relevant are also considered to have minds (see Frimer, this volume). Many of the things that we seek to protect, such as rainforests, rivers, or reefs are unlikely to be thought of as possessing the capacity to think or feel. This raises an important question: what are the qualities that people are interested in protecting in these cases? As we alluded to earlier, qualities such as uniqueness and beauty are also commonly referred to when seeking to raise the status of a particular entity to a level that affords it the right to be protected from harm, and by harm we mean its destruction. We argue that mind, beauty, and uniqueness are all qualities that contribute to a particular entities' *intrinsic value*. To understand the full extent to which morality is caught up in our reasoning about resource use we need to broaden our scope beyond mind perception alone: we need to begin to consider the broader ways in which things may be attributed with intrinsic value.

Indeed the notion of intrinsic value has traditionally been thought to lie at the heart of ethics. For philosophers, the intrinsic value of something is related to the value that that thing has in itself, for its own sake, or in its own right. This can be contrasted with the concept of extrinsic value: that which is valuable not for its own sake, but for the sake of something else to which it is related. These two forms of value bring to light an important distinction along which resource conflicts often arise. Those concerned about the intrinsic value of a rainforest are opposed to others who see that forest as an important source of extrinsic value (see Brandt, Wetherell, & Crawford, this volume, for a discussion of how these differences may become polarized). Put differently, the value of a rainforest as a thing of beauty and uniqueness is pitted against its value as a source of wood for building and construction. Critically, when people assign intrinsic value to a particular entity they are motivated to protect that thing from harm, indicating that it has, at least to some extent, become something that has moral relevance in their world—it matters in its own right.

Of course, these two forms of value are rarely completely independent. For instance, preserving a rainforest is also of extrinsic value in terms of its production of oxygen and its value as an ecosystem that supports biological diversity. Nonetheless, as is evident in the mandate of UNESCO, World Heritage Sites are protected because they are sources of intrinsic rather than extrinsic value. To this extent, we argue that a broader focus on intrinsic value, which includes qualities such as mind, beauty, and uniqueness, is critical for understanding when a resource may be viewed as morally relevant.

## What Predicts Moral Concern Regarding Resource Use?

When we begin to talk about moral concern for resources we are clearly referring to the more distant reaches of moral thinking. The morality of protecting our own children from harm is somehow more potent, and obligatory, than the morality of protecting rainforests. Nonetheless, as we noted earlier there is an increasing tendency to import more distant entities into our moral worlds. Indeed, the idea that people are expanding their moral universe to include more distant nonhuman entities has been noted by a number of prominent theorists (Lecky, 1869; Singer, 1981). While this trend has been observed historically and has been argued for ethically, the ability to directly capture this psychological tendency (to include an increasing number of entities within the boundaries of moral concern) has been missing from the psychological literature.

Recent work by Crimston, Bain, Hornsey, and Bastian (in press) has made significant progress in capturing individual differences in the extent to which people's moral worlds are either more or less expansive. The Moral Expansiveness Scale was developed to assess the relative size of an individual's moral world. Specifically, it involves asking people to make judgments about the moral standing of a range of entities within four clearly defined boundaries. Drawing from a list of 30 entities ranging from "family" to "plants," people are asked to decide where each entity exists in their moral world. To achieve this, people are provided with four "moral spaces" and asked to place each of the entities into one of them. The "inner circle" is defined as pertaining to those entities worthy of the highest level of moral concern and standing, where there is an obligation to ensure their welfare and a sense of personal responsibility to ensure their moral treatment.

The "outer circle" is defined as pertaining to entities that certainly hold moral standing but which people may be less likely to feel personal responsibility for. The "fringes" are defined as pertaining to entities that may have some moral rights and standing, but where there is a definite lack of personal concern and responsibility about their moral treatment. "Outside the moral sphere" is defined as pertaining to entities without any moral standing. Higher scores are given to entities placed in the inner circle (3) and decreasing for each subsequent moral space (outer circle = 2, fringes = 1, outside = 0). People who place more entities closer to the center of their moral worlds receive higher scores. Such individuals are referred to as high in moral expansiveness.

The key question for research on moral expansiveness is to understand how this individual difference shapes decision making around resource allocation and resource protection. In general, most people would indicate a desire to allocate resources to their own family, and may even make significant self-sacrifices for them. Of interest is whether this same tendency might extend to more distant entities, even if to a lesser degree, and whether moral expansiveness could predict this.

Across a number of studies Crimston et al. (in press) found that those high in moral expansiveness indicated a preference for spreading resources to more distant others, as opposed to keeping them for themselves or for those closest to them. For example, when asked whether they would choose to make medicines available to those overseas who cannot afford them (e.g., AIDS victims in Africa) versus ensuring the US had the best hospitals in the world, Americans high in moral expansiveness supported the first option more than the second. Similarly, when asked if they would prefer to safeguard the habitats of chimpanzees and the other great apes around the world versus ensuring that the cost of living remains stable in the US, those high in moral expansiveness supported the needs of animals over their fellow citizens.

Crimston et al. (in press) also examined whether moral expansiveness might predict behaviors that run against an individual's immediate self-interest. To this end, they found that moral expansiveness predicted the willingness to donate a kidney to a variety of non-kin human targets (e.g., refugees, criminals) and the tendency to make greater financial contributions to a range of animal welfare and environmental causes. Perhaps most powerfully, they also found that moral expansiveness predicted the willingness to sacrifice one's own life in order to protect a variety of targets, ranging from members of one's hometown to Africans and prisoners, but also extending beyond humans to coral reefs and redwood trees. Importantly, Crimston et al. (in press) found these effects when controlling for other "nonmoral" variables such as the capacity for empathic concern and perspective taking (Davis, 1983), extended identification with humanity (McFarland, Webb, & Brown, 2012), and connection to the natural world (Mayer & Frantz, 2004), as well as other "moral" variables such as variations in moral intuitions

(Haidt, 2012), moral identity (Aquino & Reed, 2002), or endorsement of universalism values (Schwartz, 2007).

This paper by Crimston et al. provides two important insights. First, it suggests that moral expansiveness is an important variable that predicts the tendency to prioritize protection of more distant entities even when this is pitted against narrower self-interest. Second, it demonstrates that these issues are indeed moral issues. The way in which people structure their moral worlds predicts their tendency to allocate resources and make self-sacrifices for nonhumans. To this end, the research highlights the inevitable tension between expanding our moral universe to include nonhumans and our desire to provide for and protect those closest to us, including ourselves.

Ongoing work on moral expansiveness will hopefully encourage new insights and research directions. Scholars such as Singer (1981) have identified the idea that each person has a moral universe or moral circle that can be either expanded or contracted to be more or less inclusive of others, yet a measure tapping individual differences in this tendency has been missing. The work by Crimston et al. (in press) provides for novel psychological insights into the individual, situational, and ecological factors that cause people to expand or contract their moral universe.

## Human Need Satisfaction and the Shifting Moral Universe

Although it appears that there may be important individual differences in how people make decisions about resource use and their moral concern for both humans and nonhumans, there are also powerful situational determinants of these decisions (see Miller & Monin, this volume). While people may seek to protect the needs and rights of nonhumans, the motivation to do so may be moderated by the personal costs associated with doing so. Put differently, although moral expansiveness may predict the tendency to make self-sacrifices to protect nonhumans from harm, it is also likely that when human needs and desires conflict with the desire to protect resources from harm, the satisfaction of those needs may win out. In this way, we argue that decision making around resource use is flexible and shifting, often motivated by our own particular needs and perspectives.

This is especially evident when we consider the practice of eating meat. Work in this area has highlighted what is referred to as the meat-paradox: how people can both love animals and enjoy eating meat. Most people are horrified by the sight of animal cruelty (Allen et al., 2002; Plous, 1993), and in general most people are not particularly comfortable with the killing practices necessary to bring meat to their supermarkets and dinner tables (Herzog, 2010; Joy, 2010; Singer, 1975). Nonetheless, the vast majority of people continues to eat meat. This appetite for meat is indeed no recent phenomenon, with meat consumption predating human civilization (Rose & Marshall, 1996). The question is, how do we continue this widespread consumption of meat at a time when we are also increasingly becoming more sensitive to concerns over animal welfare?

This example of conflicting interests—the human appetite for meat and animal welfare—provides a critical case study into how people may shift their moral worldviews when their concern for others interferes with their own need satisfaction. Research has examined how people are able to resolve the meat-paradox thereby reducing discomfort associated with their meat-eating practices. In one study, Bastian, Loughnan, Haslam, and Radke (2012) asked people to rate the extent to which 32 animals possessed a range of mental capacities as well as their willingness to eat each animal. What they found was that people's willingness to eat an animal was negatively related to the extent to which they thought that animal possessed mental capacities. Ruby and Heine (2012) found this same relationship between edibility and mind attribution across diverse samples, including American, Canadian, Hong Kong Chinese, and Indian consumers.

Whilst these correlational studies provide little insight into motivational process, other research has provided compelling evidence. A study by Loughnan, Haslam, and Bastian (2010a) randomly assigned participants to consume either beef or nuts, and subsequently report their moral concern for animals and to rate a cow's capacity to suffer. What they found was that after consuming beef, participants reported a more restricted moral concern for animals in general, and specifically rated a cow as less capable of suffering. It would seem that this response may work to reduce any negative feelings that people experience when they are eating meat (see also Bratanova, Loughnan, & Bastian, 2011).

To test this possibility directly, Bastian et al. (2012) had participants provide some ratings of the mental capacities of a cow, amongst a range of other measures. They were then led to believe that they would be participating in a consumer survey and would either be sampling meat or green apples. Right before they were about to sample the food, participants were asked to briefly fill in the same measure of mind attribution to the cow and they also rated their positive and negative emotions. Participants who anticipated meat consumption attributed the cow lesser mental capacities, right before they were about to eat meat. This was compared to their perception of a cow's mind at the beginning of the experiment, which was similar to the amount of mind attributed by the control group at the beginning of the experiment and also right before they were about the sample the apples. Those who were about to eat meat, but not those who were about to eat fruit, strategically diminished their perception of the cow's mind right at a time when it would most interfere with their meat consumption.

This finding is consistent with previous research showing that both situational and chronic meat consumption lowers mind attribution (Bilewicz, Imhoff, & Drogosz, 2011). Importantly, people in the meat condition who ascribed diminished mental capacities to the cow reported less negative emotion when anticipating meat consumption. This finding suggests that by diminishing their perceptions of an animal's mental capacities (making them seem less human-like), people can alleviate unpleasant feelings aroused by meat consumption.

Meat-eating provides an excellent example of a context in which human needs conflict with the needs or rights of a particular resource, and how those needs may motivate people to perceive the world in a way that allows them to satisfy those needs. As we note, however, moral motives may also extend to concerns over the use of less sentient resources such as the protection of rainforests, rivers, or reefs. Indeed, others have also argued that the protection of these environmental entities is understood by many as a moral issue (Feinberg & Willer, 2013; Markowitz & Shariff, 2012; Singer, 2002). Yet, just as in the case of meat, the protection of these environmental entities may also come at a cost.

The motivation to satisfy human needs appears to shape people's reasoning and judgments around the use of resources that are capable of satisfying those needs. This occurs by shifting attitudes and perceptions in ways that facilitate need satisfaction. Specifically, by diminishing the extent to which resources are viewed as morally relevant, which may entail denying their possession of morally relevant qualities, people are less troubled by the use of those resources to satisfy their needs.

It is perhaps interesting to draw a parallel between work on meat-eating and work on sexual objectification. Although people are by no means resources in the same way that animals can be, the use of others for the satisfaction of sexual desire can certainly shape our perceptions of others so that they are viewed as more resource-like. Indeed, the satisfaction of sexual desire is a strong motivator of a large proportion of human behavior, and different lines of research have shown that when attuned to sexual desires men view female targets in more instrumental ways—they objectify them.

Providing direct support to this process, Vaes, Paladino, and Puvia (2011) showed that activating the goal of sex led men (although not women) to view female targets in more objectified ways: sexual attraction shifted a man's focus away from a women's personality and onto her body, triggering a diminished perception of her human qualities. This work suggests that viewing women as less human-like may allow men to satisfy their sexual desires by treating them as instruments of need satisfaction rather than full human beings that are valuable in their own right. Providing converging support for this process, Loughnan et al. (2010b) showed that objectified women (those who were shown wearing minimal clothing or whose body was the focus in photographs), as well as objectified men, were attributed with fewer mental capacities and rated as deserving less moral concern: they were literally viewed as more like objects than people.

This work on objectification, together with the other research reviewed here, shows that both humans and nonhumans are sometimes used as resources in order to satisfy people's needs or drives. When human need satisfaction conflicts with our moral consideration for other entities, people are motivated to find ways to change their perceptions of those entities in order to satiate their needs. Whether those needs relate to hunger, sexual desire, or financial gain, they moderate the extent to which moral standards, considerations, or concerns shape behavior.

## A "Third Dimension" to Resource Dilemmas?

Our analysis suggests that there are, at least some, cases where our decisions over resource use are shaped by a moral consideration of the resources themselves. The morality of resource allocation and resource use is not only tied up in how those decisions affect (human) consumer needs, but also in the rights and wrongs of resource use itself. As we noted earlier, we believe this line of thinking has been largely absent from work focusing on how resource dilemmas are resolved.

Traditionally, scholars have focused on resource dilemmas as social problems that exist between the competing needs of two human parties (also referred to as "commons dilemmas" or the "tragedy of the commons"; Axelrod, 1984; Dawes, 1980; Kollock, 1998). This approach is adequate for cases where resources are only of extrinsic value. For instance, in most games designed to test how people resolve resource dilemmas, numerical points, or at most money, are used as the focal resource (Van Lange, Joireman, Parks, & Van Dijk, 2013). This is, of course, not reflective of resource dilemmas in the real world. As we noted at the beginning of this chapter, resources such as rainforest, rivers, and reefs invite a range of other considerations, as does the use of animals for food. While coal or iron ore may be reducible to numbers or monetary value, the impacts of mining cannot. Resource dilemmas are not simply defined by egalitarian approaches to the maximization of extrinsic value; rather, they are powerfully shaped by intrinsic qualities such as sentience, beauty, and uniqueness. The value of a rainforest cannot be accounted for in terms of its wood, and the value of a river cannot be defined by its potential to provide irrigation and produce hydroelectricity. Just so, the value of an animal cannot be accounted by its ability to provide meat, and the value of a person cannot be accounted for by their ability to provide sex.

We argue that considering the intrinsic value of resources brings a necessary third dimension to resource dilemmas. Focusing only on selfishness and altruism between interacting human parties is no longer sufficient for understanding how resource issues are resolved (e.g., Fehr & Fischbacher, 2003). In the real world, people's consideration of the intrinsic value of resources themselves impacts on decision making regarding resource allocation and resource use. To date, however, we know of no research to explicitly take up this challenge. We believe that taking account of this third dimension promises to provide fertile territory for novel research endeavors. Next we outline some of our own current research directions on this issue and the specific research questions that are motiving them.

What happens when we introduce a focus on the intrinsic value of resources to resource dilemmas? How would this critical change to common resource dilemma paradigms affect people's tendency to cooperate together? We suggest that framing resources as intrinsically valuable should have a number of important effects. First, it should lead to less greed in taking resources for oneself. Maximizing the amount of money or points that one receives has implications for reciprocal cooperation from others; however, maximizing the number of old-growth trees, or number of cows for personal meat consumption, may also come with other more moral implications. These may range from personal discomfort with one's own greed to reputational concerns, extending beyond the willingness to cooperate with others to one's motivation to prevent harm.

Second, we suggest that a focus on intrinsic value should also moderate the ways in which people respond to defectors. When others take more points or money for themselves the best response is to do the same in return. Indeed it was exactly this strategy—the tit-for-tat strategy (Axelrod, 2006)—that was found to be most robust in promoting cooperation in the prisoner's dilemma game. Yet, when we consider the dilemma faced by environmentalists and logging companies over the use of forests for wood, this strategy is unlikely to be adopted. Imagine the environmentalists cutting down more trees to punish the loggers every time they take too many for themselves. When people are focused on the intrinsic value of a resource, and as such are motivated to prevent its destruction, they will seek ways to *prevent* its use rather than to *equalize* its use. This suggests that such individuals will aim to influence the behavior of others in less direct ways. For instance they may continue with their own strategies, hoping to lead by example, or they may engage in self-sacrificial behavior, either by taking less for themselves or by expending their own resources to prevent further harm. When focusing parties on the intrinsic as opposed to the extrinsic value of a resource, cooperative strategies are likely to be more robust against defection. This may, of course, produce other problems in the longer term—such as occurs when perpetrators are not punished appropriately—yet it nonetheless suggests that how a resource is valued can fundamentally change how resource dilemmas are resolved.

Third, we argue that a focus on intrinsic value should not only ensure that cooperation is more robust against defection, but should also promote increased cooperation, and potentially even some level of self-sacrifice, when it comes to first offers. If motivated to protect a resource, people will be motivated to ensure that they will be able to establish cooperation from other parties. To achieve this, first offers may be used to communicate cooperative intent, as well as perhaps conservational intent. To this extent, people will be more egalitarian, and perhaps more conservative, in their initial allocation of resources where other parties are able to make resource allocation decisions in return.

We believe that further exploration of these possibilities holds a number of promising and important insights. Specifically, it suggests that although the needs of humans and nonhumans often collide in the course of resource conflicts and resource decision making, focusing on the intrinsic qualities of resources may promote increased cooperation between humans. Of course, this may not lead to increased satisfaction of human needs, but it would lead to the increased preservation of resources themselves.

Our own work is currently investigating these research questions in a variety of ways, from attempts to understand how people conceptualize intrinsic value and seek to protect intrinsically valuable entities, to the ways in which the introduction of such value may change economic decision making. We believe that uncovering the various ways in which people value resources, and how this may in turn affect human cooperation, is a research question that has significant practical and theoretical value.

## The Future of Resource Conflicts: Implications for Policy

We believe that a moral psychology of resource use would make a valuable contribution to the fields of moral psychology and environmental psychology. Beyond its capacity to generate new knowledge, however, we also think that it would provide valuable insights into policy development.

Perhaps the most obvious is the link between how resources are framed in terms of their value and the implications that this might have for resource conservation and human cooperation. Indeed, such is the approach employed by environmental groups when seeking to protect old-growth forests or other natural resources. These groups seek to focus people's attention on the historical importance, the uniqueness, and the irreplaceability of natural entities. In doing so they seek to remind people that old-growth forests are not simply unharvested wood, but that they are intrinsically valuable and deserve to be protected as things of value in and of themselves. This same approach is evident in the case of groups who advocate for animal protection and animal rights. Reminding people that animals are sentient and intelligent creatures is a powerful way to interrupt their use of them for food or other instrumental purposes. Understanding the psychology behind these strategies could provide important avenues through which policy makers can seek the protection of resources that are either scarce or whose destruction has become unpalatable.

A less canvassed contribution is the link between a focus on intrinsic value and human cooperation around resource consumption. These links have yet to receive solid empirical attention, and as such many of the policy implications are yet to be realized. Nonetheless, should the tendency to focus on intrinsic rather than extrinsic value shape human cooperation, this insight would provide valuable and immediate inroads into managing resource dilemmas globally.

Most critically, however, is the role of psychology in guiding and directing policy around resource bottlenecks. As we noted at the beginning of this chapter, there is a pressure cooker effect that is already well on its way to overheating. Increased human population means that more resources are required, some of which are becoming scarce, and when this is paired with expanding moral concern for an ever-growing list of entities it suggests that conflicts around resource allocation, resource consumption, and resource protection will become increasingly prominent in the years to come. These issues will become the focal point for social policy in the near future and the greater the role that moral psychologists and moral psychology are afforded, we believe, the better the outcomes.

## Conclusions

Our world is growing, not only in terms of those who are competing over resources, but also in terms of those who are considered to have a right to protection from harm. A moral psychology of resource use is needed to successfully navigate the various pressure points that are increasingly sensitive within this debate. We have offered some general insights into the nature of these issues, and some initial research findings. The field of moral psychology is growing, as is the field of environmental psychology, and we believe that by bringing these two bodies of knowledge together it will be possible to make an important contribution, not only to the literature, but also to public policy and public debate.

## References

ABC. (2014, December 22). Captive orangutan Sandra has human right to freedom, Argentine court rules. Retrieved from http://www.abc.net.au/news/2014–12–22/captive-orangutan-has-human-right-to-freedom/5983440

Allen, M., Hunstone, M., Waerstad, J., Foy, E., Hobbins, T., Wikner, B., & Wirrel, J. (2002). Human-to-animal similarity and participant mood influence punishment recommendations for animal abusers. *Society & Animals, 10,* 267–284.

Amiot, C.E., & Bastian, B. (2014). Toward a psychology of human-animal relations. *Psychological Bulletin, 141*(1), 6–47.

Aquino, K., & Reed, A. (2002). The self-importance of moral identity. *Journal of Personality and Social Psychology, 83*(6), 1423–1440.

Axelrod, R. (1984). *The evolution of cooperation.* New York: Basic Books.

Axelrod, R. (2006). *The evolution of cooperation* (Rev. ed.). New York: Basic Books.

Bastian, B., Laham, S.M., Wilson, S., Haslam, N., & Koval, P. (2011). Blaming, praising, and protecting our humanity: The implications of everyday dehumanization for judgments of moral status. *British Journal of Social Psychology, 50*(3), 469–483.

Bastian, B., Loughnan, S., Haslam, N., & Radke, H.R. (2012). Don't mind meat? The denial of mind to animals used for human consumption. *Personality and Social Psychology Bulletin, 38*(2), 247–256.

Bilewicz, M., Imhoff, R., & Drogosz, M. (2011). The humanity of what we eat: Conceptions of human uniqueness among vegetarians and omnivores. *European Journal of Social Psychology, 41*(2), 201–209.

Bratanova, B., Loughnan, S., & Bastian, B. (2011). The effect of categorization as food on the perceived moral standing of animals. *Appetite, 57*(1), 193–196.

Crimston, D., Bain, P.G., Hornsey, M.J., & Bastian, B. (in press). Moral expansiveness: Examining variability in the extension of the moral world. *Journal of Personality and Social Psychology.*

Davis, M.H. (1983). Measuring individual differences in empathy: Evidence for a multidimensional approach. *Journal of Personality and Social Psychology, 44*(1), 113–126.

Dawes, R.M. (1980). Social dilemmas. *Annual Review of Psychology, 31*, 169–193.

Duffy, C. (2012, June 14). World's largest marine reserve network unveiled. *ABC News.* Retrieved from http://www.abc.net.au/news/2012–06–14/burke-announces-marine-parks-reserve/4069532

Epley, N., Akalis, S., Waytz, A., & Cacioppo, J.T. (2008). Creating social connection through inferential reproduction: loneliness and perceived agency in gadgets, gods, and greyhounds. *Psychological Science, 19*(2), 114–120.

Epley, N., Waytz, A., & Cacioppo, J.T. (2007). On seeing human: a three-factor theory of anthropomorphism. *Psychological Review, 114*(4), 864–886.

Fairbrother, A. (2012). I, River: In New Zealand, the Whanganui river becomes a legal person. *Takepart.com.* Retrieved from http://www.takepart.com/article/2012/09/13/new-zealand-river-becomes-person

Fehr, E., & Fischbacher, U. (2003). The nature of human altruism. *Nature, 425*(6960), 785–791.

Feinberg, M., & Willer, R. (2013). The moral roots of environmental attitudes. *Psychological Science, 24*(1), 56–62.

Ford, S. (2012, December 19). Tarkine mine to begin development in "near future": Shree, *Advocate.* Retrieved from http://www.theadvocate.com.au/story/1195747/tarkine-mine-to-begin-development-in-near-future-shree/

Gray, K., Young, L., & Waytz, A. (2012). Mind perception is the essence of morality. *Psychological Inquiry, 23*(2), 101–124.

Haidt, J. (2012). *The righteous mind: Why good people are divided by politics and religion.* London: Allen Lane.

Hardin, G. (1968). The tragedy of the commons. The population problem has no technical solution; it requires a fundamental extension in morality. *Science, 162*(3859), 1243–1248.

Herzog, H. (2010). *Some we love, some we hate, some we eat: Why it's so hard to think straight about animals.* New York: Harper.

Joy, M. (2010). *Why we love dogs, eat pigs and wear cows: An introduction to carnism.* Enfield, UK: Conari Press.

Kollock, P. (1998). Social dilemmas: The anatomy of cooperation. *Annual Review of Sociology, 24*, 183–214.

Lecky, W.E.H. (1869). *History of European morals from Augustus to Charlemagne* (Vol. 1). London: Longmans, Green.

Loughnan, S., Haslam, N., & Bastian, B. (2010a). The role of meat consumption in the denial of moral status and mind to meat animals. *Appetite, 55*(1), 156–159.

Loughnan, S., Haslam, N., Murnane, T., Vaes, J., Reynolds, C., & Suitner, C. (2010b). Objectification leads to depersonalization: The denial of mind and moral concern to objectified others. *European Journal of Social Psychology, 40*(5), 709–717.

Markowitz, E.M., & Shariff, A.F. (2012). Climate change and moral judgement: Psychological challenges and opportunities. *Nature Climate Change, 2*(4), 243–247.

Mayer, F.S., & Frantz, C.M. (2004). The connectedness to nature scale: A measure of individuals' feeling in community with nature. *Journal of Environmental Psychology, 24*(4), 503–515.

McFarland, S., Webb, M., & Brown, D. (2012). All humanity is my ingroup: A measure and studies of identification with all humanity. *Journal of Personality and Social Psychology, 103*(5), 850–853.

Pinker, S. (2011). *The better angels of our nature: Why violence has declined.* New York: Viking.

Plous, S. (1993). Psychological mechanisms in the human use of animals. *Journal of Social Issues, 49*(1), 11–52.

Rose, L., & Marshall, F. (1996). Meat eating, hominid sociality, and home bases revisited. *Current Anthropology, 37*, 307–338.

Ruby, M.B., & Heine, S.J. (2012). Too close to home. Factors predicting meat avoidance. *Appetite, 59*(1), 47–52.

Schwartz, S.H. (2007). Universalism values and the inclusiveness of our moral universe. *Journal of Cross-Cultural Psychology, 38*(6), 711–728.

Singer, P. (1975). *Animal liberation: A new ethics for our treatment of animals.* New York: Random House.

Singer, P. (1981). *The expanding circle: Ethics and sociobiology.* New York: Farrar, Straus & Giroux.

Singer, P. (2002). *One world: The ethics of globalisation.* Melbourne: Text Publishing.

Stern, P.C., & Dietz, T. (1994). The value basis of environmental concern. *Journal of Social Issues, 50*(3), 65–84.

Vaes, J., Paladino, P., & Puvia, E. (2011). Are sexualized women complete human beings? Why men and women dehumanize sexually objectified women. *European Journal of Social Psychology, 41*(6), 774–785.

Van Lange, P.A.M., Joireman, J., Parks, C.D., & Van Dijk, E. (2013). The psychology of social dilemmas: A review. *Organizational Behavior and Human Decision Processes, 120*, 125–141.

Waytz, A., Gray, K., Epley, N., & Wegner, D.M. (2010). Causes and consequences of mind perception. *Trends in Cognitive Science, 14*(8), 383–388.

# 17

# OF BABOONS AND ELEPHANTS

## Inequality and the Evolution of Immoral Leadership

*William von Hippel, Richard Ronay, and*
*William W. Maddux*

*Moral judgments and behaviors lie at the heart of numerous human social activities, including interpersonal relationships, political judgments, intergroup relations, and prosocial behavior (Brandt, Wetherell, & Crawford; Frimer; Graziano & Schroeder; and Simpson, Farrell, & Marshall, this volume). In this chapter we focus on the morality of group leaders, asking what causes leaders to behave in a moral or immoral fashion. Clearly there are numerous situational and dispositional factors that induce leaders to be moral or immoral. One such factor is the presence of inequality of opportunity within the group. We suggest that increasing inequality makes immoral individuals more attracted to leadership positions and also makes individual leaders more likely to behave in an immoral fashion. To explore this possibility we take an evolutionary perspective on the development of cooperation and competition within and between groups.*

## On Human Origins

Humans and chimpanzees shared a chimp-like common ancestor approximately six million years ago. Although there are only clues in the fossil record about what might have caused the split between us and our chimp cousins, one speculative but compelling theory that links together much of the evidence is the "East Side Story" (Coppens, 1994). According to this account, the critical event that led to the evolution of *Homo sapiens* was a shift in the tectonic plates that led to the Great African Rift Valley approximately eight million years ago. As a consequence of this change in geology, the rainforests on the east side of the Rift Valley began to dry out and were replaced by savannah. It was the necessity of adapting to this savannah that presumably led our proto-chimp ancestors to diverge down the pathway that led to modern humans.

Chimpanzees occupy a dominant position in the rainforests, with very few predators that can hunt them successfully in the canopy (particularly when they are with other members of their group; Boesch, 1991). In contrast, chimps are relatively easy prey on the ground as they cannot move rapidly, and their comparatively small size makes them vulnerable to attack by large cats such as lions and leopards and other predators such as hunting dogs and hyenas. The replacement of the rainforest with savannah would have put enormous pressure on our proto-chimp ancestors, as they would have found themselves much more vulnerable to predators than they were in the rainforest they had once occupied. No doubt most of the proto-chimps would have perished in this new environment, but one possible response to this newfound vulnerability to attack would have been collective action. A single chimp throwing stones at a hungry predator is likely to end up in the belly of an angry beast, but many chimps throwing stones could potentially drive off lions, hyenas, and other potential predators. Thus, proto-chimps who survived this evolutionary pressure cooker were likely those who had the capacity or innate tendency to be particularly cooperative with each other, thereby initiating the evolution of modern humans.

Although this account clearly goes well beyond what the fossil record can tell us, it is consistent with anatomical changes that have emerged between us and our chimp cousins. For example, chimpanzees cannot lock their knees, but the fossil evidence suggests that our ancestor *Australopithecus afarensis* (who roamed East Africa 3 million years ago) probably could (Crompton et al., 2012). Locked knees, in turn, provide a much better platform for hard and accurate throwing of projectiles, and consistent with this line of reasoning, *A. afarensis* shows evidence of adaptations in the hand for precise and forceful throwing (Marzke, 1983). Relatedly, chimps and our other great ape cousins have eyes that are entirely brown, whereas the sclera of our eyes is white, providing a readily detected signal of gaze direction. Such a change in eye color could easily be an adaptation to a world in which it was advantageous for us to communicate to our fellow group members where we are looking rather than to hide that information. In other words, the creation of the savannah might have also created a niche for apes who cooperate with each other more than they compete with each other.

The advantage of the emerging ability to read behavioral cues, such as where others' attention is directed, is supported by another profound anatomical difference between humans and our primate cousins: our impressively developed brains (Dunbar, 1998). The human brain is a resource-hungry piece of neural architecture. Although constituting only about 2% of our body weight, our brains consume roughly 20% of our daily caloric intake. These costs suggest that large brains will only develop when the selection factors in their favor are sufficient to overcome the steep cost gradient associated with their maintenance. This striking development in humans is due in large part to the dramatic expansion of our neocortex, a piece of neural architecture that facilitates our capacity for understanding others' thoughts, feelings, and motivations. This capacity to understand others, known as theory of mind, provides profound advantages for cooperative enterprises. The evolution of language also provides us with direct means of probing others' goals, prescribing and enforcing behavioral norms, and generally coordinating behavior in ways that facilitate efficient solutions to problems of collective action (Alvard & Nolin, 2002; Boehm, 2000; Pinker, 2010).

If we accept that this evolutionary story, or something like it, represents our ancestral pathway to the present, we can see the potential for group leadership in humans that is a blend of self-serving and group serving. On the group-serving side, *Homo sapiens* have been successful in large part due to our ability to work well as a team, and thus human leaders are likely to depend upon, exemplify, and facilitate the group orientation that such teamwork demands (Van Vugt, 2006). On the self-serving side, however, natural selection acts on individual organisms to maximize their inclusive fitness, and thus any benefits that accrue uniquely to group leaders as a function of their leadership role are likely to nudge human leaders to consider their personal and nepotistic desires ahead of those of their group. For the purposes of the current chapter, it is this tension between group- and self-orientation that determines the morality of leadership. Moral leaders are those who act in their group's interest, and thus benefit from their decisions only to the degree that their group benefits. We refer to such moral leaders as *elephants*. Immoral leaders are those who act out of self-interest, and thus benefit from their decisions at the expense of the group. We refer to such immoral leaders as *baboons*.

## Elephants and Baboons

Adult male elephants are formidable creatures. With few if any natural predators, they live either alone or in somewhat fluid groups with each other, and thus long-term elephant groups are composed exclusively of adult females and juvenile males and females. In principle, the strongest male elephant could impose himself as leader over the herd, but there is no incentive for him to do so. Their plant food sources are not readily monopolized, and females announce their fertility to all males in their vicinity, and so males must compete for sexual access whether they are in the group or reside miles away. Thus, the leader of long-term groups of elephants is typically one of the oldest females in the group (i.e., the matriarch), and she is relied upon to coordinate group movements, migration, and responses to threats (McComb, Moss, Durant, Baker, & Sayialel, 2001; McComb et al., 2011). Because leadership does not give her preferential access to food sources or mating opportunities, the elephant leader does not gain fitness benefits from her position at the top of the dominance hierarchy (Archie, Morrison, Foley, Moss, & Alberts, 2006). Rather, leadership in elephant groups provides a mutual benefit to all members of the group in a manner that is predominantly group serving. For these reasons, elephants are by nature "moral" (i.e., group-serving) leaders.

Baboons sit on the other end of the continuum. Despite their intimidating canines, because of their relatively small size baboons are preyed upon by hyenas and large cats such as leopards and lions. Consequently, there is safety in numbers, and male and female savannah baboons live together in troops of varying sizes. Although baboon troops do not have leaders in the sense of an individual who provides guidance or protection to group members, they do compete fiercely for dominance over one another. Females' position in the dominance hierarchy is inherited from their mother, but males leave the troop of their birth to join another group, and so must attempt to dominate other members of the troop through continual threats or acts of aggression.

Because the alpha male provides no guidance to the troop, the goal of dominance over other baboons is entirely self-serving. The benefits available to group members (access to fertile females, preferred foods, shady resting spots, etc.) are impossible to monopolize, but they are nonetheless disproportionately dominated by the alpha male (Sapolsky, 2007). Although it is clearly not beneficial to other members of the baboon troop to be dominated in such a manner, they are largely unable to prevent this outcome. Traits such as physical size, aggression, and an indomitable disposition have been selected for in baboon males as they facilitate dominance of the troop, which in turn provides reproductive opportunities that permit these traits to flourish (Sapolsky, 2007). For these reasons, baboons are by nature "immoral" (i.e., self-serving) leaders.

One takeaway from the contrasting examples of elephant versus baboon leadership is that resources matter (see also Bastian & Crimston, this volume). With regard to diet, the inability of herbivorous elephants to monopolize the abundant and widespread plant matter necessary to meet their massive energy needs contrasts with that of baboons and their omnivorous diet. The relative scarcity of high-calorie foods (particularly meat) available to baboons imposes strong selective pressures on dominance. Baboons compete fiercely for food, and control over food sharing even allows baboon leaders to buy and maintain allies (Silk, 2005), which can be critical to maintaining alpha status.

Perhaps more importantly, differences in opportunities for reproduction contribute to the type of leader that emerges. Because elephant leaders are female, they experience no reproductive advantage as a consequence of their role, and (as noted earlier) the social structure of elephant herds excludes the possibility of males usurping the leadership position. On the other hand, approximately 50% of the variance in reproductive success of male baboons is accounted for by their rank in the hierarchy (Cowlishaw & Dunbar, 1991; Alberts, Watts, & Altmann, 2003), which imposes strong selective pressure on achieving a dominant position within the troop. Disgruntled troop-mates can either mount a challenge or try to join another group where they might be more successful. Either way, the troop provides important protection and more eyes to detect predators, and so non-dominant males still prefer group living to trying their chances alone.

## Elephants and Baboons as Types of Leaders

There is a tension between the self-serving and group-serving goals of all human leaders, and most human leaders are a blend of baboon and elephant. Some saintly leaders, like Nelson Mandela, seem to be elephant through and through, and some despotic leaders, like Robert Mugabe, seem to be baboon through and through. Elephant-like leaders seem to maintain a group orientation under most circumstances, but baboon-like leaders are very sensitive to threats to their leadership, and thus they shift in their group orientation versus self-orientation depending on internal and external threats.

The clearest example of such situational shifting can be found in the work of Maner and colleagues. For example, Maner and Mead (2010) demonstrated that when baboon leaders (i.e., those high in dominance orientation) feel that their leadership position is threatened by subordinates, they limit their information sharing with their group and exclude talented members, at a cost to group performance. Case and Maner (2014) went on to demonstrate that baboon leaders also rely on the tried-and-true "divide and conquer" strategy when they feel their leadership position is threatened by talented team members. Such leaders restrict intragroup communication, particularly with talented group members, and try to prevent them from bonding with one another. The immorality of this leadership strategy is highlighted by their efforts to exclude and isolate only the talented; highly talented group members are the most capable of helping the group, and thus these actions place the leader's goals in direct opposition to their group's goals. Furthermore, these immoral leadership behaviors disappear when baboon leaders are assured of their leadership position, again providing evidence that baboon leaders know how to enhance group performance but choose not to do so when their own stature is at risk.

Immoral leadership behaviors also disappear when baboon leaders find their group in competition with other groups. Under such circumstances, even baboon leaders rally round to act in their group's interest (Maner & Mead, 2010), as group and leader goals—even baboon leader goals—are brought into alignment by the fact that failure in intergroup competition could lead to extermination of the entire group (or at least all the males in the group). This sort of intergroup competition is a challenge that humans have faced over evolutionary time, and it has shaped our psychology to accept and even prefer more dominant leaders during times of intergroup rivalry (Van Vugt & Spisak, 2008). Such psychological responses to intragroup and intergroup pressures might easily be adaptations to group living in a species that shows substantial cooperation within groups but often ruthless competition between groups.

Experiments such as those of Case and Maner (2014) and Maner and Mead (2010) provide compelling evidence for the sensitivity that leaders have to different types of threats to their leadership positions, but they do not indicate when leadership positions will be particularly attractive to baboon versus elephant types. Our brief account of the causal role played by resource availability and distribution in shaping the contrasting "leadership" styles of baboons and elephants might offer just such a perspective through which to examine the emergence of moral or immoral leadership in humans. In particular, one way to address this question is to look to our ancestral past by examining the styles of leadership that emerge in small-scale societies of the type in which we are thought to have evolved and spent most of our history. We consider two such groups here: hunter-gather groups as exemplified by the Hadza (description based on Marlowe, 2010) and hunter-horticulturalist groups as exemplified by the Yanomamö (description based on Chagnon, 2013).

## The Hadza and the Yanomamö

The Hadza are hunter-gatherers who live in northern Tanzania (a section of East Africa in which *Homo sapiens* is thought to have evolved). They live in relatively small and fluid groups of individuals (mean = 30, median = 21) who set up temporary camps for a few weeks or months at a time. The Hadza typically move to a new location when the local water hole dries up, or the women have exhausted the local resources and must travel uncomfortable distances to gather foods. Because of their nomadic lifestyle, the Hadza only own as much as they can carry, and thus the total sum of their individual possessions is very limited (e.g., jewelry, clothes, knives and axes, and bows and arrows among the men; jewelry, clothes, digging sticks, and cooking pots among the women).

The Hadza make all of their group decisions through discussion, and they have no explicit leaders. Older men and women are given a degree of deference, but do not actually lead, and individuals who try to dominate others quickly find themselves shunned. Because individual Hadza can change groups at their own discretion, would-be leaders have very little power to enforce their will over group members. Hadza are largely egalitarian and peaceful, with violence within or between groups being the exception rather than the rule. Hadza are also monogamous with female choice, and a couple are considered to have married when they set up house together. In his survey of childbirths, Marlowe (2010) found the range in the number of children born to individual men to be from zero to 16 (mean = 4.5).

The Yanomamö are hunter-horticulturalists who live in the Amazon basin of Venezuela and Brazil. Their villages also move on occasion, but much more rarely than the Hadza. As a consequence, their domiciles are more permanent structures and they tend to own more implements. Their villages also grow to a much more substantial size than those of the Hadza, sometimes over 300 individuals in a single village. Most people prefer to live in smaller villages of the size typical of Hadza camps (and for the same reason that the Hadza prefer smaller groups: because they lead to less bickering), and the headmen in such smaller villages tend to lead by example rather than force. Nevertheless, some leaders wield a great deal of power and prevent their groups from fissioning despite the wishes of their group members. Part of the motivation of the group leader to maintain group membership is that many of the villages are in a near constant state of war with each other, and larger villages have an advantage in this regard over smaller ones.

Many leaders among the Yanomamö are despotic and cruel. Such leaders hold group members in sway through the threat of personal violence, and typically rely on a network of male kin as their power base. Conflicts are resolved through various forms of violence, from side slapping and wrestling for minor disputes, through ritualized club fights, ending in deadly tit-for-tat raids between villages. Yanomamö are polygynous, often with very little female choice, as powerful males have systems of trading their female kin with each other for wives. Wives are treated very poorly by many such men, who abuse them at will. Violence appears to be a predominant route to obtain both leadership positions and wives, as men who have killed another (*unokais*) have more wives (mean = 1.63) than men who have not (mean = .63). Commensurate with their greater number of wives, *unokais* also have more children (mean = 4.91) than men who have not killed (mean = 1.59). By virtue of their large numbers of wives, some Yanomamö leaders have very large numbers of children (e.g., Chagnon, 2013, documents one leader as having 43 children and 229 grandchildren).

## Inequality and the Emergence of Baboon Leaders

Why are Hadza egalitarian and peaceful *elephants* while Yanomamö leaders are often despotic and violent *baboons*? No doubt many factors are involved, but opportunity for monopolizing resources appears to play an important role. Reminiscent of the ever-grazing elephants described earlier, individuals within nomadic societies such as the Hadza encounter fewer opportunities for accumulating and controlling resources than those in more sedentary hunter-horticulturalist societies such as the Yanomamö. When resources can be controlled and used to leverage deference and compliance from others, they give rise to the more competitive and self-serving aspects of our psychology. Indeed, the historical shift from hunter-gatherer societies to more settled horticulturalist practices was a critical point in the shift from egalitarianism to despotism in many human societies (Boehm, 1993; Diamond, 1997).

One critical feature allowed by a horticultural lifestyle is the capacity to afford more than one wife. The differential reproductive success of Yanomamö men as a function of whether they have killed another and are high in the dominance hierarchy is not possible among Hadza men, who are almost never capable of provisioning more than one wife. In this manner, female choice and monogamy that emerges among the Hadza (largely because of their nomadic hunter-gatherer lifestyle) leads to an elephant leadership style, whereas polygyny and lack of female choice that emerges among the Yanomamö (largely enabled through their more sedentary hunter-horticultural lifestyle) leads to a baboon leadership style. Indeed, this potential for polygyny likely plays a critical role in shaping the morality of leaders that emerge across very different types of societies (Betzig, 1982).

Immediate return societies like the Hadza, in which people consume what they hunt and gather on a daily basis, typically rely on community-wide sharing and egalitarianism, as it is in everyone's interest for hunters to share their bounty. Even the best hunters are frequently likely to come home empty-handed, and so mandated sharing serves as an insurance policy against a series of failed hunts (Kaplan & Gurven, 2005). Successful hunters who brag about their spoils are also criticized, and so humility too becomes normative, even among the most skilled (von Rueden, 2014). When individuals do display self-aggrandizing behavior, coalitions of subordinates quickly form to ostracize the conceited, thereby stymieing any coercive influence such individuals might otherwise develop over the group (Boehm, 1999).

The resultant enforced equality of Hadza society—with hunters required to share their kill, normative humility, people owning very few possessions, and women free to choose their own partners (and thus reproductive success spread relatively evenly across society)—means that there is little to be gained for the self through despotic leadership. Not only does such despotism meet stiff resistance from others who have equal access to resources and thus are not dependent on would-be leaders (see Boehm, 1999), but there are no additional resources that can be garnered by such a strategy. Rather, wise counsel can help the group be more successful, and all individuals benefit to the degree that their group benefits. Indeed, to the degree that individuals gain anything by offering their leadership during group decision making, it is through the increased prestige they garner by demonstrating wisdom, compassion, and so forth. Thus, leadership can only be obtained momentarily and situationally in Hadza society, and *the goals of would-be leaders are of necessity aligned with their group*. Another way of expressing this concept is that the inherent selfishness that is part of human nature and the inherent group orientation that is also part of human nature are aligned by the structure of Hadza society: toward elephant leadership (or *prestige-based* leadership, in the terms of Henrich & Gil-White, 2001; see also Cheng, Tracy, Foulsham, Kingstone, & Henrich, 2013).

In contrast, even though the Yanomamö also have few possessions, as noted earlier there is the potential for substantial inequality in Yanomamö marriage systems. This inequality raises the possibility that men can be rewarded for their dominance and status seeking, as wives are obtained in part through violence against others (particularly other groups) and in part through alliances that can be more readily controlled by those in leadership positions. As a consequence, violent and despotic leaders have substantially greater reproductive success than nonviolent individuals and people who are not in leadership positions. Thus, in sharp contrast to Hadza society, the structure of Yanomamö society allows the selfishness inherent in human nature to oppose the group orientation inherent in human nature. The result of this motivational tension is a leadership style that varies both with circumstance and with the personalities and proclivities of individual leaders. Particularly in smaller villages, a group orientation is common and leadership is often elephant-like. But because Yanomamö society has the potential for great inequality, a self-orientation is rewarded and the resultant leadership is often baboon-like—based on dominance over others rather than helpful guidance (or *dominance-based* in the terms of Henrich & Gil-White, 2001).

## From Small-Scale Societies to Large-Scale Corporations

If we fast-forward to modern corporations, we can see many of the same inequality-based dynamics of Yanomamö society at work; modern corporations are structured in a manner more similar to the Yanomamö than the Hadza, and as a result they incentivize baboon-type leadership. For example, the average CEO salary of the top 350 companies in the world was $14.1 million in 2013 (DePillis, 2013). As a consequence, competition for such roles can be fierce (Jacquart & Armstrong, 2013; Jensen & Murphy, 1990; Malmendier & Tate, 2009), and elephant leaders are often insufficiently motivated to go head-to-head with baboon leaders who are less ethically constrained and more strongly motivated by status, power, and financial reward (although followers are, of course, highly motivated to select elephant leaders). Baboon leaders also benefit from the fact that enormous financial rewards can accrue irrespective of performance. Aligning the goals and interests of the leaders (e.g., CEOs) and followers (e.g., stockholders) via equity motivates leaders to make value-maximizing decisions for the firm (Harris & Raviv, 1979; Holmstrom, 1979; Jensen & Murphy, 1990), but such alignment appears to be the exception rather than the rule. For example, in one study that incorporated data across five decades and thousands of CEOs in 1,400 publicly listed companies, overall CEO compensation was found to be largely unrelated to corporate performance, with little disparity in financial outcomes between successful and failed CEOs (Jensen & Murphy, 1990).

This takeover by baboons is not limited to the leadership structure of modern corporations. Similar effects can be seen across entire societies: inequality within countries brings out the baboon aspects of our psychology, as inequality makes people increasingly desperate to be one of the haves rather than the have-nots. The clearest example of this effect can be seen in the data of Loughnan et al. (2011), who show that self-enhancement increases linearly in society as a function of income inequality (measured by the Gini coefficient). For example, they show that Japan—whose citizens are famously self-effacing for reasons long thought to be associated with their high levels of collectivism—anchors the low end of the self-enhancement continuum. But Germans, who are much more individualistic, show similarly low self-enhancement to the Japanese, and Germany and Japan also happen to be countries with a high degree of economic equality. In contrast, Peru and South Africa anchor the high end of the self-enhancement continuum, and are also countries with the highest levels of inequality. These data suggest that income inequality can exacerbate our baboon psychology, as it leads people to claim to be much more than they really are. Such inflated self-claims presumably emerge in unequal societies as people strive to convince others of their abilities in an effort to be chosen for the few lucrative opportunities that exist (see von Hippel & Trivers, 2011).

One reason that self-enhancement features so prominently in baboon leaders' psychology is that it increases their perceived self-confidence, a quality that people strongly prefer in their leaders (Hogan, Curphy, & Hogan, 1994). In contrast to self-improvement, which leads to greater confidence via greater performance, self-enhancement leads to greater confidence via overconfidence, but people are largely incapable of distinguishing between confidence and overconfidence in others in the absence of objective evidence (Anderson, Brion, Moore, & Kennedy, 2012). As a consequence, people with unrealistically grand self-concepts have an advantage in leadership competitions.

For example, in a recent study by Ronay, Oostrom, and Lehmann-Willenbrock (2015), professional recruitment consultants interviewed and then rated the overconfidence of job candidates who were vying for actual leadership positions. As expected, consultants' perceptions of candidates' overconfidence were negatively related to their perceptions of the candidates' competence. Consultants' ratings of candidates' overconfidence were unrelated to an independent measure of candidates' overconfidence, however, and candidates' actual overconfidence was *positively* related to favorable leadership evaluations made by the consultants. These data suggest that perceptions of being overconfident are detrimental, but actual overconfidence facilitates leadership acquisition.

While self-enhancing tendencies may help baboons secure leadership roles, these tendencies do little to promote their effectiveness within such positions. Overconfident leaders tend to make poor decisions, ignore obvious flaws, and continue with failing plans (e.g., Schrand & Zechman, 2012; Simon & Houghton, 2003). Such inflated self-views also result in leaders who are inclined to overreward themselves due to their exaggerated sense of their own abilities. For example, narcissism (a form of self-aggrandizement) among CEOs is related to higher pay disparities between themselves and other members of their leadership teams (O'Reilly, Doerr, Caldwell, & Chatman, 2014). The fact that these pay disparities increase with the tenure of narcissistic CEOs suggests that self-aggrandizing corporate leaders are looking out for themselves at the expense of their group—a defining trait of immoral leadership.

## *What Can Be Done to Enhance Moral Leadership?*

This discussion of the evolutionary origins of immoral leadership leads naturally to a question about what can be done to rein in baboonism and promote elephantism. Given the role of inequality that has been highlighted here, an obvious answer to this question is to minimize inequality, particularly with regard to the rewards given to leaders versus other members of their group (of course, baboon leaders tend to enhance inequality and fiercely resist such efforts). In all likelihood, CEO positions would still be highly sought after even if they did not pay an average annual salary of $14 million. In the presence of such inequality, however, linking pay as tightly as possible to performance outcomes—especially long-term performance outcomes—provides a more elephant-like means of remuneration, as it aligns the interests of the leader to those of their group (Harris & Raviv, 1979; Holmstrom, 1979; Jensen & Murphy, 1990). Baboon leaders might not be attracted to CEO positions that pay only slightly more than the salary of the average employee in their corporation, or that pay a salary that is closely aligned to group performance, but that is precisely the point. Elephant leaders are likely to be willing to take on the mantle of leadership even when the financial compensation for doing so is modest and entirely dependent on their performance.

The research of Maner and Mead (2010), Van Vugt and Spisak (2008), and others (e.g., Bornstein, Gneezy, & Nagel, 2002; Sherif, 1966) also provides an avenue for minimizing immoral leadership. Ironically, conflict with other groups makes baboon leaders behave in a more moral fashion (putting their groups' interests ahead of their own), and thus intergroup conflict could provide an important avenue for enhancing leader morality. In modern corporations this sort of conflict is the basis of the market economy, as corporate collusion is forbidden by antitrust legislation. The resulting market competition facilitates success, at least to a point (Aghion, Bloom, Blundell, Griffith, & Howitt, 2005). Silicon Valley thrives on a culture of competition, in part because there is also a local culture of egalitarianism that motivates employee buy-in. Eric Schmidt (2014), executive chairman at Google, describes how the spoils of success and the weight of losses tend to be similarly shared. And this pecuniary incentive is matched by a company ethos of striving to be the best, and "do cool things that matter," a motivational slogan splashed across Google's pages and offices.

Of course, conflict-based psychological mechanisms that cause leaders to prioritize their group's goals also enable duplicitous and immoral leaders to induce their followers to prioritize their group's goals, even while the leaders themselves do not. By raising the specter of intergroup conflict, or by creating actual intergroup conflict, baboon leaders can generate greater group loyalty among their followers, even at the expense of group goals. Autocratic and dictatorial leaders throughout human history have used the generation of conflict and the creation of enemies as a strategy to reaffirm and justify their baboon leadership. This strategy is itself an example of baboon leadership, as the mere creation of unnecessary intergroup conflict is often harmful to group goals. Thus, intergroup conflict has the potential to enhance moral leadership while also serving as a cynical tool in the hands of immoral leaders.

A different sort of answer to this question can be found in the anthropological literature. That is, leaders can be controlled by their followers. Somewhere along the way, our distant ancestors who discovered that danger might be warded off by collective action, such as throwing stones at predators, also realized that despotic leaders could be deposed through collective action. Indeed, stoning unpopular leaders might well have been a strategy that followed directly from experience with stoning potential predators. More generally, in small-scale societies followers control their leaders through a variety of means (Boehm, 1993, 1999; von Rueden, 2014). At the mild end of the continuum, group members bring their leaders in line through the threat of negative public opinion, criticism, and ridicule. When this proves ineffective, group members move to disobedience and desertion. Particularly noxious leaders are subjected to exile or execution.

These strategies can be highly effective, but of course despotic leaders have their own counterstrategies available. Baboon leaders who are politically astute can survive and thrive by strategically distributing resources to allies (a strategy adopted by actual baboons), by inculcating fear in their followers (another strategy of actual baboons), and by preventing their followers from forming coalitions (a strategy that is probably too complex for monkeys but that is evident among chimps; de Waal, 1982). All of these strategies make it difficult for followers to depose their leaders.

Nevertheless, a case study of baboons in Kenya provides a gleam of hope in this regard. Sapolsky and Share (2004) describe a troop of baboons that established its territory next to a tourist lodge garbage dump. As the dump provided a steady source of food, rule of fang soon decreed it the dominion of the fiercest males, leaving the less combative to eke out a more meager existence in the adjacent forest. Then, in an ironic twist of fate, these aggressive males proved to be fighting over meat tainted with bovine tuberculosis, which soon killed them all. With the most belligerent summarily removed, the stage was reset and a new culture emerged. Left behind were the males who had been too submissive to try their luck among the dump brawlers, along with the females and infants. This change in the dominance structure ushered in a cultural shift toward pacifism and a relaxing of the characteristically fierce baboon hierarchy, a shift that has endured across more than two decades of new males entering the troop from the outside.

This case study suggests that culture really does matter, and that leaders—even those within actual baboon troops—do indeed set the "tone at the top," shaping the ethical climate of their organizations (Clinard, 1983; Treviño, 1990; Treviño, Butterfield, & McCabe, 1998; Victor & Cullen, 1988). For this reason, understanding the antecedents and predictors of immoral leadership could prove to be a first step toward bolstering leadership ethics, organizational fairness, and even corporate effectiveness.

# References

Aghion, P., Bloom, N., Blundell, R., Griffith, R., & Howitt, P. (2005). Competition and innovation: An inverted U relationship. *Quarterly Journal of Economics, 120*, 701–728.

Alberts, S.C., Watts, H.E., & Altmann, J. (2003). Queuing and queue-jumping: Long-term patterns of reproductive skew among male savannah baboons. *Animal Behavior, 65*, 821–840.

Alvard, M.S., & Nolin, D.A. (2002). Rousseau's whale hunt? Coordination among big game hunters. *Current Anthropology, 43*, 533–559.

Anderson, C., Brion, S., Moore, D. A., & Kennedy, J. A. (2012). A status-enhancement account of overconfidence. *Journal of Personality and Social Psychology, 103*, 718–735.

Archie, E.A., Morrison, T.A., Foley, C.A.H., Moss, C.J., & Alberts, S.C. (2006). Dominance rank relationships among wild female African elephants, *Loxodonta africana*. *Animal Behaviour, 71*, 117–127.

Betzig, L.L. (1982). Despotism and differential reproduction: A cross-cultural correlation of conflict asymmetry, hierarchy, and degree of polygyny. *Ethology and Sociobiology, 3*, 209–221.

Boehm, C. (1993). Egalitarian society and reverse dominance hierarchy. *Current Anthropology, 34*, 227–254.

Boehm, C. (1999). *Hierarchy in the forest: The evolution of egalitarian behavior*. Cambridge, MA: Harvard University Press.

Boehm, C. (2000). Conflict and the evolution of social control, *Journal of Consciousness Studies, 7*, 79–101.

Boesch, C. (1991). The effects of leopard predation on grouping patterns in forest chimpanzees. *Behaviour, 117*, 220–242.

Bornstein, G., Gneezy, U., & Nagel, R. (2002). The effect of intergroup competition on group coordination: An experimental study. *Games and Economic Behavior, 41*, 1–25.

Case, C.R., & Maner, J.K. (2014). Divide and conquer: When and why leaders undermine the cohesive fabric of their group. *Journal of Personality and Social Psychology, 107*, 1033–1050.

Chagnon, N.A. (2013). *Noble savages: My life among two dangerous tribes—the Yanomamö and the anthropologists*. New York: Simon and Schuster.

Cheng, J.T., Tracy, J.L., Foulsham, T., Kingstone, A., & Henrich, J. (2013). Two ways to the top: Evidence that dominance and prestige are distinct yet viable avenues to social rank and influence. *Journal of Personality and Social Psychology, 104*, 103–125.

Clinard, M.B. (1983). *Corporate ethics and crime*. Beverly Hills, CA: Sage.

Coppens, Y. (1994). East side story: The origin of humankind. *Scientific American, 270*, 88–95.

Cowlishaw, G., & Dunbar, R.I.M. (1991). Dominance rank and mating success in male primates. *Animal Behavior, 41*, 1045–1056.

Crompton, R.H., Pataky, T.C., Savage, R., D'Août, K., Bennett, M.R., Day, M.H., ... Sellers, W.I. (2012). Human-like external function of the foot, and fully upright gait, confirmed in the 3.66 million year old *Laetoli* hominin footprints by topographic statistics, experimental footprint-formation and computer simulation. *Journal of the Royal Society Interface, 9*, 707–719.

DePillis, L. (2013, June 26). Congrats, CEOs! You're making 273 times the pay of the average worker. *Washington Post*. Retrieved July 25, 2014, from http://www.washington post.com/blogs/wonkblog/wp/2013/06/26/congrats-ceos-youre-making-273-times-the-pay-of-the-average-worker/

de Waal, F.B.M. (1982). *Chimpanzee politics: Power and sex among apes.* New York: Harper & Row.

Diamond, J. (1997). *Guns, germs and steel.* London: Vintage.

Dunbar, R. (1998). The social brain hypothesis. *Evolutionary Anthropology, 6,* 178–190.

Harris, M., & Raviv, A. (1979). Optimal incentive contracts with imperfect information. *Journal of Economic Theory, 20,* 231–259.

Henrich, J., & Gil-White, F.J. (2001). The evolution of prestige: Freely conferred deference as a mechanism for enhancing the benefits of cultural transmission. *Evolution and Human Behavior, 22,* 165–196.

Hogan, R., Curphy, G.J., & Hogan, J. (1994). What we know about leadership: Effectiveness and personality. *American Psychologist, 49,* 493–504.

Holmstrom, B. (1979). Moral hazard and observability. *Bell Journal of Economics, 10,* 74–91.

Jacquart, P., & Armstrong, J.S. (2013). The ombudsman: Are top executives paid enough? An evidence-based review. *Interfaces, 43,* 580–589.

Jensen, M.C., & Murphy, K.J. (1990). CEO incentives: It's not how much you pay, but how. *Harvard Business Review, 3,* 138–153.

Kaplan, H., & Gurven, M. (2005). The natural history of human food sharing and cooperation: A review and a new multi-individual approach to the negotiation of norms. In H. Gintis, S. Bowles, R. Boyd, & E. Fehr (Eds.), *Moral sentiments and material interests: On the foundations of cooperation in economic life* (pp. 75–113). Cambridge, MA: MIT Press.

Loughnan, S., Kuppens, P., Allik, J., Balazs, K., de Lemus, S., Dumont, K., . . . Haslam., N. (2011). Economic inequality is linked to biased self-perception. *Psychological Science, 22,* 1254–1258.

Malmendier, U., & Tate, G. (2009). Superstar CEOs. *Quarterly Journal of Economics, 124,* 1593–1638.

Maner, J.K., & Mead, N.L. (2010). The essential tension between leadership and power: When leaders sacrifice group goals for the sake of self-interest. *Journal of Personality and Social Psychology, 99,* 482–97.

Marlowe, F. (2010). *The Hadza: Hunter-gatherers of Tanzania.* Berkeley: University of California Press.

Marzke, M.W. (1983). Joint functions and grips of the *Australopithecus afarensis* hand, with special reference to the region of the capitate. *Journal of Human Evolution, 12,* 197–211.

McComb, K., Moss, C., Durant, S.M., Baker, L., & Sayialel, S. (2001). Matriarchs as repositories of social knowledge in African elephants. *Science, 292,* 491–494.

McComb, K., Shannon, G., Durant, S.M., Sayialel, K., Slotow, R., Poole, J., & Moss, C. (2011). Leadership in elephants: The adaptive value of age. *Proceedings of the Royal Society B: Biological Sciences, 278,* 3270–3276.

O'Reilly, C.A., Doerr, B., Caldwell, D.F., & Chatman, J.A. (2014). Narcissistic CEOs and executive compensation. *Leadership Quarterly, 25,* 218–231.

Pinker, S. (2010). The cognitive niche: Coevolution of intelligence, sociality, and language. *Proceedings of the National Academy of Sciences, 107,* 8993–8999.

Ronay, R., Oostrom, J.K., & Lehmann-Willenbrock, N. (2015). *The overconfidence prescription: Self-deceptive overconfidence buffers social stress and boosts social status in leadership selection.* Working paper.

Sapolsky, R. (2007). *A primate's memoir: A neuroscientist's unconventional life among the baboons.* New York: Simon and Schuster.

Sapolsky, R., & Share, L.J. (2004). A Pacific culture among wild baboons: Its emergence and transmission, *PLOS Biology, 2*(4), e106.

Schmidt, E. (2014). How Google works. Retrieved April 21, 2015, from http://www. slideshare.net/ericschmidt/how-google-works-final-1

Schrand, C., & Zechman, S. (2012). Executive overconfidence and the slippery slope to financial misreporting. *Journal of Accounting and Economics*, *53*, 311–329.

Sherif, M. (1966). *In common predicament: Social psychology of intergroup conflict and cooperation.* Boston: Houghton Mifflin.

Silk, J.B. (2005). The evolution of cooperation in primate groups. In H. Gintis, S. Bowles, R. Boyd, & E. Fehr (Eds.), *Moral sentiments and material interests: On the foundations of cooperation in economic life* (pp. 43–73). Cambridge, MA: MIT Press.

Simon, M., & Houghton, S.M. (2003). The relationship between overconfidence and the introduction of risky products: Evidence from a field study. *Academy of Management Journal*, *46*, 139–149.

Treviño, L.K. (1990). A cultural perspective on changing and developing organizational ethics. In R. Woodman & W. Passmore (Eds.), *Research in organizational change and development* (Vol. 4, 195–230). Greenwich, CT: JAI Press.

Treviño, L.K., Butterfield, K.B., & McCabe, D.L. (1998). The ethical context in organizations: Influences on employee attitudes and behaviors. *Business Ethics Quarterly*, *8*, 447–476.

Van Vugt, M. (2006). Evolutionary origins of leadership and followership. *Personality and Social Psychology Review*, *10*, 354–371.

Van Vugt, M., & Spisak, B.R. (2008). Sex differences in the emergence of leadership during competitions between and within groups. *Psychological Science*, *19*, 854–858.

Victor, B., & Cullen, J.B. (1988). The organizational bases of ethical work climates. *Administrative Science Quarterly*, *33*, 101–125.

von Hippel, W., & Trivers, R. (2011). The evolution and psychology of self-deception. *Behavioral Brain Sciences*, *34*, 1–16.

von Rueden, C. (2014). The roots and fruits of social status in small-scale human societies. In J. Cheng, J. Tracy, & C. Anderson (Eds.), *The Psychology of Social Status* (pp. 179–200). New York: Springer.

# 18

# GROUPS CREATE MORAL SUPERHEROES TO DEFEND SACRED VALUES

*Jeremy A. Frimer*

*What role do moral heroes (e.g., Nelson Mandela, the Dalai Lama, Osama bin Laden) play in ideological movements? One possibility is that they function as leaders and agents, making key decisions. In this chapter, I examine an alternative possibility—that moralistic groups help create moral superheroes out of relatively ordinary individuals to serve as mascots, symbolizing the group's objectives and modeling self-sacrifice. Taking a social functionalist perspective, I describe the motive behind this practice. As symbols of self-sacrifice for the group's sacred values, moral heroes help bind together adherents into powerful collectives. Seemingly nonsensical group practices of sacralizing objects or rituals serve an adaptive function by helping adherents identify one another. Both ideologically right-leaning and left-leaning groups rely on sacredness for this purpose. I then describe a mechanism by which moral heroes come to represent self-sacrifice for these sacred values—the inspiring, prosocial speech. Along with gossip, ingroup favoritism, and altruistic punishment, hero creation may be an evolved moral "technology" that helps humans form large, powerful groups of non-kin.*

South Africa was once under racist, apartheid rule until a small group of dissidents attracted a larger following, which fought for and won universal suffrage in 1994. Decades later, under the perceived threat of Western imperialism in the Middle East, a small group of Sunni Muslims joined together, attracted adherents, and seized control of a swath of land in Iraq and Syria the size of Belgium. The anti-apartheid movement and Islamic State are but two examples of "successful" moralistic groups. Not all moralistic groups succeed, however. Under threat of income inequality, Occupy Wall Street showed a promising start in 2011 and then dwindled. One of the features that the former, successful movements had that the latter one lacked was a deified moral superhero—Nelson Mandela and Abu Bakr al-Baghdadi in the former cases, respectively.

In this chapter, I explore the possibility that successful moralistic groups make use of a number of evolved "technologies" that bind group members together and to the cause. Among a larger set of social and psychological adaptations is the tendency for moralistic groups to manufacture moral heroes. These heroes serve as mascots, symbolizing the core messages of the group; the effect of their presence is the promotion of loyalty, obedience, and even self-sacrifice from members of the tribe. I begin by taking a social functionalist perspective to understand how the seemingly nonsensical group practices of sacralizing objects and rituals serves an adaptive, binding function. I then explore one mechanism by which groups transform relatively ordinary persons into self-sacrificial mascots.

## Moralistic Groups: A Social Functionalist Perspective

Militaries and social movements are uniquely human (Haidt, 2012). Although non-human animals form small groups of non-kin (e.g., a pack of wolves), only humans managed to form large cooperative groups of non-kin. Humans form these groups simply because large, cooperative groups are advantageous: compared to lone individuals and discordant groups, they are better at gaining and defending resources, raising the adaptive fitness of individual members (Pinker 2012). No other species forms such large groups perhaps because they cannot: they lack the cognitive ability for symbolic thought necessary for complex cooperation. For a large group to work and remain viable, group members must cooperate with strangers. Only humans have figured out how to get such large groups of nonrelatives to cooperate.

A key challenge in maintaining group cohesion is dealing with free riders. Each group member is tempted to cheat on the group, behaving selfishly while still collecting benefits from group membership (see also von Hippel, Ronay, & Maddux, this volume). Doing so raises the cost of group membership to other adherents; they too become tempted to cheat. Disintegration becomes inevitable. For the group to succeed, it must find a way of preventing individuals from acting out of selfishness. The key to the formation of large, powerful groups is social glue: a set of operative social mechanisms that turns individuals into team players. A suitable name for the collection of such social and mental mechanisms is "morality" (Haidt, 2007). Along with gossip (Feinberg, Willer, & Schultz, 2014), altruistic punishment (Fehr & Gächter, 2002), and ingroup favoritism (Brewer, 2007), sacred values and the moral heroes that defend them help bind together individuals into powerful, cooperative groups.

### Sacred Values Identify Group Members

For large groups to succeed, members need to know whether a stranger is an ally. Only if the individual is an ally is the stranger worthy of trust and cooperation.

Humans may have solved this problem of stranger identity, in part, with sacred values (Durkheim, 1915/1995; Haidt, 2012; Smith, 1759/1976). The heuristic is that only allies share one's sacred values.

A sacred value is a special kind of good thing. Most values are amenable to tradeoffs and instrumental sacrifice: people treat them as tools. For example, a person who values money may sacrifice $20,000 in hopes of making $30,000 (e.g., on the stock market) or trade it for another thing (e.g., a car). Knowing that Ingrid values money is a poor method of knowing whether she is a friend or foe, because she values money *instrumentally*. Sacred values are a special kind of goods, ones that are immune to tradeoffs and exchanges (Tetlock, 2003). Sacred values are ones that seem to have *inherent* value (see also Bastian & Crimston, this volume). Life itself is a commonly held sacred value in the West; people who hold life as sacred are repulsed by the thought of sacrificing a child for material gain (e.g., from life insurance) or even to save the lives of five children needing an organ donor. Life is not universally sacred, however. The Nazis did not and ISIS does not treat all human life as sacred, by regarding their prisoners' lives as mere instruments for inciting fear and recruiting new members.

Other examples of sacralization are Catholics sacralizing traditional marriage, Hindus sacralizing the cow, and Jews sacralizing the Sabbath. Sacred values tend to be outlandish and bizarre to outsiders (Atran, Axelrod, & Davis, 2007). They imbue individuals with a sense of moral righteousness, wherein "our" cause is good and "theirs" is bad. The ends of defending the integrity of sacred values come to justify the means. This may even occur within social psychology, wherein scholars misinterpret findings to advance a social agenda, such as the advancement of social justice (see Fiedler; and Jussim, Crawford, Stevens, Anglin, & Duarte, this volume).

Protecting the "natural" state of sacred entities, even when rational calculus would favor tradeoffs and revision, is costly. For example, Hindus forgo a readily available food source by sacralizing the cow. Why sacralize then? The seemingly irrational nature of the sacrosanct may serve a social function. No rationally acting individual, operating on simple cost/benefit calculation, would protect the original state of another group's sacred values. By this logic, anyone making personal sacrifices for a sacred object or practice must be a group member. And in the eyes of the ingroup, anyone who treats the sacrosanct callously, as a mere tool, is evil and must be stopped, as was recently demonstrated by Islamic militants killing journalists for disrespecting their prophet.

## Sacred Values of the Political Left

Do only certain groups, namely ones that cling to antiquated, discriminatory dogma, protect their own version of the sacrosanct? The examples of Catholics, Hindus, Muslims, and Jews sacralizing align with this intuition. And findings from

Moral Foundations Theory suggest that political conservatives use sanctity and purity more than do liberals when making moral judgments (Graham, Haidt, & Nosek, 2009). Conservatives are more sensitive to disgust, a reaction to the violation of the sacred (Inbar, Pizarro, & Bloom, 2009). Does this mean that leftist groups, such as environmentalists and people fighting against the discrimination of minorities, also cohere into groups without the use of sacred values?

If sacred values serve an adaptive function, then their application should be universal, applying to ideologically Right-leaning and Left-leaning groups alike. The crux of this culturally universal versus culturally relative issue is whether Left-leaning groups (also) hold certain cherished entities as sacred. Evidence is emerging that they do: the Left condemns changes to the environment (e.g., the Keystone XL pipeline) as first and foremost a desecration of nature and sacrilege of the Earth (Frimer, Tell, & Motyl, 2015; see Bastian & Crimston; and Brandt, Wetherell, & Crawford, this volume). In fact, another proposed oil pipeline leaving the Albertan tar sands travels westward to the Pacific Ocean, through a region aptly named the "Sacred Headwaters." Does this necessarily mean that the Left sacralizes the environment? Perhaps environmentalists understand that environmental destruction causes humans and other animals to suffer; they condemn environmental changes for the harm they cause (Gray, Schein, & Ward, 2014), and use sanctity/purity/disgust rhetoric merely for dramatic effect in persuading others of their conclusion (Haidt, 2001).

Does the Left condemn environmental destruction merely on the basis of rational, utilitarian principles such as for the suffering it exacts? If so, then the Left ought not condemn environmental destruction that causes no suffering. This is a challenging question because most environmental degradation occurs to ecosystems that involve at least some sentient beings. In oil spills, pelicans gasp for air. With climate change, humans are displaced, starve, and go to war; polar bears starve. Environmental desecration and suffering are normally conflated in the real world.

To test whether the environment truly is sacred to the Left, we needed a context in which environmental destruction occurred with no sentient beings present. A recent mountain climbing controversy in Argentina ideally suited this purpose. In 1970, an Italian climber tried to make the first ascent of a majestic peak, backed by a small army of climbers and a gas-powered drill. He installed hundreds of bolts into the side of the lifeless, sterile granite flanks of the mountain Cerro Torre. The international climbing community condemned the bolting as a desecration of the mountain. A systematic analysis of an online forum discussion about the bolting, and a survey of climbers themselves (who identified as social liberals) confirmed that concerns about the sanctity of the mountain—and not pain and suffering—explained their outrage (Frimer, Tell, & Haidt, 2015). The environment is merely the latest "sacred" issue; previously, left wing, antiestablishment ideologies sacralized equality, tolerance, dignity, and so forth. Both the political Right and the Left sacralize; they do so because sacred values provide a reliable indicator of group membership.

Evidence is building that the Left and the Right are more symmetric in their social cognition and moralizing than previously thought. Both the Left and the Right sacralize their own objects and practices (Frimer, Aquino, Gebauer, Zhu, & Oakes, 2015), discriminate against the "other team" (Wetherell, Brandt, & Reyna, 2013; Brandt et al., this volume), and assign blame to perpetrators when the perpetrator is from an outgroup (Morgan, Mullen, & Skitka, 2010). Along with these features of moral judgment, I propose that the Left and the Right also manufacture and worship their own moral heroes.

## Moral Heroes as Mascots

What role did Nelson Mandela play in the anti-apartheid movement, Osama bin Laden in Al Qaida, and Al Gore in the environmental movement? Moral heroes may have been the behind-the-scenes *drivers* of their respective movements. As "masters of puppets," they may have imagined and designed objectives and strategies, actively recruited and organized followers, and managed internal discord (see von Hippel, Ronay, & Maddux, this volume). Moral heroes may also fill a *passive* role. As mascots, they served as the public face of the movement. To serve as effective mascots, moral heroes must have certain marketable qualities. What are the reputational features that make up a moral hero? Next, I will make the case that at least two features—sacred values and self-sacrifice—are necessary perceived feature of moral heroes.

## Moral Heroes as Symbols of Sacred Values

Evidence is emerging that moral heroes serve a symbolic function. Both the Left and the Right have their own moral heroes that symbolize the group's sacred values (Frimer, Biesanz, Walker, & MacKinlay, 2013). American professors judged the legacy—as promoters of social hierarchy (a Right-wing value) versus promoters of social equality (a Left-wing value)—of 40 influential figures of the 20th century from *Time* magazine's lists. The most hierarchy-promoting figures were Pope John Paul II, Winston Churchill, Margaret Thatcher, Ronald Reagan, and Billy Graham, whereas the most equality-promoting icons were Ché Guevara, Rosa Parks, Emmeline Pankhurst (UK suffragette), Margaret Sanger (Planned Parenthood), and Harvey Milk (first openly gay US representative). Another sample of Left- and Right-leaning professors judged the moral character of the 40 figures; the Right idolized the hierarchy promoters and vilified the equality promoters. Moral heroes of the Right symbolized religion, nationalism and military might, and free-market economics. The Left did the exact opposite; their moral heroes promoted a society that treated women, racial minorities, the poor, and sexual minorities as equals and their villains promoted social hierarchy.

## Moral Heroes Model Giving

Moral heroes must epitomize goodness. Goodness may have both group-relative features (e.g., sacred values promoting hierarchy vs. equality for ideological groups) but also more universal features of giving to the cause. Research from both intergroup and interpersonal research has reliably found that the single most important question that people ask when deciding whether another person is good or bad is whether or not they are warm and prosocial (Abele & Wojciszke, 2007; Cuddy, Fiske, & Glick, 2008; Fiske, Cuddy, Glick, & Xu, 2002; Graziano & Schroeder, this volume). Simply put, people like givers and dislike takers. To illustrate how this might influence moral hero perception, imagine learning that, behind the scenes, Nelson Mandela was cold and harsh with his team, and quietly exploited his position within the anti-apartheid movement to become a multimillionaire. This is counter to the common conception of Mandela, because most people think of him as both a social equalizer (symbolic of a Leftist sacred value) and a self-sacrificial giver.

We see this tendency for both the Left and the Right to revere givers in judgments of influential figures. The prosocial dimension nearly perfectly distinguished moral heroes from moral villains for both Left- and Right-leaning judges (Frimer et al., 2013). That is, both leftist and rightist Americans judged the most prosocial figures (Martin Luther King Jr., Mohandas K. Gandhi, Eleanor Roosevelt, Nelson Mandela, and Mother Teresa) to be more moral than the least prosocial figures (Adolf Hitler, Mao Zedong, the Ayatollah Khomeini, Margaret Thatcher, and Vladimir Lenin).

How do people come to their impressions about whether other people are givers or takers? One possibility is by observing behavior. However, the social intent of a given behavior can be ambiguous. Burning people at the stake for the sake of their eternal souls was considered prosocial in the age of the Inquisition. Nazis framed the extermination of the Jews as a charitable deed to protect humanity. Islamic terrorists kill innocents in the name of higher moral values. Written or spoken words offer another information source, and can explain the social intent of complex behavior. Consider the following self-defense by a known and admitted saboteur and bomber:

> I have fought against white domination, and I have fought against black domination. I have cherished the ideal of a democratic and free society in which all persons live together in harmony and with equal opportunities. It is an ideal which I hope to live for and to achieve. But if needs be, it is an ideal for which I am prepared to die.

Nelson Mandela gave this speech in 1964 while on trial for sabotage (he was found guilty and sentenced to prison). Mandela claimed that the seemingly antisocial behavior means (setting off bombs) may have served a prosocial end. Sacred values (equality) and the ultimate form of giving for the cause are evident in his speech, giving the impression that he is both selfless and symbolizes sacred values of the Left.

In the next section, I will review evidence that moral heroes have a generalized tendency to talk about giving to the cause, just like Mandela did here. I will then describe how audiences cannot help but use this information to form impressions about the speaker, and how these impressions feed into the process of moral hero manufacturing.

## Moral Heroes Have the Giver's Glow

Moral heroes tend to talk about helping others. In one study (Walker & Frimer, 2007), each of the moral heroes in the study had received a national award, given to "the unsung heroes who volunteer their time, their efforts and a great deal of their lives to helping others, and who ask for nothing in return." To name a few of their accomplishments, these moral heroes had raised funds for sick children, helped immigrants adjust to their new homes, connected young offenders to role models, or helped young single mothers return to their studies. We sat down with 25 awardees and asked them about their lives. To test whether these moral heroes were different than the population, we recruited and interviewed a demographically matched comparison group.

The heroes told remarkable stories (Walker & Frimer, 2007). Their stories were rich in self-empowered themes of agency, "helper" figures to whom they recalled having a secure attachment style, optimism, and redemptive turns wherein a bad event gave way to a good outcome. Moreover, caring heroes talked about helping others as if these efforts were intertwined with their own desires for power and achievement (Frimer, Walker, Dunlop, Lee, & Riches, 2011; Frimer, Walker, Riches, Lee, & Dunlop, 2012). Their stories made it sound as if they were helping others out for a sense of personal fulfillment or meaning, rather than out of obligation. Personality variables coded from verbal measures yielded more pronounced differences between moral heroes and the comparison group than did self-report personality inventories.

To get a sense of how people normally responded to interview questions, consider the following excerpt from an interview with a participant in the comparison group. The interviewer prompted this "ordinary" person for a high point event in his life:

INTERVIEWER: Is there some event that signals a particular high point in your life, for you?

PARTICIPANT: It's probably easier to signify the low points.

INTERVIEWER: Well, let's try the high points first. I'm looking for one that stands out.

PARTICIPANT: The highest point of my life probably, other than my marriage, would be the day I won the [local] Drama Festival, as the director. It was my debut as a director, and I brought a play down from [my home town] down here to [the city] to go into the [local] Drama Festival. We drove for twenty-two hours getting here. Bunch of complete amateurs as actors who came up against the best that the rest of [the region] could offer, and . . . and won. It was one of those things that I had a feeling for. I felt I could do something with this play; I felt I could associate with this play; I felt I could make this play work. I had to teach everybody how to act and teach everybody how to emote, how to interreact, and it became a great teaching experience for me, and in the end it was very rewarding because we won five of the seven awards that were given out in the festival.

This comparison group participant describes a drama festival. The central theme he communicated was pride in a personal achievement and recognition; connecting or helping others seems to merely be a means to an end of winning the drama festival.

By contrast, the moral heroes' stories were extraordinarily prosocial. The following is an excerpt of an interview from Sam (a pseudonym), a Caring Canadian Award recipient. Sam also describes winning a prize, but with importantly different social meaning.

The first time I received some public acknowledgment was a high point. We were working diligently to raise funds for the Big Brother association in [the city]. Drew and I were the two . . . I guess we'd call ourselves the cofounders of it. . . . We were frantically working away at organizing a boxing match in [the city]. We had fighters lined up; we had a lot of different things going on, a lot of promotion and advertisement. . . . And Drew, that night . . . just before the last fight was on, he said, "Now I have a special recognition." And he said, "The motto of Big Brothers: No man stands so straight as when he stoops to help a fatherless boy." And Drew said, "The man who stands straightest with me right now is Sam, who's helped us put on . . . "—and he mentioned all the different events.

(Frimer et al., 2011, p. 155)

For Sam, achievement and recognition seem to only be valuable insofar as they reflect beneficence toward fatherless children. His story may send shivers down the spine of some readers, giving them a feeling of moral elevation (Vianello, Galliani, & Haidt, 2010) and the impression that Sam is a giver. The story communicates an intrinsic desire to see disadvantaged children flourish, giving the impression that Sam has a kind of glow about him. Systematic analyses found that this glow (the tendency to communicate desires to help others) generalizes across a variety of different stories that moral heroes tell (e.g., early memories, turning point event, future goals; Mansfield & McAdams, 1996; Walker & Frimer, 2007).

## The Function of Prosocial Rhetoric

Are the glowing speeches and stories of moral heroes a symptom of an underlying disposition to put others' needs ahead of their own? If so, then people who talk about helping others would actually tend to help other people. Applied to the case of Sam, his speech about helping fatherless boys would be a reliable indicator that he really is a giver. Ongoing, systematic tests are finding that this is *not* the case.

In one study, participants described their personal goals, which naturally vary in how much they were about helping others. We measured this variability with validated computerized content analysis called Linguistic Inquiry and Word Count (LIWC; Pennebaker, Booth, & Francis, 2007) and a set dictionary of prosocial words (Frimer, Schaefer, & Oakes, 2014). Naïve judges read the goals and guessed how prosocially each person would behave in an economic game. The judges guessed that people who described prosocial goals would behave prosocially. But they were mistaken. People who described prosocial goals were no more likely to behave prosocially to a stranger in than people who described self-serving goals. Even with a large sample ($N > 3,500$), meta-analyzed, prosocial talk remained undiagnostic of prosocial action (Frimer, Zhu, & Decter-Frain, 2015).

To illustrate, a participant who described goals like "I would like to have a legacy of being a charitable person. It means a lot because some close to me have died of cancer and I would like to help those in need" behaved totally selfishly in the economic game. And another participant who said that he wanted "to save enough money to pay for my own car. I need to pinch a few pennies to make this happen. This will enable me to be independent and to go where I want" behaved extremely generously. A person's words make a poor indicator of a person's constitution. The correspondence bias may explain this discrepancy (Jones & Harris, 1967). Audiences mistakenly interpret a speaker's words as being a reflection of the speaker's internal disposition because audiences fail to recognize and correct for the force of situational demands on the speaker. A person's words seem to be a product of a person's context and motivation, but not their enduring qualities.

Why, then, do moral heroes give such elevating, prosocial speeches if these speeches do not reflect their inner dispositions? The simple answer is because it works. That is, prosocial, cooperative language impresses an audience and leads to social approval. Moral heroes may even have implicit knowledge of this, and craft their speeches to impress. Lab studies are finding that assigning a speaker to write down their goals that are about helping others (vs. any goals) and then read them out loud to an audience reliably enhances the audience's impression of the speaker.

This effect of prosocial language as a tool for impression management scales up to explain how governments gain the confidence of the governed (Frimer, Aquino,

Gebauer, Zhu, & Oakes, 2015). A text analysis of all ~124 million words spoken during floor debates in the US Congress found that prosocial language strongly predicted public approval ratings by the American public 6 months into the future, suggesting that the language of Congress may *influence* public sentiment. In 1996, when transcription of Congress began, public approval was modest (~30%). It climbed over the next few years to peak around 50% in 2002, before undergoing a precipitous decline to record-low levels of approval (10%) by 2014. The trend in prosocial language followed the same trend, beginning at 2.3% in 1996, climbing to 2.6% in 2002, and dropping to 2.0% by 2014. Even controlling for a raft of alternative factors (e.g., the economy, the efficacy of Congress at passing bills, conflict within Congress, exogenous world events), prosocial language remained the strongest unique predictor. Congressional language may sway the public directly (a surprisingly large segment of the public watches floor debates on the C-SPAN channel) and through the media.

Together, these findings suggest that the inspiring, prosocial language of moral heroes is not reflective of who they are as persons. Rather, their language serves to persuade others and galvanize support for the cause. That is, perhaps individuals become moral heroes as a *consequence* of giving uplifting, prosocial speeches. Groups may select inspiring speakers to become their moral heroes, regardless of their private shortcomings. Nelson Mandela's marital infidelity and lackluster presidency aside, he was a moving and charismatic public speaker.

## Conclusion

Sacred values help identify group members. By giving uplifting speeches, moral heroes come to personify self-sacrifice for these sacred values. These heroes help bind together group members in their common moral cause. Adherents may simply copy the group-centric, self-sacrificial behavior of moral heroes. Group members may also follow the instructions, demands, and even orders of their moral heroes. And when other group members fail to follow orders, adherents may demand obedience. Both the Left and the Right demand obedience when the authority represents their own ideology (Frimer, Gaucher, & Schaefer, 2014). More generally, reanalyses of the original Milgram shock experiments suggest that obedience to authority is more about a sense of collusion between commander and commanded and less about blind deference to the "man in charge" (Reicher & Haslam, 2011). Moral heroes create a sense of "we," which invites adherents to willingly self-sacrifice for the cause.

## References

Abele, A.E., & Wojciszke, B. (2007). Agency and communion from the perspective of self versus others. *Journal of Personality and Social Psychology, 93,* 751–763.

Atran, S., Axelrod, R., & Davis, R. (2007). Sacred barriers to conflict resolution. *Science*, *317*, 1039–1040.

Brewer, M. (2007). The importance of being we: Human nature and intergroup relations. *American Psychologist*, *62*, 726–738.

Cuddy, A.C., Fiske, S.T., & Glick, P. (2008). Warmth and competence as universal dimensions of social perception: The stereotype content model and the BIAS map. In M.P. Zanna (Ed.), *Advances in experimental social psychology* (Vol. 40, pp. 61–149). San Diego, CA: Academic Press.

Durkheim, E. (1995). *The elementary forms of religious life* (K.E. Fields, Trans.). New York: Free Press. (Original work published 1915)

Fehr, E., & Gächter, S. (2002). Altruistic punishment in humans. *Nature*, *415*, 137–140.

Feinberg, M., Willer, R., & Schultz, M. (2014). Gossip and ostracism promote cooperation in groups. *Psychological Science*, *25*, 656–664.

Fiske, S.T., Cuddy, A.C., Glick, P., & Xu, J. (2002). A model of (often mixed) stereotype content: Competence and warmth respectively follow from perceived status and competition. *Journal of Personality and Social Psychology*, *82*, 878–902.

Frimer, J.A., Aquino, K., Gebauer, J., Zhu, L., & Oakes, H. (2015). A decline in prosocial language helps explain public disapproval of the U.S. Congress. *Proceedings of the National Academy of Sciences*, *112*, 6591–6594.

Frimer, J.A., Biesanz, J.C., Walker, L.J., & MacKinlay, C.W. (2013). Liberals and conservatives rely on common moral foundations when making moral judgments about influential people. *Journal of Personality and Social Psychology*, *104*, 1040–1059.

Frimer, J.A., Gaucher, D., & Schaefer, N.K. (2014). Political conservatives' affinity for obedience to authority is loyal, not blind. *Personality and Social Psychology Bulletin*, *40*, 1205–1214.

Frimer, J.A., Schaefer, N.K., & Oakes, H. (2014). Moral actor, selfish agent. *Journal of Personality and Social Psychology*, *106*, 790–802.

Frimer, J.A., Tell, C., & Haidt, J. (2015). Liberals condemn sacrilege too: The harmless desecration of Cerro Torre. *Social Psychological and Personality Science*, *6*, 878–886.

Frimer, J.A., Tell, C., & Motyl, M. (2015). *Sacralizing liberals and fair-minded conservatives: Ideological symmetry in the moral motives fuelling the Culture War*. Manuscript under review.

Frimer, J.A., Walker, L.J., Dunlop, W.L., Lee, B., & Riches, A. (2011). The integration of agency and communion in moral personality: Evidence of enlightened self-interest. *Journal of Personality and Social Psychology*, *101*, 149–163.

Frimer, J.A., Walker, L.J., Riches, A., Lee, B., & Dunlop, W.L. (2012). Hierarchical integration of agency and communion: A study of influential moral figures. *Journal of Personality*, *80*, 1117–1145.

Frimer, J.A., Zhu, L., & Decter-Frain, A. (2015). *Do givers leak their social motives through what they talk about? Maybe not*. Manuscript under review.

Graham, J., Haidt, J., & Nosek, B.A. (2009). Liberals and conservatives rely on different sets of moral foundations. *Journal of Personality and Social Psychology*, *96*, 1029–1046.

Gray, K., Schein, C., & Ward, A.F. (2014). The myth of harmless wrongs in moral cognition: Automatic dyadic completion from sin to suffering. *Journal of Experimental Psychology: General*, *143*(4), 1600–1615.

Haidt, J. (2001). The emotional dog and its rational tail: A social intuitionist approach to moral judgment, *Psychological Review*, *108*, 814–834.

Haidt, J. (2007). The new synthesis in moral psychology. *Science*, *316*, 998–1002.

Haidt, J. (2012). *The righteous mind: Why good people are divided by politics and religion*. New York: Random House.

Inbar, Y., Pizarro, D.A., & Bloom, P. (2009). Conservatives are more easily disgusted than liberals. *Cognition and Emotion, 23*, 714–725.

Jones, E.E., & Harris, V.A. (1967). The attribution of attitudes. *Journal of Experimental Social Psychology, 3*, 1–24.

Mansfield, E.D., & McAdams, D.P. (1996). Generativity and themes of agency and communion in adult autobiography. *Personality and Social Psychology Bulletin, 22*, 721–731.

Morgan, G.S., Mullen, E., & Skitka, L.J. (2010). When values and attributions collide: Liberals' and conservatives' values motivate attributions for alleged misdeeds. *Personality and Social Psychology Bulletin, 36*, 1241–1254.

Pennebaker, J.W., Booth, R.J., & Francis, M.E. (2007). Linguistic Inquiry and Word Count: LIWC [Computer software]. Austin, TX: LIWC.net.

Pinker, S. (2012). The false allure of group selection. *Edge.org*. Retrieved from http://edge.org/conversation/the-false-allure-of-group-selection

Reicher, S., & Haslam, S.A. (2011). After shock? Towards a social identity explanation of the Milgram "obedience" studies. *British Journal of Social Psychology, 50*, 163–169.

Smith, A. (1976). *The theory of moral sentiments*. Oxford: Oxford University Press. (Original work published 1759)

Tetlock, P.E. (2003). Thinking the unthinkable: Sacred values and taboo cognitions. *Trends in Cognitive Sciences, 7*, 320–324.

Vianello, M., Galliani, E.M., & Haidt, J. (2010). Elevation at work: The effects of leaders' moral excellence. *Journal of Positive Psychology, 5*, 390–411.

Walker, L.J., & Frimer, J.A. (2007). Moral personality of brave and caring exemplars. *Journal of Personality and Social Psychology, 93*, 845–860.

Wetherell, G., Brandt, M.J., & Reyna, C. (2013). Discrimination across the ideological divide: The role of perceptions of value violations and abstract values in discrimination by liberals and conservatives. *Social Psychology and Personality Science, 4*, 658–667.

# INDEX

Note: Page numbers in italic indicate tables or figures.